P9-DTT-430

Women in India

India—Political Map

Courtesy of Natraj A. Raman

Women in India
A Social and Cultural History

Volume 2

SITA ANANTHA RAMAN

PRAEGER

An Imprint of ABC-CLIO, LLC

A B C 🛆 C L I O

Santa Barbara, California • Denver, Colorado • Oxford, England

Copyright 2009 by Sita Anantha Raman

Library of Congress Cataloging-in-Publication Data

Raman, Sita Anantha.
   Women in India : a social and cultural history / Sita Anantha Raman.
      p. cm.
   Includes bibliographical references and index.
   ISBN 978–0–275–98242–3 (hard copy (set) : alk. paper) — ISBN 978–0–313–37710–5
   (hard copy (vol. 1) : alk. paper) — ISBN 978–0–313–37712–9 (hard copy (vol. 2) : alk.
   paper) — ISBN 978–0–313–01440–6 (ebook (set)) — ISBN 978–0–313–37711–2 (ebook
   (vol. 1)) — ISBN 978–0–313–37713–6 (ebook (vol. 2))
   1. Women—India. 2. Women—India—Social conditions. I. Title.
HQ1742.R263   2009
305.48'891411—dc22   2008052685

13 12 11 10 09 1 2 3 4 5

This book is also available on the World Wide Web as an eBook.
Visit www.abc-clio.com for details.

ABC-CLIO, LLC
130 Cremona Drive, P.O. Box 1911
Santa Barbara, California 93116-1911

This book is printed on acid-free paper ∞

Manufactured in the United States of America

YOKED OXEN

Pipes played, drums rolled
the chant of mantras
cleansed the air
as showered with flowers
we took seven steps
together, you and I
two oxen, one yoke
Since that day
pebbles on my path
became
petals on a rug

For dear Babu

CONTENTS

PREFACE

This history is really dedicated to the numerous women whose narratives I have tried to record as accurately as possible. On a personal plane, I thank the inspirational teachers, stimulating colleagues, and close family who watched over me as I wrote this book. I deeply regret that a lack of space precludes my acknowledging each by name. Two inspirational *gurus* at UCLA shared their vision of history as truth with me years ago. Mentor and friend Stanley Wolpert steered my research directly to the study of women and gender in India. Damodar SarDesai broadened my understanding of Asia and encouraged me in my early career. My fascination for women's history thrived in conversations with my good friend Brenda Ness of Santa Monica College. At Santa Clara University, I shared innumerable hours of enjoyable discussion on women and world history with Barbara Molony, Jo B. Margadant, Thomas Turley, and Timothy O'Keefe. My many students gave me insights into how to make this complex region and its multifaceted women comprehensible. I specially thank Mini Krishnan of Oxford University Press in Chennai for having promoted my work in India. Praeger editors Brian Foster and Hillary Claggett helped to breathe life into these two volumes. Christy Anitha, Haylee Schwenk, Diana Andrews, Valentina Tursini, and Anthony Chiffolo of ABC-CLIO gave them their final look and shape. I acknowledge the assistance of archivists at the Theosophical Society, Adyar, Tamil Nadu, the Government of Tamil Nadu Archives at Chennai, the National Archives of India at New Delhi, the Jawaharlal Nehru Memorial Museum and Library at New Delhi, the Madras Institute of Development Studies at Chennai, and the research librarians at Santa Clara University, UCLA, and University of California at Berkeley. I thank Shilpa Sankaran, Nandita (Sankaran) Geerdink, and Sonya Sankaran for allowing me to put their picture in Bharata Natyam dance pose on the cover of Volume 1. I especially thank my dear husband Natraj Raman for his two valuable maps, as well as for his patient humor and perceptive comments. I dedicate the book to him, and to my sons, daughters-in-law, granddaughters, sisters, brothers, nieces, nephews, and friends.

INTRODUCTION

It is not surprising that women in India are often described as having two sharply contrasting aspects. In a region famous for goddesses with multiple visages, identities, and functions, the first façade is of the serene, primordial mother Great Goddess (Devi), Primal Energy (Shakti), and Nature (Prakriti), a gentle boon-giver who also slays demons. The other is the clouded face of the domestic handmaiden trailing behind men in life expectancy, nutrition, health, education, pay, and other rights on the subcontinent.[1] However, behind this colorful essentialization of Indian women lies the complex reality of myriads of feminine personas in a sea teaming with self-sacrificing heroines like Sita in the epic *Ramayana*, modern feminists in the guise of Shakti, and the victims of gender, religious, caste, and class inequalities.

This poses several dilemmas to the historian. What could an engendered history then include, which female narratives would one recount, and how does one retrieve the voices of the apparently voiceless? A work of this scope cannot cover all the narratives, since such a vast undertaking would lose its critical edge, and its diluted or descriptive litany may be unreadable. Due to the longevity of Indian history, this study of women is therefore divided into two broad chronological sections, i.e., the premodern era from antiquity to the early medieval Hindu kingdoms and the later era under Turko-Afghan and Mughal dynasties, colonial rule, and the independent state after 1947. The four interrelated themes focus on gender and female sexuality, viz., premodern social, religious, cultural, political paradigms of women in male-authored texts; their later resurrection by men and women for contemporary political and social purposes; women's narratives in their social contexts; and the contentious issues of female agency and objectification.

TEXT, CONTEXT, AND RE-CREATED TEXTS

No matter how unassailable texts and material artifacts appear to be, the historian views them as contested territory. This work attempts to be critical in its assessment of the primary evidence from literature, art, and archaeology, as well as of secondary scholarship on women in Indian history. As it is almost impossible to read all the archaic texts entirely in their original languages, some scholarly translations have been used judiciously. However, it is clear that within ancient meanings lie embedded the unconscious biases of later translators steered by their own theoretical or cultural reasons to retell India's history. The values they attributed to ancient gender norms were often remodeled in later eras for contemporary purposes, and these crystallized into paradigms for modern women. Therefore, in order to trace the evolution of gender norms, it is imperative to reexamine India's complex historical tapestry and to re-create a new narrative concerning its women.

Ancient and classical texts reveal that in the preeminent interface between Aryan and local Dravidian-aboriginal cultures, the core value crystallized across the subcontinent. This was the high honor given to female chastity, a virtue whose luster almost exceeded that of women's natural intelligence in archaic texts, and there were numerous ambiguities, as the texts were composed by multiple male authors separated by centuries. Moreover, the genres of hymnal, epic poetry, and *shastra* (scripture, religious manual) facilitated several typologies of women as divine, heroic, maternal, saintly, victimized, lustful, or manipulative. The divine maternal appears early (ca. 3000 BCE) in pre-Aryan artifacts of the Indus Civilization, and it also appears in the Sanskrit scriptural *Vedas* (1600–300 BCE). In the early first millennium BCE, society also began to accord high respect to male and female celibate hermits (*sanyasins*). Thus, the utterances of the woman sage Gargi and the questions of Maitreyi to her sage husband Yajnavalkya were carefully recorded in the *Brihad Aranyaka Upanishad*.[2] Unlike the *Vedas*, the popular epics *Mahabharata* and *Ramayana* contain socially pertinent messages on the honor given to faithful wives. Thus, while Indians celebrate the *Mahabharata* heroine Savitri for outwitting Death, the annual fast by Indian wives is a reminder that their chastity ensures the husband's longevity. Similarly, the *Ramayana* makes it clear that male strictures on female sexuality were paramount, so that even guiltless Sita had to be punished for residing as a hostage in Ravana's fortress.

This schizophrenia about women became more rigid in the classical era (250 BCE–500 CE) when India witnessed waves of immigrants and conquerors. The newcomers jostled for a high rung on the Sanskritic caste ladder and took local women whose husbands and male kin agonized over the lost "purity" of caste lineages. New texts by elite men reined in mortal women's sexuality, but exalted the feminine divine as the Devi. As local cults to divine female guardians were subsumed into the traditions of Devi worship, the Sanskrit hymn Devi Mahatmya celebrated the supreme goddess Durga's martial triumphs over demons. An echo of semidivine female fury also occurs in the Tamil epic *Silappadikaram* in which a chaste wife Kannaki sets Madurai city ablaze as a malediction for the unjust killing of her husband.

Meanwhile, ordinary women were kept in their domestic place by the misogynist authors of *Manu Smriti,* which may have been simply a normative manual but which some later Hindus regarded as their sacrosanct law code.

The long experience of gender inequality on the subcontinent prevents its dismissal as mere feminine fancy. Despite the persistence of local pockets of aboriginal and Dravidian matrilineal societies, and enclaves of Buddhist, Jaina, and Hindu nuns, the many layers of mainstream patriarchal society were cemented by adopting Sanskritic values (or "Sanskritization") due to foreign invasion, immigrant settlement, and internecine feudal wars. These occurred centuries before Islam and European Christianity infused their own patriarchal features into Indian society. However, women did rebel quietly through nonconformism and loudly through religious literature. The most famous examples are the Kannada hymns of Akkamahadevi (twelfth century), a woman saint who rejected caste and gender inequality; the *padas* (songs) in three languages of Rajput saint Mira (sixteenth century) who cast aside prescribed norms of feminine and royal behavior; and the *yakshagana* folk songs of the Telugu widow Tarigonda Venkamba (nineteenth century) who was compelled by society to be a recluse. Other women worked from within the patriarchal order to negotiate with elite men through their writings. Betrayed in love, Chandrabati (sixteenth century) composed Bengali ballads against unjust social laws; the Mughal princess Gulbadan Begam (sixteenth century) wrote *Humayun Nama,* a biography of her brother in Persian; and courtesan Mahlaqa Bai Chanda (eighteenth century) composed Urdu *ghazal* poetry.

Exotic, Colonial Accounts of Sexual Mores

During tumultuous, colonial wars over hegemony in India (seventeenth to nineteenth century), women retreated further into private courtyards and *zenanas,* constrained further by earlier child marriage, bigamy, widow abuse, and a widow's enforced immolation on her husband's funeral pyre (*sati*). Colonial evangelical commentaries based on a bird's eye view of misogynist customs fueled Victorian complacency over Western superiority. In 1829, Governor-General Bentinck passed a law outlawing *sati,* partly influenced by Utilitarian James Mill's popular *The History of British India* (1826). Although Mill had not visited India, he described its civilization as "rude" and its women as "generally degraded." He smugly concluded, "Nothing can exceed the contempt which Hindus entertain for their women."[3] These initial images of India left an indelible mark upon Europeans.

Colonial officials and a growing elite class of Indian reformers drew upon Orientalist translations of Indian texts, missionary accounts of Hinduism, colonial statistics, and the summations of Western anthropologists about

tribal and matrilineal societies in India. Indian reformers felt abashed by
their partial truths, but they did not discard them easily. If scholarly Orientalists revealed the common origin of Aryan languages, pseudoscientific
Social Darwinism cataloged linguistic groups as separate "races." Racial
theory validated European imperialism for having brought material
advancements, and as being genetically the fittest to rule. A corollary
deemed the high-caste "Aryan" Indian as a heathen "brown stepbrother"
to Europeans; but it delegated darker Dravidian and aboriginals to the ranks
of the least civilized on the subcontinent. Twentieth-century discoveries of
sophisticated, pre-Aryan cities at Mohenjo Daro and Harappa on the Indus
river compelled a reexamination of these colonial fantasies. While Victorian
anthropologists assiduously cataloged India's manifold tribal and Dravidian
matrilinies, and the worshipers of indigenous goddesses, many were dismis-
sive of their religions and sexual norms favorable to women. A rare scholar
was Verrier Elwin (1902–64) who lived among the matrilineal Gonds and
sympathized with their "melancholy" when their forests were confiscated
by the colonial state. Elwin married a Gond wife in a sensational public marriage, but callously discarded her once the novelty wore off.[4] E. B. Thurston
(1855–1935) documented his personal fascination for non-Aryan tribes and
castes who performed "primitive" blood sacrifices to goddesses. W. H. Rivers (1864–1922) focused on exotic matrilineal and "promiscuous" customs
among the Todas of south India.[5] Higher-caste Hindus were a trifle higher
on the scale of civilization, as their peculiar practices included female subjugation, caste, and the worship of strange deities. Victorian prudery was especially shocked by the uninhibited views on sexuality in precolonial India. A
century of imbibing Raj attitudes in schools and offices resulted in greater
sexual puritanism among elite-caste Indians who often lauded the chastity
of high-caste women and decried lower-caste female promiscuity. Thurston's assistant K. Rangachari argued that "primitive" tribalism must
"evolve" into a more refined, *brahmanical* Hinduism. A. S. Altekar echoed
this in his authoritative work, *The Position of Women in Hindu Civilization*
(1938), and he exaggeratedly praised ancient Hindu women with these
words:

> Women were honored in ancient India, more perhaps than among any
> other nation on the face of the globe. They were considered the intel-
> lectual companions of their husband.[6]

Both India and Indian women were the objects of male political contestations during the Raj. While Indian aspirations for a national renaissance
were more commendable than British imperial ambitions, Eastern and
Western patriarchs selectively read classical texts to arrive at diametrically
opposing views on Indian women. Evangelicals exaggerated women's abject
condition to justify their conversion; while Indian reformers used women's

customary constraints to negotiate their own place in the Raj, making women fodder for the nationalist engine, while improving female literacy and legally restricting *sati* and child marriage. Nationalist Hindu "matriots" lauded Indian epic women as the paradigm for modern womanhood, maternal and chaste, educated companion and activist, the pure soul (*jivatma*) of goddess Mother India.[7] These appear in Bankim Chandra Chatterji's Bengali hymn *Bande Mataram* (1882), C. Subramania Bharati's *Nattu Vanakkam* (1907) in Tamil, and Abanindranath Tagore's painting of Mother India (1905) as an ascetic four-armed goddess with white lotuses at her feet. These sentiments were expanded by nationalist-feminists like Sarojini Naidu in *Ode to India* (1904).[8]

Hindu and Muslim nationalists tried to improve female literacy and social life, but they simultaneously reified patriarchy and religious identities. Thus to counter Western contempt for Hinduism, Swami Vivekananda (1863–1902) idealized ancient Aryan mores of universal tolerance. Yet, neoconservatives later distorted his inclusive philosophy to advocate Hindu superiority and majority rule. B. G. Tilak hoisted the petard of militant Hindu patriarchy when he vehemently attacked feminist Pandita Ramabai for ostensibly preaching Christianity and when he opposed a moderate law to raise the female age for marital sex.[9] Religious extremists in the Arya Samaj supported female education, but also anti-Muslim drives. Modern Muslim consciousness was similarly divisive when it came to women's education and seclusion through the veil (*pardah*). Thus, Maulana Thanawi's *Bihishti Zewar* (Jewelry of Paradise, 1906), a conservative guideline for modern Muslim women, defused feminism by supporting women's education and also the veil.[10] In the present era, defensive, resurgent Islamic movements often curtail women's rights and social spaces.

To what extent then can we accept the narratives of colonial, nationalist, and postmodern Western scholars? Western educated scholars sometimes use the colonial-nationalist dialogue as a benchmark to gauge women's status, often relying on Western models and theories without cultural specificity for India. For example, in their anxiety to declare war on religion and capitalism, some Marxists fault Hinduism, its caste system, and patriarchy for delaying the dialectical process in India. However, recent studies on the emergence of capital prior to colonial rule have undercut these theories.[11] Some liberal histories describe reformers as indebted to Western secular and Christian thought, without reference to their early education in humanist Indian scriptures.[12] Several downplay sectarian coexistence without serious conflagrations in early India. Yet, it is well known that Indian reformers would cite Hindu-Muslim-Buddhist-Jaina ideas on universalism to implant recent ideas from the West on social equality. For example, Tamil reformers Vedanayakam Pillai and A. Madhaviah frequently quoted the Jaina sage Tiruvalluvar (ca. 100 CE) on gender and caste equity, as well as the Enlightenment philosopher Voltaire on equality.[13]

Despite their championship of Indian feminism, Western feminists have sometimes interpreted Indian texts using Western models. Victorian-Edwardian women wrote rosy biographies of saint Mirabai and princess Gulbadan Begam (sixteenth century), but they infused their lives with contemporary European ideals on feminine virtue. Recent Western feminist translations of Indian texts are considerably more sophisticated, and they shed light on the multiplicity of female narratives. Yet, even these scholars either do not place the texts within the social context of India's living traditions or read early texts through the lens of modern Western feminist theory. This reminds us that historians must be cautious when applying Western models upon studies of Indian women, and second, avoid attributing modern value judgments to premodern societies.

SHAKTI, SAINT, OR SLAVE?

Were all Indian women saints and powerful agents, or hapless victims throughout history? This history attempts to avoid simplistic portrayals of victims and heroines of mythical courage, as these are socially dangerous. It notes that women are subordinate in India from the evidence of a declining sex ratio, lower literacy rates, poorer nutrition, and higher mortality rates than for men. However, it suggests that women have been both objects and agents, occasionally both on different fronts. It will show examples of their active resistance, avenues for self-expression, negotiations with patriarchy, and even their support of oppressive traditions.

It is also worth noting that before the emergence of feminism in Europe over two centuries ago, women asserted themselves in India and other cultures. Moreover, the idea of a universal sisterhood gained credence only in the last century, and today's feminists highlight sisterhood as a bond transcending parochial and national boundaries. Some scholars suggest that in view of its importance in determining women's social and domestic roles, gender is the sole marker of feminine identity, and that it bifurcates the horizontal stratifications of caste, class, and ethnicity, each with its regional, religious, or chronological variations. However, I suggest that women have multiple identities besides being female, and that they are often dissuaded from uniting in a generic sisterhood due to their strong loyalties to family, caste, class, nation, or religion. It must also be remembered that women's loyalties have been historically more local and communal, than national or international. Not all women are ardent feminists; some sit on the fence, some are even misogynist. Women have often quietly accepted domestic constraints either because they wish to protect the family even at cost to themselves, or because they are relatively powerless in specific situations, or because in the domestic pecking order, even lowly daughters-in-law can eventually become powerful mothers-in-law.

Despite their multiple identities, such a study is validated simply because, historically, women's experiences have been uniquely their own, whether in segregated female spaces or integrated public forums. Their agency or objectification is specific to each era, region, culture, economy, polity, and religion. Thus, this book examines the narratives by and about Indian women in the context of their regional history. To study India's women, we must come to terms with Indian patriarchies and the region's contradictions of power and pathos, beauty and ugliness, compassion and cruelty, serenity and chaos.

OUTLINE OF CHAPTERS

Volume 1 contains chapters 1 through 7. Chapter 1 introduces the subcontinent, its women, and its ethno-linguistic matrix of pre-Aryan aboriginal, Dravidian, and Sanskritic cultures; polyandrous, matrilocal, and matrilineal societies; local goddesses and their influence on mainstream societies; Indus Valley artifacts and influence upon later Hinduism. Chapter 2 discusses the coming of the Indo-Aryans, the Vedic era, and effects on women's education and roles; Vedic goddesses and women as authors of scriptures; the mergers between Aryan and local non-Aryan cultures; the connections between caste, gender hierarchies, and gender norms. Chapter 3 is on non-Vedic scriptures (*smritis*) like the epics *Ramayana* and *Mahabharata,* and their paradigms of motherhood, female sexuality, and education. Chapter 4 is on Buddhism and Jainism, nuns, lay devotees and donors. Chapter 5 examines women's representations in Hindu and Buddhist art, Sanskrit and Tamil literature during the classical era; the making of Indian society through streams of immigrants, their implications for gender and caste, elite responses in *The Laws of Manu,* and its resurrection by colonialists and nationalists. Chapter 6 is about Devi traditions in mainstream Hinduism, Tantric Hinduism, and Vajrayana Buddhism; images of Devi in Hindu, Buddhist, Jaina literature and art. Chapter 7 is on medieval devotional (*bhakti*) women saints and their hymns; feudal norms of *sati* and domesticity; philanthropic queens and courtesans in north and south India. Volume 2 begins with Chapter 1 on Islam, its textual references to women; arrival and history on the subcontinent; women's involvement in Shia and Sufi festivals; Turko-Afghan and Mughal princesses and courtesans till 1700. Chapter 2 is on colonial rule (sixteenth to nineteenth century), the impact of hegemonic wars, sexual intermingling between Europeans and Indian women; nineteenth-century missionary impact on education for girls and boys; Victorian influence on elite Indian men and women, and dual patriarchies; legal changes affecting women. Chapter 3 is on Indian male reformers and nationalists and their views on women; female victimization and agency; attempts to pass laws favorable to women on *sati,* marriage, and divorce; male reformers' work to educate Hindu, Christian, Muslim women; working-class women. Chapter 4 is on Indian feminism, suffrage, Indian nationalism, women nationalists, feminists in international forums and as freedom fighters alongside Mahatma Gandhi and Jawaharlal Nehru. Chapter 5 is on postindependence issues such as declining sex ratio, violence, globalization, and key political and legal controversies; women's education and employment; postmodern feminism; women in environmental and working-class struggles; women in politics and the arts; conclusion.

NOTES

1. The ratio of females to 1000 males declined from 945 (1991) to 927 (2001) in all states, except for Kerala and Pondicherry, despite the Prenatal Techniques Regulation and Prevention of Misuse Act (1994). The highest decline was in Punjab (874), Haryana (860), Chandigarh (773), Gujarat (921), Delhi (820), *vide,* Government of India, Office of the Registrar General and Census Commissioner, *Census of India 2001,* Series 1, India, vol. 4 (Primary Census Abstract, and Total Population Table A-5), vol. 9 (Report and Tables on Age C-14), New Delhi: Controller of Publications, 2003; Asha Krishnakumar, "Doomed in the Womb?" *The Hindu,* December 14, 2003, 14. Cities with a steep decline in the sex ratio are Delhi, Mumbai, Pune, Amritsar, Patiala, Ambala, Gurgaon, Faridabad, Kurukshetra, Ahmedabad, Vaddara, Rajkot, Jaipur, Satara, Nagpur, Salem, Tiruchi, Cuddalore, and Vellore, *vide,* Shefali Vasudev, "Missing Girl Child," *India Today* 28, no. 45, November 10, 2003, 16–22; T. K. Rajalakshmi, "A Dangerous Trend," *Frontline* 20, no. 23, November 21, 2003, 95–96. Female literacy rates rose significantly, but women's education still lags behind men.

	1947	1991	2001
India	6%	39.19% (f)–64.13% (m)	54.28% (f)–75.96% (m)
Kerala (highest)		86% (f)–93.62% (m)	87.86% (f)–94.20% (m)
Rajasthan (lowest)		20.44% (f)–54.99% (m)	44.34% (f)–76.46% (m)

See Sita Anantha Raman, "Walking Two Paces Behind: Women's Education in India," in *Ananya: A Portrait of India,* ed. Sridhar Rao and Nirmal Mattoo (New York: SUNY Press, 1996), 375–96.

2. *The Brhadaranyka Upanisad* (Chennai: Sri Ramakrishna Math, 2000), chap. 4, 6, and 8.

3. James Mill, *The History of British India* (1826), 2 vols. (New York: Chelsea House, 1968), 309–10.

4. Verrier Elwin, *Leaves in the Jungle* (1936; repr., London: Oxford University Press, 1968); Ramachandra Guha, *The Unquiet Woods: Ecological Change and Peasant Resistance in the Himalaya* (Berkeley: University of California Press, 1989), 57.

5. Edgar Thurston, *Castes and Tribes of Southern India,* assisted by K. Rangachari, vols. 1–7 (Madras: Madras Government Publications, 1909); W. H. Rivers, *The Todas* (repr., Jaipur: Rawat Publications, 1986).

6. A. S. Altekar, *The Position of Women in Hindu Civilization* (1938; repr., Delhi: Motilal Banarsidass, 1999).

7. Personal communication with Vasantha Surya, author of *A Word Between Us* (Chennai: Sandhya Publications, 2004).

8. The watercolor painting on paper with the Rabindra Bharati Society, Calcutta is depicted in Vidya Dehejia, *Indian Art* (London: Phaidon, 2002), 410.

9. Meera Kosambi, *At the Intersection of Gender Reform and Religious Belief: Pandita Ramabai's Contribution and the Age of Consent Controversy* (Bombay: Research Centre for Women's Studies, 1993).

10. Barbara Daly Metcalf, "Islamic Reform and Islamic Women: Maulana Thanawi's *Jewelry of Paradise*," in *Moral Conduct and Authority: The Place of Adab in South Asian Islam,* ed. Barbara Daly Metcalf (Berkeley and Los Angeles: University of California Press, 1984), 184–95; Shaheeda Lateef, *Muslim Women in India: Political and Private Realities, 1890s–1980s* (New Delhi: Kali for Women, 1990), 55–94; Gail Minault, "Women, Legal Reform and Muslim Identity in South Asia," in *Jura Gentium: Centre for Philosophy of International Law and Global Politics,* ed. Claudio Augustino, Anil Mishra, and Antonella Roninone (1998), http://www.juragentium.unifi.it/en/surveys/rol/minault.htm.

11. K. N. Chaudhuri, *Asia before Europe* (Cambridge: Cambridge University Press, 1997).

12. Ainslie Embree, ed., *Sources of Indian Tradition: From the Beginning to 1800,* vol. 1; Stephen Hay, ed., *Sources of Indian Tradition: Modern India and Pakistan,* 2nd ed., vol. 2 (New York: Columbia University Press, 1988).

13. Sita Anantha Raman and Vasantha Surya, *A. Madhaviah: A Biography and a Novel* (Delhi: Oxford University Press, 2005); also Sita Anantha Raman, "Old Norms in New Bottles: Constructions of Gender and Ethnicity in the Early Tamil Novel," *Journal of Women's History* 12, no. 3 (Fall 2000): 93–119.

ABBREVIATIONS

AIADMK	All India Anna Dravida Munnetra Kazhagam
AIWC	All India Women's Conference
AS	Arya Samaj
BJP	Bharatiya Janata Party
BS	Brahma Samaj
INC	Indian National Congress
ML	Muslim League
NA	National Archives, New Delhi
NMML	Nehru Memorial Museum and Library
PS	Prarthna Samaj
SEWA	Self-Employed Women's Association
TNA	Tamil Nadu Archives, Chennai
TSA	Theosophical Society Archives
VS	Vedanta Society
WIA	Women's Indian Association

1

MUSLIM WOMEN IN PREMODERN INDIA

And recite what is rehearsed to you in your homes, of the Signs of Allah and His Wisdom: for Allah is All-Subtle, All-Aware.

For Muslim men and women, for believing men and women, for devout men and women, for true men and women, for men and women who are patient and constant, for men and women who humble themselves, for men and women who give in charity, for men and women who fast, for men and women who guard their chastity, and for men and women who engage much in Allah's remembrance, for them has Allah prepared forgiveness and great reward.

Qur'an 33:34–35[1]

INTRODUCTION

Arab traders introduced Islam into South Asia in the seventh century after the death of its founder, the Prophet Muhammad (570–630 CE). In life, the gentle mystic had contended against warlike adversaries over polytheism, female infanticide, and the denial of female inheritance rights. His revelations from Allah are recorded in the *Qur'an,* which contains some humane guidelines on the treatment of women and girls. Islam emphasizes the individual's moral imperative and vouchsafes spiritual equality to all believers, irrespective of gender or class. Early Arabic women took the scripture's chapters (*suras*) and verses seriously, questioned male authority, ran businesses, voiced opinions in public, and fought battles. The *Qur'an*'s panaceas for gender justice thus remain relevant for India whose female Muslim population (62.85 million) is five times greater than that of Saudi Arabia (12.25 million).[2]

Islam marked a shift from the tribe to the family and the Muslim brotherhood or *umma* (*Qur'an* 2:143). However, as Allah and *umma* are envisaged as male, Islam inherited the patriarchy of its Arabic forbears; political crises often raked up controversies over women's social space and etiquette.

Medieval clerical pronouncements on some ambiguous *suras* favoring men became institutionalized. Ambiguity also stemmed from the nonchronological arrangement of the *suras,* since Muhammad received the revelations over 20 years (610–632), sometimes in critical life phases. For example, the verses from Medina reflect his preoccupation with war and marriage (622–630), but they reaffirmed pre-Islamic polygamy and the female veil (*hijab* [Arabic]).[3] Muslims consider two other sets of texts sacred, namely the *Hadith* comprised of the Prophet's sayings recorded by his companions, and the Sharia laws derived from the *Qur'an* and the *Hadith.* Female inheritance, marriage, divorce, and the veil have been defined by five schools of Sharia jurisprudence. These are the Sunni schools of Hanafi in north India, and Shafi in south India; and the Jafari school for Shias. The Prophet tried to reform Arabic society, but he could not predict that medieval clerics would reinterpret *suras* to penalize women, that gender perspectives would change in the modern era, or that Islam would spread to remote regions whose local customs would compound the problems of Muslim women.

This is the case in South Asia where Arabs first brought Islam to the Malabar coast and later occupied Sind (711) through the fiat of the religious head (Khalif) at Baghdad. Islam was the vanguard religion of later Turko-Afghans and Mughals who established kingdoms (sultanates) at Delhi (1206–1526), Deccan, Bengal, Gujarat, and the later Mughal empire (1526–1857). Although kings (sultans) periodically forced conversions, most lower castes were swayed by Islam's promise of social equality and by Sufi mystics who preached a love for God that is akin to Hindu *bhakti.* The long history of Islam on the subcontinent has resulted in layers of genetic admixtures through marriage or cohabitation, and cultural and linguistic exchanges within each region.[4] The regional bonds of language, food, custom, and art between Muslims and Hindus in one region sometimes exceed those with coreligionists elsewhere. In this adaptive process, Muslim women were agents of change by bridging the gulf between secluded female quarters (*zenana*) and the outside world of Hindu traders, artisans, and servants. Cultural exchange is visible in their speech patterns (*begamati zabaan*) that are different from those of men.[5]

Yet, Muslim women's legal advantages eroded in the Indian milieu, and they were inhibited by the *hijab* (*pardah* [Persian]) and the *zenana.* Despite such constraints, women painted, wrote, read, sewed, took part in female rites, and even rode horses wearing the *hijab.* Today, they contend with three sets of patriarchal constraints, viz., Islamic laws reinterpreted by medieval clerics; preexisting gender relations in India; and reconstructed gender stereotypes as religious identities crystallized in the modern nation-state. As both women and members of a religious minority in India, they are subject to dual discriminations. This chapter describes some female social and legal problems by disentangling the gender dilemmas from the *Qur'an*'s ethical intent[6] and by placing their narratives in the context of India's medieval history.[7]

ARABIC ANTECEDENTS

Islamic Tenets and Gender

Islam means peace after "submission" to Allah, indicating that the believer's personal relationship with God needed no intermediaries. The first of five tenets (*shahada*) unequivocally declares that Allah is One, and that Muhammad was His Messenger (*rasul*), the final "seal" of Biblical prophets. Muslims thus also believe in the Old Testament, its prophets from Abraham to Jesus, archangels, a Day of Judgment with heaven and hell, and injunctions against engraved images.[8] The *Qur'an* decries three pre-Islamic Arabic goddesses as mirages and false creations. These verses possibly shaped Muslim antipathy to the worship of icons and goddesses in India:

> Have you seen Lat, and 'Uzza? And another, the third (goddess) Manat? What? For you the male sex, and for Him, the female? Behold, such would be indeed a division most unfair!
>
> *Qur'an* 53:19–22[9]

The second tenet (*salat*) is of prayer five times daily facing Mecca where Muhammad was born. This can be alone at home or in congregation at a mosque, as the site is less significant than the believer's spiritual attitude. The early mosque was adjacent to nine rooms where Muhammad resided with his wives and family. He occasionally entered the prayer room after arising from his conjugal bed, perhaps to challenge earlier restrictions on menstruating women or on prayers immediately after intercourse.[10] However, in tune with contemporary customs, the *Qur'an* forbids menstrual intercourse as "a hurt and a pollution" (*sura* 2:222), but it advises sexual purity for both genders.[11] The Prophet's peers also commented upon his kindness and gentle respect for women. The third Islamic tenet (*zakat*) is a charitable tithe for the *umma;* the fourth is a month of fast during *Ramadan* when Muslims refrain from sex, alcohol, and impure thoughts and actions; and the fifth is a pilgrimage to Mecca (*hajj*) at least once in a lifetime.[12]

Prophet and Women

Having lost his mother Amina in childbirth and his father Abdu'llah as a child, Muhammad was raised by his uncle Abu Talib.[13] His reputation for honesty attracted the attention of Khadija Bint Khawaylid, a wealthy female caravan owner who employed and then married him. Muhammad was 25, several years younger than Khadija, but the marriage was happy, since she believed in him and became his first convert. Of seven children, the daughters Ruqayya and Fatima alone survived, so that their descendents stem from a female line in an otherwise patriarchal society. In 610, Muhammad began to meditate at Mount Hira where he received his first revelation (*sura* 96) through the voice of Archangel Jibreel (Gabriel). At first, the bewildered Prophet entreated Khadija to cover him, as he feared he was going mad. He had divulged his anxiety to her, rather than to his male companions, but Khadija reassured him of his mystical uniqueness.[14] The deaths of Khadija and his uncle lost him the support of the Meccan elite, and he fled to Medina (*hejira*) in 622. The next eight years of political tensions were marked by 26 battles and marriages to several women. He returned in triumph to Mecca after his views gained credence, and died peacefully two years later.

Muhammad never claimed to be more than a human, and he showed his interest in worldly affairs. He treated his wives courteously, and their importance is reflected in their title as the "Mothers of Islam" (Umm-al-Momineen). The *Qur'an*'s rules on polygyny, divorce, and the veil were formulated with reference to his wives, some being much older than him like Khadija and Sawda. Several were far younger like his favorite A'isha, a brilliant, fiery personality and author of 1,000 Hadiths; Umm Salama, a 29-year-old widow with four children, and a friend who inspired his revelations on women; and the beautiful divorcee Zaynab Bint Jahsh who led him to verses that reified the *hijab*. A few were war captives whom he freed, like Juwayriyya, Safiyya the Jew, and Maria the Copt whose son died in infancy.[15] One of his first male converts was his cousin Ali who married his daughter Fatima the mystic. Other friends and relations through marriage who succeeded him as Khalif were his friend Abu Bakr whose daughter was A'isha; Umar whose daughter Hafsa was also Muhammad's wife; and Uthman who married his daughter Ruqayya. Muhammad's death resulted in a sectarian schism between orthodox Sunni Muslims led by Abu Bakr and A'isha, and dissident Shias led by Ali and Fatima.

Muslim women accord respect to three female role models, since Muhammad often relied on them for advice. They were his wife Khadija who diplomatically handled tribesmen, Fatima the first woman mystic, and A'isha. Wives Umm Salama and A'isha often accompanied him into battle and offered their views on political strategies. After a victory, Muhammad received several women captives whom he freed but also occasionally married to legalize his protection, so that they were more friends rather than wives. He disliked taking captives and wept upon discovering that a prisoner was the sister of his wet nurse Halima. After hearing her story, he gave her freedom and gifts.[16] Muslim women often draw special inspiration from Umm Salama's questions that led to revelations on female spiritual equality (*Qur'an* 33:34–35), since divine rewards accrue from faith and virtue, not from gender. These verses led to another chapter named entirely for women (*sura* 4, An-Nisaa). Umm Salama was ready to die for Islam as the new religion decried the capture of women as booty in war.[17]

Qur'an: Medieval Text, Modern Relevance

Islam recognizes no miracles except the *Qur'an,* which states that the genders are spiritually equal as both have souls. However, as women were socially inferior, their legal rights are explained in *suras* 2:221–241 (The Heifer); 4:1–43 (The Women); 16:57–59 (The Bee); 24:1–34 (The Light); and 33:28–37, 49–55 (The Confederates). This verse condemns pre-Islamic female infanticide (16:58–60):

> When news is brought to one of them, of (the birth of) a female child, his face darkens, and he is filled with inward grief! With shame does he hide himself from his people, because of the bad news he has had! Shall he retain it on (sufferance and) contempt, or bury it in the dust? Ah! What an evil (choice) they decide on! To those who believe in the Hereafter, applies the similitude of evil: to Allah applies the highest similitude, for He is the Exalted of Power, full of Wisdom.[18]

Female Inheritance Rights

The *Qur'an* forbids men to treat women harshly or as inherited property (*sura* 4:19), stipulating special rules for the upkeep of orphans (4:6–9); widows' inheritance (2:240); widow remarriage after four months (2:234); female divorce and alimony (2:237);[19] women's right to privacy (24:27) and chastity, through the *hijab* (24:31).[20] *Qur'anic* rulings were later amplified by the *Hadith* and codified into the five schools of Sharia laws (four Sunni, one Shia) in the medieval era. The *Qur'an* emphasizes a father's financial responsibility to maintain his daughters, and his moral duty to marry them to believers (*sura* 2:221), if he wished to avoid hell.

The chapter on women (*sura* 4) was intended to prevent female destitution by ensuring that daughters and widows inherited property. It urges men not to dissipate the wealth of heirs and orphans but to treat children kindly (4:2, 10). Although daughters inherited half the sums received by sons (4:10–12), this was a praiseworthy innovation in the medieval era. Another verse requires men to give their wives a dowry or *mehr* upon marriage (4:4). A later chapter asks men who divorce their wives to "release them in a handsome manner" with a gift (33:49).[21]

However, after recommending the *mehr* for the wife, the next verse (4:5) warns men not to entrust their property to "the weak-minded" (*al sufaha*) but to clothe, feed, and speak words of kindness to them. Since Muhammad himself valued the opinions of his intelligent wives, he may have perhaps added this cautionary verse not to trust ignorant women, since few were literate in his era. However, misogynists have seized upon these words to denigrate women as incapable of managing property, especially since the *sura* also solemnly declared that "Men are the protectors and maintainers of women" as Allah had given them greater strength, and that righteous women should remain "devoutly obedient" to their husbands (4:34).[22] The medieval verses advocate kind paternalism, but they do not guarantee equality by today's norms.

Relevance for Modern Indian Women

Recent events show that the *Qur'an*'s injunctions to return the wife's *mehr* upon divorce are sometimes disregarded in South Asia. This reduces women to destitution, as seen in the famous case of Shah Bano whose husband divorced her but withheld her *mehr* (1985). Although the Indian civil court ruled in her favor, this was overruled by Muslim clerics. The Indian government then placated its Muslim voters with a law potentially detrimental to women's rights.[23] In Kerala, Mappila Muslims have virtually given up their matrilineal customs by reducing *mehr* to nominal amounts and have also adopted the patriarchal Hindu custom of paying a dowry to the bridegroom. Women are thus made more financially vulnerable.[24]

Polygamy, Divorce, and Wives

Tribal antecedents are reflected in the *Qur'an*'s support to polygamy (4:3; 33:50–51) and to gender inequality. Men were allowed up to four wives by formal contract (*nikah-nama*) to be witnessed by Muslim clerics, but nomadic Arabic traders often took "temporary" wives during long absences. The Prophet was an exception as he was allowed more wives (33:50), and he used this authority to save female captives after war. The *Qur'an* sternly admonished men to treat them with "kindness and equity." It banned incest and "lewdness" (4:19–23), and it also stated:

> O ye who believe! Ye are forbidden to inherit women against their will.
> Nor should you treat them with harshness.
>
> *Qur'an* 4:19[25]

The *Qur'an* views marriage as a contract between adults, although child marriages were common in Muhammad's era. The Prophet's wives were adult, except for A'isha who was six when she married him when he was a 40-year-old widower, although the marriage was probably consummated only on her menarche. However, this *Qur'anic* precedent has made it difficult to overturn Muslim child marriages in India. Muslim women have greater customary rights than Hindu women, as they can initiate divorce for legitimate reasons, remarry as widows, and no impunity is attached to marriages between older women and younger men.

However, these particular rights were not given to the widows of the Prophet. Muhammad remained monogamous until after Khadija's death, and tradition points to his restraint from conjugal relations with wives whom he valued as companions or did not love. The *Qur'an* advises his "consorts" not to esteem "the life of this world, and the glitter," but to "stay quietly in your houses, and make not a dazzling display" (33:28–33), be exceptionally chaste as they were "not like other women" (33:32–33), but the "mothers" of the *umma*. It also cautioned men not to cast eyes on his wives (33:53) or widows.[26]

Such injunctions reified docile domesticity for women. Yet, the Prophet's wives felt that the *Qur'an* freed them from pre-Islamic male domination, as he tacitly encouraged his wives' independent opinions. Muhammad's wife Umm Salama resisted interference from his companion Umar who preached docility to his women.[27] Muhammad then ruminated alone for 29 days before receiving a revelation that stated that in gender disputes, diplomacy was preferable to authoritarianism.

Relevance for Modern Indian Women

The *Qur'an*'s reforms were a response to medieval gender inequalities, but as proscriptive scriptural laws, they are rigidly enforced despite changed modern circumstances. Recent Indian Muslim feminists have therefore demanded a reconsideration of Islamic laws on divorce. The *Qur'an* does not favor divorce but allows women to divorce husbands for legitimate reasons such as cruelty or physical defects in a spouse. Men cannot reclaim the dower (*mehr*) they had given the wife at marriage, thus enabling the divorced woman to sustain herself independently. Sharia laws do not allow outside agencies or civil judges to separate couples who have signed the marriage contract (*nikah-nama*). Sharia requires a waiting period of three months (*iddah*) before reconciliation or separation in order to detect a possible pregnancy.

Yet, the Sharia laws on divorce make it significantly easier for men to obtain divorce. Three methods for men to initiate a divorce (*talaq*) can be undertaken without the wife's consent. While Sunnis and Shias file for male *talaq* through different legal methods, a reprehensible method of triple *talaq* has existed since Muhammad's era. This consists of the husband simply uttering "*talaq*" three times even without his wife's knowledge, but he must return her *mehr*. Although Muhammad disapproved of this type of *talaq*, it continues in India and elsewhere. Female instituted divorce (*khula*) requires a wife to return her *mehr* to the husband as compensation, thus buying back her freedom. Although the *Qur'an* allows men up to four wives, individual couples can insert a clause against bigamy in the *nikah-nama*, and this legally entitles the wife to ask for *khula*. According to the *Hadith*, some marriages were so displeasing to God that they could be dissolved for no other reason. The *Qur'an* made an attempt to reform divorce customs in Arabia, but Muslim women still face unequal laws in South Asia and elsewhere.[28]

Hijab or *Pardah*

Although the *Qur'an* declared gender equality (33:35), it advised a screen (*hijab*) between the genders when they conversed (33:53). Ninth-century accounts describe the episode in which a boorish guest Anas bin Malik remained in the presence of Muhammad's bride, Zaynab Bint Jahsh, despite the Prophet's request of privacy. Muhammad left the chamber to ruminate on this offensive behavior until he received the revelatory *sura* on the *hijab,* which advised men not to transgress upon female privacy. The verses express Allah's anger over insensitivity to his Messenger, caution men to respect women, and advise a "curtain" of modesty between the genders. This had a subtle implication, that veils cannot hide humans from God. The verses state:

> 33:53. O ye who believe! Enter not the Prophet's houses—until leave is given you—for a meal, (and then) not (so early as) to wait for its preparation: but when ye are invited, enter; and when ye have taken your meal, disperse, without seeking familiar talk. Such (behaviour) annoys the Prophet as he is shy to dismiss you, but Allah is not shy (to tell you) the truth. And when ye ask (his ladies) for anything ye want, ask them from before a screen: that makes for greater purity for your hearts and for theirs. Nor is it right for you that ye should annoy Allah's Messenger, or that ye should marry his widows after him at any time. Truly such a thing is in Allah's sight an enormity.
> 55. There is no blame (on those ladies if they appear) before their fathers or sons, their brothers, or their brothers' sons, or their sisters' sons, or their women, or the (slaves) whom their right hands possess. And, (ladies), fear Allah; for Allah is Witness to all things.[29]

Another verse advises women also to use the head scarf or *hijab* when venturing outside the home, as protection from lecherous men (33:59):

> O Prophet! Tell thy wives and daughters, and the believing women, that they should cast their outer garments over their persons (when out of doors): that is most convenient, that they should be known (as such) and not molested: And Allah is Oft-Forgiving, Most Merciful.[30]

A vehement chapter also warns men not to slander women's chastity (24:1–31), probably as a response to false allegations of adultery against A'isha. This led to an injunction to women to use the *hijab* to cover both head and bosom. The veil's original intent was to promote sexual "purity," but it has historically constrained Muslim women's freedom of movement and often secluded them.[31] Later Muslim clerics argued that seclusion guarded women from harsh worldly affairs, but it legitimized male agency and female passivity. Muslim girls are thus often constrained from attending schools, even those in mosques. This led modern Indian feminists to campaign against *pardah* as an outdated, medieval practice that inhibited their equal right to education.[32]

Sects and Early Women Martyrs

Muhammad's death led to a religious schism between Sunni supporters of Abu Bakr as leader (Khalif) and dissident Shias who favored Ali, Muhammad's son-in-law. Muhammad's wife A'isha fought bravely but unsuccessfully against Shias in the Battle of the Camel. Sunnis thus regard her as "a pearl amongst women," as she composed about 1,000 Hadiths. However, Shias accuse A'isha of intensifying the rift through undue female interference. Shias revere Fatima for her devoted care of the Prophet, after whose death, she died from grief. Shias also lament the Prophet's descendents through Fatima and Ali. They were their martyred sons Hasan and Husayn; their daughters Zaynab and Umm Khultum, and granddaughter Fatima Khubra, all three bridal widows; and Sakina, a four-year-old granddaughter who died from Sunni inflicted wounds.[33] During the somber festival of Muharram, Shia women and men resurrect these events by singing dirges and through bloody rites of self-flagellation. Shia Muslims also conduct mournful laments and ceremonies within the *zenana*.

QUEENS IN INDIAN SULTANATES

Settlement and Gender

Arab traders initially disseminated Islam along the Konkan, Kerala, and Tamil coasts, and in neighboring islands where they settled with local wives. This was qualitatively different from later Perso-Arabic court practices like the *hijab/pardah* and segregated female quarters or haram/*zenana,* introduced by sultans across India. In 711, the Khalif of Baghdad invaded Sind to retaliate against the Hindu raja's plunder of Arab vessels, and a new era of cultural fusions began. West Asian men and women wore full-body shifts, and their courts were notable for female seclusion through *pardah* and the haram. Although the *Qur'an* requires a head-bosom scarf or *hijab* but not a face veil (*niqab*), West Asian women moved outside the haram in a full-body cloak (*burqah*) that shrouded them from the public eye. These clothes became marks of elite culture in Indian sultanates (post–twelfth century) and the Mughal empire (post–sixteenth century).[34]

Historical antecedents have shaped Muslim women's lives, since female inheritance, divorce, and *mehr* are affected by regional customs and the specific school of Sharia for local groups. Thus, northern Sunni women follow the Hanafi school, while the Shafi school of laws prevails in the south.

Shia laws are based on the Jafari school, but there are differences among sub-sects like the Isna Ashari, Bohra, and Ismaili/Khoja.[35] While most Indian Mus-lims are descended from local converts, there was an infusion of West and Central Asian genes due to marriage, cohabitation, or rape during war. The elite or *ashrafs* of north India can trace Turkish, Afghan, or Persian forbears, while some are descended from Ethiopian Habshis who married women in the Deccan. There were Sunni kingdoms in the north and Shia sultanates in Multan, Kathiawar, Kashmir, Oudh (now Uttar Pradesh), and the Deccan (Bijapur and Hyderabad).[36]

Sultans often converted subjects to impress court clerics or *ulama* (*alim* [singular]), or to justify their pillage of local temples. However, most Muslims are descended from voluntary converts swayed by Sufi mystics (*pirs*) whose royal patrons included Akbar (1556–1605).[37] Many aristo-cratic Muslim women were devotees of *pirs,* and their practices could devi-ate from more conservative methods required by the *ulama*. Despite Islam's promise of equality, Muslim society was stratified by ethnicity and class, and dominated by foreign-born *ashrafs*.[38] Muslim political interac-tions with Hindu Vijayanagar, the Rajput, Maratha, Nayaka, and Sikh states also brought about religious, linguistic, and cultural mergers. Hindus adopted the *pardah* in north India, while the *zenana* became a feature of their courts after the thirteenth century.

Women and Politics

Sultan Raziyya (1236–40)

The Delhi Sultanate (1206–1526) was the center of Islamic authority on the subcontinent. Its first important ruler was Iltutmish (1211–36) whose religious zeal to convert Hindu subjects did not equal that of the court *ulama*. Thus, during territorial wars with Hindu kingdoms, Muslim sultans periodi-cally went on conversion sprees to satisfy the *ulama* and ambitious Turkish nobles (*amirs*). Upon the death of his first son Nasir-uddin Mahmud in 1229, Iltutmish appointed Raziyya as sultan (1236–40), as she was his oldest child and daughter by his first queen. Iltutmish deemed his other sons to be dissolute or incapable. Raziyya was the only Muslim woman to rule on her own merit in India, a remarkable feat since she called herself sultan instead of begam (queen). The main source on her short regime of three years, six months, and six days is Minhaj Siraj Juzjani's *Tabaqat-I-Nasiri*. Raziyya appointed Juzjani as chief judge or *qazi,* and principal of the first Muslim college in Delhi. Juzjani respected his patron, but as he addressed her as sultan, he obviously felt that she was qualified to be a military ruler (Juzjani I:457).[39] Moreover, since he was also the *qazi* for subsequent rulers, he does not seem to have been unduly biased. Juzjani attributed Raziyya's downfall to her gender, rather than to structural weaknesses in the Delhi Sultanate.[40] Juzjani wrote this summation of Raziyya:

Sultan Raziyya was endowed with all the admirable attributes and qualifications necessary for kings; but, as she did not attain the destiny, in her creation, of being computed among men, of what advantage were all these excellent qualifications to her?[41]

The powerful vested interests of nobles and some *ulama* threatened Raziyya's legitimate claim to the throne. The *ulama* relied on charitable gifts and endowments for a training college from the royal family of Iltutmish, Raziyya, and Shah Turkan Khatun, a concubine whom Iltutmish married and elevated to queen. After Nasir-uddin Mahmud's death, Turkan Khatun's ambitions escalated for her own son Rukh-nuddin Firuz to become sultan, and she wooed the *ulama* through "many offerings and much charity on learned men, *saiyids,* and devotees." The *ulama* chose sides in this quarrel, with their eyes on the candidate most likely to succeed, while the nobles resented Raziyya's opposition to established conventions. The Turkish *amirs* belonged to a clique of "The Forty" who had elected Iltutmish to power and in return had received life-term land grants (*iqtas*) and posts as provincial governors (*maliks*).

According to Juzjani, Iltutmish left a document declaring Raziyya as his heir, citing the precedent of earlier Muslim queens in Persia and Egypt.[42] Iltutmish distrusted Rukh-nuddin, a frivolous youth addicted to drink and concubines, yet placated him with the post of governor in an important province. Although many *amirs* distrusted Turkan Khatun, they supported Rukh-nuddin, while a faction led by the *amir* Junaydi favored her other son Ghiyas-uddin. The most ambitious was Balban who supported Raziyya whom he hoped to manipulate as a figurehead. A few nobles supported Qutb-uddin, another of Iltutmish's sons, but he was cruelly blinded by Turkan Khatun when her son Rukh-nuddin served as sultan for a few months.[43] Raziyya had diplomatically relinquished her claim to Rukh-nuddin, but with some allies, she overthrew her brother in a coup that year.

Raziyya's success led to the formal declaration of allegiance by *amirs* and the *ulama,* including Juzjani. Her initial coins bear her name along with that of Iltutmish (1237–38), but after this date, she boldly dispensed with her father's name. Raziyya seems to have been free of contemporary racial prejudices, as she distrusted her Turkish countrymen and raised respected non-Turks to positions of importance. She thus appointed an Afghan as governor, and she raised the rank of Jamal-uddin-Yaqut, an Ethiopian Habshi, to that of chief *amir* and advisor.[44]

She also dispensed with the veil and appeared in public in male attire but with the head turban, as required by the *Qur'an.* Juzjani states that she rode upon elephants, and that she exhibited the qualities of "military leader." Clearly, Raziyya wished to highlight her preeminent position as Sultan and to downplay her femininity to show that she was not a puppet of the Tajik and Turkish nobility. Raziyya may also have had the support of the local

denizens of Delhi. Contemporary rumors of an affair between Raziyya and
Yaqut are indicated in Juzjani's statements. Juzjani wrote that the Ethiopian
"acquired favor or closeness in attendance upon the Queen with the result
that the Turkish *amirs* and *maliks* became jealous of him."[45] At this point,
she had completely alienated the prominent *amir* Ikhtiyar-uddin-Aytegin.
In 1239 she could quell an uprising by the *amir* Kabir Khan in Lahore. However, next year, she was unable to subdue a more serious rebellion by
Aytegin and Altuniya who governed the region of Tabarhindh.[46] Altuniya
killed Yaqut in battle, took Raziyya prisoner, and installed her brother
Bahram as sovereign. However, Altuniya fell in love with Raziyya who
married him, perhaps seeking an ally in her renewed bid for the throne.
Although Raziyya and Altuniya marched toward Delhi, their allies deserted
them, the campaign floundered, and they were killed by Hindu highway
robbers on October 14, 1240.[47]

What were the consequences of Raziyya's exceptional challenge to male
authority? Raziyya had made a short but courageous move to establish
women's right to be sovereigns on their own merit. However, her failure
to remain in power served to deter later women who aspired to be queens
in medieval India.[48] Contemporary sources indicate that kings and nobles
distrusted women as leaders, and in this frontier Islamic state in India,
mutual dependency bound Turkish or Afghan sultans to powerful military
amirs. In the chaotic decades between 1240 and 1266, Balban served as
the de facto ruler until formally appointed sultan (1260–87). He then
relegated women to the *zenana* and curbed their political "meddling."

The *amirs* and many *ulama* distrusted Raziyya and saw her overthrow as
proof that women could not hold sovereign power alone. Thereafter, princesses wielded power through minor sons, but their authority was confined
to the *zenana* in the Delhi Sultanate. Due to royal polygamy, there was no
dearth of offspring from minor queens and concubines, making contests
for the throne commonplace in medieval India. Muslim clerics therefore
decried women's power in their texts on governance. The scholar Isami
(ca. 1350) thus declared that Raziyya should have made "cotton her
companion and grief her wine-cup," as "a woman's place was at her spinning wheel" (*charkha*).[49] Despite this venomous indictment of sultan
Raziyya, the African humanist Ibn Batuta (1333–45) noted that her tomb
was a popular pilgrimage site.[50]

Pardah Politics in the Delhi Sultanate

There were some royal women who struggled for control over the throne
during the first century of the Delhi Sultanate. However, their strivings took
place in the *zenana* walls, and few were successful or as talented as Raziyya.
As Mongols encroached on the empire from the northwest, there was
another contest among Iltutmish's male heirs and the Turkish nobles.

Raziyya's stepsister, as well as a widow of Iltutmish who bore the title of "Malika-i-Jahan" (Mistress of the World), used women's *Qur'anic* rights to divorce and remarriage to realign the factions behind the throne. Malika was deeply ambitious for her own son Nasir-uddin Mahmud, an ascetic prince in prison. Her ally was the *amir* Qutlugh Khan whom she married, and she pressured the dissolute sultan Ala-uddin Masud Shah to release his uncle Nasir-uddin Mahmud from prison. The unwary Ala-uddin Masud Shah agreed, after which Malika and Qutlugh Khan incited nobles to overthrow him and to crown Nasir-uddin as sultan. As Nasir-uddin's father-in-law was the powerful Balban, he was successful in ascending the throne.[51] Eventually tiring of his mother's authority, Nasir-uddin appointed Qutlugh Khan governor of Bihar and exiled his mother and her husband from Delhi. The couple finally sought refuge with Mongol kings in Central Asia.[52]

An important source was scholar Zia-uddin Barni (1285–1357) who wrote accounts of Jalal-uddin Khalji (1290–96) and his nephew Ala-uddin Khalji (1296–1316). Although the subjects were largely Hindu, Barni described his vision of the ideal Muslim kingdom and monarch in his political document, *Fatawa-yi-Jahandari.* Barni drew a line of male authority originating in Allah, proceeding to Prophet Muhammad as his emissary, and ending with the Delhi sultan as Allah's earthly representative. The repeated emphasis on the word "king" reminded the sultan of his responsibility to uphold Islam, that Allah was the real king, and that earthly "kings" were merely instruments of "His Decree and Divine Power" (folio 143).[53] Barni underscored political patriarchy by claiming that "the head of religion and the head of government are twin brothers" (folios 247b–248a).[54] Finally, Barni drew a parallel between the "Divine Throne" and "Godlike attributes" of a perfect "king" (folios 193a–195a).[55] As women were excluded from this discourse, female political ambitions could be pursued only in the *zenana.*

Ala-uddin Khilji cruelly murdered his uncle Jalal-uddin Khilji and seized the throne. His first years as sultan witnessed a rebellion by his widowed aunt Malika-i-Jahan (no relation of the earlier queen by that title). The widow tried to claim the throne for her son Rukh-nuddin Ibrahim Shah. In his historical, *Tariq-i-Firuz Shahi,* Barni described Malika-i-Jahan as "the silliest of the silly" as she could not outmaneuver Ala-uddin Khalji and was ultimately a failure.[56] Distrustful of women, Ala-uddin kept his *zenana* under close supervision. A misogynist irritated by women's customary rites during marriage and childbirth, Ala-uddin may have had a homosexual relationship with the eunuch convert Malik Kafur whom he appointed as his deputy and chief general. Other sources describe his lust for Rajput queens Padmini of Chittor, who eluded him through *jauhar,* and Kamladevi of Gujarat whom he captured and married as a trophy wife.[57]

Historian Isami informs us that at least one Turko-Afghan queen was famous for pious philanthropy. She was Mahduma-i-Jahan, dowager queen of Ghiyas-uddin Tughlaq (1320–24), and mother of sultan Mohammad bin Tughlaq (1325–51). Mahduma-i-Jahan established several free hospitals where patients and visitors were fed regularly. She also founded hostels for foreign visitors who were given free elegant repasts and gifts of silk, linen, and cotton cloths embroidered with gold thread.[58]

Maldive Matriliny

A different scenario of Islamic acculturation and gender relations emerged in Dravidian regions with earlier matrilineal traditions. When southern communities adopted Islam, Arab traders often married the daughters of wealthy converts. Since matrilineal traditions favored them as sons-in-law, they did not question such customs, so that there ensued an eclectic mix of social matriliny and Islamic religious patriarchy. This is seen in the Muslim Mapillas of Kerala, and the Muslim inhabitants of the Maldive Islands who embraced Arabic Islam but not Persian court customs of north India. In the fourteenth century, visitor Ibn Batuta noted admiringly that a queen ruled the Maldive Islands, a rarity in Muslim kingdoms where women's political authority was restricted to the *zenana*. Ibn Batuta wrote:

> One of the wonders of these islands is that they have a woman for their ruler, viz., Khadijah, daughter of Sultan Jalal-ud-din Umar, son of Sultan Salal-ud-din Salih-ul-Bangali.[59]

Ibn Batuta also praised customs favorable to women in the Muslim kingdom of Hanaur on the Konkan coast near modern Goa. He praised Hanaur Muslims for starting as many schools for girls as for boys, indicating that girls were viewed as an asset, and not a burden. He wrote:

> I saw in Hanaur thirteen schools for the instruction of girls, and twenty-three for boys, a thing I have not seen anywhere else.[60]

Sultana Chand Bibi of Ahmadnagar

One of the most remarkable Muslim queens was Chand Bibi (1550–1600), or Chand Sultana of Ahmadnagar, one of five sultanates eventually absorbed by the Mughal empire. Chand Bibi's fame rests upon her regency for under-age sultans in Bijapur (1579–84) and later in Ahmadnagar (1591–1600), and also for her legendary resistance to the siege by the Mughal emperor Akbar (1556–1605). Chand Bibi was killed in an internecine struggle among her own officers shortly before Ahmadnagar succumbed to an apparently "savage" Mughal attack.[61]

Chand Bibi's parents were sultan Husayn Nizam Shah and queen (begam) Khonza Humayun in Ahmadnagar. Chand Bibi was married at the age of 12 to Bijapur's sultan Ali Adil Shah as a part of a treaty to realign the Deccan Muslim kingdoms. The alliance was cemented by the marriage of Chand Bibi's brother Burhan Nizam Shah II, future sultan of Ahmadnagar, to a Bijapur princess. After her husband's assassination in 1579, dowager Chand Bibi became regent for his nine-year-old son by another wife, the later celebrated sultan Ibrahim Adil Shah II (d. 1626) of Bijapur. Factional disputes were common in the Deccan among foreign-born *ashrafs*, Habshis, and local Muslims called Dakkhinis, and these struggles were often provoked by powerful eunuchs in the courts. Chand Bibi governed wisely with the help of Ikhlas Khan, a Habshi minister who also influenced her ward Ibrahim Adil Shah whose later reign was notable for its tolerance and innovation.[62]

In 1584, Chand Bibi returned to her home state of Ahmadnagar. In an effort to centralize his empire, Akbar sent missions in 1591 to Ahmadnagar and Bijapur. Ahmadnagar's sultan Burhan Nizam Shah II repulsed his emissaries and refused to cede the province of Berar to the Mughals. However, upon his untimely death, Chand Bibi became regent for her infant nephew; and under her leadership, Ahmadnagar resisted the Mughal siege. When bombs were detonated to bring down the fort in 1595–96, Chand Bibi successfully repaired the walls and continued to hold out until relief forces arrived from Bijapur and Golconda.[63] The Mughal army was weakened by squabbles between Akbar's generals and his alcoholic son Murad. In 1599, Akbar personally pitched camp outside Ahmadnagar with his 80,000 troops to take command over the siege. In August 1600, the Mughals breached the fort, and in the ensuing commotion, Chand Bibi was killed by jealous officers. Ahmadnagar then ceded to the Mughal empire.[64]

WOMEN IN THE MUGHAL ERA

Bridging Gendered Spaces

The Mughals were descended from nomadic Chagatai Turks and Mongols whose women had authority and ownership rights. Although the Mughal empire in India has been called a "patrilineal military state," its rulers prized an earlier Persian Muslim tradition of regnant queens. European visitors and later historians often described the engendering of space, with the public court being dominated by men, and female seclusion through *pardah* within the haram (*zenana*). Yet, public and private worlds were not as discrete as once imagined, as several royal women wielded considerable authority from within the haram, and they were immensely wealthy in their own right. While Mughals respected the haram's sanctity and their women as the "veiled ones," these gendered spheres were scenes of female activity, not passivity, with permeable boundaries. There existed bridges of communication, as the advice of senior royal women on political (public) issues and family (semi-private) matters had ramifications for the state.[65] The haram itself consisted of two sections, that is, private chambers solely for women, and common areas where close family men congregated to celebrate births, birthdays, female rites at marriage, and other occasions.

Moreover, royal women were not excluded from knowledge of public events, dramas, or sermons which they often watched through grilled trellises in the haram. They had opportunities for intellectual stimulation and were often accomplished women who read, wrote poetry, and painted. Several were patrons of painters, architects, and writers. Female *Qur'anic* scholars (*ustad bis*) instructed them as girls; and they had access to Akbar's vast library with books on world religions and on secular Persian, Turkish, and Indian literature. They sewed, played board games like chess and Parcheesi, played polo, and hunted outdoors. Contemporary accounts, paintings, and architecture inform us about this magnificent period in Indian history.

Early Mughal Women

Babur led a semi-nomadic life of political turmoil before he founded the Mughal empire at Agra in 1526. During battles, he was accompanied by his wives, children, and extended family of female relations who went from one base camp to another in covered litters or palanquins, and camped in *pardah* within closely guarded, opulent tents. In her work *Ahval-i-Humayun Badshah,* his gifted daughter Gulbadan Begam (1523–1603) describes *pardah* tents as lined with cloth-of-gold and having exotic comforts like silk cushions, deep carpets, a jeweled throne, jeweled drinking cups, and ewers for rose water.[66] While enjoying these luxuries and fine foods in temporary shelters, senior women helped to plan the military strategies of princes-in-waiting. It was in this atmosphere that Gulbadan was born to her mother Qut-luq-nigar Khanim before the conquest of northern India.[67]

In his autobiography *Babur Nama,* Babur referred respectfully to the "royal ladies." He paid particular tribute to his loyal wife Qut-luq-nigar by writing: "She was with me in most of my guerilla expeditions and throne-less times."[68] Qut-luq-nigar learned Turki and Persian from her erudite father, and bequeathed love of literature and composition to Gulbadan. Babur also thanked his maternal grandmother Aisan Daulat Begam for her wise counsel when he was a 12-year-old prince in search of a kingdom.[69] Aisan Daulat Begam had warned him that a Hasan-i-Ya'qub would prove traitorous. Babur wrote:

> Few amongst women will have been my grandmother's equal for judgment and counsel. She was very wise and farsighted and most affairs of mine were carried through under her advice. She and

my mother were (living) in the Gate-house of the outer fort; Hasan-I-Ya'qub was in the citadel.[70]

Gulbadan Begam

There is a paucity of real histories, and almost none by women in premodern India. This makes Gulbadan Begam's *Ahval-i-Humayun Badshah* a rare historical document.[71] The senior Mughal princess wrote this memoir of her half brother Humayun (d. 1556) upon the request of her nephew Akbar (1556–1605), who also asked for other people's accounts of his father (*Humayun-namas*). Although she inherited her father's literary talent and was devoted to Humayun, she initially pleaded a lack of scholarship. However, she eventually composed *Ahval-i-Humayun Badshah* in elegant Persian, the *lingua franca* of the Mughal court, interspersed with many Turkish phrases.[72]

Gulbadan's work was shadowed by the more famous *Ain-i-Akbari* by Akbar's close friend Abul Fazl; and her memoir was praised by later British historians in India. While many historians have overlooked it as simply an account of haram affairs, Gulbadan's *Ahval* is replete with information on politics in the early empire and on the adventures of Babur and Humayun (1530–56).[73] However, Gulbadan ends her work after describing Humayun's efforts to regain his empire, after having lost it to his treacherous half brother Kamran. Gulbadan's loyalty to Humayun far outweighed her sense of duty to her own weak husband Khizr Khan.

Ahval is also unique as it gives details of haram life and how her female relations in *pardah* assisted their men to establish the empire. This compels us to discard the earlier view of separate, gendered spheres of activity, since these worlds actually converged in the *zenana,* which was not as isolated as imagined. Notions of womanhood, wifehood, and motherhood were also not irrevocably fixed in the haram but altered due to political and social pressures.[74] Once this is acknowledged, however, it must be stated that the *zenana* later became a private female refuge during crises like invasions and colonial wars for hegemony over India (eighteenth to nineteenth century). While several Hindu and Muslim women were prominent figures, most ordinary women saw a shrinking of their public personas due to confinement in *pardah*.

Gulbadan describes the marriage alliances and relationships in detail, and a complex *zenana* hierarchy reflected in female duties and obligations. She reveals that despite seclusion, Mughal women freely articulated opinions, and that princes heeded the advice of seniors like Gulbadan and Hamida Begam, Humayun's wife and Akbar's mother, who performed administrative functions for the empire. For many, same-sex friendships were more binding than heterosexual relationships. A few did not consider homoerotic feelings incompatible with married love. Women candidly expressed their feelings about prospective husbands in a royal culture of political alliances often sealed with marriages. This is seen in Hamida Begam's early refusal to marry Humayun, who wooed her again and was later accepted. The events reveal that despite gender inequalities in political power, women had their own spheres of influence and rules of etiquette.[75] Humayun was a prince with a promising future, yet as a noblewoman, Hamida made this candid and trenchant comment:

> For forty days the begam resisted and discussed and disagreed. At last her highness my mother, Dil-dar Begam, advised her, saying, "After all you will marry someone. Better than a king, who is there?" The begam replied, "Oh yes, I shall marry someone; but he shall be a man whose collar I can touch, and not one whose skirt it does not reach."
>
> *Ahval-i-Humayun Badshah*[76]

Gulbadan's work is not a litany of frivolous concerns but a document that fills a void on the formative empire with minute details of Babur's relationship with the Uzbegs of Samarqand, and Humayun's struggles. It also describes the bartering of royal women for territory or peace, so that even Babur's exalted sister Khanzada Begam fell as a marriage pawn for the enemy.[77]

Mughal Heyday (1556–1707)

Politics and the *Zenana*

Mughal royal women were adept in the political game, questioned male decisions, and sometimes neglected marital duties for more permanent natal ties. Princesses were married more commonly before Akbar consolidated his empire. Thereafter, they often remained single, since high-ranking suitors complicated the struggles for succession. Although resident in the haram, they bridged the private and public worlds by interceding for rebellious princes or by conspiring with favorite brothers in the unceasing competition over the throne, complicated by royal polygamy. Several women wielded considerable power and negotiated state policies and family matters affecting the state. Less ambitious women were spectators who watched public events through the *zenana* trellises.[78] Their lives were hardly private, since political interests were reflected in their architectural commissions, letters and poetry, and pilgrimages to holy sites.

Gulbadan thus served as Akbar's trusted emissary in his contentious relations with the Portuguese whose maritime empire was based in Goa, Daman, Diu, and Surat. Their vouchers (*cartazes*) were needed for all ships sailing to and from India to the Persian Gulf, including those with *hajj* pilgrims to Arabia. In 1580, Akbar invited three Jesuits to Agra, one of whom was Antonio Monserrate who left a record of his visit. Monserrate describes the extent of Gulbadan's imperial authority and states that Gulbadan handed over the region of Bulsar to the Portuguese before leaving on a royal women's *hajj* organized by her. In October 1576, Gulbadan and a contingent of senior royal women sailed from Surat on the vessels *Salimi* and *Ilahi*, which Akbar had commissioned.[79] As Gulbadan was in *pardah*, these negotiations probably took place across the trellises overlooking the public hall. Gulbadan was accompanied by a granddaughter, a stepdaughter, her sister-in-law Salima Begam, and several others, and they returned three and a half years later after a perilous journey. Monserrate also states that as Gulbadan governed the major province of Delhi, her responsibilities devolved upon Hamida Begam during her absence.[80]

While many colonial histories attribute Gulbadan's pilgrimage to her piety, few state that this was the first imperial *hajj,* and that it transpired soon after Akbar's conquest of Gujarat (1573), which not only consolidated his empire but opened a port for maritime traffic to Mecca. Gulbadan's *hajj* thus marked a strategic imperial act for Akbar who commissioned the ships, arranged substantial funds, and provided thousands of sets of clothes for distribution among the pious in Mecca. Upon their return, Gulbadan was escorted in a magnificent palanquin across roads paved with silken cloths, and thousands of subjects were fed.[81] As religious policy, Gulbadan's *hajj* soothed a restive, conservative *ulama* after Akbar and Abul Fazl formulated their new eclectic sect Din-I-Ilahi which was inspired by Sufism, Zoroastrianism, and Hindu spiritualism.[82] While Gulbadan's piety may have led her to undertake the *hajj,* her trip validated Akbar's Muslim piety shortly after his new, controversial policy of religious toleration.

While historians focus on the Mughal military bureaucracy in which Rajputs were senior officials (*mansabs*), far less has been written about Rajput queens whose sons inherited the throne or on the political implications of having many Hindu princesses in the haram. Although Sunni Muslims, Akbar and his successors married three Hindu women from prominent Rajput dynasties, so that the *zenana* became central to his policy of social integration. Akbar's chief wife was the Rajput princess of Amber, Manmati/Harkha/Maryam-i-Zamani, and their son Salim later became emperor Jahangir (1605–27). One of his senior Rajput queens was Man Bai of Amber, also called Shah Begam (Imperial Wife), the mother of his eldest son Khusrau.[83] Although Khusrau's charm made him popular in the haram, his later rebellion so shamed Shah Begam that she committed suicide.[84] The beauty and wit of Jahangir's wife Jagat Gosain (Jodh Bai) of Jodhpur endeared her to the populace. Jodh Bai was the mother of his third son Khurram who was later crowned Shah Jahan (1627–56). Jahangir's Rajput wives included the Rathor mother of his daughter Bihar Banu Begam, a Bundela princess from Bikaner, Malika Jahan of Jaisalmer, and a Jaipur princess whom he wooed with an enormous sum.[85] Jahangir's brother Daniyal also married Rajput women; and several aristocrats took Hindu concubines. Even the conservative Sunni emperor Aurangzeb (1656–1707) relied on his Rajput relations as allies. Aurangzeb even claimed Rajput ancestry for his Circassian concubine Udaipuri Mahal whom he married and elevated to a queen. She was the mother of his favorite son Kam Baksh.[86] The Mughal haram was a multicultural universe whose internal politics reflected the court.

Mughal queens heard petitioners, issued minor edicts (*hukms*) on the release of prisoners and property transfers, and issued imperial orders (*firmans*). Such queens often interceded for rebellious princes beginning with Babur's sister Khanzada Begam who begged Humayun to forgive his recalcitrant brother Askari. Akbar's mother Hamida Begam also issued *hukms* and appealed for Jahangir when he rebelled. Three queens issued *firmans* with the royal seal, and they had royal titles or were honored with mausoleums. They were Jahangir's mother Harkha, his last wife Nur Jahan Begam (1611–45), and Shah Jahan's wife Mumtaz Mahal. Nur Jahan's name appeared with Jahangir's on gold coins, and she was the de facto ruler after he lost interest in governance due to opium addiction.[87] Born Meherunissa Begam, she received the title Nur Mahal (Light of the Palace) at marriage and of Nur Jahan (Light of the World) four years later.[88] Emperor Shah Jahan called his favorite daughter Jahanara Begam (Mistress of the Universe). European Jesuits and merchants from Portugal, Venice, Holland, France, and England left accounts of the Agra court, *zenanas,* and princesses like Nur Jahan, Jahanara, and Zebunissa.

Nur Jahan (1578–1645)

Although he had several wives and four sons as emperor in 1605, Jahangir became enamored of the 34-year-old widow, Meherunissa Begam, daughter of Itimad-ud-daula, an immigrant Persian noble. As Jahangir was bored by governance but interested in several intellectual pursuits, he agreed to make her chief queen. As the de facto sovereign in 1611, Nur Jahan Begam elevated her father and brother Asaf Khan to posts, heard courtiers' petitions, and stamped the royal seal on land grants. The court chronicle, *Iqbal-nama-i-Jahangiri,* states that she favored women property holders and gave generous dowries to orphan girls upon their marriage.[89]

Like Jahangir, Nur Jahan was not particularly devout, but she performed the traditional charities of a Muslim queen. She accompanied him to the shrine of the Sufi *pir* Moinuddin Salim Chishthi to whom Akbar had asked for prayers before the birth of his heir. He rewarded Salim Chishthi by naming his son Salim (Jahangir). At the annual feeding ceremony, Nur Jahan assisted her husband in serving the poor, and her presence was much remarked.[90] On another occasion, she and a skeptical Jahangir visited a Jaina shrine, where they debated with the chief monk on the merits of asceticism. It is not known whether Nur Jahan appeared in public with a *hijab,* full facial veil (*niqab*), or body cloak (*burqah*). Her attire would indicate if she conformed to conservative traditions or if she emulated Raziyya Sultana. As Nur Jahan performed the customary prayers for the royalty, she clearly did not wish to risk alienating the Sunni *ulama* in a period of growing conservatism after Akbar's radical reforms.

Nur Jahan's regime was momentous, as her name appeared with Jahangir's on gold coins, perhaps in emulation of Chandra Gupta I and Rani Kumaradevi (310 CE). Nur Jahan's talents included poetic compositions and sports like hunting and polo. A magnificent miniature shows her wielding a long musket, with her hair discretely under a cap, a long shift (*kameez*), and loose pants (*shalvar*) modestly covering her limbs.[91] She probably shared Jahangir's interest in nature and accompanied him into jungles to observe birds and wild animals. Nur Jahan's architectural commissions were a famous tomb to her father in Delhi, a tomb to her brother in Lahore, her gardens, and palaces like Nur Mahal in Agra. A talented businesswoman, she acted as her own ship's agent when importing English embroidery and exporting Indian textiles and jewelry. An affluent landowner, she used her personal fortunes to benefit destitute girls.

Despite these talents, she acquired an unsavory reputation for manipulating Jahangir and for deftly pitting one prince against another in the scramble for succession. Nur Jahan first tried to woo the talented third son Khurram (later emperor Shah Jahan) with opulent presents and by arranging his marriage to her niece Mumtaz Mahal. However, these acts failed to guarantee his friendship or that of Jagat Gosain, Khurram's mother and her chief rival in the haram. Nur Jahan then tried to entice the heir Khusrau to marry Ladli Begam, her only daughter from her first marriage. When that failed, she poisoned Jahangir's mind against Khusrau, in favor of the second son, the alcoholic prince Parviz. She later discarded Parviz for Shahariyar, the fourth prince whom she wedded to her daughter Ladli Begam. Jahangir appears to have been blissfully unaware of her intrigues, as he was lost to addictions and to his preoccupation with painting, science, and poetry. Western visitors to Agra commented that Nur Jahan drove a wedge between the emperor and Khurram, his favorite son.[92] Thomas Roe, the English merchant ambassador, jotted in his diary that public business "slept" unless she took notice of it, and astutely remarked: "She governs him and wynds him up at her pleasure."[93] Francisco Pelsaert, the Dutch agent in Agra (1618–25), maliciously described her as "a crafty wife of humble lineage" who used her "persuasive tongue" to manipulate the inebriated emperor.[94] The queen did twist the mind of an aging monarch, but the comments may reflect the merchant's jealousy over Nur Jahan's wealth and power. As she was only as opportunistic as other Mughal monarchs and certainly less bloodthirsty than some ambitious princes, it would be unfair to apply higher moral standards for female sovereigns than for kings.

Zenana Life

As instruction in the *Qur'an* was essential for good Muslims, *mullah* clerics taught both girls and boys in the mosque or in orphanage schools (*anjumans*). A miniature painting (sixteenth century) shows such a *mullah* teaching girls and a few boys, while naughty boys play nearby.[95] However, due to the emphasis on rote memorization in poor schools, illiteracy was more common among lower-class girls, as it was feared that having learned to write, they would pen clandestine love notes.

This was not the case with wealthy or aristocratic girls who were instructed in the *zenana* by learned *ustad bis* and elderly male *ustads*. Contrary to some accounts, aristocratic women did not languish in boredom, as they were taught not only the scripture but also other secular works. Thus, Jahanara, eldest daughter of emperor Shah Jahan, was taught by Satti Khanum, sister of court poet Talib-I-Amuli.[96] Zebunissa, emperor Aurangzeb's eldest daughter, was an able poet, who studied with the female tutor Hafiza Maryam. Emperor Aurangzeb paid the princely sum of 30,000 gold pieces to the *ustad bi* for having taught his cherished daughter well.[97] Women had access to libraries of illuminated handwritten manuscripts, which in Akbar's reign numbered in the thousands. They wrote verses, sometimes under a pseudonym, and recited the *Qur'an* and Persian poetry. Salima Sultan Begam, a granddaughter of Babur and the widow of Bairam Khan, composed Persian poetry under the popular pseudonym "Makhfi" (Hidden). Childless and scholarly Salima Sultan perused books for hours in Akbar's library. Yet, it was not her erudition but her "purity and nobility of disposition" that invited praise from Abul Fazl.[98] Jahanara's interest in Hindu philosophy was acquired through discussions with her favorite brother, the mystical Dara Shikoh.[99] Jahanara was also spiritually inclined, becoming a devotee of the Sufi *pir* Mullah Shah for whom she constructed a seminary and a mosque. Zebunissa imbibed her interest in spiritualism from her favorite aunt Jahanara.[100] Zebunissa also composed a book of poems under the pseudonym of Makhfi. She was a generous patron of religious poets who were women and men.[101] Zebunissa's library was inspired by Akbar's collection, which had the *Qur'an,* Hindu and Jaina scriptures, Greek mythology, Persian texts, travel accounts of the scholarly Alberuni, translations of the Bible, and contemporary writings about her ancestors.[102]

Medieval miniatures show women riding, hawking, and even hunting with guns, as seen in the painting of Nur Jahan holding a long musket. Like her, other Mughal women went riding and were adept at polo.[103] Jahangir shared his keen interest in natural science with his family women by venturing into the jungle to observe wild animals, birds, and plants. A delicate miniature shows the Hindu rani Roopmati of Sarangapur and her Muslim husband Sultan Raz Bahadur of Mandu (1564), riding with falcons on their wrists and gazing on a lake with storks.[104] Their love story is celebrated in a palace at Mandu and in legends (1508).[105]

Of sedentary pastimes such as cards, chess, and Parcheesi (*chaupar*), Zebunissa's favorite was Parcheesi. Women often played the lyre (*dilruba*) and listened to musicians from behind their trellised screens. They also watched puppetry and live animal shows, and were entertained by actors and storytellers. Devout women would hear sermons by *mullahs* and Sufi *shaikhs* from behind the *pardah* trellises.[106] They traveled outdoors in covered palanquins with attendants and went on pilgrimages to the tombs of Sufi saints (*dargahs*).

The haram had its own hierarchies of power with the aristocratic women at the top, served by ranks of female servants, each with norms of etiquette and decorum. The haram housed wives, female relatives, concubines, girl children, and underage male children who lived in nearby rooms. If earlier emperors had four wives and several concubines, Akbar had many wives. When informed by the *ulama* that he exceeded the numbers of contractual marriages (*nikah*) allowed by the Qur'an, theologian Badauni gave him a loophole, namely that law did not restrict "temporary" marriages (*mut'a*).[107] As Shias followed this custom, Akbar circumvented religious law by marrying many women, including Rajput Hindus who were not compelled to convert. The Mughal *zenana* thus comprised about five thousand women with their own entourages of wet nurses (*anaga*), deaf-mute female slaves, and chaste women superintendents (*daroghas*). Ethiopian or Uzbek women guards and eunuch guards guarded the *zenana*, and even Jahangir (1605–27).[108] The luxurious haram contained running water and pools; marble tiled floors, spacious rooms, gardens, wall murals of birds, flowers, and *sura* verses in calligraphy. It had its own kitchens with cooks, scullery maids, and bearers. A woman housekeeper (*mahaldar*) organized the servants, her authoritative position a source of envy and fear. Elite *ashraf* women avidly sought the post of royal wet nurse, who was crucial to the survival of the royal child, so that she often claimed princely favors for her own children, raised like royal foster siblings. The ambitious nurse Maham Anaga thus manipulated an underage Akbar into favoring her son Adham Khan, who blatantly misused his power. Mother and son also murdered rivals, so that Akbar killed Adham Khan and pensioned off his old nurse.[109]

What aristocratic women did not enjoy was the freedom to move unveiled outside the *zenana*, but even this was modified under protected conditions, if we can believe paintings. Women did not veil their faces in the *zenana*, and wore unrestrained clothes such as a long *kameez* with loose *shalvar* (pants) and undergarments. The *kameez* was of heavy silk or woven wool in winter, and even diaphanous cotton or silk during the summer. Paintings depict Mughal women with a thick shawl over the bosom and head, while younger women wear a wisp of a veil attached to an elongated cap ornamented with jewels and a feather. Although they lived behind the *pardah*, women received male relatives. They would then drape the shawl over the head to partially cover the face or appear completely unveiled.

As Islam forbids engraved images, at first Muslim artists in India did not depict the human face. However, this rule was broken by Mughal rulers in their collection of masterpiece miniature portraits. The habit of portraying the emperor developed after Akbar's advisor Abul Fazl claimed that "royalty is a ray of light emanating from God."[110] This new interpretation of divinely ordained royal authority became popular during Jahangir's reign (1605–27) when Muslim and Hindu artists painted emperors with haloes and unveiled royal women.[111]

In a compelling painting of the *zenana*, Akbar's Rajput queen Manmati/ Maryam-i-Zamani lies prone on a bed beneath a raised curtain, perhaps as a metaphor for women's unveiling. The women admire the infant Jahangir brought by Hindu women with scarves (*dupattas*) while Mughal women with jeweled caps watch benignly.[112] A full-length portrait shows a beautiful royal woman (ca. 1630) in a translucent gown to her ankles, her *shalvar* faintly visible, beaded necklaces, and a long cap with a fluttering ornamental veil. Another magnificent image shows Nur Jahan in a pensive mood, hair streaming down her back, a feathered cap, her bosom visible through a transparent, tight blouse. It is unlikely that male artists entered the *zenana* to paint royal women, and this portrait was probably an idealization.[113] Another possibility is that a woman painted or sketched the drawing, which was later finished by a male artist. There also exist some pictures by the woman painter Sahifa Banu (ca. 1620) whose work was admired. A sketch from the reign of Shah Jahan shows a female artist with other women before a drawing board.[114] It is conceivable that there were more women painters in the Mughal court, since Zebunissa (1638–1702), daughter of Aurangzeb, was praised for her calligraphy,[115] and other royal women were known for their artistic skills.[116]

Jahanara and Roshanara

Mumtaz Mahal bore 14 children for emperor Shah Jahan before she died in childbirth in 1631. She met the annual demands of pregnancy with aplomb, and yet managed to read and supervise all official documents, which she closed with the imperial seal in her possession. Deeply moved by her death, Shah Jahan commissioned the Taj Mahal as her mausoleum, a flamboyant tribute to a loyal wife. Despite such high honors on death or huge pensions and inheritances in life, Mughal women's lives were marked by political and sexual constraints. After Akbar's reign, most Mughal princesses remained single, mainly out of royal fears that high-ranking suitors would claim the throne. Patrilineal succession also restricted the princesses' right to the throne, and they became vicariously involved in the fratricidal rivalries of their brothers.

For example, in the succession battles among Shah Jahan's sons, his daughters conspired with their favorite brothers and shared their antithetical views on religion. His elder daughter Jahanara Begam (1613–80) sided with Dara Shikoh (d. 1659), the heir whose love for mysticism she shared. Dara introduced her to various books and philosophical ideas, and to a favorite Sufi *pir,* and Jahanara declared that their empathy made them "one soul in two bodies and one spirit in two physical forms."[117] Believing in the universality of human religious impulse, Dara tried to understand Hinduism by translating the *Upanishads* into Persian. He also allied himself with Rajput relations disaffected with Aurangzeb's conservative, Sunni beliefs and policies. During their struggle for the throne, Aurangzeb's claim was supported by Roshanara Begam (1617–71), a sister who acted as his spy in court. Roshanara's letters informed him of their father's distrust and kept Aurangzeb abreast of the latest political maneuvers to enable him to seize power. He then imprisoned Shah Jahan, crowned himself emperor, and beheaded his brother Dara for apostasy to Islam.

Rather than detailing Roshanara's political views or loyalty to Aurangzeb, Western accounts focused on her sexual escapades. Nicolao Manucci, a Venetian in Agra (1653–1708), thus described Roshanara as frivolous, "bright, mirthful, fond of jokes and amusement."[118] Frenchman Francois Bernier (1656–68) gossiped about her promiscuous affairs, including secreting lovers into the haram.[119] Roshanara inherited her father's streak of cruelty and insisted upon Dara's execution as a member of the council that tried him for apostasy to Islam. Roshanara argued that if Dara were imprisoned instead of killed, he would continue with his heresies, and conspire against Aurangzeb.[120]

Jahanara Begam was the first child of Shah Jahan to whom she was greatly devoted, and she nursed Mumtaz Mahal in her final illness. After her mother's death in 1631, the 18-year-old princess took over the care of her father to whom she remained loyal till he died 20 years later. The gossip monger Bernier hinted that such filial devotion was based on an incestuous relationship, as she was "passionately beloved by her father," and their "attachment reached a point which is difficult to believe." Bernier blamed Jahanara for conniving to dominate the aged emperor, and he sympathized with Shah Jahan for entrapping her suitors out of jealousy. Although Manucci was often salacious, he did not credit rumors of incest, but he felt that the princess manipulated her father while he grieved for his wife.[121] Despite their gossip about Jahanara's love of wine and sexual escapades, they also described her as pious and dignified. Her piety earned her the title of Padshah Begam (chief Mughal princess); Jahanara frequented the shrines of Sufi saints of the Chishthi and Qadiriyya orders to whom she donated munificently. She thanked Dara Shikoh for introducing her to *pir* Mulla Shah through whom she had a spiritual experience. She described this eloquently:

I then sat down in a corner facing Mecca, and concentrated my mind on the picture of my master, whilst at the same time keeping a description of our holy Prophet before my eyes. While occupied with this contemplation, I reached a spiritual state in which I was neither asleep nor awake. I saw the holy community of the Prophet and his first disciples with the other holy ones; the Prophet and his four companions were sitting together . . . I also noticed Mulla Shah. He was sitting near the Prophet, his head resting on his foot, whilst the Prophet said to him, "O, Mullah Shah, for what reason have you enlightened this Timurid girl?" When I came to my senses again, my heart opened like a rose bud under the impact of this sign of God's grace . . . Oh what exceptional good fortune, what unheard of happiness he has vouchsafed to me, a weak and unworthy woman! I bring thanks and endless praise to the Almighty, the unfathomable God, who, when my life seemed all set to be wasted, allowed me to devote myself to the quest for Him.[122]

Despite these religious feelings, Jahanara was not a rigid moralist as she enjoyed both liquor and light entertainment. On one occasion, she sustained serious burns when her favorite dancer's clothes caught on fire while twirling near candles. Jahanara flung herself upon the dancer to put out the flames. Severely injured on the chest, Jahanara was critically ill for a considerable time, while her father prayed beside her bed. Upon her recovery, she visited a Sufi shrine in Ajmer. Jahanara used her immense fortunes for charity, especially to widows. Like her father, she commissioned monuments and gardens, and a bathhouse and palaces in Old Delhi. She supported writers and artists, and delighted in Persian literature. Jahanara endeavored to prevent Aurangzeb's persecution and beheading of his elder brother Dara. However, Aurangzeb killed him and eliminated his other brothers to ascend the Peacock throne. As emperor, he banned alcohol and music at court, so that Jahanara tried to convince him that such austere injunctions promoted hypocrisy and clandestine drinking. One account states that she invited the wives of clerics to her chambers, and then plied them with wine till they lay in a stupor. She then led Aurangzeb to view the women, "lying drunk and in disorder," and he was forced to reevaluate his methods to reform a profligate court.[123] Ironically, his favorite daughter Zebunissa Begam was influenced by her aunt Jahanara's proclivity for poetry and Sufi mysticism.

Zebunissa's Rebellion

The most notable of Aurangzeb's several daughters was Zebunissa Begam (1638–81), daughter of his first wife Dilras Begam whose marriage was promoted by Jahanara. Zebunissa was born in the Deccan during her father's military campaign during Shah Jahan's reign. Her first teacher was the poetess Hafiza Maryam, who also taught her sisters to recite the *Qur'an.* Upon hearing his seven-year-old daughter's rendition of the sacred verses, Aurangzeb showered Hafiza Maryam with 30,000 pieces of gold and appointed her son to a high post. Zebunissa was also taught Persian poetry by her great-grandmother Salima Begam, and she soon composed poetry.[124] Zebunissa accompanied her favorite aunt Jahanara and uncle Dara Shikoh to the hermitage of the *pir* Mulla Shah with whom Dara engaged in deep conversations. Unhappy over her separation from her father Aurangzeb, Zebunissa became attached to Dara who encouraged her to pursue calligraphy, an art form popular among devout Muslims. Zebunissa also began to paint and read extensively under Dara's influence, especially from Akbar's vast library to which Dara had added non-Muslim Indian texts. She shared her father's fascination for astrology and religious subjects, but was influenced by Dara's eclectic vision. Zebunissa wrote mystical, mournful verses under the pseudonym of "Makhfi." They reflect her sense of alienation, which may have stemmed from knowledge of her father's murder of Dara and several cousins.[125] An example of her poetic themes is given here:

> Behold the pages of my book of life!
> Its record blotted, black with sin and strife,
> As if the woe of all the world should be
> Ever following and pursuing me.
> *Diwan* 11[126]

As Zebunissa loved the gardens in Agra and Delhi, a Garden of Zebunissa in Lahore is named for her. She financed poor poets, even sending them on *hajj* to Mecca. She and her sister Zinatunissa commissioned mosques in Delhi and Agra.[127] However, the life of this talented woman changed due to a succession struggle in the Rajput state of Marwar. Aurangzeb challenged the autonomy of this traditional Mughal ally and threatened to convert the infant heir to Islam. When Marwar resisted, Aurangzeb sent his forces under his son Mohammad Akbar. Akbar was deeply devoted to his sister Zebunissa, since his mother had died at his birth (1657). The disaffected Rajputs convinced Mohammad Akbar of their support if he rebelled against his father's conservative rule. Mohammad Akbar corresponded frequently with Zebunissa who supported her brother's rebellion.[128] There was a deep dissatisfaction against Aurangzeb among the Rajputs, Marathas, Sikhs, and Shia Muslims.[129] Prince Mohammad Akbar crowned himself emperor in 1681 with the help of the Rajputs and his brother Moazzam. However, the surrender of his battalions led to his flight to the Marathas, and later to Persia. As Mohammad Akbar's rebellion failed, Zebunissa was imprisoned for complicity, and she died in prison in 1702.

Oriental Women through Western Eyes

India's contacts with Europe date from the third century BCE, but the arrival of Vasco da Gama's Portuguese ships on May 20, 1498 at Calicut ushered in an era of less congenial relations. By 1509, the Portuguese had established a maritime trading empire based in Goa, Diu, and Daman on the western coast. These ports became Catholic missionary centers with Dominican, Franciscan, and later Jesuit monks in 1542. Akbar's invitation to some Jesuits to his court set the stage for European visitors to Agra. Although the men were quite different in their responses to India, several described the Mughal haram as a den of luxury, intrigue, and sexual mayhem. The Portuguese were initially tolerant toward Hindus as allies against Muslim states, but this changed, especially during the Counter Reformation (ca. 1540) when the Catholic Church instituted the Inquisition (1560–1812) in Goa and elsewhere. A few like the Italian humanist Pietro della Valle who visited Agra in 1623 praised Shah Jahan for honoring his female relations. Others resembled Sir Thomas Roe, the Protestant emissary of the English East India Company at Jahangir's court. Roe commented on Mughal princesses and their luxuries, but did not seriously acknowledge the business acumen of senior women. The Jesuit Monserrate (in Agra in 1580) so distrusted Islam that he viewed Akbar's international haram as a sign of Oriental excess, rather than as an unusual political ploy to unite a multiethnic empire. Monserrate commented that Akbar had "more than 300 wives," each in a separate suite, but did not seem to understand how there were "only three sons and two daughters."[130] He also did not appear to have considered the possibility that a multiethnic *zenana* promoted cultural harmony, and not Oriental promiscuity. Yet, Monserrate reported that Gulbadan was Akbar's emissary to the Portuguese, and that she governed Delhi.[131] Such views later fueled British descriptions of Asia as the unfathomable Orient, a continent that was *essentially* alien to Christian Europe.[132] A rare British historian suspected that Akbar's haram was a "parliament of religions," and regretted that no one had described its "probable debates."[133]

Some Western writings are replete with secondhand anecdotes passed off as eyewitness accounts. This is the case of the Florentine Francesco Carletti (ca. 1600) who recounted the mass *sati* for a Vijayanagar king 40 years after the event.[134] Others were laced with supercilious judgments on Indian customs. Few Western men actually entered the *zenana*, except for the French doctor Francois Bernier (in Agra, 1658–64). However, Bernier's Eurocentric views make his account less than objective. Bernier explains how he was taken into the *zenana* to treat a woman too ill to come to the gate, writing with distaste about being swathed in a long shawl from head to toe, and led "as if I were a blind man" by a eunuch.[135] Bernier's gossip about Shah Jahan's incestuous love for Jahanara has been related earlier. The truth probably was that after watching the homicidal rivalry of his sons, the aging ruler could only trust this daughter. Aurangzeb later imprisoned his father and crowned himself emperor. Bernier wrote:

> Rumour has it that his attachment reached a point which is difficult to believe ... [and that] *Chah-Jehan* reposed unbounded confidence in this his favorite child ... It is not surprising, therefore, that her ascendancy in the court of the *Mogol* should have been nearly unlimited.[136]

Some writers indulged in fantasies about the mysterious *pardah*, yet these have been read as eyewitness accounts of the *zenana*. Few men entered the actual female chambers, but some foreigners ate with nobles in the *zenana* dining halls. Nicolao Manucci, a Venetian gunrunner and medical quack (1656–1717), described the Mughal court in *Storio Do Mogor*. He wrote of women patients lying prone behind a *pardah*, like pieces of flesh without will, mechanically sticking out the appropriate limb for examination, sometimes calling for a consultation simply to indulge in flirtations. Manucci also gossiped about the drinking orgies of Jahanara and Roshanara, particularly maligning the latter as starved for sex, and enticing men into the haram disguised as women. He described how Roshanara escaped for trysts outside the palace.[137] To his credit, however, Manucci also reported two incidents that portray Jahanara favorably. He described her unselfish aid to a woman dancer whose clothes caught on fire, and then engulfed the princess. He also related how Jahanara exposed court hypocrisy when the *ulama* urged Aurangzeb to outlaw alcohol. Jahanara invited the clerics' wives, served them intoxicants, and called her brother to witness them asleep in stupor.[138]

Dutch merchant Francisco Pelsaert (1620–27) described palace women as preoccupied with jewelry, clothes, shallow intrigue in *Remonstrantie*. However, he incidentally betrayed his own Puritan repressions in his descriptions of the "burning passions" driving the "wretched women" to use eunuchs. Such myths of the Orient probably shaped later Hollywood writers whose films often depicted voluptuous Muslim women lounging in the haram.[139] Pelsaert wrote:

> The *mahals* are adorned internally with lascivious sensuality, wanton and reckless festivity, superfluous pomp, inflated pride, and ornamental daintiness, while the servants of the lords may be justly described as a generation of iniquity, greed and oppression ... As a rule they have three or four wives, the daughters of worthy men, but the senior wife commands most respect. All live together in the enclosure surrounded by high walls, which is called the *mahal*, having tanks and gardens inside. Each wife has separate apartments for herself and her slaves of whom there may be ten, or twenty or 100, according to her fortune.

Each has a regular monthly allowance for her expenditure. Jewels and clothes are provided by the husband according to the extent of his affection. Their food comes from one kitchen, but each wife takes it in her own apartments; for they hate each other secretly, though they seldom or never allow it to be seen, because of their desire to retain the favour of their husband, whom they fear, honour, and worship as a god rather than a man. Each night he visits a particular wife, or *mahal,* and receives a warm welcome from her and from the slaves who, dressed specially for the occasion, seem to fly, rather than run about their duties ... In the cool of the evening they drink a great deal of wine, for the women learn the habit quickly from their husbands, and drinking has become very fashionable in the last few years. The husband sits like a golden cock among the gilded hen until midnight, or until passion, or drink sends him to bed. Then if one of the pretty slave-girls takes his fancy, he calls her to him and enjoys her, his wife not daring to show any signs of displeasure, but dissembling, though she will take it out of the slave-girls later on.[140]

Yet, his ideas of sexual repression may have been partially true, as the profusion of co-wives and concubines made princely conjugal visits infrequent for each wife. This partly explains why senior queens did not easily conceive male legitimate heirs. Kings also married noblemen's widows, but royal widows rarely remarried, and as few high-ranking loyal nobles could be trusted to marry princesses, there were many single women in the *zenana.* These frustrations are reflected in the eighteenth-century miniatures of lesbianism in the *zenana,* and in textual references to women's use of phallic objects (*apradavyas*) of gold, silver, various metals, ivory, and wood.[141] For many men and women, the closest bonds were same-sex friendships, without or with erotic desire, but they met in the *zenana* for other amusements besides sex and procreation. Royal men entered to dine, listen to music, watch dancers, or to simply converse with the women. Here Shah Jahan (1627–56) spent his days with his wife Mumtaz Begam, and his daughter Jahanara attended to him in his final years. Lesser nobles relaxed with family women, and sometimes invited European guests to dine. It is thus likely that Pelsaert, Roe, and chaplain Edward Terry (seventeenth century) probably saw serving maids, and perhaps just briefly met veiled noblewomen.[142]

Sufi and Shia Women

Sufi Traditions in North India

If rank and file Sufi *pirs* spread Islam in the countryside, Sufi intellectuals and poets in court interwove *Qur'anic* beliefs with local legends. They invented syncretic literary traditions whose ideals of gender and sexuality were adapted from Indian traditions. Indian Muslim sultans were their patrons, and they too drew upon pre-Islamic precedents of court culture.[143] For example, Sufi poets in Bihar's Jaunpur sultanate (fourteenth to seventeenth century) composed a new epic form in the Awadhi or eastern Hindavi language. The narrative was similar to the Sanskrit-Indian epic love story ("prem-kahani"), but they interwove the theme of divine love from the Sufi poet Ibn al-Arabi's (eleventh century) elusive epistle, "Fususal-hikam" (Jewels of Wisdom). Hindavi poets gave a Sufi twist to a theme common in *bhakti* poetry. Self-absorbed human lovers thus became a metaphor for a devotee's "self-annihilation" *(fana)* into Allah. Poet Maulana Daud (1379) borrowed a lower-caste legend of Lorik and Canda to weave the first Hindavi romance, *Candayan,* with this theme. In *Mirigavati* (1503), poet Qutban told the sensual tale of Chandragiri (Moon Mountain) and Mirigavati (Doe woman), underscoring the message about ethical choices. The separated lovers are reminiscent of Rama and Sita in the Hindu *Ramayana;* the heroine's name reminds us of Sita's illusory deer, while the hero's ascetic journey reinforces his duty to God, just as Rama's travails to recover Sita reestablished *dharma* on earth.[144]

Sufi tombs *(dargahs)* sanctified Indian soil for many Muslims who could not make the *hajj* to Mecca. Women, the ill, and the destitute found it especially impossible to seek this spiritual benefit, and pilgrimages to *dargahs* became a simpler alternative. Women found the *hajj* daunting, as it entailed an expensive entourage of guards and servants, with palanquins as *pardahs.*[145] Women thus often made these visits to Sufi shrines, and if converts they transposed pre-Islamic traditions onto the new rites. North India's important *dargahs* for Sufi Shaikhs were for Mu'in-uddin Chishthi (Punjab); Nizam-uddin Auliya (d. 1325) and Baba Farid-uddin Ganj-I-Shakar (Delhi). Local customs of royal fealty were transposed upon Muslim ideas on paying honor *(adab),* for example, by Jat caste converts at Baba Farid's *dargah.*[146] *Dargahs* are also pilgrimage sites for Hindus who revere all saints.

While more scholarship is needed on the effects of Sufism on Muslim women, one scholar has shown that the hymns of *pirs* were sung by medieval women in the Deccan while performing their chores of child and family care.[147] Women sought comfort from mystical poetry and composed their own oral verses, which are unfortunately often unavailable to the historian.[148] Despite spiritual equality in Islam, medieval women were in the periphery of religious authority, and class distinctions were rife. Few Indian women could seek spiritual counsel from *mullahs,* unless these were elderly men allowed inside the *zenana.* Girls in the *zenana* were taught only by old men or learned female teachers *(ustad bi).* However, devout women often listened from behind the trellises to sermons by ascetic Sufis whose message of love was more relevant to female life than that of young *mullahs* in mosques. One such Sufi saint was Nizam-uddin Auliya whose concern for the paucity of *Qur'anic* female scholars led him to praise spiritual women like his mother and Bibi Sharifa, the daughter of Baba Farid who could not obtain the legal credentials of a Sufi Shaikh despite her great erudition.[149] Despite their relative exclusion from religious authority, devout women emulated female mystics like the Prophet's daughter Fatima; the Sufi Rabi'a of Iraq (eighth century); and Indian mystics like Bibi Sharifa, and Hazarat Zaccha Bibi of south India.[150] Poor but with great spiritual grace, women Sufis resembled the Hindu servant woman Janabai whose *bhakti* for Krishna lifted her above a crippling caste system. Legends about disenfranchised saints often inspired Indian women.

Islam and Gender in South India

South Indian Sufi saints integrated Islam into Dravidian culture, often connecting the *pirs* (or Hazarats) with female power or *shakti*. While most *pirs* were men, there are some important *dargahs* to female mystics in southern India. Two shrines to women *pirs* are located in Porto Novo near Thanjavur, Tamil Nadu. The first is to Hazarat a-Quraish Bibi (seventeenth century) whose *shakti* enabled her to conquer snake and scorpion bites. The second is to Hazarat Zaccha Bibi regarded by women as assisting them during pregnancy, depression, and other female sorrows. The shrine continues to draw pilgrims since a hospital was built next to it.[151]

A third is a famous *dargah* to Hazarat Mira Sahib and his wife Sultana Bibi (sixteenth century) at Nagapattinam, and it is visited by Muslim and Hindu pilgrims. The tombs lie beside each other, decorated with marigold garlands from devotees with "*bhakti*," according to the site booklet.[152] Women are frequently found sitting in prayer beside the tombs. A medieval Tamil Muslim devotional poem, *Nakaiyan-antatim*, is addressed to the saints of the *dargah* in the genre of Tamil *bhakti* poetry. Male *mullahs* say prayers in Tamil and Arabic, burn incense and smear sacred ash on the devotee irrespective of sect, while the worshipper gives flowers, coconuts, fruits, sweets, and meat to the saints. Except for the meat, these offerings resemble Sanskrit *puja* to Hindu gods in temples.[153]

The motifs at other Tamil *dargahs* such as to Kat Bava, Nathar Wali, and Alimullah Qadiriyya resemble Hindu legends for Devi/Amman, Shiva, and Vishnu, respectively. The myth of Kat Bava shrine concerns seven holy maidens, like the Hindu myth of seven goddesses (*sapta matrikas*) who emanated from Durga. Muslim and Hindu devotees refer to the Sufi shrine's mystique (*barakat*) as its "*shakti*" (energy or strength), and as "*shakti*" is another name for Amman or Shakti Devi in south India, some devotees identify the *pir* with the Goddess.[154] Islam was grafted onto Dravidian societies through curious mergers of local and Sufi ideas. One Tamil theoretical school draws on the parallel veneration of Amman as Shakti, and early Islamic maternalism. It suggests that Prophet Muhammad married several women out of genuine concern for their welfare, so that his wives are exalted in the *Qur'an* as "Mothers of Islam" (Umm-al-Momineen). Another school draws dual inspiration from Ibn al-Arabi's semi-erotic Sufi text, "Fususal-hikam," and from Tantric ideas of goddess Devi's primal *yoni* or womb. This theology suggests that al-Arabi's hidden message of sacred sexuality is a metaphor for ecstatic union with God, thus acknowledging a primal female in the universe.

Shia Women's Rites

Each year during Muharram in Lucknow, Uttar Pradesh, and Hyderabad, Andhra Pradesh, Shia men and women mourn the martyred children of Ali and Fatima. A Mrs. Ali recorded these rites in 1820 during the colonial era, but they had existed for centuries earlier, and still continue. While men's public flagellations are well known, less is known about aristocratic women who beat their breasts and sing dirges within their *zenanas*. The women especially mourn Zaynab's lost veil signifying her bridal widowhood; and four-year-old Sakina's death from wounds, symbolic of her desecrated innocence.[155] Mrs. Ali confirmed that female rites were devout and powerful, although male rituals were more bloody and public. During the 10-day season, women sacrificed their usual comforts, wore dark clothes even in the intense summer, abjured jewelry and flowers, and luxuries like betel leaves (*paan*). They gathered in a room with a cenotaph for Hasan and Husayn, while educated women read Shia poetry aloud.[156]

Moreover, while men compiled the Sharia laws, women have shaped local Indian Muslim customs by retaining or borrowing Hindu customs. The Khojas of Kathiawar are the descendants of local Shia converts. Benign Khoja customs often involve wedding ceremonies shaped by women, including the habit of smearing the bride with turmeric for good luck. A cultural point of convergence is Khoja devotional songs (*ginaans*) in classical Hindu melodies to induce spiritual ecstasy (*barakat*). While many *ginaans* are attributed to men, there was at least one female composer. Saiyida Imam Begum (d. 1866?) wrote the popular *ginaan*, "Ae Rahem Raheman" (O, Merciful and Powerful), in which she regretted that she was not a Sufi *pir* like her mentor Shaikh Hasan Shah.[157] However, the Khojas also borrowed some Hindu customs that adversely affect women, such as patriarchal inheritance and the objection to widow remarriage. Khoja eclecticism is evident in the enlisting of Sunni clerics to officiate at weddings and funerals.

Muslim Musicians, Poets, and Dancers

Late thirteenth-century sultans were often entertained by dancers, instrumentalists, composer-singers called *taifa* (*tawaif* [singular]). Like Hindu *devadasis*, *taifa* artistes were highly regarded in Muslim courts, as they helped to shape new literary and musical traditions. However, later Victorian rulers equated them with English dance hall girls, and demeaned them as *nautch* women or prostitutes. This led many *taifa* to call themselves *ganevalis* (singers).[158] The *taifa* danced in the *kathak* style, whose original Indian classical postures with bent knees were replaced by straight legged poses used in Persia. Similarly, their songs (*ghazal*) used Indian melodic arrangements (*ragas*) but Urdu lyrics infused with a yearning for Allah resembling Hindu *bhakti*. Urdu is a language akin to Hindi, but enriched by Persian, and these links appear in Amir Khusrau's Urdu poems (thirteenth century). These art forms flourished due to *ganevalis* in Lucknow in Uttar Pradesh, and Hyderabad in the Deccan. The artistes became famous for their Urdu *ghazals* and *kathak* dances (*nautch*), like the woman composer Mahlaqa Chanda (1767–1824) of Hyderabad.[159] In 1790, a Hasan Shah wrote *Nashtar* on the life of Khanum Jan, another real-life *ganevali*.[160] He revealed that gifted courtesans were taught Persian, Urdu, English, and the arts, but were often dismissed as *nautch* women (dancing prostitutes) in colonial army camps.[161] Another sensitive portrayal of the *ganevali* was *Umrao Jan Ada* (1902) by Mirza Mohammad Hadi Ruswa whose talented heroine could not find a worthy husband, although her talents brought wealthy patrons.[162] Tarred by the colonial brush as prostitutes, women performers were penalized by Victorian laws, and finally "saved" by Indian nationalists.

NOTES

1. Allama Abdullah Yusuf Ali, trans., *The Meaning of the Illustrious Qur'an (Being the Textless Edition of the English Translation of the Holy Qur'an)* (1934; repr., Lahore: Shaikh Muhammad Ashraf, 1946), 354.

2. Zoya Hasan and Ritu Menon, *Unequal Citizens: A Study of Muslim Women in India* (New Delhi: Oxford University Press, 2004); Shibani Roy, *Status of Muslim Women in North India* (Delhi: B. R. Publishers, 1979); Indira Jaising, ed., *Men's Laws, Women's Lives: A Constitutional Perspective on Religion, Common Law and Culture in South Asia* (New Delhi: Women Unlimited and Kali for Women, 2005), these essays: Pratap Bhanu Mehta, "Reason, Tradition, Authority: Religion and the Indian State," 56–86; Cassandra Balchin, "Law Reform Processes in Plural Legal Systems," 87–108; Martha Nussbaum, "Religion, Culture and Sex Equality," 109–37; Sharan Parmar, "Gender Equality in the Name of Religion," 226–58.

3. Muhammad's first revelation in Mecca (*sura* 96) is placed near *sura* 98, which was revealed later in Medina. See Fatima Mernissi, *Women and Islam: An Historical and Theological Enquiry,* trans. Mary Jo Lakeland (Delhi: Kali for Women, 1991), 118–22, 125–26.

4. On Islam in India, see: Richard M. Eaton, *The Rise of Islam and the Bengal Frontier, 1204–1760* (Berkeley and Los Angeles: University of California Press, 1993), 113–34; Richard M. Eaton, ed., *India's Islamic Traditions, 711–1750* (Delhi: Oxford University Press, 2003); Susan Bayly, *Saints, Goddesses and Kings: Muslims and Christians in South Indian Society 1700–1900* (Cambridge: Cambridge University Press, 1989).

5. Gail Minault, "Other Voices, Other Rooms: The View from the Zenana," in *Women as Subjects: South Asian Histories,* ed. Nita Kumar (Calcutta: Stree, 1994), 108–24.

6. Leila Ahmed, *Women and Gender in Islam* (New Haven: Yale University Press, 1992), 79–100.

7. Ashgar Ali Engineer, ed., *Problems of Muslim Women in India* (Bombay: Orient Longman, 1995), these essays: Ashgar Ali Engineer, "The Status of Women and Social Change," 1–17; "Appendix I: Marriage Agreement—A Sample of a Nikhanama," 180–82; "Appendix II: Revised Memorandum by the Muslim Women's Research & Action Front to the Committee on Proposed Reforms to the Muslim Personal Law," 183–92.

8. Maulana Mohammad Abdul-Aleem Siddiqui, *Elementary Teachings of Islam* (Karachi: Taj Company Ltd., 1954), 6–24.

9. Ali, *The Meaning of the Illustrious Qur'an*, 463.

10. Mernissi, *Women and Islam*, 107.

11. Ali, *The Meaning of the Illustrious Qur'an*, 26.

12. Siddiqui, *Elementary Teachings of Islam*, 25–77.

13. Syed Abas A. Rizvi, *The Wonder that Was India*, vol. 2, *A Survey of the History and Culture of the Indian Sub-Continent from the Coming of the Muslims to the British Conquest, 1200–1700*, 5th ed. (1987; repr., Delhi: Rupa & Co., 1996), 2; and Wiebke Walther, *Women in Islam from Medieval to Modern Times* (Princeton and New York: Marcus Wiener Publishing, 1993), 73.

14. Mernissi, *Women and Islam*, 102–3.

15. Ibid., 149–53, 176–79.

16. Ibid., 104, 136–37.

17. Ibid., 117–20, 132–35.

18. Ali, *The Meaning of the Illustrious Qur'an*, 214–15.

19. Ibid., 28–29.

20. Ibid., 288–89.

21. Ibid., 58–59, 355.

22. Ibid., 57–58, 61.

23. Vibhuti Patel, "The Shah Bano Controversy and the Challenges Faced by Women's Movement in India," in *Problems of Muslim Women in India*, ed. Engineer, 140–48; Sita Anantha Raman, "Shah Bano Case," in *Encyclopedia of India*, ed. Stanley Wolpert, vol. 4 (New York: Charles Scribner, 2005), 44–45.

24. Prema A. Kurien, *Kaleidoscopic Ethnicity: International Migration and the Reconstruction of Community Identities in India* (Delhi: Oxford University Press, 2002), 96.

25. Ali, *The Meaning of the Illustrious Qur'an*, 59–60.

26. Ibid., 353, 356.

27. Mernissi, *Women and Islam*, 142–43; Walther, *Women in Islam from Medieval to Modern Times*, 104–6.

28. Ramala Baxamula, "Need for Change in Muslim Personal Law Relating to Divorce in India," in *Problems of Muslim Women in India*, ed. Engineer, 18–29.

29. Ali, *The Meaning of the Illustrious Qur'an*, 356.

30. Ibid.

31. Mernissi, *Women and Islam*, 162–65.

32. Walther, *Women in Islam from Medieval to Modern Times*, 71–72, quoting Ibn Sa'd's (ninth century) *Kitab at-Tabaqat-al-kabir*, vol. 8, ed. E. Sachau et al. (Leiden: 1904–21), 74n; also Mernissi, *Women and Islam*, 86–88, citing

Al-Tabari's (tenth century), *Tafsir, jami'ak-aayan 'an ta'wil ayi al-qur'an,* vol. 22 (Beirut: Dar a-Fikr, 1984), 26.

33. David Pinault, "Zaynab Bint' Ali and the Place of the Women of the Households of the Imams in Shi'ite Devotional Literature," in *Women in the Medieval Islamic World,* ed. Gavin R. G. Hambly (New York: St. Martin's Press, 1998), 70–80.

34. Ahmed, *Women and Gender in Islam,* 41–78.

35. Zenab Banu, "Muslim Women's Right to Inheritance: Sharia Law and Its Practice Among the Dawoodi Bohras of Udaipur, Rajasthan," in *Problems of Muslim Women in India,* ed. Engineer, 34–39.

36. Syed Abas A. Rizvi, "Islam in Medieval India," in *A Cultural History of India,* ed. A. L. Basham, 6th ed. (Delhi: Oxford University Press, 2002), 281–93, *vide,* 282.

37. Richard M. Eaton, "The Political and Religious Authority of the Shrine of Baba Farid," in *India's Islamic Traditions, 711–1750,* ed. Eaton, 263–84; Simon Digby, "The Sufi Shaikh as a Source of Authority in Medieval India," in *India's Islamic Traditions, 711–1750,* ed. Eaton, 234–62; and Richard M. Eaton, *Sufis of Bijapur: Social Roles of Sufis in Medieval India* (Princeton: Princeton University Press, 1978).

38. Eaton, *The Rise of Islam and the Bengal Frontier, 1204–1760,* 71–94, 238–39, 275–81.

39. Peter Jackson, *The Delhi Sultanate: A Political and Military History* (Cambridge: Cambridge University Press, 1999), 47.

40. Texts of Minhaj Siraj's "Tabaqat-I-Nasiri" are available in H. G. Raverty, ed., *A General History of the Muhammadan Dynasties of Asia, Including Hindustan (810–1260)* (1881; repr., Delhi: Oriental Books Reprint Corporation, 1970), 1:637–38; and Henry Miers Elliot and John Dowson, eds., *The History of India as Told by Its Own Historians: The Muhammadan Period* (1869; repr., New York: AMS Press, 1966), 2:332. Historian Rizvi, *The Wonder that Was India,* 2:217, 320, cites H. G. Raverty's translation, *A General History of the Muhammadan Dynasties of Asia;* and John Keay, *India: A History* (New York: Grove Press, Harper Collins, 2000), 245–46, 540 n. 17, using Elliot and Dowson's translation, *History of India as Told by Its Own Historians.*

41. Minhaj Siraj, "Tabaqat-I-Nasiri," in *The History of India as Told by Its Own Historians,* ed. Elliot and Dowson, 2:330.

42. See Rafiq Zakaria's *Razia: Queen of India* (1966; repr., New Delhi: Oxford University Press, 1999), 137.

43. Siraj, "Tabaqat-I-Nasiri," 2:330–32.

44. Jackson, *The Delhi Sultanate: A Political and Military History,* 67.

45. Elliot and Dowson, *The History of India as Told by Its Own Historians,* 2:332–37. This is questioned by Raverty in *A General History of the Muhammadan Dynasties of Asia,* 1:637–38.

46. Jackson, *The Delhi Sultanate: A Political and Military History,* 47, 67–68.

47. Siraj's "Tabaqat-I-Nasiri," 2:332–37.

48. Walther, *Women in Islam: From Medieval to Modern Times,* 121–22.

49. Keay, *India: A History,* 245; also see Irfan Habib, *The Cambridge Economic History of India* (1200–1750 CE), ed. T. Raychaudhuri and Irfan Habib (Cambridge: Cambridge University Press, 1982), 1:78.

50. H. A. R. Gibb, trans., *Travels of Ibn Battuta,* 2nd series (Cambridge and London: Hakluyt Society at the University Press, 1958), 3:632; also Jackson, *The Delhi Sultanate: A Political and Military History,* 46.

51. Siraj, "Tabaqat-I-Nasiri," 2:345–56.

52. Iqtidar Hussain Siddiqui, "Socio-Political Role of Women in the Sultanate of Delhi," in *Women in Indian History: Social, Economic, Political and Cultural Perspectives,* ed. Kiran Pawar (Patiala: Vision & Venture Publishers, 1996), 87–101, vide, 90–93; Rizvi, *The Wonder that Was India,* 2:29–31.

53. Cited by Ainslie M. Embree, ed., *Sources of Indian Tradition: From the Beginning to 1800,* 2nd ed. (New York: Columbia University Press, 1988), 1:410–11.

54. Embree, *Sources of Indian Tradition,* 1:415–16, citing Zia-uddin Barni, *Fatawa-yi-Jahandari,* Persian manuscript no. 1149 (London: India Office Library).

55. Embree, *Sources of Indian Tradition,* 1:415–16.

56. Rekha Pande, *Succession in the Delhi Sultanate* (New Delhi: Commonwealth Publishers, 1990), 94–99.

57. Siddiqui, "Socio-Political Role of Women in the Sultanate of Delhi," 93–94.

58. Ibid., 95, citing Isami's *Futuh-us-salatin,* ed. A. S. Usha (Madras, 1948), 160–81.

59. K. A. Nilakanta Sastri, *Foreign Notices of South India from Megasthenes to Mahuan* (1939; repr., Chennai: University of Madras, 2001), 220, 256.

60. Keay, *India: A History,* 267, 277–78.

61. Annemarie Schimmel, *The Empire of the Great Mughals: History, Art and Culture* (London: Reaktion Books, 2004), 143.

62. K. A. Nilakanta Sastri and G. Srinivasachari, *Advanced History of India* (Bombay: Allied Publishers, 1971), 413.

63. Rizvi, *The Wonder that Was India,* 2:83, 112–13.

64. John F. Richards, *The New Cambridge History of India: The Mughal Empire,* 6th ed. (New Delhi: Foundation Books, for Cambridge University Press, 2002), 53–54.

65. Ruby Lal, *Domesticity and Power in the Early Mughal World,* Cambridge Studies in Islamic Civilization (Cambridge: Cambridge University Press, 2005), 14–23.

66. Ibid., 127–28.

67. Schimmel, *The Empire of the Great Mughals,* 79.

68. Annette Susannah Beveridge, trans., *Baburnama in English (Memoirs of Babur)* from the original Turki of Zahiru'ddin Muhammad Babur Padshah Ghazi, vol. 1 (London: Luzac & Co., 1922), 20–21.

69. Kiran Pawar, "Role of the Royal Women in the Career of Babur," in *Women in Indian History,* ed. Pawar, 102–10, vide, 103; Schimmel, *The Empire of the Great Mughals,* 23.

70. Beveridge, *Baburnama in English,* 43.

71. On Gulbadan, see Lal, *Domesticity and Power in the Early Mughal World,* 50–68, 111–39; Schimmel, *The Empire of the Great Mughals,* 144–48, 163–64; Rekha Misra, *Women in Mughal India (1526–1748)* (New Delhi: Munshiram Manoharlal, 1967); Rumer Godden, *Gulbadan: Portrait of a Rose Princess at the Mughal Court* (New York: Viking Press, 1981); Bamber Gascoigne, *A Brief History of the Great Moguls: India's Most Flamboyant Rulers,* 2nd ed. (New York: Caroll & Graf

Publishers, 2002), 26, 28–29, 35, 42–43, 90, 117, 250–51; Rizvi, *The Wonder that Was India,* 2:200–202.

72. Susie Tharu and K. Lalitha, eds., *Women Writing in India: 600 BC to the Present* (New York: Feminist Press, 1991), 1:99.

73. Lal, *Domesticity and Power in the Early Mughal World,* 50–56.

74. Ibid., 12, 21.

75. Ibid., 105, 111–28.

76. Excerpt in Tharu and Lalitha, *Women Writing in India,* 1:102.

77. Lal, *Domesticity and Power in the Early Mughal World,* 130.

78. Ibid., 14–15, 24–29, 75–81, 128–39.

79. Sanjay Subrahmanyam, "The Viceroy as Assassin: The Portuguese, the Mughals and Deccan Politics, c. 1600," in *Sinners and Saints: The Successors of Vasco da Gama,* ed. Sanjay Subrahmanyam (New Delhi: Oxford University Press, 2000), 162–203, *vide,* 170–71.

80. Lal, *Domesticity and Power in the Early Mughal World,* 30–31, 208–10.

81. Richards, *The Mughal Empire,* 31; Schimmel, *The Empire of the Great Mughals,* 138; Godden, *Gulbadan,* 133–40.

82. Lal, *Domesticity and Power in the Early Mughal World,* 211–13.

83. Schimmel, *The Empire of the Great Mughals,* 143, 170–71.

84. Ellison Banks Findly, *Nur Jahan: Empress of Mughal India* (New York: Oxford University Press, 1993), 48–49.

85. Ibid., 124–27.

86. Annie Krieger Krynicki, *Captive Princess Zebunissa: Daughter of Emperor Aurangzeb,* trans. Enjum Hamid from the French (Oxford: Oxford University Press, 2005), 41, 120, 205 (on Aurangabadi Mahal, mother of his daughters Meherunissa and Zubdatunissa), and 103, 120, 128, 207 (on Udaipuri Mahal, mother of his favorite son Kam Baksh).

87. Findly, *Nur Jahan,* 122–23.

88. Ibid., 94, 122–23.

89. Findly, *Nur Jahan,* 46, 306 n. 30, citing Mutamad Khan's *Iqbal-nama-i-Jahangiri,* from Elliot and Dowson, *The History of India as Told by Its Own Historians,* 6:405.

90. Findly, *Nur Jahan,* 205–6.

91. Schimmel, *The Empire of the Great Mughals,* 163.

92. Ibid., 46, 143, 148–49.

93. Findly, *Nur Jahan,* 333. Findly cites Thomas Roe from W. Foster, ed., *The Embassy of Sir Thomas Roe to India, 1615–19* (London: Hackluyt Society, 1926).

94. Lal, *Domesticity and Power in the Early Mughal World,* 41. Lal cites W. H. Moreland and P. Geyl, trans., *Jahangir's India: The Remonstrantie of Francisco Pelsaert* (Cambridge, 1925), 2, 5, 50.

95. Godden, *Gulbadan,* 37, 155.

96. Schimmel, *The Empire of the Great Mughals,* 152.

97. Krynicki, *Captive Princess Zebunissa,* 4.

98. Zinat Kausar, *Muslim Women in Medieval India* (Patna and New Delhi: Janaki Prakashan, 1992), 155–56. She cites Badauni, *Muntakhab-ul-Twarikh,* trans. W. H. Lowe (repr., New Delhi, 1973), 2:389; and Abul Fazl, *Akbar Namah,* 3 vols., trans. H. Beveridge (1907–39; repr., New Delhi: Oriental Books Reprint Corporation, 1977), 3:1223.

99. Schimmel, *The Empire of the Great Mughals,* 152–53.

100. Krynicki, *Captive Princess Zebunissa,* 14–18, 59.

101. Schimmel, *The Empire of the Great Mughals,* 153–54.

102. Krynicki, *Captive Princess Zebunissa,* 61–62.

103. Schimmel, *The Empire of the Great Mughals,* 163.

104. Ibid., 159.

105. Sastri and Srinivasachari, *Advanced History of India,* 395–96.

106. R. Nath, *Private Life of the Mughals of India (1526–1803 A.D.)* (Delhi: Rupa & Co., 2005), 158.

107. Lal, *Domesticity and Power in the Early Mughal World,* 172.

108. Nath, *Private Life of the Mughals of India (1526–1803 A.D.),* 19–23.

109. Schimmel, *The Empire of the Great Mughals,* 34, 156.

110. Abu'l Fazl, "A'in-I-Akbari," in *Sources of Indian Tradition,* ed. Embree, 1:426.

111. Portrait sketch of Akbar without a halo; gilded paintings of Jahangir and Shah Jahan with haloes; portrait sketch of Aurangzeb with a halo; gilded painting of Shah Jahan with a halo in Schimmel, *The Empire of the Great Mughals,* 32, 70, 51, 200. Paintings of Jahangir and Shah Jahan with haloes in Valérie Berinstain, *India and the Mughal Dynasty* (New York: Harry N. Abrams, 1998), 64–65.

112. Berinstain, *India and the Mughal Dynasty,* 40–41.

113. Schimmel, *The Empire of the Great Mughals,* 152, 162.

114. Ibid., 158.

115. Krynicki, *Captive Princess Zebunissa,* 60–61.

116. Nath, *Private Life of the Mughals of India (1526–1803 A.D.),* 160.

117. Krynicki, *Captive Princess Zebunissa,* 59.

118. Lal, *Domesticity and Power in the Early Mughal World,* 45. Lal cites William Irvine, trans., *Storio Do Mogor or Mogul India, 1653–1708 by Nicolao Manucci Venetian* (London, 1907), 1:239.

119. Findly, *Nur Jahan,* 102, 322 n. 133. Findly cites Archibald Constable, ed., *Travels in the Mogul Empire AD 1656–1668 by Francois Bernier* (London: Oxford University Press, 1891; repr., Delhi: S. Chand & Co., 1968), 132–33.

120. Krynicki, *Captive Princess Zebunissa,* 92; Schimmel, *The Empire of the Great Mughals,* 153.

121. Lal, *Domesticity and Power in the Early Mughal World,* 43. She cites Constable, *Travels in the Mogul Empire AD 1656–1668,* 11. See also Schimmel, *The Empire of the Great Mughals,* 153; Findly, *Nur Jahan,* 103; and Krynicki, *Captive Princess Zebunissa,* 27–28, but Findly and Krynicki also cite Manucci's version.

122. Schimmel, *The Empire of the Great Mughals,* 151, citing original work in Jahanara's handwriting.

123. Lal, *Domesticity and Power in the Early Mughal World,* 46, quoting Irvine, *Storio Do Mogor or Mogul India,* 2:149–50.

124. Krynicki, *Captive Princess Zebunissa,* xi, 4–5.

125. Ibid., 57–64, 97–100.

126. Ibid., 139. Krynicki quotes Zebunissa's poems from L. Magan and Duncan Westbrook, *The "Diwan" of Zebunissa* (Lahore, 1912; repr., London, 1918).

127. Schimmel, *The Empire of the Great Mughals,* 153–54.

128. Krynicki, *Captive Princess Zebunissa,* 101–3, 160–63.

129. Richards, *The Mughal Empire,* 170–84.

130. Monserrate described Allah's laws as hypocritical, so that Akbar circum-vented Muslim law by having 300 wives, in J. S. Hoyland and S. N. Banerjee, trans., *The Commentary of Father Monserrate, S. J., on his Journey to the Court of Akbar* (London: Humphrey Milford, Oxford University Press, 1922), 196–213:

> For, to draw attention to one or two such points, he allowed incestuous unions with closely-related women, excepting only the mother and the sister. He also invented and introduced amongst the Musalmans two forms of marriage, first that with regular consorts, who may number four; and second that with those who are merely called wives, and who may be as numerous as a man's resources allow. Musalman kings employ this sanction and licence of the foulest immoral-ity in order to ratify peace and to create friendly relationships with their vassal princes or neighbouring monarchs. For they marry the daughters and sisters of such rulers ... Hence Zelaldinus [Akbar] has more than 300 wives, dwelling in separate suites of rooms in a very large palace. Yet when the priests were at the Court he had only three sons and two daughters. His sons' names are as fol-lows:– the eldest is Xecus ["Shaikh Baba," Akbar's nickname for Salim, the future Jahangir], called after the Xecus by whose advice, as has been mentioned, the King built Sequiris; for this boy was the first born after the change of capital, and thus survived infancy. The second son is Paharis [Murad, whose nickname was "Pahari" (from "pahar," or "mountain")], and the third Danus or Danialus.

131. Lal, *Domesticity and Power in the Early Mughal World*, 30–31, 35–37.

132. See Edward Said, *Orientalism* (New York: Pantheon Books, 1978).

133. Stanley Lane-Poole, *Medieval India Under Mohammedan Rule AD 712–1764* (London, 1903), 251–52, cited by Lal, *Domesticity and Power in the Early Mughal World*, 32.

134. Michel Chandeigne, ed., *Goa 1510–1685: Inde Portugaise, Apostolique et Commerciale*, Collection Memoires no. 41 (Paris: Editions Autrement, 1996), 160–80, *vide*, 166.

135. Gascoigne, *A Brief History of the Great Moguls*, 154.

136. Lal, *Domesticity and Power in the Early Mughal World*, 43.

137. Gascoigne, *A Brief History of the Great Moguls*, 154–55; Schimmel, *The Empire of the Great Mughals*, 153.

138. Lal, *Domesticity and Power in the Early Mughal World*, 45–46. Lal cites Manucci.

139. An example is the film *Road to Morocco*, 1942, with Bing Crosby and Bob Hope as American heroes, Dorothy Lamour as seductive Princess Shalmar, and Anthony Quinn as the Muslim Mullay Kasim. The script was by Frank Butler and Samuel Donald Hartman.

140. Quoted by Nath, *Private Life of the Mughals of India (1526–1803 A.D.)*, 31–34.

141. Giti Thadani, *Sakhiyani: Lesbian Desire in Ancient and Modern India* (London: Cassell, 1996), 51–66 with plates; and Nath, *Private Life of the Mughals of India (1526–1803 A.D.)*, 144–53 with plates.

142. Gascoigne, *A Brief History of the Great Moguls*, 184. Gascoigne cites Francisco Pelsaert's *Remonstrantie*, trans. W. H. Moreland (1925); *The Embassy of Sir Thomas Roe to India, 1615–19*, ed. W. Foster (1926); and Edward Terry, *A Voyage to East India* (1777).

143. Eaton, *The Rise of Islam and the Bengal Frontier, 1204–1760*, 22–32.

144. Aditya Behl, "The Magic Doe: Desire and Narrative in a Hindavi Sufi Romance, circa 1503," in *India's Islamic Traditions, 711–1750*, ed. Eaton, 180–208.

145. Eaton, *The Rise of Islam and the Bengal Frontier, 1204–1760*, 77–94; Barbara D. Metcalf, ed., *Moral Conduct and Authority: The Place of Adab in South Asian Islam* (Berkeley: University of California, 1984), 333–56; Eaton, "Introduction," in *India's Islamic Traditions, 711–1750*, ed. Eaton, 1–34; Bayly, *Saints, Goddesses and Kings*, 73–103.

146. Eaton, "The Political and Religious Authority of the Shrine of Baba Farid," in *India's Islamic Traditions, 711–1750*, ed. Eaton, 263–84, *vide*, 272, 276–80.

147. Eaton, *The Sufis of Bijapur*, 157–58.

148. Sheila McDonough, "Muslim Women in India," in *Women in Indian Religions*, ed. Arvind Sharma, 2nd ed. (Delhi: Oxford University Press, 2004), 166–88, *vide*, 171–72.

149. Siddiqui, "Socio-Political Role of Women in the Sultanate of Delhi," 97–98.

150. Schimmel, *My Soul Is a Woman: The Feminine in Islam* (London: Continuum International Publishing Group, 1997); Camille Adams Helminski, "Women and Sufism," at http://www.sufism.org/society/articles/women.html, 1–7; and "Rabi'ah al Adawiyya," at http://www.islamicedfoundation.com/poetry/rabia.htm, 1–2.

151. Bayly, *Saints, Goddesses and Kings*, 134–35.

152. J. G. Khadir Navalar and R. S. Khwaj Huhuideen, *Karunai Kadal: Kanjul Karamatu* (Nagore: Miran Sahib-Sultana Bibi Dargah Press, 1996), 1–3.

153. Sita Anantha Raman, "Popular Pujas in Public Places: Lay Rituals in South Indian Temples," *International Journal of Hindu Studies* 5, no. 2 (August 2001): 165–98, *vide*, 168, 189 n. 3.

154. Bayly, *Saints, Goddesses and Kings*, 116–19, 123–24, 131–37.

155. Pinault, "Zaynab Bint' Ali and the Place of the Women in Shi'ite Devotional Literature," 69–98, *vide*, 85–93.

156. J. R. I. Cole, "Popular Shī'ism," in *India's Islamic Traditions, 711–1750*, ed. Eaton, 311–41, *vide*, 317–26.

157. Ali S. Asani, "Creating Tradition Through Devotional Songs and Communal Script: The Khojah Isma'ilis of South Asia," in *India's Islamic Traditions, 711–1750*, ed. Eaton, 285–310, *vide*, 287, 295.

158. Sita Anantha Raman, *Getting Girls to School: Social Reform in the Tamil Districts, 1870–1930* (Calcutta: Stree, 1996), 1, 9, 10, 12, 28, 35, 111, 168, 176, 207, 209, 213, 227–30, 234, 237–39; also Dharampal, *The Beautiful Tree: Indigenous Education in the Eighteenth Century* (New Delhi: Biblica Implex, 1983).

159. Mahlaqa Chanda's verse, trans. Syed Sirajuddin, in Tharu and Lalitha, *Women Writing in India*, 1:122.

160. Qurratulain Hyder, trans., *Hasan Shah's The Nautch Girl* (New Delhi: Sterling, 2003).

161. Saleem Kidwai, "The Singing Ladies Find a Voice," 1–12, at this Web site: http://www.india-seminar.com/2004/540/540%20saleem%20kidwai.htm.

162. Mirza Mohammad Hadi Ruswa, *Umrao Jan Ada,* trans. Khushwant Singh and M. A. Husaini (Bombay: Disha Books and Orient Longman, 1982), viii, 35–38, 65.

2

WOMEN IN THE COLONIAL ERA

COLONIALISM AND GENDER

South Asia experienced two European colonial regimes, viz., the maritime Portuguese Estado da India based in Goa (1510–1961) and the British Indian Empire (1757–1947). These colonial states shared certain hegemonic assumptions that implicated Indian women, relied on the labor of women and men, passed patriarchal laws challenging Indian rules of marriage, and introduced Western missionary schools. At first simply trading ventures with Indian empires, their search for dominion led to contentions with Hindu, Sikh, and Muslim states. The Portuguese arrived in 1498, followed by rival Dutch, English, and French East India Companies (EIC) who established outposts (seventeenth century). Anglo-French wars ended with decisive British victories at Plassey (1757) and Baksar (1765). The British Empire initially comprised Bengal, Madras, and Bombay, which were ruled jointly by Parliament and EIC. Subsequent encroachments expanded the empire, but the Great Revolt of 1857 led to complete Parliamentary authority. Although regarded as Britain's "crown jewel," India attained freedom in 1947 through the efforts of patriotic women and men led by Mohandas Gandhi.

Although Asia and Europe form a single landmass with a history of migratory interaction, Western domination required the ideological construction of two racially distinct continents and unequal civilizations. Western political rule had a domino effect on gender and class in both regions. A key argument for Western rule was that it improved Indian women's social condition. However, as the chief imperial purpose was profit, Europe became affluent, and Asia's industrial modernization was postponed. Moreover, while the encounter expanded knowledge of Indian traditions in Europe and funneled secular Enlightenment ideas into India, these exchanges were filtered through the prism of cultural opposition between an emotive, mysterious, *feminine* Orient (East) and a logical, scientific, *virile* Occident (West).[1] India was thus feminized in the popular imagination.

Colonial economies thrived upon underpaid or unpaid Indian workers, and natural resources. The Estado depended upon the labor and products of Indian women and men, often slaves. Although prostitution was endemic in ports and garrisons, the Portuguese regarded this as a moral, not social problem caused by a floating male population. The Inquisition penalized Indian women prostitutes.[2] British colonial plantations also initially used Indian slaves until Parliament abolished slavery in 1807. However, a "new system of slavery" involving state-sponsored indenture of Indian "coolies" was instituted between 1834 and 1917.[3] Impoverishment and famine drove tribals and lower castes to toil long hours for little pay and no rights on sugar, tea, or rubber plantations in Mauritius, the West Indies, Fiji, Sri Lanka, and Malaya.[4] The demand for male workers led to a phenomenal gender disparity on estates. The shortage of women did not translate into higher wages, but it exposed them to rape and violence.[5] Britain's industries relied upon India's iron, wood, and coal, extracted with cheap labor, and their jute mills in India drew upon this work force. However, women earned less than half the wages of men, were restricted from forming unions, and faced sexual harassment.[6] Although female labor was essential to the colonial economy, it was almost invisible in its records.[7]

Colonial policies were not uniform or static, but were shaped by powerful ideological trends in Europe and adapted flexibly to local conditions in a relentless search for profit. Attitudes to local women depended on the colonizer's contemporary mores and on immediate circumstances. The initial paucity of Western women resulted in a large Eurasian population that merged into surrounding society or formed Luso-Indian and Anglo-Indian communities. The Estado allowed interracial marriages and liaisons, depending on prevalent biases in Portugal. Goa's state policy promoted interracial marriages,[8] but recommended fair-skinned wives,[9] and also paid dowries to Portuguese women settlers.[10] Goan society initially reflected Lisbon's permissive attitudes, but mores became straitlaced after the Jesuits arrived in 1542.[11]

Similarly, in the early British Empire, interracial liaisons and marriages were initially accepted by soldiers, civil servants, and merchants. However, these attitudes changed after 1813 with the influx of missionaries due to Parliamentary funds and during the Victorian heyday after the Revolt of 1857. The racial chasm then widened, and officials closeted interracial sex as transgressing the boundaries between rulers and subjects. Indian mistresses were thus discretely overlooked, but few Englishmen married local women.[12] Guilt mixed with anathema drove Europeans to baptize and educate biracial children, but they were regarded as social inferiors. Missionaries spread literacy, and the Gospel laced with strictures on sexual sobriety among Indian and Eurasian girls and boys.[13] Elite Indian men apologetically stapled Victorian morality onto earlier conventions of sexual tolerance.

British laws in India were based on English patriarchal models that negated local matrilineal rights. As they influenced later laws in independent India, they affect women to the present era. Yet, as colonial rule crystallized political identities based on gender, caste, and sect, it served as a catalyst for nationalist and feminist movements.

The Victorian era was also marred by pseudoscientific theories of European racial superiority through a purposeful misreading of Darwin's principles of evolution and natural selection.[14] Social Darwinism credited imperialists with altruism for having bestowed Western civilization upon the "dark races."[15] The myth is encapsulated in "The White Man's Burden" (1899) by Rudyard Kipling, an Englishman born in India. Kipling urged the United States to shoulder its Western imperialist destiny among nonwhite "fluttered folk and wild," "new-caught, sullen peoples, half-devil, half-child."[16] Imperial rhetoric was thus replete with gender and racial typologies that portrayed India as a feminine entity, supine in the arms of a virile Anglo-Saxon empire. Indian men were derided as emasculated by their climate, echoing Robert Orme's (1753) early description of the Hindu as the "most effeminate inhabitant of the globe."[17] Indian women were viewed as either voluptuous sirens or chaste, but ignorant victims requiring Christian succor.[18] If India's feminization derived from Western notions of male power, later Indian nationalists made women the centerpiece of their reform agenda and deified the "motherland" as Goddess Shakti, a womb-house of power. Yet, ordinary women remained the *objects* of this male dialogue until feminists restored their sense of historical agency.[19] This chapter examines the norms for Indian women in this era, and their changes in the Estado and the British Empire.

FEMALE PARADIGMS AND ROLES

The divine female is one of the earliest forms of Indic religion, remaining persistent in the Hindu worship of goddess Devi as Shakti (energy), who along with male divinities Vishnu and Shiva are manifestations of a universal neuter spirit (Brahman). A mystical understanding of Brahman's unity with the soul (Atman) bestows salvation or *moksha*. Indian terms for marriage (*mangalya, kalyana*) thus reflect an intrinsic awe of the female body, which despite its apparent delicacy endures the repeated stresses of menstruation, childbirth, and infant care. Women's sexuality is regarded as an auspicious power bestowing good fortune and progeny, or misfortune by evoking men's lust. To ensure caste purity and male descent lines, patriarchs devised rules to honor the virgin bride and faithful wife (*sumangali*), and placed taboos on a widow's (*amangali*) remarriage.[20] In the colonial era, high-caste girls were often married just before or after puberty.

However, the norms of premarital sexuality, marriage, widow remarriage, and female inheritance vary significantly across ethnic lines, while some customs are shared by sects in the same region. Generally, Dravidian and aboriginal cultures, the lower castes (*varnas*) and subcastes (*jatis*) give greater freedom to women than the Sanskritic high castes. Thus, while upper castes often disallow widow remarriage, they are accepted by some Deccan castes as "*pat*" or "*natra*" marriages;[21] and by other Dravidian or matrilineal lower-caste Hindu Tamils, Bants (Karnataka), Nayars (Kerala), and by Muslim Mappilas (Kerala). Widow remarriage is also permitted by tribes like the Garos (northeast India), and the Tibeto-Burman Limbu, Gurung, Tamang, and Newari (Nepal).[22] However, those aspiring for a higher status have often emulated the high castes by disallowing widow remarriages and by conducting marriages just prior to or shortly after the girl's menarche.

Widows and Property Rights

Guidelines on female roles and rights appear in the *Manu Smriti* (100 BCE–200 CE), widely regarded by many middle- and upper-caste Hindus as scriptural laws (*shastra*). Despite regional interpretations, and lower-caste and aboriginal customs on lineage and inheritance, *brahman* translators in British colonial courts enshrined *Manu Smriti* as the definitive Hindu law code. *Manu Smriti* advised the widow to remain faithful to her husband till her death and to subsist frugally on flowers, fruits, and roots (*MS* 5:157–160) as would the respected male ascetic (*sadhu*). *Manu Smriti* did not advocate widow immolation on her husband's pyre as a "true wife" (*sati*), but it repudiated widow remarriage (5:161; 3:155; 3:159). However, it conceded remarriage if the woman was yet virgin or if she was deserted before nuptial consummation (9:69–70, 9:175–176). In such cases, it advised a levirate marriage to her brother-in-law.[23] However, society generally regarded the widow as an ill omen, and few Sanskritic castes allowed remarriage. Till the twentieth century, widows were tonsured; wore drab saris devoid of a blouse, flowers, and jewelry; and were forbidden to wear a vermilion mark on the forehead (*tilak*). Thus defeminized, the unattractive widow was prevented from bearing illegitimate children. During medieval wars, institutional misogyny, especially among *kshatriya* castes, elevated the cremation of a *sati* into an honorable act. It was particularly popular among Rajputs who venerated the "true wife-mother" (*sati-mata*) as a family goddess (*kuldevi*).[24] However, in the eighteenth century, widow immolation became popular among *vaishyas* who had become affluent through commerce with the West and wished for an elevated caste rank. It also crystallized among some *brahmans* on the Ganges plains.

If Muslim women's property rights were defined by the *Qur'an* and Sharia laws, caste Hindus followed the *Manu Smriti,* which stipulates that a woman's property rights depend on her stage in life. These were as an unmarried girl under her father's care, as a wife under coverture with no share in her husband's patriarchal joint family property, and as a widow released from coverture.[25] Joint family property was bequeathed to male heirs, but a wife often received gifts from her husband's personal earnings. Such gifts along with those from her natal family constituted female property or *stridhan,* which maintains women during need and as widows. It allowed women funds to perform rituals for spiritual welfare, and it was inherited largely by female offspring. *Manu Smriti* cautioned men that they had no rights over *stridhan,* and not to cheat a woman as "a just king should punish them for theft" (*MS* 8:27), and they would suffer dire *karmic* consequences in the after-life. Important verses on *stridhan* (9:192–196; 9:198–199) are:

> Now, when the mother has died, all the uterine brothers and sisters should share equally in the mother's estate. Something should even be given to the daughters of these daughters out of the estate of their maternal grandmother, through affection and according to their deserts. A woman's property is traditionally regarded as of six sorts: what was given in front of the (marriage) fire, on the bridal procession, or as a token of affection, and what she got from her brother, mother, or father. In addition, any subsequent gift and whatever her affection-ate husband might give her should become the property of her children when she dies, (even) during her husband's lifetime. And if a father should give anything valuable to a wife, the daughter of the (hus-band's) wife of the priestly class, or her children may take it. A woman should not make a great hoard of the family property that belongs to several people, nor even of her own valuables, without her husband's permission.
>
> *Manu Smriti*[26]

The original author probably intended *stridhan* to be matrilineal property, as the verse refers to "daughters of these daughters" (9:193). An important verse stipulates: "Whatever separate property the mother has is the share of the daughter alone; if a man dies sonless, his daughter's son should take his entire property" (9:131). However, there are ambiguities in *Manu Smriti* as it was expanded by several authors over hundreds of years. Other verses thus state that daughters and sons inherit their mother's *stridhan* (9:19), and that a childless woman's wealth transfers to the husband. Moreover, there were several schools of law and interpretations of *Manu Smriti.*

Many high-caste Hindus follow the Mitakshara system of Vijneshwara (eleventh century), and some Bengal *brahmans* follow the Dayabhaga laws of Jimutavahana (twelfth century). Mitakshara laws exclude a widow from inheriting her husband's property, so that a dependent widow was at best valued as a selfless aunt, or at worst an unpaid drudge. Dayabhaga rules allow widows a share of the husband's movable or immovable estate. However, this advantage became a scourge during EIC misrule of Bengal (eighteenth century), when famines claimed horrendous tolls and private property laws created disputes. Disinherited male relatives then colluded with misogynist priests to compel widows to become *satis*. The spate led the British governor to abolish *sati* in 1829.

Sikhism and Women

Founded by Guru Nanak (1469–1539), a *nirguni bhakti* saint in Punjab, Sikhism rejects caste and gender discrimination. Nanak was inspired by Hindu devotion or *bhakti* for a formless Being as the Breath of life (*prana*), modified by Islamic Sufi emphasis on monotheism. Ten Sikh *guru* preceptors preached monogamy and respect for women, but they repudiated the iconic worship of a mother goddess. The Sikh scripture *Adi Granth* was completed under the last *guru*, Gobind Singh (d. 1708), as an eclectic collection of six thousand sayings of the *gurus* and hymns of mystics from other sects like Ramdas and Kabir. Nanak's verse shows respect for women:

> From woman is man born, inside her is he conceived;
> To woman is man engaged, and woman he marries;
> With woman is man's companionship,
> From woman originate new generations.
> Should woman die, is another sought;
> Why revile her of whom are born great ones of the earth?
> From man is born woman,
> no human being without a woman is born.
> Saint Nanak: The holy Eternal alone with woman can dispense,
> The tongue by which is the Lord praised.
>
> *Adi Granth* 473[27]

Punjab's Sikhs and Hindus believe in the *karma-samsara* cycle of the soul's transmigration and hold similar views on women's domestic roles. Their patriarchal communities view the relationship between devotee and God as analogous to that of a devoted wife to her husband. The *Adi Granth* lauds the devotee who resembles a faithful wife (*AG* 31) and "wins her Lord's pleasure" (*AG* 56).[28] The ten *gurus* preached respect for mothers and wives without whom human birth and life were impossible. Third *guru* Amardas (d. 1574) urged women to remove the veil and to attend congregational prayers at temple (*gurudwara*) by sitting apart. He also recruited a few women leaders (*peerahs*) to proselytize for the new syncretic sect.[29] Amardas and his successor Ramdas (d. 1581) also promoted widow remarriage.

While the *gurus* emphasized spiritual and social equality of both genders and all castes, these ideals were sometimes repudiated by the dominant, patriarchal Jat caste in Punjab. The mantle of leadership thus fell upon 10 male *gurus,* and there was never a female *guru* of their stature. This relegated women to playing a secondary role in Sikhism. As Punjab is the avenue through which invaders entered the subcontinent, its culture places a premium on male valor and female chastity. Girls were regarded as burdens even during Nanak's time. Therefore, despite the *gurus'* teachings, society expected widows to remain chaste, and it practiced female infanticide, child marriage, and polygamy. Nanak's remedy was *bhakti,* while Gobind Singh (1666–1708) forbade female infanticide. He also reinforced the martial ethic by initiating men and women into the army of the Khalsa (Pure) to resist oppression. Caste names were forbidden for the Jat, Khatri, and Mahzib communities that adopted Sikhism. Initiation rites were uniform for men who were given the honorific of Singh (lion) and for women whose title is Kaur (princess). Sikh identification is through long hair (*kesh*), covered by women under a shawl (*dupatta*), and swathed by men beneath a turban; a comb (*kanga*) to keep the hair in place; an undergarment (*kaccha*); a steel bracelet (*kadha*); and a small sword (*kirpan*).

While the *gurus* forbade polygamy and *sati,* Sikh history indicates that aristocrats practiced polygamy, and practiced *sati* immolation when the British Empire absorbed Indian kingdoms (eighteenth to nineteenth century). The most significant ruler to negotiate successfully with the British was Maharaja Ranjit Singh (1780–1839), often called "the Lion of the Punjab." Ranjit Singh took pride in his haram of 22 wives, and upon his death, his chief wife Rani Guddun Kaur, three other wives, and seven mistresses or serving women became *satis.* Despite romantic Western accounts of their voluntary immolation, their genuine state of mind is unknown. The women may have possibly succumbed to prevalent myths of empowered *satis,* as they feared a harsh widowhood. Some historians suggest that two minor wives of the later Maharaja Kharak Singh (d. 1840) also became *satis,* but that his chief widow Chand Kaur lived on to assume the title of sovereign Maharani. However, at least one Sikh prince refused to bow to the widow on the throne and to apply the *tilak* on her forehead as a mark of his fealty.[30]

Devadasis: From Temple to Court in South India

In medieval south India, a class of Hindu dancers-musicians were ritually espoused to the temple deity. Falling outside the common parameters of worldly marriage, the temple woman was called the "eternally auspicious wife" (*nityasumangali*) or the handmaiden of god (*teyvadiyal/devadasi*). Temple women stemmed from various castes, including royalty during the Chola empire (ninth to fourteenth century). As they filled a ritual, artistic niche, they were maintained by royal endowments to the shrine, to which *devadasis* made donations.[31]

A growing market economy and court culture transformed the *devadasi* tradition in the sixteenth century under the Vijayanagar Empire (1336–1565). A text on dance (*natya*) by Goppa Tippa reveals that the venue for Karnatak music and dances had shifted from the temple to royal courts (*sadir*).[32] Once the honored wife of the temple deity, many *devadasis* now sought the mundane patronage of kings and aristocrats. A new etiquette evolved allowing only married, elder sons to serve as artistic patrons for *devadasis*. Yet, the death of a reputable *devadasi* was mourned, her body was garlanded as an auspicious wife (*sumangali*), and temple kitchen fires ignited her funeral pyre.[33] During the annual Ram Navami festival processions in Vijayanagar, *devadasis* attracted the attention of merchants, officials, and Portuguese visitors like Domingo Paes (ca. 1518) and Fernao Nunes (ca. 1535). Paes described women functionaries, dancers, musicians, and royal guards, indicating that *devadasis* enjoyed a conspicuous secular presence:

> After this is over you will see issuing from the inside twenty-five to thirty female door-keepers, with canes in their hands and whips on their shoulders; and then, close to these come many eunuchs, and after these eunuchs come many women playing trumpets and drums and pipes (but not like ours) and viols, and many other kinds of music, and behind these women will come some twenty women-porters, with canes in their hands all covered with silver, and close to them come women clothed in the following manner . . . They carry in their hands vessels of gold each as large as a small cask of water; inside these are some loops made of pearls fastened with wax, and inside all this is a lighted lamp. They come in regular order one before the other, in all perhaps sixty women fair and young, from sixteen to twenty years of age . . . In this manner and in this array they proceed three times round the horses and at the end retire into the palace.[34]

After Vijayanagar fell in 1565, the *devadasis'* secular venue widened under their dynastic patrons, the Wodeyars of Mysore; the Nayakas and Marathas of Thanjavur and Madurai; and the matrilineal kings of Travancore, Kerala.[35] Learned *devadasis* at court composed Sanskrit, Telugu, and Tamil literature, and educated their daughters in temple verandah (*pyal*) schools with boys. Their court compositions marked a transition from earlier *bhakti* texts which proclaimed the supremacy of spirit over sensory desire. Their *bhakti* texts used the sensory/erotic/ornamental mode (*sringara rasa*) to exalt the body as the medium for spiritual salvation (*moksha*). Moreover, the growth of a market economy is visible in their emphasis on a transactional relationship between devotee and God. The *sringara* mode became an ideal voice for *devadasi* composers and provided a repertoire for performers. Their court based art similar to the tradition of female Kathak dancers in northern Muslim and Hindu kingdoms.

Meanwhile, temple *devadasis* maintained the Karnatak music and dance traditions of south India, inspiring maestros like Muthuswami Dikshitar (1775–1835). Some of Dikshitar's masterpieces were dedicated to a gifted dancer at Tiruvarur temple in Thanjavur, where his own father had studied music from another gifted *devadasi*.[36] Such artistes ritually served the temple deity and transmitted their art to *devadasi* daughters. Under their matrilineal tradition, their chief heirs were daughters, and musician sons were therefore less powerful.

However, other *devadasis* used skills and personal charms to please mortal men. Foreign merchant accounts inform us that Indian ports and towns teemed with wealthy clients and courtesans, as parents sold daughters to temples or as performers for the affluent. Their tradition deteriorated when colonial powers absorbed small kingdoms and temples lost their royal endowments in the eighteenth century.[37] British missionaries viewed *devadasis* with opprobrium, male nationalists were apologetic, and women nationalists tried to save their fallen sisters.

Women Court Poets

Wodeyars, Nayakas, and the Marathas patronized *devadasi* dancers and composers, and also working women poets. Sanciya Honamma thus held the menial job of rolling betel leaves with areca nuts (*paan*) for Rani Devajamanni, chief wife of Chikkadevaraya Wodeyar (1672–1704). At the same time, she composed the guideline for women, *Hadibadeya Dharma* (Duties of a Devoted Wife), in the Kannada language. As a lower-caste poet, Sanciya Honamma made concessions to the elite men at court, so that she won accolades from a senior poet. However, it is likely that such praise may not have been given, if she had challenged orthodox male authority.[38]

Three *devadasis* composed Sanskrit poetic drama (*kavyas*) at the Nayaka and Maratha courts. Their bold feminine style in the ornamental *sringara* mode affirmed the sensory world and earthly desire as a metaphor for a spiritual love of God. Ramabhadramba of Thanjavur was thus honored as "Kavita Sarvabhauma" (Queen of Poetry) for her epic *Raghunathabhyudaya*.[39] She was probably a courtesan, although Indian nationalist Annie Besant (1847–1933) believed that she was the daughter of king Raghunatha Nayaka (b. 1612). Ramabhadramba's poem pays tribute to this famous royal patron of literature, architecture, and sculpture by identifying him with god Rama/Raghunatha whose name he bore. Ramabhadramba's genius fused an archaic Tamil veneration for the king as god with medieval *bhakti* for God as king.[40]

The other two courtesan poets who used the sensual *sringara rasa* to relate spiritual themes were Rangajamma (seventeenth century) at Thanjavur and Muddupalani (eighteenth century) at Madurai. In her Telugu epic *Radhika Santvanamu* (Appeasing Radhika), Muddupalani boldly declared that a king's valor was enhanced through intimacy with a gifted courtesan.[41] *Radhika Santvanamu* consists of 584 poems in which god Krishna's love for Radha became the erotic medium to express a mortal woman's desire.[42] Wealthy *devadasis* at Maratha courts performed public rituals in their names and established shrines and villages in honor of scholarly *brahmans* to whom they gave grants. Clearly, *devadasis* still occupied a respected social niche in this era.

Philanthropic Queens

Royal women were usually educated and accomplished in the arts. Many elite-caste women were taught Hindu scriptures and languages in domestic seclusion. The Maratha queens of Thanjavur, Tamil Nadu also administered substantial religious charities (*chattrams*), which comprised whole villages, verandah (*pyal*) schools, colleges, shrines, infirmaries, feeding and rest homes for pilgrims on the road to the sacred site of Rameshwaram.[43] Obviously considering educational charity as the highest form of *dharma,* Maratha kings established 20 such endowments between 1743 and 1837, prior to British takeover in 1852. Among the students at the *pyal* schools were *devadasi* girls, and boys of various castes.[44]

As the *chattrams* often bore the queens' names, it is likely that they administered the charities, especially since Thanjavur queens held matrilineal inheritance rights from the inception of Maratha rule in 1677. At that time, Rani Dipamba had convinced her husband Raja Ekoji (d. 1686) to purchase Thanjavur's freedom with jewels and money to forestall the armies of his half brother Shivaji of Maharashtra (d. 1680). In return for Dipamba's diplomacy in averting a military clash, Shivaji granted her land revenues in Bangalore, to be inherited as matrilineal property (*stridhan*) by her female descendants. The six types of *stridhan* stipulated by the *Manu Smriti* (9:194–195) were primarily to enable women to undertake rituals for their spiritual welfare, to support themselves if necessary, and to bequeath sums to their daughters.[45] The text thus states that a husband cannot touch his wife's *stridhan* without her acquiescence; nor can she set aside a portion of his patrilineal family property without his permission.[46] Thanjavur *chattram* documents indicate no gender conflict on the issue of matrilineal inheritance, as the system began with Shivaji. Two *chattrams* started in 1776 by Raja Tulsaji (1763–87) were named for his chief ranis, Rajasamba Bai and Sakhavaramba Bai. Other *chattrams* were named for royal women Rajakumara Bai, Mohanambal, Sulakshanambal, Draupadambal, Yamunambal, Sakwarambal, Muktambal.[47] Thanjavur was politically threatened by the British after 1799, and king Sarabhoji (Serfoji; d. 1832) finally handed over the *chattram* administration to the colonial government. Sarabhoji's letter to the British government confirmed that *chattrams* were royal matrilineal properties. He wrote that they descended "from the elder to the younger queen, that it remained in the hands of the senior queen until her death, and then descended to the wife of the reigning Raja."[48]

Despite the loss of sovereignty, south Indian kings and princesses donated lands and sums for girls' and boys' schools, irrespective of sect. Grateful for

Muslim merchants who enriched Thanjavur, the rajas gave revenue lands to mosque schools.[49] Tulsaji bequeathed enormous sums to Christian Frederick Schwartz (d. 1798), the Danish missionary.[50] Also in memory of Schwartz, Sarabhoji gifted large sums and the entire village of Kannathangudi to educate "fifty poor Christian children."[51] In 1871, his granddaughter Vijaya Mohana Muktambal donated Rs. 7,000 to the colonial government's Lady Hobart School for Muslim girls.[52] In 1877, the same princess donated money to the Society for the Propagation of the Gospel (SPG) for the Lady Napier School for Hindu girls, although conversion was central to the SPG mission.[53] Other rulers supported girls' and boys' schools, irrespective of sectarian affiliation. The Muslim Nawab of Arcot gave the munificent sum of Rs. 80,000 to Lady Campbell's Female Orphan Asylum, run by a Reverend Gericke and 12 directresses for 62 Eurasian girls. During war in 1790, there were 200 students, including orphan Indian girls.[54] In matrilineal Travancore, ranis Lakshmibai (in 1814) and Parvatibai (in 1821) donated rich paddy lands and coconut estates to the Church Missionary Society for girls' and boys' schools. Such institutions often relied upon funds from the sale of the girls' embroidery and lace.[55]

Female Servitude: "Stri-Dharmapadhati"

Despite eighteenth-century Thanjavur's female composers, administrators, and philanthropists, some of the orthodox male elite resented women's public presence. This is evident in the work "Stri-Dharmapadhati" (Guide to the Religious Status and Duties of Women), a manual for female subservience composed by a *brahman* named Tryambakayajvan. This author urged women not to flaunt their authority, remain at home, abstain from public activity. He drove home his point by citing *Manu Smriti,* which declared that "nothing should be done independently by a woman, either as a child, a young girl, or an old woman, even in her (own) home."[56] "Stri-Dharmapadhati" advised women of their roles and property rights, as delineated by *Manu Smriti.* Although other lawgivers had elaborated and advised different views on *stridhan,* and many tribal, Dravidian, and low-caste communities did not consider *Manu Smriti* prescriptive, Tryambakayajvan reiterated its guidelines on female conduct. His orthodox views had appeared earlier in *Dharmakuta,* a commentary on the *Ramayana* (ca. 1715).[57] However, by drawing specific attention to *Manu's* laws in "Stri-Dharmapadhati," Tryambakayajvan paved the way for *brahman* translators in colonial courts to declare the *Manu Smriti* as the preeminent Hindu laws.

Tryambakayajvan's work indicates that women had largely receded from public life in south India, perhaps in response to colonial wars. He argued that women's minds were fickle, that their menstrual cycles kept them perpetually impure, but these flaws could be remedied if the wife worshipped her husband and performed menial chores with religious merit. He thus advised her to present an auspicious face to him each morning, labor on household tasks, collect cow dung with her hands, and smear it on the walls, sort grain till nightfall. The low caste had little relevance for this misogynist work, but its weight fell heavily upon elite women.[58]

WOMEN IN THE PORTUGUESE ESTADO

When Vasco da Gama's fleet docked at Calicut, Kerala, he did not realize that his nation's empire would outlast other Western colonies in India. The Portuguese were propelled by two colonial visions that shaped their views on non-European women, after a Papal Bull (1492) directed the Iberians to discover new trade routes and to spread Catholicism. A medieval antipathy to Muslims ("Moors") and Jews on the Iberian Peninsula was fueled by Arab mercantile successes in the Indian Ocean. Demographics shaped their colonial policy, compelling them to take local convert wives. Portugal's population of one million was often decimated by epidemics, and it lacked the manpower to run an empire from a distance. It could thus ill afford the high rates of shipboard mortality due to poor hygiene or the loss of entire fleets on perilous oceans.[59] In his 1572 epic, *The Lusiads* (The Portuguese), poet Luiz de Camoes praised his countrymen as being "so strong, though you are so few" (7:3), and for surmounting these obstacles.[60] He failed to mention that without Indian women, the Estado was doomed from the start.

Intermarriage Policy

Until the Counter Reformation, there were widespread prostitution, homosexuality, and common law marriages, even among monks and nuns in Portugal. The near absence of women on ships made homosexuality inevitable, and the crew rushed to local women immediately after disembarking at colonial ports.[61] Similar mores also prevailed in Goa, despite the interracial Marriage Policy (Politica dos Casmentos) instituted in 1510 by Viceroy Afonso de Albuquerque (1453–1516). The new policy did not stem from lack of racial bigotry, but from the Viceroy's desire to legalize marriages with Indian women who were sexually necessary. Yet, adultery continued even under the eagle eyes of Jesuits during the Inquisition in Goa (1560–1812).

A large contingent of Indian women had accompanied Albuquerque's forces after their temporary loss of Goa to Bijapur Sultanate in 1502. Observing that his soldiers enjoyed Indian mistresses, he became convinced that such promiscuity was a waste of national energy, and that his nascent colony could only survive through state-sponsored marriages. Accordingly, after he regained Goa in 1510, he informed King Dom Manuel that he had baptized the women, and that a friar had married "a hundred and fifty people."[62] The plebeian Konkani women were more amenable to interracial marriages than high-caste women in Cochin and Calicut. The Marriage Policy is unique in India's colonial history, as soon after it was instituted, there were about 450 biracial couples in Goa.[63] Albuquerque felt that legal marriages would produce stable families of householders (*casados*) who as the backbone of the Estado would induce Indians to convert to Catholicism. However, Albuquerque was a pragmatist who was not averse to using prostitution to stabilize his empire. In at least one instance in 1513, he sent eight prostitutes to his guards at a warehouse (factory) and informed the Portuguese merchant that he would send more women after four months.[64]

The settlers who benefited from the Marriage Policy were artisans, clerks, masons, soldiers, and a few convict settlers who began life anew in the colonies. The Viceroy asked his king to supply funds, and he rewarded the men with land, cattle, houses, minor offices, and the woman as chattel.[65] Thus, a Fernao de Basto received money and an Indian woman slave as his marriage gift. Another soldier married the governor's maid and received a huge sum, a house, and a job. Albuquerque also occasionally punished his wealthy opponents by demanding a dowry for a couple to start their household. For example, he compelled his captain Diogo Mendes Vasconcelos and the merchant Francisco Corvynell to pay a substantial sum to a Pedro Vas who married a Goan woman.[66] Although the demand for such marriages and gifts far exceeded the availability of women, Albuquerque stated his preference for fair-skinned converts from affluent or powerful Indian families in Goa. Fresh evidence shows that the women were primarily from lower castes for whom conversion meant social ascendancy. Their political power was also augmented as they now belonged to the ruling elite.[67]

Albuquerque's letter enthusiastically reminded Dom Manuel of a conversation in Lisbon about intermarriage as a colonial policy. He flattered his distrustful royal patron by giving him credit for a farsighted plan, but the idea originated with Albuquerque. He wrote:

> With regard to the people here whom Your Highness has ordered to marry, it seems to me that this would be doing a great service both to God and to yourself. If Your Highness could see how great an inclination and desire the people have to marry in Goa, you would be amazed. There seems to be something divine about the wish that Portuguese men have to marry and settle in Goa. As God is my salvation, I believe that Our Lord has ordained this and inclined men's hearts towards something that is hidden from us, but is of great service to him. Your Highness should give every encouragement to this business, and whoever you have here as governor and captain-general should watch over it with great care and give it his protection. I assure Your Highness that the devil is greatly concerned to

oppose and thwart this scheme and gnaw away at the tender shoot to prevent its growing.[68]

Albuquerque's enemies included insubordinate monks, and officials jealous over Goa's preeminence over Cochin. He complained that "very few" were ready to set up monasteries, arrange intermarriages, or ensure that recently convert wives were good Christians. He was particularly exasperated by a Dominican friar whom he had misguidedly left as the vicar of Goa. The friar "stole more than seven hundred *cruzados* from the fund for the deceased," excommunicated some soldiers, and refused to marry them to Indian wives.[69] Moreover, as conversion was a central goal, Albuquerque drove Hindus out of Goa and Cochin to prevent social or sexual contact with converts.[70] He wrote to Manuel in 1512:

When I arrived at Cochin, it seemed to me right for the service of God and Your Highness that I should put an end to certain evils that were being committed here involving your people and the new Christians. I issued a proclamation saying that any heathen, man or woman, should withdraw from our settlement and go and live outside it. I did this, Sire, because these newly converted Christian ladies had ten, fifteen, twenty people in their households, cousins and brothers and other relations, who were not Christians but had dealings with them, and there were other heathen houses where the Moslems of Cochin came to sleep with the Christian women. Then there were houses which gave shelter to heathen and Moslem men from outside the city, whose occupation it was to entice male and female slaves to rob their masters and flee. Moreover, some of your people, weary of sleeping with Christian women, have gone to live with these heathen women.[71]

Gender, Sect, and Race in the Estado

The Marriage Policy represented European racial pragmatism in sixteenth-century India. While the Estado was a male enterprise, it came to fruition through complicit Indian women, and ensuing generations of Catholic Luso-Indians (*mestiças/mestiços*). Although Albuquerque advised his men to marry fair Muslim women, few such women left the *zenana* unless taken captive in war. Similarly, few elite-caste women would have converted unless they were widows or captives. However, in the next centuries, more elite families perhaps converted because they benefited in various ways from their connections to the Portuguese rulers in Goa.

Although society placed a premium on fair-skinned wives, Portuguese men apparently enjoyed dark-skinned mistresses they acquired in the slave trade between Mozambique (Africa), Goa (India), and Brazil (South America). Seventeenth-century accounts thus give lascivious details about the dark bodies and unrepressed desires of non-European women.[72] Frenchman Francois Pyrard (ca. 1603) described Goa's slave auction on Rua Direita where "some of the most beautiful girls of all the nations of India" were sold as menials and sexual companions. Pyrard specifically described their swarthy, olive, and white bodies, the values of their products, their gift with musical instruments, and their skill in sewing dainty garments. He wrote of their gourmet cooking talents, and that their preserves were sold in the market, carried by slave women. He stated also that while the women cost little, "the greatest profit and riches of the people of Goa proceeds from the work of their slaves." They were dressed attractively in lengthy silk cloths and bodices to entice customers to buy their goods, and to offer themselves as prostitutes. Clearly, female slavery, prostitution, and crafts were inextricably bound together in Goa's economy.[73]

For Camoes, the ideal of feminine beauty was the "fair" European with "angelic hair" and "shoulders white as ivory" (TL 3:102).[74] It is also believed that during his stay in Goa, he was attracted to a local woman named Luisa Barbara to whom he wrote verses. Yet, in his trenchant work Disparates na India (Follies of India), he dismissed Goan women as low-class speakers of a pidgin language. He also vented his poetic spleen against Muslims whom he described as traitors (2:7) of "shameless, barbaric blood" (3:75), and ranted against Hindu "heathen idols" (2:51) as "abominations base" (7:47).[75] However, Camoes had exaggerated praise for Kerala's products and polyandry. This sexual hyperbole convinced European visitors of the easy availability of docile women and wealth in India. Camoes wrote (TL 7:41):

> Women are held in common, but they are
> In this restricted to the husband's kin.
> Happy that race, under a kindly star,
> Who feel no pang of jealousy within.
> Such practices, the men of Malabar,
> Like others odder yet, esteem no sin.
> And the land fattens on all trade the while,
> Which the seas fetch from China to the Nile.[76]

In a strange prejudicial twist, although Portuguese soldiers feared "white" Jews and Muslims, Albuquerque wished them to marry fair Muslims, not dark Malabari Hindus.[77] Yet, newly converted dark Catholics ranked higher than fair Jews and Muslims in the Estado.[78] In the bloodthirsty war with Bijapur in 1502, Albuquerque mercilessly set fire to a Muslim ship, but saved 20 children for conversion. In his second battle over Goa in 1510, Albuquerque cut off the noses and ears of 6,000 Muslim men, women, and children in a fishing village. Widows converted when soldiers threatened rape.[79] The Portuguese had mixed feelings about Hindus (gentias [f]; gentios [m]) whom they first mistook for "fallen" Christians, and the humanist Tome Pires even saw similarities in Hinduism and Christianity in 1623. Albuquerque wooed Hindus as allies against Muslims, but despised them as heathen idolaters. Hindu men and women were stoned in Malabar, and banished from Goa where temples were zealously razed, especially after St. Francis Xavier arrived (1542) as harbinger of the Counter Reformation.[80] Xavier separated soldiers from Hindu lovers, baptized Indians en masse, weeded out lax converts, and recommended the Inquisition, which was implemented in 1560, six years after his death.[81]

Inquisition and Goan Women

The Inquisition lasted for roughly 250 years in the Estado, and Hindu, Muslim, and Jewish converts were targeted. Women were penalized for simple social acts, including birth control. In 1774 it was outlawed by the Marquis of Pombal, a dictator in Portugal, but reinstated in 1778 by Queen Maria, and finally abolished in 1812.[82] Over 16,000 women and men were tortured, imprisoned, or burnt alive for presumed offences against the Church.[83] Hindus later paid a poll tax to live in Goa, but faced restrictions on rites, names, and attire. Women could not wear their traditional blouses (choli), men the cotton nether garment (dhoti) as being sexually provocative.[84]

Women were prosecuted for breaking the ban on social functions during weddings. They were jailed for prostitution, using contraceptives, and abortion. Thus, in 1771 the widow Luisa was jailed for aborting her fetus. Although a convert, the tribunal viewed her with suspicion, especially as she was listed as being of the "sudra class." Convert women Flomazia, Maria, and Esperanca were imprisoned for prostitution.[85] Midwives or widows were accused of necromancy and for faith in non-Christian superstitions when delivering infants. Catherina, Anna Maria Telles, and Luiza Fernandez thus performed penance, and Anna Pinto was confined at a garrison jail.[86]

Women were jailed for celebrating female life rituals during pregnancy or a girl's menarche. These festivities were banned in 1736, but observed secretly, and then in open after the Inquisition ended.[87] Male Inquisitors also banned residual, but innocuous Hindu wedding customs such as anointing the bride with turmeric and coconut water (1736), and covering the bride's face (1780). A bride could no longer wear a nose-ring or jewelry gifted by the groom's parents. The parents of the bride were not permitted to follow the tradition of washing their son-in-law's feet, nor could they exchange gifts of betel leaves and areca nuts (paan).[88]

Portuguese Women Settlers in Goa

Between 1550 and 1750, the Portuguese state and the Catholic Church sent destitute orphan girls (orfas) and reformed prostitutes to Goa and Brazil. If the state saw them as a drain on the exchequer, the Inquisitors were

determined to stamp out prostitution and homosexuality in Goa, and to produce stable *casado* families. The females were between 14 and 30 years of
age, and they were given dowries upon marriage to *casados* in Goa.[89] The
dowries came from royal subsidies and special taxes, but also from the
women's personal finances. Prior to departure in groups of three to five,
the women were housed in special shelters like the Ricolhimento do Castelo
at Sao Jorge. Sometimes there were older women who were slated to marry
junior colonial officials who requested Portuguese wives. The *misericordia*
was the main supervisory institution for the *orfas* until marriage, while
another government agency searched for suitable husbands. So many
orfas arrived in Goa in the sixteenth century that the Estado passed
special taxes and used a royal subsidy to build the shelter, Recolhimento
da Nossa Senhora da Serra. In 1610, the Ricolhimento de Santa Maria
Madalena was established for reformed prostitutes, while Convent of Santa
Monica in Goa catered to those who wished to be nuns.[90]

While the Estado promoted white female immigration, some officials felt
that it counteracted Albuquerque's original policy of intermarriages with
Indians. Interestingly, over time, the *orfa* dowry became a type of female
inheritance. For example, a woman named D. Clara Maria Torres was given
a naval notary position in honor of her father in lieu of a dowry, and this
could be transferred to the husband. Women also occasionally inherited
valuable villages with large incomes if they married elite officials born in
Portugal but settled in Goa (*reinos*).[91]

Women in Multiethnic Goa

Unlike the later English and Dutch, the Portuguese viewed their Indian
colony as an extension of their national identity, ensuring that their men
married convert Indian wives and raised families. Despite such marriages,
Portuguese and *mestiço* sailors continued to consort with slave and free mistresses from Brazil to Malaya. This long history of sexual traffic has left
multiracial descendants and Creole cultures in peninsular India and Sri
Lanka.[92] A permissive life style was also shared by Goa's military nobility
(*fidalgos*), householders (*casados*), and male soldiers (*soldados*), whose
social status depended upon birth, as among Hindu castes. The highest ranks
were born in Portugal (*reinas* [f]/*reinos* [m]), followed by Portuguese born in
India (*castiças/castiços* or *Indiaticas/Indiaticos*), Eurasians (*mestiças/
mestiços*). After the eighteenth century, Hindus and Muslims were allowed
to reside in Goa, but they ranked lowest.

Prostitution and venereal diseases like syphilis were thus widespread in
Goa. The Jesuits tried to curb prostitution, realized its impossibility, and
finally just collected a tax from the women.[93] Fear of prosecution by the
Inquisition drove homosexuality underground, and lip service was paid to
sexual sobriety. This is apparent in the scholarly account of John Huygen

van Linschoten, a Dutch physician who studied Goa's customs, women, and systems of medicine (1583–88). While he probably did not intend to titillate, his writings provide a glimpse into early Western views on the "primitive savage" and dark women's animal appetites. Linschoten does not blame European men for their lust, but the tropical climate and Indian women's lewd attire. Yet, he felt that even intercourse with dark women was preferable to sodomy. He wrote:

> The women go altogether naked onely with a cloth before their privie members, which openeth chewing all they have, which is by them ordayned to the ends that by such means it should tempt men to lust after them and to avoid the most abominable and accursed sin of Sodomie.[94]

Linschoten also described the use of clove and other spices, and even marijuana or *ganja* to increase desire. Similarly, the seventeenth-century French visitor Francisco Pyrard de Laval described Goa's sexual mores, which allowed women to drug their husbands with datura to enjoy trysts with Portuguese and Eurasian lovers.

With such widespread promiscuity, the formal ranks overlapped across the centuries. When ensuing generations of soldiers settled in Goa with Indian wives and when affluence increased in the early Estado, some *Indiaticas/Indiaticos* and *mestiças/mestiços* became as powerful as *reinos*. Thus, by 1524, there were about 450 *casados,* including those with Indian wives. They had increased to 1,800 by 1540, many now powerful *mestiços.*[95] *Mestiças/mestiços* with high-caste Catholic mothers often retained their caste status.[96]

During the eighteenth-century European hegemonic wars, the Dutch, French, and English prized the beauty and wealth of *Indiatica/mestiça* wives whose knowledge of India gave them a distinct political advantage. Despite the policy on interracial marriages, the fair-skinned enjoyed a higher status in Goa. Laws prohibited the smuggling of Portuguese women on ships from Lisbon, but this was common in the first decades. When three women were caught in 1524, Viceroy da Gama ordered their public flogging and return to Europe in fetters. Although he later gave dowries for marriage, he refused to pardon them.[97]

Many wealthy *fidalgos/reinos* openly maintained Indian mistresses, and adultery was also common among aristocratic Goan women.[98] This was especially true of senior officials who came without their wives to India on a short tenure until 1750, when the Marchioness of Tavora accompanied her husband the Viceroy to Goa.[99] Ordinary soldiers, lesser functionaries, and merchants settled permanently in India with local wives, as they could not afford periodic visits to Portugal, so that inevitably within decades, many *casados* were *mestiços*. Their wives were most often women from the lower castes, as *brahman* women would not risk losing their high caste through intermarriage, although they were taken as war captives or forced to be the mistresses of powerful officials. Albuquerque also convinced some elite Indian families to marry their daughters to his men and to convert to Catholicism.

Despite the interracial Marriage Policy, neither the genders nor the races were equal. In a patriarchal culture that thrived on slavery, women and slaves of all hues were considered necessary for colonial existence. What is significant, however, is that Catholic *mestiços* were given a legal standing in the Estado. The dictator of Portugal in 1773 was the Marquis of Pombal who outlawed slavery in the Estado and legalized *mestiço* inheritance rights. *Mestiços* were also allowed to hold official posts in Goa. This inspired Francisco Luis Gomes (b. 1829), a Goan doctor who wrote the biography, *Marquis de Pombal*, in which he praised Pombal for repudiating Jesuit excesses in the Inquisition.[100] Gomes's novel *Os Brahamanes* derided the elitism of Hindu priests and of European colonials. Yet, illicit slavery thrived despite Pombal's enactments until the Portuguese Civil Code (Part I, Article 7) finally, but effectively eradicated it in 1869.[101]

Female Education and Rights in Goa

The absence of state schools and paucity of private girls' schools meant that female illiteracy was widespread until the mid-nineteenth century. The affluent had private teachers instruct their daughters in the precepts of Catholicism, some rudimentary reading and arithmetic, and in sewing, embroidery, and lace-making. This is seen in the popular work, *Carta de Guia de Casados* (Guidelines for Casados), by Dom Francisco Manuel de Melo (1606–66), a *fidalgo* patriarch who advised that women be taught only handicrafts and domestic skills.[102] In 1846 the state finally established a girls' primary school in Goa, but few families enrolled their daughters in the first decades. However, after more liberal laws were passed in 1910, female literacy rates began to ascend, as they did elsewhere in India. Polygamy and *sati* were banned in 1567, stimulated by Catholic horror at heathen customs, although the Inquisition exacted its own brand of penalties upon women. On the positive side, however, Christian girls were married at a later age, so that their mortality rates in childbirth were lower than that of Hindu women.[103] A liberal Portuguese Civil Code (1869) allowed widows to remarry, and wives to annul unhappy marriages, although only with Ecclesiastical Court approval. When Portugal became a republic in 1910, the Estado instituted more egalitarian statutes on female rights in marriage, remarriage, divorce, and guardianship over children. While praiseworthy, the laws were enacted after four hundred years of racial, sectarian, and gender discrimination in the Estado.[104]

WOMEN IN THE BRITISH EMPIRE

Wars and Women's Lives

British colonialists and Indian nationalists remarked often on the low social status of Indian women. They both blamed outdated Indian traditions, but the problems had exacerbated during the eighteenth-century Anglo-French wars for colonial domination. Moving armies and modern weapons left a trail of widows, *sati,* rape, and Eurasian orphans. Fearing the loss of caste, orthodox caste men tightened the rules governing women's sexual lives, education, and public appearance. High-caste women now retreated further into households, valued primarily as reproducers, so that their labor became invisible in official records. Early marriages meant more progeny, but they also resulted in greater female mortality in childbirth.

In south India and the Deccan, high-caste girls were married before puberty, but consummation occurred after puberty and a secondary ritual. The literate castes, especially those with liberal propensities, instructed daughters in the epics and *Bhagavad Gita,* sometimes seated in the inner rooms of verandah schools, while boys sat outside and learned the *Vedas.*[105] Prepuberty marriages reduced women's chances to study, while working women remained largely illiterate. However, *devadasi* girls attended *pyal* schools with boys in south India. In Bengal, elite girls were taught at home by women performers (*vaishnavis*) versed in the epics and *Puranas.* In her work, *Sekele Katha* (Tales of Olden Days), Swarnakumari Thakur (1855–1932) described an earlier generation taught by *vaishnavis* who entered their inner rooms. Swarnakumari's educational opportunities were due to her father Debendranath Thakur, a reformer in the Brahma Samaj (BS; 1828).[106]

In the agricultural northwest, patriarchal Hindus, Sikhs, and Muslims welcomed male children as seasonal rain to the farm, as boys were future wage earners obliged to care for aged parents.[107] Girls were financial burdens, since village exogamy required daughters to be married with fanfare and sent away. Female infanticide was common among high-ranking Jats and Rajputs, and lower-caste Khatris until the colonial Prohibition of Female Infanticide Act (1872). The sex ratio became less disproportionate in Punjab by 1901.[108] Despite this misogynist custom, natural affection led parents to undertake expenses for daughters whose departure they mourned after the wedding, knowing that separation could be permanent. Punjabi Hindus and Sikhs also practiced levirate marriage (*karewa*) in which the widow remarried her deceased husband's brother. She then regained her married status, and *karewa* safeguarded her children. Unfortunately, such marriages did not require her acquiescence, especially if the husband's family wished to retain her dowry.[109]

Women's clothing varied according to region, caste, and sect. In south India, Muslim women wore a light veil (*pardah*) over head and face; but

Hindu women did not, although they covered the bosom carefully and lived sheltered lives at home. Women of working castes wore unrestricted saris for labor and movement. In the north, east, and west, Hindu and Sikh women draped heads and bosoms with the *sari* or a *dupatta* (shawl), which also served as a partial *pardah*. Muslim women wore similar attire, but observed *pardah* more completely, and when in public they wore a body cloak (*burqah*). Many homes across India had separate women's chambers in the inner section, while men stayed in outer rooms. Family and close friends met in a central courtyard where Muslim women sometimes shed the veil.[110] *Pardah* reinforced the gender division of labor among rural Hindus, Sikhs, and Muslims. Women attended to household chores, sorted crops, and cared for the livestock, but as they did not get paid, their labor was not recorded in documents. Upon acquiring some wealth, rural families withdrew their women from harsh field work. Social esteem rose when women could remain family reproducers, although they also did all domestic chores, cared for children, and nursed the elderly.[111]

Few Muslim girls attended mosque schools (*maktabs*) along with boys, and there was gender segregation in the few classes which they did attend. Here most often girls learned to recite, but nor read the *Qur'an*. In the nineteenth century, segregated girls' *maktabs* numbered eleven in Bengal, and only six around Delhi, so that many working-class women were illiterate.[112] As a preparation for marriage, girls helped their mothers with cooking, sewing, and caring for younger siblings and the elderly. As most elite Muslim girls were in strict *pardah*, they did not attend the *maktabs*. However, older male teachers (*maulvis*) did enter their homes to instruct young girls and boys on the *Qur'an*, moral tales from Persian texts, and elementary arithmetic. After maturity, elite girls were taught separately at home by female scholars (*ustad bis*).[113] The education of elite class Muslim and Hindu girls largely depended upon patriarchal favor. While the enlightened taught their daughters to read the scriptures, the conservative feared that other literature would lead women astray, and the feudal feared that literacy would tempt girls to write clandestine notes to lovers.[114] A popular Persian classic cautioned parents to teach girls the scripture and laws, but not how to write, as such knowledge would be "a great calamity."[115] The time spent in the classroom for Muslim girls was as limited as for Hindus, since the former were sometimes engaged as children, but married after puberty. This section focuses on women's education, two colonial laws affecting women before the 1857 Indian Revolt, working women in the empire, and Eurasians in the British colonial state.

Colonial Rulers, Laws, and Indian Women

After Parliament assumed joint control with the EIC, the empire's new moral arbiters were the Evangelicals led by William Wilberforce

(1759–1833). Wilberforce accused EIC officials of licentiousness with Indian women, for banning missionaries from their territories, visiting Hindu temples on festivals, and promoting European scholars of Indian texts (Orientalists). Wilberforce reiterated Britain's obligation to "improve" India by sending Christian chaplains and schoolmasters, and charged Hinduism with condoning idolatry, infanticide, and *sati*.[116] Many officials were now convinced of the superiority of Western society (Anglicists), and many espoused Jeremy Bentham's (d. 1832) Utilitarian views on government efficiency. Despite the numerous errors in *The History of British India* (1806) by EIC Director James Mill, who never visited India, his derogatory views on Hinduism and its women were widely accepted in Britain. A Parliamentary grant to missionary enterprise in India led to an influx of missionaries after 1813. They implicitly believed these words by Mill:

> Nothing can exceed the habitual contempt which Hindus entertain for their women ... they are held in extreme degradation, excluded from the sacred books, deprived of education and (of a share) in the paternal property.[117]

A Dual Patriarchy: British Officials and Indian Reformers

Having acquired an empire through dubious means, which remained necessary for this profitable enterprise, the British sought to reduce their culpability by enacting moral laws in India, many affecting women. However, these measures depended on the support of educated Indian men (*bhadralok*) like Ram Mohan Roy (1772–1833) and Ishwar Chandra Vidyasagar (1820–91). Anchored in Indian and Western texts, Ram Mohan Roy and the BS's *bhadralok* believed that *sati*, polygamy, and constraints on widow remarriage deviated from the humane ideals of early Hinduism. Roy's pamphlets against *sati* strengthened the decision of Governor-General William Bentinck (1828–33), an evangelical and Utilitarian, to pass the Bengal Sati Regulation Act XVII (1829). Bentinck also banned highway robbery (*thuggi*) in the name of goddess Kali. Similarly, Vidyasagar's petitions on widow remarriage enabled Governor-General Dalhousie (1848–54), another Utilitarian, to enact Widow Remarriage Act XV (1856). However, orthodox Hindus protested the measures as religious interference by foreign rulers.

After the 1857 Revolt, the British hesitated to pass religiously intrusive laws, but did enact others on women's marriage, inheritance, and other rights. These were the Indian Divorce Act (1869), Special Act of 1870 for the Suppression of Female Infanticide, Special Marriage Act (1872), Married Women's Property Act (1874), the Age of Consent Act (1860; amended in 1891), and Child Marriage Restraint Act (1929). Indian reformers spearheaded the last two laws which raised the age of consensual sex and marriage for girls to 12 years. They followed the view of Sir William Jones, a judge and Orientalist scholar, that earlier Hindu texts took precedence over later works, and that textual laws took precedence over local customs of marriage, inheritance, and other rights. This recognized Sanskrit textual laws in *Manu Smriti* over India's labyrinth of regional ethnic customs.[118]

This interpretation was accepted by British officials and elite Indian men who both believed that India would modernize through colonial rule. While some laws were beneficial to Indian women, others negated their rights, but their long-term effects appear in the laws of independent India. However, elite-caste reformers disagreed with the British that premodern Indian laws were uniformly unjust and outmoded. They argued instead that ancient Vedic ideals of universalism and justice had eroded over the millennia, and needed rectification. Despite good intentions, patriarchy won the day. Colonial laws were based in English common law which guaranteed male property rights, as this resonated in the *Manu Smriti*. However, they negated some Indian matrilineal traditions on female property rights. Moreover, for reasons unknown, the British court denied *Manu Smriti*'s fair stipulation that widows be maintained from the husband's joint family property.[119]

Altruism and self-interest governed the dual patriarchy of elite British officials and Indian reformers. The former tried to validate an illegal empire through benign laws, and the latter initially focused only on customs inhibiting elite women. Reformers labored under feelings of cultural inferiority, with a schizophrenic defense of enlightened Indian traditions with apologies over its misogynist customs. The Bengal *bhadralok* tried to instill their new Western knowledge in women (*bhadramahila*), who were proudly introduced into the Calcutta's colonial society.[120] However, both reformers and officials ignored issues peripheral to their interests, viz., the problems of working women and of Eurasians. The former threatened British bourgeois views and were ignored by Indians seeking a niche in the new regime. Both elites derided Eurasians as misfit "half-castes," as they were an uncomfortable reminder of British sexual dependence on local women and of Indian women's unchaste complicity with foreign men.

However, humanists like Ram Mohan Roy, Rabindranath Thakur (1861–1941), and A. Madhaviah (1872–1925) were genuinely disturbed by gender and caste inequities. They sought homologies between premodern Indian universalism and recent Western ideals of equality in their writings in Indian languages and in English. Rabindranath of Bengal and Madhaviah of Tamil Nadu explored gender issues through fiction, entering into women's minds to explore their frustrations over educational neglect, seclusion, child marriage, and widow abuse. Thakur assumed a woman's voice to describe marital cruelties from which the only escape was religious pilgrimage ("A Letter from a Wife," 1912). In one novel, he compared the caged bird to a woman in *pardah*. If suppressed women remained gullible children, colonial chains reduced India to a gullible nation (*Home and the World*, 1915). Madhaviah charged Hindus with subordinating women through illiteracy, marital rape, and widow abuse (*Padmavati Charitram*, 1898; *Muthumeenakshi*, 1903). He also accused unscrupulous Bible women of converting unwary females (*Satyananda*, 1909) and elite Christians of discriminating against lower-caste converts ("Padmavati Charitram Munram Bhagam," 1924).[121] A rising class of women reformers emulated Pandita Ramabai Saraswati (1858–1922) who educated women of all castes; Savitribai Phule (1831–97) who taught Dalit women with her husband Jotiba Phule (1827–90); and Rokeya Sakhawat Hossain (1880–1932) who started schools for Muslim girls. They form the subject of a later chapter.

Women's Education

Girls in Indigenous Schools (Madras)

With its large population of high-caste *brahmans* and non-*brahmans*, *devadasis*, Muslims, and Christian converts, multilingual Madras Presidency provides insights into indigenous schools and colonial policies on female education. Upper-class Muslim girls were taught at home by women scholars (*ustad bis*), and at local mosque schools (*maktabs*) meant primarily for boys, although a few girls' schools were scattered across north India. Fearing missionaries, upper-class Hindu and Muslim parents did not send daughters to Western schools until the late nineteenth century. As Muslim girls also did not attend Muslim colleges (*madarssas*), they were largely invisible in the first British educational survey (1822) conducted by Governor Thomas Munro in Madras. The collectors who gathered data on indigenous education concluded that the only girls visibly in attendance in verandah or *pyal* schools were *devadasis*. Oral history shows that caste girls may have escaped the collectors' eyes, as they studied in rooms next to verandahs where *devadasi* girls sat with boys. They studied the regional language, arithmetic, *Bhagavad Gita,* the Sanskrit epics, and the *Puranas,* and the high-caste boys learned the *Vedas*. Yet, the girls often imbibed some sacred *Vedic* verses (*mantras*) chanted by boys. In her autobiography, Vedavalli, a *brahman* woman (1901–89), described how she learned *mantras* at the age of four, and Sanskrit two years later:

> The day began at 4:00 a.m. when my father woke me, my elder sister, and my younger brother, and took us to the temple. There he taught us to recite holy chants (*slokas*) in Sanskrit. Only after I had learnt them did we return home and break our fast. I learnt to read Sanskrit when I was six. I went to school for six months in Karuthattangudi School, the raja's school, and for another year in Nagapattinam when I was seven.[122]

Savitri Rajan (1908), descendant of a *brahman* musicologist, described the classes on the verandah of her ancestral home. She said:

> Girls could not learn the Vedas, but they were taught literature and music. They sat inside the house and the boys remained in the verandah. My great-grandmother, who was born around 1860, was known to be so well-versed in the *Manusmriti* that her two brothers, who were lawyers, often asked her advice on Hindu law.[123]

Missionaries and Girls' Education

An increasing number of male missionaries arrived after 1813, often accompanied by wives or sisters who started classes for girls. They belonged to Protestant organizations like the Church Missionary Society (CMS), London Missionary Society (LMS), Scottish Presbyterian Mission (SPM), the Wesleyan Mission, and the American Madura Mission. Later female missionaries arrived on their own, enthusiastic about their work as teachers, nurses, and doctors for Indian women. Early girls' classes were begun in south India by Mrs. Bailey at Kottayam, Travancore (1816); Mrs. Rhenius at Palayamkottai, Tirunelveli (1823); Mrs. Drew at Vepery, Madras (1832); Mrs. Eckard in Madurai (1835). They provided a network for Indian Christian women whom they trained as "suitable wives for pastors and teachers."[124] Spinster Mary Anne Cooke began an early Protestant girls' school in Bengal in 1821, and then set up 30 others.[125] At the age of 12, a Bengali woman convert named Hannah Catherine Mullens (1826–61) taught girls at Bhawanipore Mission School, left this to write Christian literature, and possibly married a British missionary.[126] Mission curriculum consisted of reading, writing, arithmetic, Gospel teachings, sewing, and knitting, the last being taught even in tropical south India.[127] Western women missionaries braved poverty, intense heat, and other adversities to teach Indian women, and their work with low castes raised their literary rates. Seeing low-caste girls as victims of *brahmans,* they attempted to convert them with such vigor that the high castes kept their own daughters away. As the poor were drawn to mission schools through gifts of rice and other benefits, especially during famines, they were often called "rice Christians." However, most Hindu and Muslim girls at mission schools did not embrace Christianity. Knowing the role of women in transmitting traditions at home, they feared that cultural identity could be lost through conversion. Missionaries also knew this and thus relied on "Bible women" converts to preach to the family, and village women. In 1821, LMS reverend Thomas Nicholson wrote to colleagues:

> While they continue in Heathenism, it does not appear that will undergo the *disgrace* of allowing their girls to be educated. The only

plan that I think remains is to take in girls who are orphans, and support them entirely, which would require an establishment of such expense that I know not to whom we could look for supplies of money ... to raise the females of India ... is of great importance as it regards the spread of the Gospel.[128]

The absence of caste girls from Western schools appeared in colonial records, so that officials were convinced that Hindu women were universally illiterate. Missionaries like Isabella Thoburn (1840–1901) felt motivated to teach, imagining Indian girls to be worse off than they really were. Her biographer wrote this exaggerated summary:

> The sad history of Indian womanhood, as seen by those brought up in the free air of Christly teachings, has been pathetically summed up in *three brief sentences,* which though all apothegms, not wholly true, still contain so much truth as to afford a severe arraignment of Brahmanism. This terse history is, "Unwelcomed at birth, unhonored in life, unwept in death." No heavier burden lies upon life in India than the inhuman and debasing treatment of womanhood by the religious prescription of the ruling faith.[129]

Female conversion did not remove the stigma of caste or widowhood, since converts continued to cling to caste ranks. However, the example of literate Bible women as preachers for other women was more persuasive than even Christian theology for villagers. Spiritual and material salvation went hand in hand, since converts learned to read the Bible and incidentally escaped child marriage or perpetual widowhood. The American Madura Mission's example of "Bible women" became a stirring example of how women converts could win a whole village. This missionary summed up the view that women were the best teachers:[130]

> It has always been an article of the creed of every people that the mothers make the nation. To educate and Christianize the makers of the Hindu nation was the work that thus opened out before the women of our Christian lands. Almost immediately the wives and daughters of our missionaries began to visit the zenanas in the towns where they were situated. This movement became a recognized feature in our Indian campaign.[131]

Yet, missionaries frowned upon women's innocent pleasures, like the red vermilion *tilak* on the forehead, love of flowers, nose-rings, necklaces. They forbade female rites for watershed life events such as menarche, marriage, and childbirth. Their biases were evident in a school for orphan and low-caste boys and girls run by J. W. Lechlar and Rosa Lechlar in 1848 in Salem, Madras. Four high-caste girls studied with them in the morning and sewed in the afternoons, and their handiwork helped with finances. However, the Lechlars bemoaned the caste girls' fondness for jewelry and the ignorance of their Hindu parents. Rosa Lechlar described the girls as "beseeching" her to convert them, so that when their work was rewarded with cash, they had to promptly donate it to the Bible Society.[132]

After 1840, women missionaries expanded their network of free classes for Hindu and Muslim girls, and opened boarding schools in temple towns like Kanchipuram and Puri. Habitually short of funds, they began teaching elite women at home, since these women did not attend formal schools in this era. Zenana missions were started in 1857 by the Church of England Zenana Mission Society (CEZMS), and also by LMS and SPG.[133] Since male teachers could not enter the women's chambers, zenana missions employed European and later Eurasian women to read stories, teach sewing, lace-making, and knitting, while they spread the Gospel. Despite evangelical zeal, their teaching was impeded by unfamiliarity with local languages and cultures. They often suffered due to heat, fell ill, died at an early age, or returned to Britain. Women missionaries were respected as part of the ruling European elite, and they earned more than governesses in Britain. Yet, like other women, they earned half the pay of male counterparts, and marriage even to a missionary meant losing both their jobs and the return fare to Britain. The quick turnover in women teachers impeded the success of zenana missions, and although elite women appreciated the classes, few became converts.[134] This remained true also of mission schools which had large numbers of elite girls after 1885, but few converts. More successful were village schools, innovative deaf and dumb industrial schools, and teacher training schools such as the Sarah Tucker College in Tirunelveli.[135] Mission women's instructional methods were adopted in secular government schools, and later by nationalists in their efforts to spread female education.

Government Girls' Schools

The colonial state did almost nothing for girls' education until the mid-nineteenth century when it began to subsidize secular private schools with grants-in-aid. Female literacy rates remained low until Indians established girls' schools, after which government increased its efforts. A new official policy to promote secular education began with Sir Charles Wood, later the secretary of state for India. In the momentous Despatch of 1854, Wood advised special taxes to raise funds for government schools, but grants for private institutions. Primary education was to be in the local language, and English for secondary classes, mostly for boys. However, Wood noted "with pleasure the evidence which is now afforded of an increased desire on the part of many of the natives of India to give a good education to their daughters." He also praised a Maghanbhai Karamchand for starting two girls' schools in Ahmedabad.[136] Officials corresponded on how to implement the

policy, while a Reverend Richards of Madras made the definitive pro-
nouncement that "the education of girls [was] a thing generally unknown
among the Hindus."[137]

Yet, at Calcutta in 1849, a Ram Gopal Ghosh and Babu Jaikissen
Mookherjee gave land and money to start the secular Hindu Balika Vidyalaya
(Hindu Girls' School) with lessons in Sanskrit, Bengali, and English taught by
Indians and Europeans.[138] Its patron was J. E. Drinkwater Bethune, law
member of Dalhousie's Council, and Mrs. Bethune, so that the institution
was called Bethune School. Its first secretary of school was Ishwar Chandra
Vidyasagar, whose petitions led Dalhousie to sign the Widow Remarriage
Act in 1856.[139] The first hint of Wood's subsidies led to a similar experiment
in Madras in 1852 by elite men. The Royapettah Hindu Female School was
started and operated by a T. Gopalkistnah Pillay and his colleagues. For the
next three years, Gopalkistnah Pillay wrote to the Madras governor for
grants, but received one letter stating that the governor viewed the school
"with gratification, and wished for its prosperity and emulation by others."
However, neither the Bethune nor the Royapettah girls' school were given
enough aid, and struggled for survival.[140] Such schools were few, as the
colonial government gave a low priority to girls' education until 1930.

In 1866, Mary Carpenter, an educationist friend of Ram Mohan Roy, visited India to gauge Indian views on government girls' schools. Impressed by
Maharaja Hindu Girls' School started in Madras by the Vizianagaram raja,
Vijayaram Gajapathi, Carpenter aggressively corresponded with officials on
starting similar teacher training schools for women. She respected Indians
and strongly advised against religious interference, and her efforts promoted
a major shift in government policy on women's secular education. In 1868,
Carpenter published *Six Months in India*, with a portrait of Ram Mohan
Roy. She stated:

> The grand obstacle to the improvement of female schools, and to the
> extension of them, is the universal want of female teachers. Nowhere,
> except in Mission Schools, are any trained female teachers to be found;
> and even in them, the supply created by the training of teachers in the
> institutions themselves, is not sufficient to meet the demand. The girls'
> schools are taught entirely by male teachers! This has long been felt to
> be a great evil by the inspectors, the intelligent native gentlemen, and
> the mothers of the children; but there has been no possibility, in the
> existing state of things, of remedying the evil.[141]

Emulating the Maharaja Hindu Girls' School, government opened the
Presidency Teachers' Training School (PT School) in 1870 in Madras.
Its first 19 students were Hindu and Christian orphans, and virgin widows
who became a resource for teacher training schools over the coming decades.[142]
In her address to Parliament in 1877, Carpenter described the support

to women's education by "enlightened Indians," and that widows were a potential resource:

> [T]he ignorance of Hindu women of a suitable age is one great impediment, and the difficulty of finding any such, except widows, who would be able and willing to be trained as teachers, is another.[143]

The first major census in 1871 revealed that although Christians formed just 1 percent of the population, they comprised 32 percent of the students in Madras schools. Caste girls were often literate, but in this era did not attend public government schools.[144] Madras reformers voiced concern that women from the literate castes would lag behind Christian girls. Over the next 40 years, elite-caste girls were sent to public schools, where 12 percent were *brahmans,* 8.5 percent were Christians, Muslims were 8 percent, and all other groups were 2 percent.[145] Yet, colonial expenditure on girls' education was a fraction of what was spent for boys.

In the early twentieth century, Indian nationalists started schools with an India-centered curriculum, including its languages and texts, English, mathematics, science, hygiene, and geography. Feminists also began schools for girls of all communities, so that after 1921, female literacy rates inched forward, but the most significant improvements occurred only after independence in 1947.

Educating *Devadasis*

After the British began absorbing smaller Indian kingdoms, the rulers lost the revenue needed for endowments to temples and to village schools. As *devadasis* depended upon the endowments for survival, they increasingly sought commercial patrons. The decline of village schools also meant that the performing women had less opportunities to study Indian languages, epics, *Puranas,* and *bhakti* texts which formed the repertoire for their dances. In the first survey of indigenous schools in Madras in 1822, Governor Thomas Munro's revenue collectors noted that *pyal* schools had begun to deteriorate in Tamil-, Telugu-, Kannada-, and Malayalam-speaking districts. They were the first to record the presence of *devadasi* girls at village schools.[146]

The situation worsened after missionary schools proliferated in India after 1813. The evangelicals were highly suspicious of *devadasis,* nor did the girls enroll in Christian institutions that did not teach them Hindu legends.[147] As the Victorian century progressed, *devadasis* also faced the censure of officials, and Indian reformers eager to "cleanse" society of its permissive traditions. *Chattram* schools attended by *devadasis* were also taken over by the British administration. In 1877, Nidamangalam *chattram's pyal* school in Thanjavur was converted into a government girls' school that catered to the elite favored by the British. In a newspaper letter, Sir W. Robinson pleaded with Victorian prudery that "brothel girls" be excluded from colonial schools. He pointed out that the maharaja of Vizianagaram had excluded *devadasis* from his model girls' school, fearing that caste girls would be tainted by "depraved prostitutes" even before puberty.[148] He sanctimoniously declared:

> I know the feeling to be genuine amongst the respectable people of this country from a lifetime spent amongst them ... It has been my painful duty, with reference to a large female school of which I had charge years ago at Narsapur, to personally inquire into those brothel exercises and filthy communications from which these infants pass to school for a few hour only in a day.[149]

Despite their misfortunes, talented *devadasis* maintained the Karnatak music and dance legacy, but were often compared to English dance hall girls. Elite Indian men accepted their art, but not the women. The term "*nautch* girl" (dancing prostitute) was used derogatively by reformers like Viresalingam Pantulu (1848–1919), an educator of widows and women, who aggressively undertook anti-*nautch* campaigns in Madras.[150] Such attitudes were imbibed by the feminist Dr. Muthulakshmi Reddi (1886–1968) who glossed over her maternal *devadasi* ancestry. Dr. Reddi later helped legally to abolish the dedication of *devadasis* to temples.[151] Feminists and male reformers united to abolish the practice in Mysore (1909), Travancore (1930), Bombay (1934), and Madras (1929, 1937, 1947). Many *devadasis* became dependent on male relatives for concert arrangements. These men became prominent musicians in south India, and they coined their new political-caste identity as *isai vellalas*.[152]

Colonial Laws and Women

Sati Regulation Act of Bengal (1829)

The feminine for "*sat*" (Truth; Skt.) is *sati,* connoting goddess Sati-Devi, but in the medieval era it referred to a true wife (*sati*) who died upon her husband's pyre. A feudal culture thus sought to balance wartime deaths of *kshatriya* warriors by demanding a comparable sacrifice of true wives. Nineteenth-century colonial debates used the term *sati* not for the widow, but for her immolation, thus reducing her from agent to victim object.[153] *Sati* immolation is not sanctioned by the scriptural *Vedas* and *Bhagavad Gita,* and it is not required by law manuals like *Manu Smriti.* It was also not practiced initially by *brahman, vaishya,* and *shudra* castes.[154] However, in the late seventeenth century, a few *vaishyas* who grew affluent through commerce began to practice *sati* immolation as a status symbol. In the eighteenth-century colonial wars, some northern *brahmans* adopted it for venal reasons. Historically, widow burnings occur during social upheavals that threaten group survival or during conflicts over women's inheritance (*stridhan*). Under such circumstances, orthodox men have imbued *sati* with false religious symbolism to reinforce cultural identity.[155]

Many higher-caste Hindus follow regional systems of law, such as Mitakshara and Dayabhaga, based on interpretations of the *Manu Smriti*. *Manu* stipulated that *stridhan* was property gifted to a woman from her father, mother, brother, husband, and that it was meant for female maintenance. As matrilineal property, the chief heirs of a woman's *stridhan* were her daughters and maternal granddaughters, but also occasionally sons, as the woman had flexibility concerning its dispensation. In contrast, Hindu joint family property is patrilineal, devolving upon male heirs for four generations. While a wife can be maintained by her husband's share of such family property, she cannot inherit a share.[156]

In Bengal after the twelfth century, some *brahmans* followed the Dayabhaga system. Dayabhaga laws allowed the widow a small share of her husband's movable or immovable property in the absence of a son. Recent studies reveal that this advantage was wrested from widows in the eighteenth century, after the EIC acquired revenue rights in Bengal, which then included modern Bihar, Orissa, and Bangladesh. EIC extortions were so severe that poverty, famine, and cholera decimated the population by a third by 1770. Alarmed at the spate of widow claimants, disinherited male relations conspired with *brahman* priests to force widows to become *satis*. Reformer Ram Mohan Roy also pointed out that the spate of *sati* burnings coincided with property litigations after the British Permanent Land Settlement (1793), a revenue policy that privatized real estate.[157] Although the British blamed Hindus for maltreating women, the colonial regime was immediately culpable for the upsurge in widow burnings. Yet, equally venal were orthodox *brahmans* who used spectacles of sacrificial *satis* and the myth of their empowerment as demigoddesses to woo back devotees who had strayed to plebeian Shakti cults.[158]

Late eighteenth-century EIC courts employed Muslim clerics to translate Sharia laws, and Hindu pandits to interpret the *Manu Smriti*. Although Governor Warren Hastings (1770–84) forbade religious interference, Anglicists enforced British laws over Indian legal systems. Humane officials also voiced concern that a growing number of widows were being coerced to ascend the husband's pyre. In 1789, revenue collector M. H. Brooke asked permission to obstruct a widow's burning, but was refused as his prohibition would make *sati* more popular. In 1805, a Bihar official also asked the right to intercede, but court legalist Ghanashyam Sharma offered his advice. The ensuing writ then stated that:

Women who desire to join their husband in the funeral pyre can do so provided they have no infant children to look after; they are not pregnant, or not in the period of menstruation, or are not minors. The rule applies to women of all castes. If a woman having an infant-child can make proper arrangements for the rearing of the child, she can burn herself along with the dead body of her husband. But it is against the Shastras or customs to apply drugs or intoxicants and to make a woman lose her senses.[159]

Four circulars were circulated between 1797 and 1829 on whether to inter- fere in a burning. These debates were more intense after 1813 when evangelical ideas had percolated into the Calcutta government. A district official was given permission to intercede if the widow were young, intoxi- cated, or had children under three years of age.[160] A distinction was now made between the social practice as murder, and ritual suicide based on Hindu laws, although Ram Mohan Roy dismissed the latter in public speeches as an invalid argument. As the public, the elite *bhadralok* of Bengal were concerned, as 55 percent of the cremated widows in Bengal were *brahmans* who constituted just 11 percent of the population.[161] The numbers tripled in Bengal from 378 (1815) to 838 (1818), with fewer inci- dences among those who did not follow Dayabhaga laws.[162] There were just 170 cases in Madras (1818), and 50 in Bombay (1819–27).[163] Governor- General Bentinck outlawed widow immolation in the Bengal Sati Regulation Act XVII (1829).

Reformer Ram Mohan Roy (1772–1833)

Men from the literate high castes became influential and affluent in the early British Empire, especially in Bengal. Besides studying Sanskrit, Bengali, and Persian texts, the urban middle class (*bhadralok*) took delight in reading English translations of Enlightenment works. Among them was Ram Mohan Roy, the pioneering activist who supported women's education and rights. He vigorously opposed *sati* and polygamy in tracts and speeches, which con- vinced Governor Bentinck that liberal Indians favored a law against *sati*. While praising the British for their rule of law, Roy criticized the censorship of Indian newspapers and the overzealous Christian missionaries.[164] Roy stressed Vedic Hindu monism and its similarities to Sufism and Unitarian Christianity. Although Roy had a Persian mistress and waged a legal battle over inheritance with his mother, these personal enigmas cannot trivialize his seminal contributions for women.

Roy supported widows' rights based on Hindu law codes, which give both widow and her sons shares in the husband's estate. His resistance to *sati* prob- ably began when he witnessed his sister-in-law's con-cremation in 1812. In 1815 he began campaigning against *sati* in his Amitya Sabha (Friendship Society), which became the Brahma Samaj in 1828. He wrote Bengali pam- phlets and translated these into English for officials. On November 30, 1818, he published his first dialogic tract, "A Conference between an

Advocate for and an Opponent of the Practice of Burning Widows Alive," in which he was the opponent. His first statement was pungent:

> Those who have no reliance in the Shastras, and those who take delight in the self-destruction of women, may well wonder that we should oppose that suicide which is forbidden by all Shastras and by every race of man.[165]

The advocate for *sati* cited the legendary chaste wife Arundhati and verses from the *Brahma Purana*. Roy assumed the voice of the opponent by quoting the *Manu Smriti* (5:157–160) which advised the widow to live on, but abstemiously. He also showed that monism in the *Upanishads* preceded priestly *Puranic* rituals to justify *sati* speciously. On February 20, 1820, Roy published, "A Second Conference between an Advocate for and an Opponent of the Practice of Burning Widows Alive," dedicating it to Governor Hastings's wife in an effort to publicize the *bhadralok*'s opposition to *sati* immolation. He now cited the *Bhagavad Gita* to prove that the highest goal for Hindus was enlightenment, not promises of a dubious heaven through *sati*. To the accusation that women were pleasure-seeking, Roy retorted that men's desire for pleasure led them to steal women's wealth. He compared women's courage and physical endurance to men's fear of death, and argued that women had more control over passions, while men had many wives and mistresses. Roy accused polygamist Kulin *brahmans* of lust for marrying, then neglecting their several young wives. The widows were later compelled to become *satis*. Roy wrote:

> Women are in general inferior to men in bodily strength and energy; consequently the male part of the community, taking advantage of their corporeal weakness, have denied to them those excellent merits that they are entitled to by nature, and afterwards they are apt to say that women are incapable of acquiring those merits.[166]

In 1822, Roy published, "Brief Remarks Regarding Modern Encroachments on the Ancient Rights of Females According to the Hindu Law of Inheritance." In this tract, Roy made the public connection between the Permanent Land Revenue Settlement, increased property litigation, and the spate of *sati* burnings. He also praised ancient lawgivers Yajnavalkya and Katyayana for stipulating the widow's right to inherit a part of her husband's estate, but accused men of stealing these rights if the women were childless. Bengali *brahman* women had lost their traditional rights through Dayabhaga law. He also attacked polygamy as harsh upon widows, as many women chose death over penury.[167]

Roy wished to use logic to persuade his countrymen to change, as he feared that a British law would popularize *sati* among orthodox *bhadralok* in the Hindu Dharma Sabha. After Bentinck read Roy's pamphlets, he invited him for a discussion, as he was considering the law against *sati* immolation. Roy refused at first, but later accepted Bentinck's second invitation. Clearly, the debates on *sati* and widow remarriage did not stem from the reformers' patriarchal wish to objectify women. Rather, they were a *bhadralok* challenge to the rulers not to dismiss all Indian traditions as regressive or complacently assume that all British laws were progressive. On his part, Bentinck wished to erase "a foul stain upon the British rule," but unlike Roy whose pamphlets focused on women, Bentinck made no reference to them in his "Minute on Suttee" to EIC Directors on November 8, 1829. As an evangelical he denounced the inhumane custom, but justified his law as "enlightened Hindus" (men like Roy) recommended it. Bentinck wrote:

> The first and primary object of my heart is the benefit of the Hindus. I know nothing so important to the improvement of their future conditions as the establishment of a purer morality, whatever their belief and more just conception of the will of God. The first step for this better understanding will be dissociation of religious belief and practice from blood and murder ... I disown in these remarks, or in any measure, any view whatever to conversion to our own faith. I write and feel as a legislator for the Hindus and as I believe many enlightened Hindus think and feel ... Descending from these higher considerations, it cannot be a dishonest ambition that the Government of which I form a part should have the credit of an act which is to wash out a foul stain upon the British rule, and to stay the sacrifice of humanity and justice to a doubtful expediency ... The practice of Sati or of burning of and burying alive the widows of Hindus, is revolting to the feelings of human nature; it is nowhere enjoined by the religion of the Hindus as an imperative duty, on the contrary, a life of purity and retirement on the part of the widows is more specially and preferably inculcated.[168]

However, as widow burnings ceased, Roy believed that the Bengal Sati Regulating Act was effective. Orthodox Hindus denounced Roy as a renegade, but he published a rejoinder in the press a few years before his death. He also praised the law in an open letter to Bentinck on January 18, 1830, and in another letter dated November 15, 1930. Declaring that numerous Hindus expressed "satisfaction at the abolition of the horrible custom," he wrote:

> Even in Bengal a greater number of the most intelligent and influential of the natives, landholders, bakers, merchants, and others, felt so much gratified with the removal of the odium, which the practice had attached to their character as a nation, that they united in presenting an address of thanks and congratulation.[169]

Sati Myths in the West and East

Sati myths became a romantic theme in European operas and literature by the irreverent Voltaire (d. 1798), Romantics like Goethe (1797), and Baptists like William Carey.[170] Carey translated Bentinck's 1829 proclamation and saw "heathen murder" as inspiration for sermons.[171] Benign patriarchs like Roy and Bentinck were similarly repulsed by widow sacrifice, but orthodox *brahmans* and Christians used *sati* to promote their own religions.[172]

European women also found the myth convenient to their purposes. The romantic Christian Mrs. General Mainwaring (ca. 1830) suggested in a lurid novel, *The Suttee, or the Hindu Convert,* that conversion could cure the disease of *sati*. Romantic Orientalists like Mrs. Speier of Calcutta blamed *brahmans* for women's decline after the Vedic era. In her monograph, *Life in Ancient India* (1852), Mrs. Speier gushed about brave *satis* and heroic Vedic women, "as free as Trojan dames or the daughters of Judaea."[173] Christine Bader's (1867) monograph on Hindu women's spirituality presaged later Theosophists like Annie Besant and feminist Margaret Cousins, author of *The Awakening of Indian Womanhood* (1922).[174]

Although men and women nationalists lauded abolition, the idea of *sati* sacrifice became a theme through which these Indians highlighted two messages from Indian history. They drew a parallel between tyrannical Turkish sultans and British imperialists in India, and they also described two contestations. The first was for India as the motherland and goddess (Bharat Mata). The second paradigm was of chaste Indian women patriots ("matriots"?) whose bodily sacrifices would free the motherland. In journals and speeches, nationalists re-evoked the romantic view of *sati* as female sacrifice, and retold feudal legends about Rani Padmini (thirteenth century) who died in a conflagration with palace women (*jauhar*) to prevent her capture by the Muslim enemy.[175] Cultural jingoism blinded famous art historian Ananda K. Coomaraswamy who mythologized the *sati* as "the ideal Hindu wife" in a paper to the British Sociological Society in 1912. Grandiloquently quoting patriarchal texts, Coomaraswamy claimed that Indians married not from passion, but from "religious duty," and that women's roles differed from those of men, since society "asks of women devotion to men; of men devotion to ideas."[176] Eighty years after Roy's campaign against *sati*, Coomaraswamy obviously thought his vision was clearer than that of the pioneer who fought against burning widows:

> Let us now return to the Indian Sati, and try to understand her better. The root meaning of the word is essential being, and we have so far taken it only in a wide sense. But she who dies for a husband is also called *Sati* in a more special sense. It is in this special sense only that the word is well known to European readers. It is this last proof of

the perfect unity of body and soul, this devotion beyond the grave, which western critics have chosen as our reproach. They were right in attaching so much importance to it; we only differ from them in thinking of our Satis with unchangeable respect and love, rather than pity.[177]

Nationalist-feminists also glorified Indian woman (Bharatiya nari) as spiritual and unselfish, and praised *jauhar* as the ultimate female sacrifice for the nation. While Sarojini Naidu (1879–1948) balked at condoning widow immolation, her poem, *Suttee,* suggested that loyal women would not wish to survive their husbands. She asked provocatively, "Shall the flesh survive when the soul is gone?"[178] In her 1917 address to the Indian National Congress (INC), Sarojini Naidu also validated the *sati* myth by referring to Rani Padmini's *jauhar*. She intended to stir the men and women delegates with dramatic tales of female courage, but her regressive metaphor handicapped the feminist movement. She said:

> Womanhood of India stands by you today ... When your hour strikes, when you need torch-bearers in the darkness, standard-bearers to uphold your honour ... the womanhood of India will be with you as holders of your banner, sustainers of your strength. And if you die, remember that the spirit of Padmini of Chittor is enshrined with the manhood of India.[179]

Widow Remarriage Act (1856)

In 1832, English became the *lingua franca* of British India, enabling those who mastered the language to seek minor positions in the bureaucracy. In Bengal, the elite *bhadralok* attended Western schools where they studied European literature and history. In contrast, elite women (*bhadramahila*) who were versed in Indian texts were often unable to converse in English. Liberal men, who wished more modern, conjugal companions, thus employed zenana teachers to instruct their wives and enable them to move in Calcutta's colonial society.[180] The men opposed child marriage, restrictions on widow remarriage, and polygamy among Kulin *brahman* community. In an era of high youth mortality due to epidemics, child brides often became child widows. Fortunately, most Bengalis belonged to lower castes that practiced later marriages, widow remarriage, and did not penalize women for cohabiting with men of their choice.[181]

By mid-nineteenth century, in India, the intelligentsia began to send girls to schools, but few allowed widows to remarry. The widow remarriage movement was spearheaded in Bengal by Ishwar Chandra Vidyasagar who had been moved by their plight in Calcutta. He lobbied to remove the prejudice in caste society and to challenge the decrees of EIC courts, which

depended on *brahman* scholarly translators. Like Ram Mohan Roy, Vidyasagar initially published a Bengali tract to prove that the most sacred texts
allowed widow remarriage. This led to heated debates with orthodox
Hindus, but the lower castes who allowed widows to remarry sang his
ideas as street ballads and wove them into cloth. Vidyasagar translated his
pamphlet into English to distribute among colonial officials with whom
he had contact, as he was secretary of the Bethune School for girls. Convinced that other enlightened Indians agreed that colonial laws would
reverse outdated customs, in 1855 Vidyasagar petitioned Governor-
General Dalhousie to legalize widow remarriage. Law member J. P. Grant
introduced a bill into Dalhousie's Council, and the Widow Remarriage Act
(1856) was promulgated.

The Widow Remarriage Act had some flaws that made it less successful
than the law against *sati* immolation. Its preamble revealed that official Victorian mores on sexual restraint often derived from missionary views on
Indian women as permissive. These Western moralities now percolated into
elite Indian society. For example, Baptist William Ward's conviction that the
law would save unmarried widows from prostitution is reflected in the preamble. This stated that "the removal of all legal obstacles to the marriage
of Hindoo Widows will tend to the promotion of good morals and to the
public welfare."[182] The Western assumption was that unattached widows
corrupted men, not that corrupt men preyed upon single women. Moreover,
the Widow Remarriage Act was merely advisory and did not inflict penalties
on those who did not arrange for family widows to remarry. A law to *allow*
remarriage was thus difficult to police and eradicate. This differed from the
earlier law *outlawing* widow immolation, so that *sati* was effectively policed
and eradicated. Another flaw was its negative effect upon Hindu widows'
customary rights to *stridhan* and maintenance by the husband's family.
The second clause of the Widow Remarriage Act stipulated that unless a
dying husband permitted his widow to remarry, or if the caste allowed it, a
widow lost her right to maintenance from his family property. If a widow
wished to dispute this, she had to appear before the magistrate. Since high-
caste women, especially widows, rarely appeared in public in this era, they
relied on male relatives to plead their case and lost their customary rights.[183]
Similar fine legal distinctions became loopholes for family men to dispossess
the widow of her customary rights. The law thus further marginalized
Hindu widows if they remarried.[184] The long-term implications of this act
were removed only a hundred years later in 1956, when women were given
equal inheritance rights in free India.

In the meanwhile, however, the Widow Remarriage Act of 1856 also
tempted some non-Hindu men to adopt Hindu customs for their material
benefits to men. In the rich agricultural province of Punjab, as Hindus and
Sikhs already allowed widows levirate marriages (*karewa*), the law was an
anomaly. This patriarchal society and also the British administration

disapproved of females inheriting agricultural land, so that remarriage
became a disadvantage to some widows. Moreover, under the law, a remarried woman lost her *stridhan* and her customary maintenance rights from
her deceased husband's family property.[185] Despite its severity, the Widow
Remarriage Act in India must be viewed in the context of contemporary
British laws which in 1857 granted women right to divorce but not maintenance. Only after 1882 were divorced British women able to hold property
separately from men.[186]

As the Act of 1856 in India could not eradicate cruelty to widows, social
reformers sought to change customs through persuasion and precept.
Widow activist Pandita Ramabai Saraswati promoted female education,
even converting to Christianity to break free of Hindu patriarchs. In Madras
Presidency, Justice S. Venkatadri Naidu promoted widow remarriage in the
1860s, and Justice T. Muthuswami Iyer founded the Widow Marriage
Association (1872); while in the 1880s, Raghunatha Rao, Viresalingam
Pantulu, and his wife Rajyalakshmi worked assiduously for widow education and remarriage.[187] In Bombay, D. K. Karve (1858–1962) began a
remarriage association, married widow Godubai Joshi in 1893, and started
a girls' school where widow Parvatibai Athavale became an inspirational
teacher. In 1912, the virgin widow R. Subbalakshmi Ammal (1886–1969)
opened a Madras home where she trained widows as teachers for women.

Working Women

Although reformers focused on elite women, working-class/lower-caste
women faced more severe problems of subsistence and survival. Females often
worked from childhood, performing outside wage labor, and household farm
chores and family care. There was often little respite during pregnancy, childbirth, and illness. Poverty mean inadequate nutrition, but women's lives were
more seriously affected by unequal gender distribution of food. Girls were
socialized early to feed others before themselves, making anemia and chronic
ailments rife among females. Poor hygiene and medical care in confinement
made them susceptible to famines and epidemics which haunted the colonial
centuries. Census records after 1901 show that female birth rates and sex
ratios (females per 1000 males) declined steadily. These figures reveal that
the sex ratio fell steadily between 1901 and 1941: 1901 (972), 1911 (964),
1921 (955), 1931 (950), 1941 (945).[188] A cultural preference for male children was because men were the primary wage earners and the mainstay of
aged parents. Males were thus fed better than females who worked at home
in diverse ways important for subsistence. However, a patriarchal colonial
state and economy exacerbated these gender preferences. As women's domestic farm labor contributed to the family's resources, but did not bring in
a wage, their work did not appear in official records.

Women's survival was also jeopardized by the colonial exploitation of
Indian labor through low wages and by the state's failure to buttress poverty

through subsidies and irrigation programs where most needed. For example, British wages for miners and construction workers in India and indentured laborers in overseas colonies were a pittance compared to the profits from these industries. Women were paid half the wages of men. While the colonial state invested in irrigational projects in riverine areas of Punjab, it neglected its arid region of Haryana, where droughts and ensuing famine severely affected the population. Women and girls were often the first casualties, victims both of unequal food distribution in a patriarchal society and of an exploitative state.[189] Moreover, in epidemics, such as the disastrous 1918 influenza epidemic, more female infants died at birth, and the overall deaths among females rose due to malnutrition and poor hygiene. Censuses between 1901–11 and 1911–21 from Madras Presidency reveal two phenomena: a declining sex ratio from 958.3 to 955.9, and an increased rate of female deaths from 961.2 to 979 per 1000 males. The female population clearly declined in these colonial decades, with the most significant losses among the marginalized.[190]

Indenture and Gender

Initially, eighteenth-century British planters used Indians as slaves on their estates in Mauritius and Guyana until 1807 when Parliament abolished slavery. However, the use of Indian slaves persisted for at least a decade, since in 1818 in Mauritius, one-seventh were south Indians. Many were smuggled into Mauritius from the French island of Reunion where they had been transported from Pondicherry on the subcontinent.[191] In 1834, the British government formalized the indenture system through which India's tribals and impoverished lower castes were recruited for overseas plantations. Heavy taxation and the decline of India's weaving and other industries under British rule caused widespread internal rural migrations and patterns of overseas emigration, which corresponded to 12 or more disastrous famines.[192] A stream of indentured Indians toiled for a pittance on sugar, coffee, or tea plantations in Mauritius, Guyana, Trinidad, Jamaica, Sri Lanka, Fiji, and Malaya until indenture was legally terminated in 1920.[193]

The indenture experience was marked by a significant sexual disparity on colonial estates, as owners preferred male workers. Thus, in Mauritius, the first Indians were 72 women and 1,182 men (1835); 353 women and 6,939 men (1838); 10 women and 73 men (1842) due to harsh local laws and conditions. Similarly, in Guyana, the first group consisted of 5 women, 6 children, 233 men (1838), but the women were refused formal contracts, although they toiled for 10–12 hours to clear dense forests for sugar fields. As mortality was high, many returned to India after the five-year contract ended.[194] In Jamaica, only one-third of the indentured were women, since Europeans wanted male "breadwinners." Despite evidence on hard-working women farm workers in India, British officials argued that they were "not nearly the equals of the men as agricultural labourers." This predilection for male workers was satisfied by Indian recruiters who received less for female workers.[195] Male biases appeared in other ways, after Indian nationalists protested that fewer women meant more prostitution, although like men, women emigrated for work and a new life. Yet, like Indian urban women workers who occasionally supplemented inadequate wages with prostitution, women also resorted to it on overseas estates.[196] In any case, the bourgeois nationalist argument based on "moral" considerations swayed Victorian officials, who in turn convinced planters to employ 40 women per 100 men.

Planters often accused women of being unreliable due to the demands of pregnancy. However, this was also an exaggeration, since evidence shows that they toiled for 10–12 hours until confinement, returning to work soon after delivery, as the family depended upon their daily wages. Women often carried infants to the fields, since childcare was not offered by the planters, an impediment that was partly remedied only in 1913 in Jamaica.[197] Planters also often employed young children in the fields, although it was illegal to indenture a person before the age of 16. Class and patriarchal biases framed the wage scales, with women earning roughly half the pay of men for the same hours of work. Labor was divided according to gender, with women being given the least remunerative, but not necessarily the least arduous jobs. The coterie of European planters-colonial officials did not apparently value the indentured woman either for her labor or as the reproducer of the workforce.[198]

Planters ignored the social consequences of the sex disparity, i.e., rape, domestic violence against women, short-term marriages, alcoholism, and suicide. Protests by Indian nationalists led to the British recruitment of more women to later colonies like Fiji. Thus, in 1891, 2,470 Indian women accompanied nearly 5,000 men to Fiji; however, the social problems of sexual misuse and violence continued. After 1920, former indentured Indians were permitted to remain in the colonies as permanent residents, and they began to multiply naturally. Thus, censuses show that in Fiji the India-born constituted 70 percent of the Indians in 1911, but only 50 percent in 1921. Over the next decade, unfettered by indenture, the sex ratio of Fijian Indians became nearly equal.[199]

Several reasons drove Indian women to emigrate to the colonies as indentured laborers. They frequently accompanied husbands, since separation to a distant colony like Guyana or Trinidad was likely to be permanent. Those who were socially outcast like widows or prostitutes often sought opportunities elsewhere. Cataclysmic events like the 1857 Revolt or devastating famines in 1867 and 1890 compelled many women and men to emigrate. There were also a few positive aspects of the gender disparity in the colonies where women could leave an unhappy marriage and abusive husband with greater facility. Women living outside India faced less censure if they remarried, even if they had a second or third husband. The shortage of women meant that men with wives enjoyed a higher status than single men, while caste and patriarchal marriage customs became less significant. For example, the dowry was a burden on parents of the bride, but it was replaced in the colonies with gifts to the bride, a custom mistaken by some to be a "bride-price." Yet, these normative changes in gender relations also conflicted with the persistence of patriarchal authority in the household. Domestic violence, marital rape, alcoholism, and suicide were features of life in the colonies. The briefest suspicion of female infidelity often resulted in "coolie wife-murder," as evident in Trinidad where 65 of the 87 murders between 1872 and 1900 were of wives by jealous husbands. A wife's infidelity meant loss of social esteem for men who were often driven to alcoholism or suicide. These residual effects of indenture still plague Indian society in the former colonies.[200]

Women Workers in India

In India's precolonial and colonial economies, women performed a variety of productive functions, which included animal husbandry, collecting fodder and water, sowing, reaping, harvesting, sorting, and drying crops. This is encapsulated in a pithy Punjabi proverb which states that a single man cannot manage a farm without a wife.[201] Rural women bought and sold goods, and worked as barbers, midwives, cooks, and as servants in large homes. They were the producers and sellers of 15–20 percent of cottage goods such as handmade woven baskets and pottery, spun thread, and dyed cloth.[202] Although in Bengal, women did not work on cotton looms, they often wove jute.[203] In south India, *kaikkolar* women of a weaving subcaste (*jati*) often handled looms. Most female manufactures were connected in some way to the family or *jati* unit. Women vendors of fish and milk thus depended on their family men for these products, while weavers, potters, laundry workers all belonged to specific *jatis*. Midwives alone were independent of family men, although they too often belonged to a specific *jati,* such as that of the leather workers (*chamars*) in Bengal. In the late nineteenth century, there was a decline in handspun cotton made by rural women and in their crafts using simple tools, as these products could not compete with the precision of machined products.[204] Gandhi's emphasis on handicrafts found expression on a state-supported handicraft industry after Indian independence.

Indian women also worked in coal and iron mines, gathered forest products like gum and wood, and worked on tea and coffee estates in India and Sri Lanka. Planters and mine owners liked to employ women and children in the labor-intensive tea industry, ostensibly due to the delicacy of the plucking operation. Often laborers were extremely marginalized Adivasi tribals ready to low-paying jobs. Children were the cheapest to employ, followed by women, and then by men. Women workers in mines received 40 percent of the wage given to men, as managers regarded female wages as merely supplemental family income. On the "coolie lines" or slum houses near mines, living conditions were deplorable, but rarely investigated. Women washed and cooked in pit water, and breathed the noxious air. There were no latrines, and pigs were the only scavengers, so that disease was rampant, and mortality rates were high.[205]

The nineteenth century was marked by a decline in Indian agriculture and industry, while the economic policy of *laissez-faire* favored mechanized industries in Britain. Only after 1850 were the first mechanized jute and cotton mills established in India by Europeans, and later by wealthy Indians.[206] Scholars have shown that the trajectory of industrialization differed in a colony like India in comparison with independent European nations. After a long neglect, British capitalists began to invest in specific industries in India, but the colonial state expedited this process without ensuring social safeguards for women and families. Moreover, Indian women were not immediately employed in mechanized mills, and when they were hired, they were not allowed to operate machines or to perform better paying technical jobs, unlike women in Europe.[207]

At first, Indian women could not be enticed to leave their small farms for mill work in Calcutta or Bombay. Women's rural work on subsistence farms provided the basic food for the family, although it brought almost no cash. Men largely migrated to work in urban textile and jute mills. As women's farm labor had little remunerative value, official records devalued their work in comparison to that of men.[208] When the subsistence farm eventually ceased to provide even the basic necessities for the family, women migrated with their children to the city in search of work at the mills. However, their wages fell far short those of men, so that women sometimes resorted to prostitution to supplement their meager mill wages. Recruitment for jobs was conducted through personal acquaintance, and women sometimes repaid male recruiters with sexual favors for a mill job. The better paying jobs were weaving and spinning, which were invariably given to men, who in turn recommended their male relatives for such jobs. An extended family of four or five male members could bring in a larger income pool than a single man and a woman, as women largely occupied the lower cadres of mill work. Moreover, the family's social esteem rose by keeping its women at home in *pardah,* in the narrow streets of the crowded workers' slums of Calcutta and Bombay.[209] The fetid atmosphere of open drains, the poor sanitation, and narrow rooms were detrimental to the health of all the workers.

Despite these problems, the Bombay textile mills employed about 25,000 women, or 25 percent of the workforce, to clean, spin, reel, and dye the cotton thread.[210] In the peak year of 1929, in the Calcutta jute mills, records show that about 59,000 women and 265,000 men worked in various semi-skilled and low-skilled jobs. Around the same time, the numbers of child laborers also declined due to various investigative reports, enactments, and subsequent managerial strategies.[211] There were also part-time female migrant workers from Bihar, Uttar Pradesh, Madhya Pradesh, and Madras, and although these were perfunctorily dismissed as "dependants," such women performed many necessary functions in the mills. However, working conditions were harsh since women were often prevented from unionizing in the mills and often endured the sexual harassment of their supervisors.

In 1881 the colonial government passed its first Indian Factories Act after an enquiry by a Labour Commission into conditions in Bombay. A child was defined as a person between 7 and 12 years, and their working hours were limited to 9 hours a day with an hour's rest. However, the act did not lay down specific rules concerning women, and although amendments were proposed, they were not implemented until another act was passed in 1891. The child was redefined as one between the ages of 9 and 14 years; the women's working hours were limited to 11 per day, with a rest break for one and a half hours for domestic responsibilities such as childcare.[212] In this era, until the formation of the International Labour Organization (ILO) in 1920, the empire was governed by *laissez-faire* economics with a strong bias toward factory owners, rather than the workers. Now, after the end of World War I, the idea of a welfare state became increasingly popular in the industrialized West, which now focused on women's crucial roles within the family. Yet, the imperial government in India did not favor the welfare state, nor did it put pressure upon mill owners to apply all the ILO recommendations to safeguard women through maternity benefits and compensation during sickness and unemployment. In 1882, Pandita Ramabai Ranade, the first Indian feminist, gave evidence to the Hunter Commission, and she recommended that government improve the educational and medical facilities for Indian women. Accordingly, in 1885, the Dufferin Fund was established to provide "zenana" hospitals and clinics expressly for women. However, the zenana medical movement largely catered to affluent women in *pardah*, and little was actually done to improve health care for working women.

The rates of childbirth mortality was extremely high, as well as the rates of infant mortality. This was evident in Bengal where 50 percent of the children died at early infancy.[213] Working women were often handicapped by their dual responsibilities within the home and to maintain a job crucial for their survival. Not only did they have to report to work regularly, for fear of losing their jobs, but the mill owners did not provide any crèches for childcare, nor any private areas for mothers to breast-feed infants in the mills. Children were thus often left in the inadequate care of elderly neighbors or relatives who fed them opium to keep them quiet until their mothers returned. In 1921, a Dr. Barnes gave evidence of the widespread use of opium to drug mill workers' children in Bombay. To counter this accusation, the mill owners proposed that minor children be allowed to work, although the Factory Act intended to curb the use of child labor in mills

and mines. In that same year, a Dr. D. F. Curjel headed an investigation of
workers' conditions, and he published his report, "The Conditions of
Employment before and after Child-birth in Bengal Industries," for the
government. Curjel was dismayed by the managers' lack of interest in the
laborers' social backgrounds, living conditions, and working problems.[214]
These two studies led to two bills in the Bombay and Bengal councils which
proposed that government provide prenatal and child care, and clinics operated by trained professionals. However, the government was unwilling to
invest in these expensive schemes, and it was only in the 1930s that the
Maternity Benefit Act became effective in several provinces. However, by
now, the numbers of women in the jute industry sharply declined due to a
combination of factors. The increased pace of mechanization resulted in the
hiring of men, rather than women, while the factory legislation promoted
female domesticity over mill employment.[215] Many women drifted to the city
in search of family men during the depression when farms were further marginalized. Many were virtually single, subsisting through part-time work in
the mills, or as domestic servants, sometimes supplemented through prostitution. Although women often participated in the unions and protested against
unfavorable work conditions or the harassment of supervisors, the middle-
class feminists largely ignored their contributions to women's rights.[216]

As they constituted just 15 percent of the labor force in Calcutta and
Bombay, women could organize to unionize on their own, but they attended
the meetings organized by men, without playing a decisive role in the proceedings. However, after 1921, women participated in strikes, and accounts
of working-class militancy indicate that they retorted verbally to the supervisors (*sardars*), and even physically staved off aggressive bullies with brooms
and sticks. Evidence given to commissions of enquiry reveal that the *sardars*
intimidated both female and male workers, often took a cut of their wages,
or demanded sexual favors from the women.[217] In extreme situations,
women surrounded and held the manager hostage in his office while making
their demands. Although these protests were few in number and appeared
spontaneous, their modus operandi was well known to elicit results. However, women often found that strikes conflicted with domestic responsibilities, and that their income balanced the loss of pay during men's strikes.
Although the women hardly saw themselves as strike breakers, managers
sometimes succumbed to their demands. This happened in 1929 when
female bag sewers refused to agree to similar demands by male workers.
In Bengal, male unionists often ignored women's demands, but in Bombay,
women organized their own strikes more effectively.[218]

Eurasians: Maternal Indian Ancestry

Until the mid-nineteenth century, the near absence of white women in
India meant that most Europeans consorted with Indian and Eurasian

women who were prostitutes, long-term mistresses, or wives. In 1690, the Frenchman Robert Challe noticed that most of the two hundred men employed by the French EIC were unlikely to return to Europe as they would settle in the colonies. A royal edict in 1664 thus tried to regulate their moral welfare abroad by stipulating that no Frenchman was to marry a local woman unless she had been instructed in Catholic precepts and then baptized. The Frenchman had also to obtain permission to marry from the Mission Superiors.[219]

Despite this stern admonishment, French outposts like Pondicherry were far more tolerant than the Dutch and English colonies toward biracial relationships and informal "marriages." French egalitarianism after the Revolution is reflected in the 1790 legal document, which classified Eurasians as French, since their ancestors were European. English travelers commented on such attitudes, so obviously at variance with their own racially exclusivist society. The Dutch and English were especially severe upon illegitimate Eurasian children, although at least one Dutch-Eurasian community survived in Cochin in the 1720s.[220] In the eighteenth century, the French and English sought beautiful and wealthy Luso-Indian wives as they were familiar with Indian life. Thus, Joseph Francois Dupleix (1697–1764), the French governor, married a Goan wife, Dona Joana de Castro, who negotiated with Indian princes and helped to forge a Catholic front against the English. Her fellow diplomat was Dom Antonio Jose de Noronha, the vicar of Mylapore, and the scion of a distinguished *Indiatico* family from Goa.[221]

Englishmen occasionally even married Indian women until 1820s. They styled themselves as "nabobs" or princes (i.e., *nawabs*), dressed like Indian aristocrats, ate curries, spoke local languages, kept Indian wives. While some EIC officials were notoriously corrupt, others had a scholarly appreciation of India, and they had Indian wives. For example, Charles Metcalfe (d. 1846), the enlightened Resident of Delhi (1811–19), had an aristocratic Sikh wife and three Eurasian sons.[222] Resident William Fraser (d. 1825) of Delhi also dressed like a local and had at least one Indian wife and several mistresses, raising his numerous progeny as Hindus or Muslims, each according to her/his mother's faith.[223]

The eighteenth-century wars resulted in a growing number of Eurasian orphans, while early EIC permissiveness toward Indian customs and women was challenged by Protestant evangelicals. As early as 1707, Protestant missionaries had started a Portuguese medium school for orphan Eurasian and other children at Ft. St. George, Madras. Also at Ft. St. George in 1715, a Reverend William Stevenson began the English medium St. Mary's Charity School for 12 girls and 18 boys, the offspring of English soldiers and Indian women to be raised as Protestants.[224] Similarly, in the British siege of Madurai in 1798, a number of orphans were left under the care of the great missionary, Christian F. Schwartz. Schwartz began a school under the auspices of the SPG at Tiruchirapalli shortly before his death.[225] In 1805 and 1811, charity schools were started for low-caste, Eurasian, and English orphans at Vizhakapattinam (Andhra Pradesh), Travancore (Kerala), Bellary (Karnataka), Cuttack (Orissa), and Serampore (Bengal).[226]

However, the orphans of ordinary soldiers and Indian women in the colonial wars were stigmatized, especially after the passing of the Pitts India Act in 1784. When a bankrupt EIC requested the British Parliament for a loan, evangelical legislators urged that stricter sexual mores replace the more permissive attitudes that had prevailed among company employees in India. In 1786, Eurasians were classified as "natives of India," and not as British subjects, paving the way for their institutional exclusion from British society. Initially, Lord Clive's Military Fund and the Bengal and Madras funds supported all orphans of soldiers killed in the wars, both legitimate and illegitimate, irrespective of the mother's ethnicity. However, now the Bengal Military Orphan Society even removed orphans from Indian mothers who were suspected of thwarting the child's Christian development. English society despised biracial marriages for "mongrelizing" their race, while Indians saw them as "half-caste." In 1825, the Indian widows of English soldiers were excluded from Lord Clive's Fund for the families of deceased soldiers, as racism replaced Christian charity. The British historian F. C. Danvers (1888) echoed the racist sentiments of traveler Richard Burton who blamed Portuguese intermarriage with Indians for their losses against England. Burton dismissed Luso-Indians as an "ugly," "degraded looking race" and as "Mestici—in plain English, mongrels."[227]

British feelings were an ambivalent mix of sexual guilt and contempt for biracial children, often caused by European soldiers' rape of Indian women.[228] The skin color and maternal upbringing of Anglo-Indians effectively led to their social ostracism, although they were raised as Christians. Anglo-Indians thus learned to despise their maternal heritage, and their loyalties often rested with unknown English fathers. During the British heyday, they prided themselves on their "heritage as Britishers."[229] There was a honeycomb of separate Eurasian caste-like identities, with Anglo-Indians ranking highest (Protestants, recent British link), and Luso-Indians/Goans as lower (Catholics, remote European link). Apart from famous Indian patriots like poet Henry Derozio (1809–31) and journalist Frank Moraes (1907–74), a few famous Anglo-Indian women include Dr. Margaret Alva, a senior member of India's Parliament (1974–2007), a Cabinet minister and Congress Party official (1984); stage artist Patricia Cooper (1905–84); Bollywood film star Helen (b. 1939); and Ann Lumsden, winner of the Arjuna Award for hockey (2004). Many Anglo-Indians emigrated to other British dominions after 1947. Their poignant history is seen in their definition in the Indian Constitution (Article 366 [2]) as a person whose "male progenitor" was of European (English, Portuguese, French, or Dutch) descent living in India.

NOTES

1. Thomas Metcalf, *Ideologies of the Raj* (Cambridge: Cambridge University Press, 1995).

2. On indenture: British Parliamentary Papers, 1837–38, Vol. 52 (100), (101), (180); 1840, Vol. 37 (58), (455); 1875, Vol. 24 (100–180); 1841, Vol. 3 (137), session (66); Lord Sanderson, Report of the Committee of Enquiry on Emigration from India to the Crown Colonies and Protectorates, 1910, Vol. 27 (1), (Cmd. 5193 & 5194); James McNeill and Chiman Lal, Report to the Government of India on the Conditions of Indians in 4 British Colonies & Surinam, 1914–1916, Vol. 67 (488 & 583); Major G. St. Orde Browne, Report of the Committee of Enquiry into Labour Conditions in Ceylon, Mauritius & Malaya, Vol. 9 (659); Charles Freer Andrews, *The Indian Question in East Africa* (Nairobi, Kenya: The Swift Press, 1921); Lord Hardinge, *My Indian Years: 1910–1916* (London: Murray, 1948).

3. Hugh Tinker, *A New System of Slavery: The Export of Indian Labour Overseas, 1830–1920* (London: Oxford University Press, 1974); also N. Gangulee, *Indians in the Empire Overseas: A Survey* (London: New India Publishing House, 1947); C. Kondapi, *Indians Overseas* (Bombay and Delhi: Oxford University Press, 1951); I. M. Cumpston, *Indians Overseas in British Territories (1834–1854)* (London: Oxford University Press, 1953), 80; Panchanan Saha, *Emigration of Indian Labour (1834–1900)* (New Delhi: People's Publishing House, 1970); K. Hazareesingh, *History of Indians in Mauritius* (London: MacMillan Education Ltd., 1975); G. S. Arora, *Indian Emigration* (New Delhi: Puja Publishers, 1991); Sinnappa Arasaratnam, *Indians in Malaysia and Singapore* (Kuala Lumpur: Oxford University Press, 1979); K. L. Gillion, *Fiji's Indian Emigrants: A History to the End of Indenture in 1920* (Melbourne: Oxford University Press, 1962).

4. Arora, *Indian Emigration,* 13–17.

5. Verene Shepherd, "Gender, Migration and Settlement: The Indentureship and Post-Indentureship Experience of Indian Females in Jamaica, 1845–1943," in *Engendering History: Caribbean Women in Historical Perspective,* ed. Verene Shepherd, Bridget Brereton, and Barbara Bailey (Kingston: Ian Randle Publishers, 1995), 233–57; Kelvin Singh, *Race and Class: Struggles in a Colonial State, Trinidad 1917–1945* (Jamaica: University of the West Indies, 1994); Morton Klass, *East Indians in Trinidad* (New York: Columbia University Press, 1961).

6. Samita Sen, *Women and Labour in Late Colonial India: The Bengal Jute Industry* (Cambridge: Cambridge University Press, 1999); Geraldine Forbes, *Women in Modern India* (Cambridge: Cambridge University Press, 1996), 167–88; Dipesh Chakrabarty, *Rethinking Working-Class History: Bengal 1890–1940* (Princeton: Princeton University Press, 1989).

7. Guha, *Unquiet Woods,* 21–61; Ramachandra Guha, "Forestry and Social Protest in British Kumaun, c. 1893–1921," in *Subaltern Studies IV: Writings on South Asian History and Society,* ed. Ranajit Guha (Delhi: Oxford University Press, 1994), 54–100; Dagmar Engels, "The Myth of the Family Unit: Adivasi Women in Coal-Mines and Tea Plantations in Early Twentieth-Century Bengal," in *Dalit Movements and the Meanings of Labour in India,* SOAS Studies on South Asia, ed. Peter Robb (Oxford and New Delhi: Oxford University Press, 1993), 225–44; B. R. Tomlinson, *The Economy of Modern India, 1860–1970* (Cambridge: Cambridge University Press, 1993).

8. Letter from Afonso de Albuquerque to King Dom Manuel, 1st April, 1512, in T. S. Earle and John Villiers, eds., *Albuquerque, Caesar of the East: Selected Texts by Afonso de Albuquerque and His Son* (Warminster: Aris & Phillips, 1990), 97, 99, 137, translating Raymundo Antonio de Buhao Pato, ed., *Carats de Affonso de Albuquerque Seguidas de Documentos Que as Elucidam* (Lisbon, 1884–85), 1:29–65.

9. M. N. Pearson, *The Portuguese in India* (Cambridge: Cambridge University Press, 1987), 101–2.

10. Timothy Coates, "State-Sponsored Female Colonization in the Estado da India, ca. 1550–1750," in *Sinners and Saints: The Successors of Vasco da Gama,* ed. Sanjay Subrahmanyam (Delhi: Oxford University Press, 2000), 40–56.

11. Pearson, *The Portuguese in India,* 21.

12. Metcalf, *Ideologies of the Raj,* 102–7.

13. Raman, *Getting Girls to School;* also London Missionary Society (Letters, records, reports), 1817–52, microfilm; Church Missionary Society, *Church Missionary Intelligencer,* volumes for 1851–1930; "A.D.," *Until the Shadows Flee Away: The Story of the C.E.Z.M.S.* (London: Church of England Zenana Mission Society, 1920); Irene H. Barnes, *Behind the Pardah,* 2nd ed. (1898; repr., London: Marshall Brothers for C.E.Z.M.S., 1903); Sylvester Horne, *The Story of the London Missionary Society, 1795–1895* (London: John Snow, 1894); M. A. Sherring, *The History of Protestant Missions in India* (London: Religious Tract Society, 1884); William F. Oldham, *Isabella Thoburn* (Chicago: Jennings & Pye, The Student Volunteer Movement for Foreign Missions, 1902); C. F. Pascoe, *Two Hundred Years of the S.P.G., 1701–1900* (Westminster: Society for the Propagation of the Gospel, 1900); J. A. Sharrock, *South Indian Missions* (Westminster: Society for the Propagation of the Gospel, 1910); John S. Chandler, *Seventy-Five Years in the Madura Mission* (Madras: American Madura Mission, 1912); Narendranath N. Law, *Promotion of Learning in India by Early European Settlers up to 1800 AD* (London: Longmans Green, 1915); Kenneth Ingham, *Reformers in India, 1793–1833* (London: Cambridge University Press, 1956); R. N. Yesudas, *The History of the London Missionary Society in Travancore, 1806–1908* (Trivandrum: Kerala Historical Society, 1980).

14. Charles Darwin, *The Origin of Species by Means of Natural Selection, or the Preservation of the Favored Races in the Struggle for Life,* 6th ed. (1859; repr., New York: Appleton, 1892); and Charles Darwin,*The Descent of Man and Selection in Relation to Sex,* 2nd ed. (1871; repr., New York: D. Appleton and Company, 1898).

15. Houston Stewart Chamberlain, *The Foundations of the Nineteenth Century,* trans. John Lees (London: John Lane the Bodley Head Ltd., 1912), 2:180–81, 196–97, 222–23; also Eugen Weber, *The Western Tradition: From the Renaissance to the Present,* 5th ed. (Lexington, Massachusetts: D. C. Heath and Company, 1995), 2:49–51.

16. Rudyard Kipling, *Rudyard Kipling's Verse: Definitive Edition* (New York: Doubleday, 1940), 321–23.

17. Metcalf, *Ideologies of the Raj,* 9, 92–112, citing Robert Orme's, "Effeminacy of the Inhabitants of Indostan," in *Of the Government and People of Indostan,* ed. Orme, pt. 1 (1753; repr., Lucknow: 1971), 42–43.

18. Gayatri Chakravorty Spivak described the *sati* debate in British India as "*white men, seeking to save brown women from brown men.*" Gayatri Chakravorty Spivak, "Can the Subaltern Speak?" in *Marxism and the Interpretation of Culture,*

ed. Cary Nelson and Lawrence Grosberg (Urbana: University of Illinois, 1988), 263–305, *vide,* 297.

19. Kumkum Sangari and Sudesh Vaid, eds., "Introduction," in *Recasting Women: Essays in Colonial History* (New Delhi: Kali for Women, 1989), 1–25; Susie Tharu and K. Lalitha, eds., "Literature of the Reform and Nationalist Movements," in *Women Writing in India,* ed. Tharu and Lalitha, 1:145–86; Kumkum Sangari, *Politics of the Possible: Essays on Gender, History, Narrative in Colonial English* (New Delhi: Tullika, 1999); Vandana Shiva, *Staying Alive: Women, Ecology and Survival in India* (Delhi: Kali for Women, 1988), 62–67; Gayatri Chakravorty Spivak, "Discussion: An Afterword on the New Subaltern," in *Subaltern Studies XI: Community, Gender and Violence,* ed. Partha Chatterjee and Pradeep Jeganathan (New York: Columbia University Press, 1995), 305–34.

20. Raman, *Getting Girls to School,* 102–12; also Raman and Surya, *A. Madhaviah,* 71–87, 126–75; A. Madhaviah, *Padmavati Charitram,* 7th ed. (1898; repr., Chennai: Little Flower Book House, 1958); A. Madhaviah, *Muthumeenakshi* (1903; repr., Chennai: Vanavil Prasuram, 1984); Thiagarajan Meenakshi, trans., *Padmavati Charitram* (New Delhi: Katha Publishers, 2004); Pandita Ramabai Saraswati, "The High Caste Hindu Woman," in *Women Writing in India,* ed. Tharu and Lalitha, 1:247–53.

21. Flavia Agnes, "Women, Marriage, and the Subordination of Rights," in *Subaltern Studies XI: Community, Gender and Violence,* ed. Chatterjee and Jeganathan, 106–37, *vide,* 126–27.

22. Bina Agarwal, *A Field of Ones Own: Gender and Land Rights in South Asia* (Cambridge: Cambridge University Press, 1994), 93, 115–17, 142, 267.

23. Wendy Doniger and Brian K. Smith, trans., *The Laws of Manu* (New York: Penguin, 1991), 115–16, 59–60, 217, 205.

24. Lindsey Harlan, "Perfection and Devotion: Sati Tradition in Rajasthan," in *Sati, the Blessing and the Curse: The Burning of Wives in India,* ed. John Stratton Hawley (New York: Oxford University Press, 1994), 79–99.

25. Agnes, "Women, Marriage, and the Subordination of Rights," 107–8.

26. Doniger and Smith, *The Laws of Manu,* 154, 213, 219–20.

27. Cited by Rajkumari Shanker, "Women in Sikhism," in *Women in Indian Religions,* ed. Arvind Sharma, 2nd ed. (New Delhi: Oxford University Press, 2004), 108–33, *vide,* 116.

28. Ibid., 117.

29. Ibid., 121.

30. Khushwant Singh, *A History of the Sikhs* (New Delhi: Oxford University Press, 1966), 1:140, 2:14–15; also Shanker, "Women in Sikhism," 122–23.

31. Leslie C. Orr, *Donors, Devotees, and Daughters of God: Temple Women in Medieval Tamilnadu* (New York: Oxford University Press, 2000), 65–74.

32. T. V. Mahalingam, *Administration and Social Life under Vijayanagar* (Madras: University of Madras, 1975), 72, as quoted by Saskia C. Kersenboom-Story, *Nityasumangali: Devadasi Tradition in South India* (New Delhi: Motilal Banarsidass, 1987), 37.

33. Amrit Srinivasan, "Reform and Revival: The Devadasi and Her Dance," *Economic and Political Weekly* 20, no. 44 (November 2, 1985): 1869–76, *vide,* 1870.

34. Quoted by Kersenboom-Story, *Nityasumangali,* 35–37.

35. Velcheru Narayana Rao, David Shulman, and Sanjay Subrahmanyam, *Symbols of Substance: Court and State in Nayaka Period Tamilnadu* (Delhi: Oxford University Press, 1998), 114–17.

36. Kersenboom-Story, *Nityasumangali*, 42.

37. Raman, *Getting Girls to School*, xii, xiv–xvi n. 2.

38. Excerpts in Tharu and Lalitha, *Women Writing in India*, 1:115–16.

39. Rao, Shulman, and Subrahmanyam, *Symbols of Substance*, 53, 191–202, 224–25, 335 (Ramabhadramba); 189 (Rangajamma). Raghunatha Nayaka is associated with Rama in the Raghunatha temple, Kumbakonam, Tamil Nadu.

40. Annie Besant, *Higher Education in India: Past and Present*, Convocation Address to the University of Mysore, October, 29, 1924 (Madras: Theosophical Society, 1932). See also Raman, *Getting Girls to School*, 1, 21 n. 1.

41. Rao, Shulman, and Subrahmanyam, *Symbols of Substance*, 53, 123–24, 316 (Muddupalani).

42. Excerpts in Tharu and Lalitha, *Women Writing in India*, 1:116–20.

43. Vedanayakam Pillai, *Pratapa Mudaliyar Charitram* (The Story of Pratapa Mudaliyar; 1879; repr., Madras: Vanavil Press, 1984). Also Raman, "Old Norms in New Bottles," 93–119.

44. British Parliamentary Papers (Colonies, East India), 1831–32 (I, Public), Part B, Appendix (I), "On the Education of the Natives," Governor Thomas Munro's Minute, July 2, 1822, 413. Also see Government of Madras (Revenue), *Proceedings, Reports of District Collectors:* J. B. Huddleston, Tinnevelly (October 28, 1822), Vol. 928, Nos. 46–47, 9937; H. Vibart, Seringapatam (November 4, 1822), Vol. 929, Nos. 33–34, 10260–10262; L. G. K. Murray, Madras (November 14, 1822), Vol. 931, Nos. 57–58, 10512, 10512s, 10512b; J. Sullivan, Coimbatore (December 2, 1822), Vol. 932, No. 43, 10939–10943; R. Peter, Madura (February 13, 1823), Vol. 942, No. 21, 2402–2406; William Cooke, North Arcot (March 10, 1823), Vol. 944, Nos. 20–21, 2806–2816; E. Smalley, Chingleput (April 3, 1823), Vol. 946, No. 25, 3494; J. Cotton, Tanjore (July 3, 1823), Vol. 953, No. 61, 5347–5354; C. Hyde, South Arcot (July 7, 1823), Vol. 954, Nos. 59–60, 5622–5624; G. W. Sanders, Trichinopoly (August 28, 1823), Vol. 959, Nos. 35–36, 7456–7457A.

45. Doniger and Smith, *The Laws of Manu*, 219.

46. I. Julia Leslie, *The Perfect Wife: The Orthodox Hindu Woman According to the Stridharmapadhati of Tryambakayajvan* (Delhi: Oxford University Press, 1989), 13–14, 277–80.

47. Sita Anantha Raman, "From Chattrams to National Schools: Educational Philanthropy in South India, 18th–20th Centuries," Selected Papers in Asian Studies, #52, Western Conference of the Association for Asian Studies, 1994, 10–14. Also Government of Madras, *Note on the Past and Present Administration of the Raja's Chattrams in the Tanjore and Madura Districts* (Tanjore: Government of Madras Press, 1908), 1–5, 24–28; Government of Madras, *Manual of the Administration of the Madras Presidency, Records of the Government and the Yearly Administration Reports,* vol. 1, pt. 1, 1885, 597; T. Venkasami Row, *A Manual of the District of Tanjore,* pt. 2 (Madras: Lawrence Government Press, 1883), 235, 249, 257; and William Hickey, *Tanjore Maratha Principality in South India* (Madras: 1872), 36–37.

48. Government of Madras, *Note on the Past and Present Administration of the Raja's Chattrams in the Tanjore and Madura Districts,* 1–5, 24–28; also Row, *A Manual of the District of Tanjore,* 226–41.

49. Bayly, *Saints, Goddesses and Kings,* 88–91; also Raman, "Walking Two Paces Behind," 382.

50. Raman, *Getting Girls to School,* 2–3.

51. Hickey, *Tanjore Maratha Principality in South India,* 101–3. Also Raman, *Getting Girls to School,* 3–5, 22 n. 14; Raman, "From Chattrams to National Schools," 10–11.

52. Samuel Sattianadhan, *History of Education in the Madras Presidency* (Madras: Srinivasa Varadachari, 1896), 226–27; Raman, *Getting Girls to School,* 50; personal interview with P. Thulajendra Raja Bhonsle, raja of Thanjavur, at his palace on January 2, 1990.

53. Raman, *Getting Girls to School,* 66.

54. Government of Madras, *Manual of the Administration of the Madras Presidency,* 566; also Law, *Promotion of Learning in India by European Settlers up to 1800 AD,* 40–45.

55. Raman, *Getting Girls to School,* 3, 7; Yesudas, *The History of the London Missionary Society in Travancore, 1806–1908,* 45–46, 53–54; P. Cheriyan, *The Malabar Christians and the Church Missionary Society: 1816–1840* (Kottayam: Church Missionary Society, 1935), 190.

56. Leslie, *The Perfect Wife,* 276, 277–79.

57. Ibid., 3, 10–13, 38–43.

58. Ibid., 57–65, 248–55.

59. Fatima da Silva Gracias, *Kaleidoscope of Women in Goa, 1510–1961* (New Delhi: Concept Publishing Company, 1996), 32.

60. Leonard Bacon, trans., *The Lusiads of Luiz de Camoes* (New York: The Hispanic Society of America, 1950), 249.

61. Pearson, *The Portuguese in India,* 20–21.

62. Earle and Villiers, *Albuquerque, Caesar of the East,* 97.

63. Frederick Charles Danvers, *The Portuguese in India: Being a History of the Rise and Decline of Their Eastern Empire,* 2 vols. (1894; repr., London: Frank Cass & Co., Ltd., 1988), 1:217.

64. da Silva Gracias, *Kaleidoscope of Women in Goa, 1510–1961,* 36.

65. Earle and Villiers, *Albuquerque, Caesar of the East,* 119.

66. da Silva Gracias, *Kaleidoscope of Women in Goa, 1510–1961,* 32–33.

67. Sanjay Subrahmanyam, *The Portuguese Empire in Asia* (London: Longmans Group, 1991), 220; C. R. Boxer, *Race Relations in the Portuguese Colonial Empire, 1415–1825* (London: Oxford University Press, 1963), 77.

68. Earle and Villiers, *Albuquerque, Caesar of the East,* 137.

69. John Villiers, "Introduction: Faithful Servant and Ungrateful Master: Albuquerque and the Imperial Strategy of King Manuel the Fortunate," in *Albuquerque, Caesar of the East,* ed. Earle and Villiers, 20, 95–97, 99, 115–16, 137.

70. Pearson, *The Portuguese in India,* 116–17.

71. Earle and Villiers, *Albuquerque, Caesar of the East,* 115, 117.

72. Pearson, *The Portuguese in India,* 21–22.

73. da Silva Gracias, *Kaleidoscope of Women in Goa, 1510–1961,* 45.

74. Bacon, *The Lusiads of Luiz de Camoes,* 106.

75. Ibid., 42, 99, 53, 260–61.

76. Ibid., 259.

77. Pearson, *The Portuguese in India,* 101–5; Earle and Villiers, *Albuquerque, Caesar of the East,* 97, 99, 107, 109, 111.

78. Villiers, "Introduction: Faithful Servant and Ungrateful Master," 2, 48–49.

79. Pearson, *The Portuguese in India,* 71–72; D. R. SarDesai, "Portuguese in India," in *Encyclopedia of India,* ed. Stanley Wolpert (New York: Thomson Gale, 2006), 3:322.

80. Pearson, *The Portuguese in India,* 116–17.

81. Ibid., 101, 104–5.

82. Alfredo de Mello, "Memoirs of Goa: The Portuguese Inquisition in Goa (1560–1812)," http://www.hvk.org?articles/1103/57.html.

83. Pearson, *The Portuguese in India,* 117–20.

84. da Silva Gracias, *Kaleidoscope of Women in Goa, 1510–1961,* 41.

85. Appendix 2, "Instructions Issued by the Church in the Province of Mormugao to Improve the Moral Conditions of Women," in ibid., 154.

86. Appendix 4, "List of Women Accused, Imprisoned and Punished by the Holy Inquisition in the 18th Century," in ibid., 156.

87. da Silva Gracias, *Kaleidoscope of Women in Goa, 1510–1961,* 50–51, 53–77.

88. Appendix 3, Conselho Geral doSanto Oficio: Inquisiçao de Goa, Maço 36, no. 23, in ibid., 155.

89. Coates, "State-Sponsored Female Colonization in the Estado da India, ca. 1550–1750," 40–56, *vide,* 41.

90. Ibid., 43–47.

91. Ibid., 48–49.

92. M. H. Goonatilleka, "A Portuguese Creole in Sri Lanka: A Brief Socio-Linguistic Survey," in *Indo-Portuguese History: Old Issues, New Questions,* ed. Teotonio R. de Souza (New Delhi: Concept Publishing Company, 1985), 147–80, *vide,* 148–54.

93. da Silva Gracias, *Kaleidoscope of Women in Goa, 1510–1961,* 36–37.

94. S. K. Pandya, "Medicine in Goa—A Former Portuguese Territory," *Journal of Postgraduate Medicine* 28, no. 3 (1982): 123–48, at http://www.jpgmonline.com/text.asp?1982/28/3/123/5573. Pandya cites Dr. Bernardus Paludanus, ed., *A Dutch Physician of XVI Century on Indian Drugs. Linschoten's Account of Spices and Drugs of India* (Hyderabad, India: Osmania Medical University, 1965), 3:173–84.

95. Pearson, *The Portuguese in India,* 95.

96. Ibid., 127–30.

97. Danvers, *The Portuguese in India,* 1:367–68.

98. Pearson, *The Portuguese in India,* 94–105, *vide,* 99, 101; also Dejanirah Couto, " 'Goa Dourada,' La Ville Dorée" (Balmy Goa, the Gilded Town), in *Goa 1510–1685,* ed. Chandeigne, 40–73, *vide,* 61–68.

99. da Silva Gracias, *Kaleidoscope of Women in Goa, 1510–1961,* 35–36.

100. Pearson, *The Portuguese in India,* xv, 102, 145, 150–51; also Henry Scholberg, "The Writings of Francisco Luis Gomes," in *Indo-Portuguese History,* ed. Teotonio R. de Souza, 202–24.

101. Margaret Mascarenhas, "Goa's Civil Code: Legal Legacy," http://mmascgoa.tripod.com/id12.html.

102. C. R. Boxer, *Women in the Iberian Expansion Overseas, 1415–1815: Some Facts, Fancies and Personalities, 1415–1815* (London and New York: Oxford University Press, 1975).

103. da Silva Gracias, *Kaleidoscope of Women in Goa, 1510–1961,* 110–16.

104. Ibid., 90–100.

105. Raman, *Getting Girls to School,* 104–7.

106. See Sumanta Banerjee, "Marginalization of Women's Popular Culture in Nineteenth Century Bengal," in *Recasting Women,* ed. Sangari and Vaid, 127–79, *vide,* 151–54, 176 n. 58; and Bharati Ray, *Early Feminist of Colonial India: Sarala Devi Chaudhurani and Rokeya Sakhawat Hossain* (New Delhi: Oxford University Press, 2002), 3, 114 n. 3.

107. Prem Chowdhry, "Customs in a Peasant Economy: Women in Colonial Haryana," in *Recasting Women,* ed. Sangari and Vaid, 302–36, *vide,* 305.

108. Ibid., 306, 330 n. 11.

109. Ibid., 312–21.

110. Rabindranath Thakur's 1905 Bengali novel *Home and the World* was filmed by Satyajit Ray in 1961.

111. Sen, *Women and Labour in Late Colonial India,* 54–65.

112. Gail Minault, *Secluded Scholars: Muslim Women's Education and Social Reform in Colonial India* (New Delhi: Oxford University Press, 1998), 22–23.

113. Ibid., 23–24.

114. Raman, *Getting Girls to School,* 157–58.

115. Minault, *Secluded Scholars,* 24.

116. Lata Mani, *Contentious Traditions: The Debate on Sati in Colonial India* (Berkeley and Los Angeles: University of California Press, 1998), 87, 134–37.

117. Uma Chakravarti, "Whatever Happened to the Vedic *Dasi?* Orientalism, Nationalism, and a Script for the Past," in *Recasting Women,* ed. Sangari and Vaid, 27–87, *vide,* 35, citing James Mill, *The History of British India,* 5th ed. (London: James Madden, 1840), 312–13.

118. Yogesh Snehi, "Conjugality, Sexuality and *Shastras:* Debate on the Abolition of *Reet* in Colonial Himachal Pradesh," *The Indian Economic and Social History Review* 43, no. 2 (2006): 163–97, *vide,* 164–66.

119. Agnes, "Women, Marriage, and the Subordination of Rights," 106–37, *vide,* 119–28.

120. Meredith Borthwick, "Bhadramahila and Changing Conjugal Relations in Bengal, 1850–1900," in *Women in India and Nepal,* ed. Michael Allen and S. N. Mukherjee, Australian National University Monographs on South Asia, no. 8 (New Delhi: Oxford University Press, 1982), 108–10.

121. Raman and Surya, *A. Madhaviah,* with Surya's translation of *Muthumeenakshi,* 127–86; 82–83. Also A. Madhaviah, *Satyananda,* an English novel (Bangalore: Mysore Review, 1909), 292–93; A. Madhaviah, "Padmavati Charitram: Munram Bhagam," *Panchamritam* (Tamil journal), 2, no. 3 (1924).

122. Vedavalli, "My Life: In Reply to Sita," a personalized autobiography dated September 1987, after an interview with her in Madras, July 1987, shortly before her death. See citation in Raman, *Getting Girls to School,* 106.

123. Interview with Savitri Rajan at Madras on December 16, 1989. See Raman, *Getting Girls to School,* 104.

124. Nora Brockway, *A Larger Way for Women: Aspects of Christian Education for Girls in South India, 1712–1948* (London: Oxford University Press, 1949), 38, 50. Brockway quotes Paul Appasamy, *The Centenary History of the Church Missionary Society in Tinnevelly* (Tirunelveli: Palamcottah Printing Press, 1923). Also Raman, *Getting Girls to School*, 8–13.

125. Forbes, *Women in Modern India*, 38–39.

126. Tharu and Lalitha, *Women Writing in India*, 1:203.

127. Raman, *Getting Girls to School*, 6–13.

128. London Missionary Society, "Report of Reverend Thomas Nicholson," May 29, 1821, Box 2, Reel 274 (1817–24; microfilm).

129. Oldham, *Isabella Thoburn*, 12.

130. "Report of Reverend W. T. Sattianadhan," in *Church Missionary Intelligencer*, vol. 27, October 1876, 624. On Bible women, also see Chandler, *Seventy Five Years in the Madura Mission*, 338–40, 442–44; "A.D.," 202–4; Sharrock, *South Indian Missions*, 92–93, 222.

131. Horne, *The Story of the L.M.S., 1795–1895*, 289, 301 (photograph of Bible women).

132. Rosa Lechlar's account from Salem, December 29, 1848, *London Missionary Society Records* (1848–52), folder 1, jacket D; citation in Raman, *Getting Girls to School*, 12–13.

133. Barnes, *Behind the Pardah*, 2.

134. Geraldine H. Forbes, "In Search of the 'Pure Heathen': Missionary Women in Nineteenth Century India," *Economic and Political Weekly* 21, no. 17 (April 26, 1986), 1–8.

135. Barnes, *Behind the Pardah*, 153–59; Godfrey E. Phillips, *The Outcastes' Hope* (London: United Council for Missionary Education, 1913), 54–59, 124–28.

136. British Parliamentary Papers, 1854 (393), XLVII, 155, Charles Wood, "Despatch on the Subject of General Education in India," July 19, 1854, no. 49.

137. British Parliamentary Papers, 1857–58 (72), XLII, 339, "Further Correspondence on Education," 390.

138. M. N. Das, *Studies in the Economic and Social Development of India: 1848–1856* (Calcutta: Firma KLM, 1959); Raman, *Getting Girls to School*, 13–14.

139. Forbes, *Women in Modern India*, 38–39.

140. Government of Madras (Public), *Proceedings*, June 6, 1854, vol. 924, nos. 38 and 39, handwritten records.

141. Mary Carpenter, *Six Months in India* 2 vols. (London: Longmans Green, 1868), 2:142–43.

142. Raman, *Getting Girls to School*, 36–37.

143. British Parliamentary Papers, 1877 (185), LXIII, 427, "Report to Marquis of Salisbury by Miss Mary Carpenter on Prison Discipline and on Female Education in India."

144. Raman, *Getting Girls to School*, 25–28, 47–48.

145. Ibid., 204–5, 222–23; and Government of India (Education), G.O. 254, May 16, 1884, unpublished record; Government of Madras, *Census of India*, 1921, vol. 13 (Madras: Government Press, 1922), charts 128–29 on literacy by caste, 120–21; Government of India, *Review of Growth of Education in British India by the Auxiliary Committee Appointed by the Indian Statutory Commission*, September 1929 (Hartog Committee Report), 45, 145.

146. Raman, *Getting Girls to School,* xii, xiv–xvi n. 2; British Parliamentary Papers (Colonies, East India), 1831–32 (I. Public), Part B, Appendix (I.), "On the Education of the Natives," Governor Thomas Munro's Minute on Education, July 2, 1822, 413; Government of Madras (Revenue), *Proceedings,* Reports of District Collectors (1822–23), Vols. 928–29, 931–32, 942, 944, 946, 953–54, 959.

147. Raman, *Getting Girls to School,* 28, 35–36, 104–6, 131, 168, 176, 187.

148. Ibid., 110–11.

149. Ibid., 35–36.

150. Amrit Srinivasan, "Reform or Conformity? Temple 'Prostitution' and the Community in the Madras Presidency," in *Structures of Patriarchy: State, Community and Household in Modernizing Asia,* ed. Bina Agarwal (New Delhi: Kali for Women, 1988), 175–98.

151. Sita Anantha Raman, "Prescriptions for Gender Equality: The Work of Dr. Muthulakshmi Reddi," in *Charisma and Commitment: Essays in South Asian History in Honor of Stanley Wolpert,* ed. Roger Long (Mumbai: Orient Longman, 2004), 331–66; Raman, "Old Norms in New Bottles," 93–119.

152. Srinivasan, "Reform or Conformity?" 175–98; and Amrit Srinivasan, "The Hindu Temple-Dancer: Prostitute or Nun?" *Cambridge Anthropology* 8, no. 1 (1983): 73–99.

153. Spivak, "Can the Subaltern Speak?" 297.

154. Radha Kumar, *The History of Doing: An Illustrated Account of Movements for Women's Rights and Feminism in India, 1800–1990,* 2nd ed. (New Delhi: Kali for Women, 1997), 7–14, *vide,* 9; Ashis Nandy, "Sati: A Nineteenth Century Tale of Women, Violence and Protest," in *Rammohan Roy and the Process of Modernization in India,* ed. V. C. Joshi (New Delhi: Vikas, 1975), 168–75; Ashis Nandy, "Sati as Profit Versus Sati as Spectacle: The Public Debate on Roop Kanwar's Death," in *Sati, the Blessing and the Curse: The Burning of Wives in India,* ed. Hawley (Berkeley and Los Angeles: University of California Press, 1994), 132–49.

155. See also Ainslie Embree, "Comment: Widows as Cultural Symbols," in *Sati, the Blessing and the Curse,* ed. Hawley, 149–59, *vide,* 152; Veena Talwar Oldenburg, "Comment: The Continuing Invention of the Sati Tradition," in *Sati, the Blessing and the Curse,* ed. Hawley, 159–73.

156. Agnes, "Women, Marriage, and the Subordination of Rights," 112–13.

157. Mani, *Contentious Traditions,* 21.

158. Romila Thapar, "Perspectives in History: Seminar 342 (February 1988)," in *Sati: Dialogues by Ram Mohan Roy,* ed. Mulk Raj Anand (New Delhi: B. R. Publishing Corporation, 1989), 83–95, *vide,* 92.

159. Cited by Anand, *Sati: Dialogues by Ram Mohan Roy,* 4.

160. Mani, *Contentious Traditions,* 17–19.

161. Ashis Nandy, *At the Edge of Psychology: Essays in Politics and Culture* (New Delhi: Oxford University Press, 1980), 5; also Nandy, "Sati: A Nineteenth Century Tale of Women, Violence and Protest," 168–93.

162. Mani, *Contentious Traditions,* 21.

163. Anand, *Sati: Dialogues by Ram Mohan Roy,* 92.

164. Excerpts from Ram Mohan Roy's *English Works,* in Hay, *Sources of Indian Tradition: Modern India and Pakistan,* 2:25–31; and in B. N. Pandey, ed., *A Book of India* (New Delhi: Rupa & Co., 2000), 383–85.

165. Ram Mohan Roy, "A Conference between an Advocate for and an Opponent of the Practice of Burning Widows Alive," in *Sati: Dialogues by Ram Mohan Roy,* ed. Anand, 20–30, *vide,* 20.

166. Ram Mohan Roy, "A Second Conference between an Advocate for and an Opponent of the Practice of Burning Widows Alive," in Anand, *Sati: Dialogues by Ram Mohan Roy,* 31–64, *vide,* 54–55.

167. Mani, *Contentious Traditions,* 59, 79.

168. Anand, *Sati: Dialogues by Ram Mohan Roy,* 15–16; Mani, *Contentious Traditions,* 76, 210 nn. 93, 94, cites "Lord William Bentinck's Minute on Suttee," from J. K. Majumdar, ed., *Raja Rammohun Roy and the Progressive Movements in India: A Selection from Records, 1775–1845* (Calcutta: Art Press, 1941), 139.

169. Roy's letter in Anand, *Sati: Dialogues by Ram Mohan Roy,* 74–79.

170. Dorothy M. Figueira, "Die Flambierte Frau: Sati in European Culture," in *Sati, the Blessing and the Curse,* ed. Hawley, 57–61; and Robin Jared Lewis, "Comment: Sati and the Nineteenth-Century British Self," in *Sati, the Blessing and the Curse,* ed. Hawley, 72–78.

171. Mani, *Contentious Traditions,* 85.

172. Spivak, "Can the Subaltern Speak?" 263–305, *vide,* 297.

173. Chakravarti, "Whatever Happened to the Vedic *Dasi?*" 42–46.

174. Annie Besant, "Address to Maharani Girls' School," Mysore, December 24, 1896, *Arya Bala Bodhini* (Adyar: TS, January 1897); Annie Besant, *On the Education of Indian Girls,* pamphlet no. 25 (Benares and London: Theosophical Society, 1904); and Margaret Cousins, *The Awakening of Indian Womanhood* (Madras: Ganesh and Co., 1922).

175. S. A. A. Rizvi, "The Ruling Muslim Dynasties," in *A Cultural History of India,* ed. Basham, 252.

176. Ananda K. Coomaraswamy, "Sati: A Vindication of the Hindu Woman," November 12, 1912, reproduced in J. Mark Baldwin, ed., *The Sociological Review* (London: 1912), 119–35, *vide,* 119, 122.

177. Ibid., 123.

178. From Vishwanath S. Naravane, *Sarojini Naidu: Her Life, Work, and Poetry,* 2nd ed. (Bombay: Orient Longman, 1996), 101.

179. Ibid., 95.

180. Borthwick, "Bhadramahila and Changing Conjugal Relations in Bengal, 1850–1900," 108–10; and Meredith Borthwick, *Changing Role of Women in Bengal, 1849–1905* (Princeton: Princeton University Press, 1984), 60–108, 291.

181. Banerjee, "Marginalization of Women's Popular Culture in Nineteenth Century Bengal," 127–79, *vide,* 146.

182. Cited from "A Bill to Remove All Legal Obstacles to the Marriage of Hindoo Widows," in entirety in Kumar, *History of Doing,* 18–19.

183. Sen, *Women and Labour in Late Colonial India,* 180–86.

184. Kumar, *History of Doing,* 20.

185. Chowdhry, "Customs in a Peasant Economy," 302–36, *vide,* 312–21.

186. Agnes, "Women, Marriage, and the Subordination of Rights," 124–25.

187. Raman, *Getting Girls to School,* 119–27.

188. Government of India, Census of India, 1991, Educational Statistics, Part II-A, General Population Tables, Sex Ratio (Table 2.5).

189. Chowdhry, "Customs in a Peasant Economy," 304–6.

190. G. T. Boag, *Government of India, Census of 1921*, vol. 13, pt. 1 (Madras: Government Press, 1922).

191. Tinker, *A New System of Slavery*, 17–18.

192. Saha, *Emigration of Indian Labour (1834–1900)*, 71–73.

193. These British Parliamentary Papers: LII, 1837–1838, Enclosure from H. J. Princep to G. F. Dick, June 29, 1836; XXXVII, 1840, (58), Despatch 57 from Governor W. Nicolay to Lord Glenglg, May 4, 1839, and Despatch 62 from Glenglg to Nicolay; III, 1841, Session 66; XXXV, 1844, (356–544); XXXIV, 1875, (100–199); Thomas Curson Hansard, ed., *Hansard's Parliamentary Debates: Third Series*, Volume XLI, 1837–1838; J. Goehgan, *Report on Coolie Emigration from India* (1873); G. A. Grierson, *Report on the System of Recruiting Coolies for British and Foreign Colonies as Carried Out in the Lower Provinces of Bengal* (1883); D. W. D. Comins, *Note on Emigration from the East Indies to Trinidad* (1893); Lord Sanderson, *Report on Emigration from India to the Crown Colonies* (1910).

194. Tinker, *A New System of Slavery*, 70.

195. Shepherd, "Gender, Migration and Settlement," 237.

196. Nirmala Banerjee, "Working Women in Colonial Bengal: Modernization and Marginalization," in *Recasting Women*, ed. Sangari and Vaid, 295.

197. Shepherd, "Gender, Migration and Settlement," 244–45.

198. Ibid., 237, 243.

199. Fiji Census Records, 1891–1921.

200. Brigid Brereton, *Race Relations in Colonial Trinidad, 1870–1900* (Cambridge: Cambridge University Press, 1979), 182–83; Shameen Ali, "Indian Women and the Retention of Social Institutions in Trinidad, 1870–1940's" (unpublished paper presented at the Indian Diaspora Conference, The University of West Indies, St. Augustine, Trinidad, August 11–18, 1995).

201. Chowdhry, "Customs in a Peasant Economy," 310.

202. Banerjee, "Working Women in Colonial Bengal: Modernization and Marginalization," 271–72.

203. Sen, *Women and Labour in Late Colonial India*, 78–79.

204. Banerjee, "Working Women in Colonial Bengal," 287.

205. Engels, "The Myth of the Family Unit," 225–44.

206. Forbes, *Women in Modern India*, 167–68.

207. Banerjee, "Working Women in Colonial Bengal," 270–71.

208. Sen, *Women and Labour in Late Colonial India*, 54–55.

209. Ibid., 124–28, 138–39.

210. Forbes, *Women in Modern India*, 167–68.

211. Chakrabarty, *Rethinking Working-Class History*, 11, 78–81.

212. Kumar, *History of Doing*, 24.

213. Sen, *Women and Labour in Late Colonial India*, 5, 142–47.

214. Dipesh Chakrabarty, "Conditions for Knowledge of Working-Class Conditions: Employers, Government and the Jute Workers of Calcutta, 1890–1940," in *Subaltern Studies II: Writings on South Asian History and Society*, ed. Ranajit Guha (New Delhi: Oxford University Press, 1983), 259–310, *vide*, 290–91.

215. Sen, *Women and Labour in Late Colonial India*, 152–56, 153–76.

216. Forbes, *Women in Modern India*, 174–75.

217. Chakrabarty, *Rethinking Working-Class History*, 109–10.

218. Sen, *Women and Labour in Late Colonial India*, 222–23.

219. Cited by Adrian Carton, "The Color of Fraternity: Citizenship, Race and Domicile in French India" (paper presented to the 15th Biennial Conference of the Asian Studies Association of Australia, Canberra, June 29–July 2, 2004), 1–9. Also see Adrian Carton, "Shades of Fraternity: Creolization and the Making of Citizenship in French India, 1790–1792," *French Historical Journal* 31, no. 4 (2008): 581–607.

220. Adrian Carton's interesting article, "Beyond 'Cotton Mary': Anglo-Indian Categories and Reclaiming the Diverse Past," *International Journal of Anglo-Indian Studies* 5, no. 1 (2000): 1–12. Carton cites H. Furber, "Bombay and the Malabar Coast in the 1720's," Heras Memorial Lectures 1962, in R. Rocher, ed., *Private Fortunes and Company Profits in the India Trade in the Eighteenth Century* (Aldershot: Variorum, 1972).

221. Sanjay Subrahmanyam, "Profiles in Transition: Of Adventurers and Administrators in South India, 1750–1810," *The Indian Economic and Social History Review* 39, nos. 2 and 3 (2002): 197–231, *vide,* 201–2.

222. Philip Mason, *The Men Who Ruled India,* reprinted from *The Founders* (1953) and *The Guardians* (1954), 3rd ed. (New Delhi: Rupa & Co., 1994), 118.

223. Mason, *The Men Who Ruled India,* 103–4.

224. Law, *Promotion of Learning in India by European Settlers up to 1800 AD,* 12–15, 20–23.

225. Sharrock, *South Indian Missions,* 42.

226. Ingham, *Reformers in India, 1793–1833,* 62–67.

227. Richard Burton, *Goa and the Blue Mountains* (London: 1851), 88, 97; Pearson, *The Portuguese in India,* 103.

228. George Orwell's *Burmese Days* (1934; repr., New York: Harcourt Brace, 1962). The novel is based on Orwell's experiences as a soldier in colonial Burma, with vivid descriptions of British angst over Eurasians.

229. See Adrian Carton's interesting 12-page essay, "Beyond 'Cotton Mary,'" 2–5.

3

MALE REFORMERS AND WOMEN'S RIGHTS

In India the mother is the center of the family and our highest ideal. She is to us the representative of God, as God is the mother of the Universe. It was a female sage who first found the unity of God, and laid down this doctrine in of the first hymns of the Vedas. Or God is both personal and absolute, the absolute is male, the personal is female. And thus it comes that we now say, "The first manifestation of God is the hand that rocks the cradle" . . . and I and every good Hindoo believe, that my mother was pure and holy, and hence I owe her everything that I am. That is the secret of the race—chastity.

Swami Vivekananda[1]

REFORMERS, NATION, AND WOMEN

Introduction

Women's rights constituted a central agenda of the social reform movement, which crystallized ideas of feminism and pan-Indian nationalism in the nineteenth century. As products of missionary and government schools, elite male reformers resented comparisons between modern Europe after the Enlightenment and India's apparently feudal, moribund society. They reread Hindu-Buddhist-Jaina texts in the original or through "Orientalist" translations, and a romantic nostalgia grew apace for a bygone "golden Aryan age" when gender and caste justice prevailed in India. Through associations (*samajs*) and pamphlets they sought to abolish child marriage, polygamy, and the cremation of widows (*satis*) on the husband's pyre; and to promote female literacy and widow remarriage. After the 1857 Revolt, elite men were emboldened by promises of administrative collaboration with the Raj, but their frustrated ambitions fueled nationalist *samajs* that promised to rejuvenate India. Meanwhile, educated women formed groups to assist the larger sisterhood, although some authoritarian men preempted their agency.

This chapter describes male reformers, their impact on colonial laws concerning women, and the work of important early feminists. Twentieth-century feminism and its impact on the freedom struggle are discussed in the next chapter.

Male Reformers before 1857

The pioneering reformer was Ram Mohan Roy (d. 1833) who reexamined Hindu scriptures to challenge adverse practices affecting high-caste women. Roy used his association Amitya Sabha (1815) and the later Brahma Samaj (1828) to persuade elite Bengali Hindus (*bhadralok*) to educate women and to eradicate *sati* and polygamy. He asserted the scriptural primacy of the *Upanishads* (Vedanta), which advocate monism and spiritualism, over the *Puranas* whose later legends and rites were used to sanctify *sati*. After reading his tracts, Governor Bentinck was convinced that liberal Indians supported a legal ban, and he accordingly passed the Bengal Sati Regulation Act (1829), which became the law in British India. Similarly, Ishwar Chandra Vidyasagar petitioned administrators to legalize widow remarriage, and Governor-General Dalhousie passed the Widow Remarriage Act (1856). However, the 1829 law was more effective, as it punished those who burnt *satis,* while the 1856 law was prescriptive and could not penalize those who chose not to remarry. Both laws were humane and well-intentioned, but reflected straitlaced, Victorian Christian mores, which seeped into nationalist rhetoric. The dual patriarchy of Indian nationalists and British officials thus bolstered the colonial state as a modernizing force, precisely when imperial *laissez-faire* economics destroyed local industries and impoverished its working women and men.

Male Reformers after 1860

Later male reformers and philanthropists established three nationalist associations, which founded schools for girls and for the poor castes. A fourth reform society was founded by Westerners enamored of Indian traditions and later relocated to India where its feminist leaders promoted women's rights. The earliest was the Prarthna Samaj (PS; 1867) founded in Bombay by Judge Mahadev Govind Ranade (1842–1901), G. K. Gokhale (1866–1915), and other elite men who wished to persuade Indians to reject child marriage and enforced widow celibacy. Less apologetic about Hindu theism than the BS, members of the PS sang congregational *bhakti* hymns (*bhajans*), a legacy of medieval devotional meetings. In 1870, Ranade supervised the first widow remarriage, and through his Sarvajanik Sabha (Public Society) established schools for girls and low castes in Pune. Although male reformers did not hold legislative positions until the 1909 Indian Councils Act, Ranade and Gokhale assisted British officials in municipal and provincial assemblies to implement progressive laws like the Age of Consent Bill (1891) which criminalized sex with a girl less than 12 years of age. Although by today's standards this was a cautious bill, it was a leap forward from the 1861 Age of Consent Act allowing marital relations with 10-year-old girls. Women reformers later publicized the 1929 Sarda Bill raising the marriage age for girls to 14 years. In 1897, Gokhale warmly supported schools for women in his paper, "Female Education in India," to women at the Victoria Era Exhibition in London.[2]

Cultural nationalists of both genders took reform to another dimension by advocating a return to ancient Vedic customs of female education and adult marriages. A spate of reform associations now popularized the modern feminine paradigm of the learned, chaste mother and wife-companion. The earliest was the Arya Samaj (AS; 1875) founded in Gujarat by the ascetic Dayananda Saraswati (1824–83). It advanced women's education and widow remarriage in Punjab but also drove a wedge between Hindus and Muslims. In contrast, the Ramakrishna Mission and Vedanta Society (VS; 1887), founded in Bengal by Swami Vivekananda (1863–1902), fostered national unity and started schools for girls and boys across India. The Theosophical Society (TS; 1875) was established in Chicago by Madame Blavatsky (d. 1891), but its headquarters shifted to Madras and Benares in the 1880s. TS President Annie Besant (1847–1933), a former Irish-English radical who became a Hindu-Indian nationalist, provided a cultural blueprint for girls' schools and institutional support for the Women's Indian Association (WIA; 1917).

A similar movement to reform Islamic society redefined Muslim political identity, while providing prescriptions on female decorum. At the crux of its agenda were the female veil (*pardah*) and the practice of female seclusion in segregated rooms (*zenana, antarala*) common among Muslims and Hindus, especially in north India. A seventeenth-century movement to purge Islam of Hindu practices had led to stricter controls on female behavior. The colonial era witnessed a modernizing movement that opened paths for young men but initially curtailed opportunities for women. The leader was Sir Sayyid Ahmad Khan (1817–98), an Urdu aristocrat (*ashraf*) who wished Muslim men to acquire a Western scientific education at the Mohammedan Anglo-Oriental College in Aligarh, Uttar Pradesh. However, for women he advocated *pardah* and Islamic education within the *zenana*. As a widely respected Muslim leader, his conservative attitudes retarded girls' enrollment in schools outside the home. Fortunately, other enlightened men educated their daughters in Muslim schools, especially after 1901. The ensuing network of educated Muslim feminists later challenged child marriage and polygamy.

Motherland and Mothers of the Nation

In 1885, 73 elite men formed the INC as a forum to articulate their political concerns. Many were inspired by Bankim Chandra Chatterji's hymn,

Bande Mataram (Hail to the Motherland), in 1882.[3] This patriotic paean from Bengal was followed in 1891 by Abanindranath Thakur's painting of Mother India as a four-armed goddess (Devi) holding a drum, lamp, palm leaf scroll, and a pot, the emblems of freedom, prosperity, learning, and charity. Abanindranath's nephew Rabindranath Thakur (1861–1941) later composed India's national anthem.[4] Pan-Indian nationalist literature now abounded with metaphors of the sacred motherland and its numerous mother tongues, while the analogy between the nation as a feminine deity and its household goddesses became self-evident. Apart from such idealism, most male nationalists agreed that it was imperative to preserve the Indian patriarchal family, and that its women remain chaste mothers and wives. After the British partition of Bengal in 1905 on sectarian lines, *Bande Mataram* became popular among Hindus, but its religious symbolism alienated Muslims.

Moreover, shamed by colonial surveys that revealed the absence of elite women in missionary schools, male reformers initially endorsed the Western critique of Indian society and reinforced the rhetoric of Britain's civilizing mission. However, recent evidence suggests that under colonialism, patriarchal rules for women became more stringent due to high incidences of rape and *sati* during the Anglo-French hegemonic wars over India. Second, when the Raj absorbed small kingdoms, royal philanthropy dried up and indigenous schools decayed.[5] Elite women now retreated into the household where they were often taught informally, and religious mendicancy became an escape from extreme domestic hardship. Ironically, a gendered household existence forged ties of sisterhood, making it easy later to establish feminist networks. Moreover, Victorian society was also male dominated, and its mores demeaned the female anatomy as conducive to "weakness" and requiring the support of virile men. Bourgeois attitudes prevailed among officials and elite Indians who regarded lower-class women as having coarse sexual appetites, while colonial records dismissed rural women's hard labor as domestic chores without economic value.

In speeches, essays, and poems, progressive male reformers promoted literacy for elite and middle-class women, adult marriages, and widow remarriage. Many felt that *pardah* adversely affected female health and education, but they neither organized campaigns against women's seclusion nor supported their inheritance rights. Like cultural nationalists, many men felt that *pardah* was a safeguard against male lust, and that its purpose was not to subordinate women but to buttress them worldly realities.[6] There were some humanitarian exceptions. Rabindranath Thakur's short story, "Home and the World," compared the *antarala* to a gilded birdcage, and the cloistered women to the fettered nation. His message was clear, that if the nation wished freedom, it must first emancipate its women.[7] Similarly, Tamil poet extraordinaire C. Subramania Bharati (1882–1924) exhorted all women to

speak up, demand an education, step out of the home, shed caste, and partici-
pate in national affairs.[8]

SOCIAL REFORM MOVEMENT

Female Education

In precolonial India, elite Hindu and Muslim girls were taught either informally or formally at home and in village schools. In south India, *devadasis*
were the few girls in open attendance with boys. Boys and girls learned to
read, but memorization and oral transmission of sacred verses from the
Ramayana, Mahabharata, and *Puranas* for Hindus, and the *Qur'an* and
Persian texts for Muslims. Many Hindu girls thus maintained their cultural
traditions even when men began to focus on Western history and its literature.
When missionaries started schools for girls, the focus on literacy alone and
school enrollment changed the system of education. They equated *devadasis*
with English dance hall women and ostracized them from their schools. The
Western emphasis on literacy and enrollment in formal schools became the
chief assessment tools in later government schools. However, as most Indian
girls did not attend mission or government schools, they were rarely counted
in official records. Few middle-class/caste Hindus of south or north India
initially enrolled their daughters in mission or government schools where the
teachers were men, or women converts.[9] Officials dismissed informal instruction at home in Indian texts and household computation until the 1882
Hunter Commission of enquiry recognized this fund of knowledge among
women.[10]

Women's formal literacy began to improve only after the spread of nationalist schools in many parts of the country. Progressive Indian men were convinced that women's education spelled progress for their society and nation,
and the platform of female education remained a core component of the
reform movement. Elite men educated in Western-style schools first began
schools for girls largely to shape their wives into companions for themselves
and later to create learned mothers for the nation. This was a common feature
of the West as well, where a growing bourgeois, consumerist economy gave
women's domesticity a new glamour. These attitudes infiltrated the mind-set
of middle-class Indian men and were adopted by many Indian women. The
first modern schools for girls were established in Bengal in 1846, followed
by a school in Madras in 1848, and in Bombay. In 1819, Bengal pandit
Gourmohan Vidyalamkara wrote the first modern text on girls' education,
and this was published by the Female Juvenile Society of Calcutta.[11] Bengali
bhadramahila or elite women produced over four hundred literary compositions in this era, indicating the extent of their erudition.[12]

Between 1841 and 1900, in Madras alone, over 40 Tamil journals discussed the importance of women's education, and later issues had essays

written by women. In 1868, the Tamil Samuel Vedanayakam Pillai published the book *Pen Kalvi* (Female Education) on the importance of girls' education.[13] A Christian with eclectic beliefs, Vedanayakam dedicated his book to his learned mother Mariamma, while he addressed his daughters on their rights. In all his works, Vedanayakam portrayed educated women, frequently quoting the classical nonsectarian *Tirukkural* by Jaina saint Tiruvalluvar to argue that learned women benefited society.[14] Justice T. Muthuswami Iyer, who started the first Widow Marriage Association in Madras, gave evidence on indigenous schools in 1882 to the liberal Hunter Commission, which validated home instruction for girls. Director of Public Instruction, H. B. Grigg stated in his sympathetic report:

> Many women of the upper class had their minds stored with the legends of the Puranas and epic poems, which supply impressive lessons in morality, and in India form the substitute for history.[15]

Devadasis and Widows

This view differed from the educational plan in Western government schools. Missionary teachers and Victorian officials often erased Indian cultural features from the curriculum as morally questionable, and their staid attitudes crept into the ideology of Indian reformers embarrassed by earlier traditions of tolerance. After the Contagious Diseases Act of 1864 was instituted in India, Victorian officials equated *devadasi* courtesans with English dance hall prostitutes. When cultural nationalism grew apace after 1880, both Hindu and Muslim traditionalists frowned upon *devadasis* as "*nautch*" or dancing girls. Although the liberal Ranade and Viresalingam Pantulu (1848–1919) of Madras promoted widow remarriage and women's education, both conducted anti-*nautch* drives to cleanse society.

These bourgeois moralities also crept into the philosophy of the early feminists who worked with male reformers. Even Pandita Ramabai Saraswati (1858–1922) and Rokeya Sakhawat Hossain (1880–1932) disassociated their girls' schools from controversies surrounding women performers. The first woman legislator, Dr. Muthulakshmi Reddi (1886–1968), helped to frame a twentieth-century law against the dedication of *devadasis* to temples, perhaps because she resented her mother's own *devadasi* ancestry. However, Muthulakshmi worked idealistically to rehabilitate *devadasis* by retraining them in other occupations.[16] Once respected as temple women, *devadasis* were now derided as prostitutes or pitied as victims of patriarchy.[17]

Scholars suggest that the early struggle for women's rights in Bengal was absorbed by Hindu and Muslim revivalists into the national movement.[18] Madras and Bombay offer a contrast since the BS and PS activists worked together. They started schools for girls and campaigned vigorously for widow remarriage, especially due to high youth mortality in influenza and plague epidemics after 1890. These decades were marked by dynamic reform efforts and a growing feminist voice.

The Widow Remarriage Act of 1856 directly resulted from Vidyasagar's efforts in Bengal. This inspired reformers in Madras and Bombay to address the problems of upper-caste widows after 1860. Upper-caste girls were often wedded just before puberty, and the marriage was consummated after menarche when a formal second ritual (*ritu shanti*) was conducted. Unfortunately, in an era of high youth mortality due to influenza, small pox, and plague, the child bride was transformed into a child widow, an inauspicious blight (*amangali*) who remained celibate for life with the shaven head of an ascetic, and wearing drab mourning. Grieving parents were compelled to observe these hidebound customs or to face social ostracism. In Madras Presidency, Judge S. Venkatadri Naidu first championed widows' right to remarry, and in 1872, High Court Judge T. Muthuswami Iyer began the first Widow Marriage Association. Others like Sesha Iyengar, a *brahman* lawyer of Travancore, bravely conducted a daughter's remarriage and appealed to the public to start support associations.[19]

In the 1880s, Telugu Viresalingam Pantulu and his wife Rajyalakshmi spent their fortune in starting girls' schools and in sponsoring widow remarriage in Rajamundhry.[20] Viresalingam first tried to teach Rajyalakshmi but decided to enroll her instead in zenana classes operated by the Lutheran missionary Agnes Schade. Subsequently, Rajyalakshmi organized other women's classes in Viresalingam's ancestral home.[21] In 1881, they conducted the first widow remarriage and began a girls' school through funds donated by the rajas of Vizianagaram and Pithapuram. Two government women inspectors, Mrs. Brander and Mrs. Carr, supervised the curriculum and helped them start other schools for girls.[22]

While Viresalingam supported laws against unfair customs, conservative reformer Raghunatha Rao advocated persuasion. Rao had first supported the 1891 Age of Consent Bill, but he later cited the census to show that Madras had few virgin widows, and that they were common only to elite castes. He believed that this "microscopic minority" of just 15 percent of the population did not have many rigid conservatives. Rao ignored the multitude of poignant widows across India, as in Punjab where 25 percent of the women were widows.[23] He wrote sanguinely:

> What should a thoughtful man do in this case? He should not apply to the Legislature for a statue for the punishment of those who would not agree so to marry or of those who would not help such parties as may agree so to marry. So long, therefore, as one desires to introduce a change and wishes to associate with society, his duty would be to tell the members of that society that have incorrect ideas on the subject and that the prohibition of widow marriage has been working very injuriously to our society by making it immoral.[24]

Pandita Ramabai and Other Early Women Reformers

As early as 1880s, some radical women activists resisted the dictates of conservative and liberal reformers. The pioneer feminist was Pandita Ramabai Saraswati, a Sanskrit scholar and widow whose distaste for Hindu social customs partly influenced her decision to convert to Christianity. In 1889 at Bombay, Pandita Ramabai opened a widows' home and girls' school, naming it Sharda Sadan in honor of the Hindu goddess of learning. She later relocated her school to Pune where she inspired the male reformer Dondo Keshav Karve to also start a widows' school. Ramabai's spirited resistance to patriarchy and the attacks of Hindu nationalist B. G. Tilak mark her as India's first feminist.

Feminist writer Tarabai Shinde's (ca. 1850–1910) satirical Marathi tract, "Stri Purush Tulana" (A Comparison between Women and Men), in 1882 protested the court's decision against a *brahman* widow who had killed her illegitimate child.[25] Tarabai accused men for hypocritically blaming women for moral turpitude, when the prisons overflowed with male convicts. Tarabai's pamphlet was endorsed by the egalitarian reformer Jotiba Phule (1827–90) and his wife Savitribai Phule (1831–97).[26] In 1873, the Phules founded Satyashodhak Mandal (Society for Serving Truth) in Pune, Maharashtra to assist the marginalized Dalit castes who were shunned as "untouchables." Savitribai was a loyal Hindu wife who bravely shielded her outspoken husband, and although less mettlesome than Pandita Ramabai, Savitribai was a renegade against unjust conventions. She had defied village censure by attending school, and opened the first Dalit girls' school where her colleague was Fatima Sheik, a Muslim woman teacher.[27]

Such feminists campaigned against child marriage, widow celibacy, and *pardah* in speeches and pamphlets. They pointed out that child wives and widows withdrew from school, and that this adversely affected their mental and physical health. They helped to raise female literacy, worked for the indigent, and undertook campaigns for suffrage. Moreover, they also helped liberal male nationalists to pass laws that prevented men from sexually exploiting girls. Feminists collaborated with male reformers to support two laws favorable to women. The 1891 Age of Consent Bill stipulated that a girl had to be 12 years of age before conjugal relations; and the Child Marriage Act (Sarda Act of 1929) decreed that the minimum age of marriage for a girl was 14 years. Feminist campaigns enabled Sarda's Bill to pass in the Central Legislative Council of British men and a handful of Indian men. Although women eventually became legislators after independence in 1947, the largely male-dominated Indian Parliament followed this precedent of men's laws for women's welfare.

The earliest women's associations were the Arya Mahila Samaj (Aryan Women's Society) started by Pandita Ramabai in 1882 in Pune with the help of M. G. Ranade and his wife Ramabai Ranade (1862–1924).[28] A year after the founding of the political group, the INC, Swarnakumari Devi (1855–1932) started Sakhi Samiti (Women's Friendship Society) to assist indigent widows. Swarnakumari was a novelist and sister of poet Rabindranath Thakur with whom she had earlier founded the patriotic journal *Bharati* (India, Land of Wisdom) in 1877. She was its chief editor in 1884.[29] In 1889, Swarnakumari Devi attended the third INC meeting at Calcutta, where some five hundred members swore to promote women's education and widow remarriage.[30] In 1887, M. G. Ranade inaugurated the Indian Social Conference (ISC, or Rashtriya Parishad) as an arm of the INC specifically geared to social reform. Yet, as women's issues were being sidelined at the ISC meetings, in 1905 the recently widowed Ramabai Ranade spearheaded a women's wing, the Indian Women's Conference (Bharatiya Mahila Parishad), as a national caucus of several hundred activists.[31]

The male reformer Dondo Keshav Karve (1858–1962), a *brahman,* emulated Ramabai by starting a school for widows and by promoting their remarriage. At Ramabai's school in 1893, he met Godubai Joshi, a widow whom he married against his family's wishes. Pandita Ramabai had begun her widows' school to help the victims in the high castes which practiced child marriage. However, conservatives misconstrued her intentions and spread the rumor that Ramabai wished to convert her students to Christians. High-caste parents rapidly withdrew their daughters, and the school failed. Having endured *brahman* ostracism by marrying Godubai, and witnessing its effect on Ramabai's school, Karve changed his tactics. He could not afford to serve the widows of orthodox castes by flaunting traditions. When Karve opened another widows' school in 1896, elite nationalists slighted Ramabai's earlier efforts and lauded Karve's venture. At Karve's home, widows were taught to think fearlessly but not to flaunt their views to conservative family members. Godubai's sister Parvatibai Athavale, who was also a widow, and other women became famous teachers and writers. Karve's success led to numerous applications to start a school for other girls. His Mahilya Vidyalaya (Girls' School) emphasized independent thought in the girls destined to become wives, companions, and mothers.[32] Karve's final achievement was to establish a Women's University in 1916. Funded by the wealthy businessman, Sir Vithaldas Thackersey, in honor of his wife Nathibai, the college was renamed Shrimati Nathibai Damodar Thackersey Indian Women's University (SNDT Women's University).[33] Schools started by Karve, Viresalingam Pantulu, and the maharaja of Mysore inspired TS President Annie Besant to write "On the Education of Indian Girls" in 1904.[34]

B. M. Malabari: Persuasion or Laws?

The main controversy was whether to slowly persuade through tracts and speeches, or to convince British officials to pass laws against unfair marriage practices. The British had passed laws on *sati* and widow remarriage with confidence before the 1857 Indian Revolt, but they now hesitated to interfere in social customs. Despite this hesitancy, other colonial laws included the Age of Consent Bill (1860) stipulating 10 years as the minimum age for a girl to have conjugal relations; the Indian Divorce Act (1869); the Special Act (1870) against female infanticide; and the Special Marriage Act (1872) to raise the marriage age for girls. However, these laws were not applicable to all communities and were often circumvented. Two major bills were passed due to the efforts of Indian nationalists, i.e., the Age of Consent Bill (1891), and the Child Marriage Restraint Act (1929) decreeing 14 as the minimum marriage age for girls. The latter received extensive publicity from feminists.

After 1884, reformers urged legal intervention. Foremost was the Zoroastrian (Parsi) reformer Behramji M. Malabari (1853–1912) whose 1887 tract, "Notes on Infant Marriage and Enforced Widowhood," horrified Victorian England.[35] Signatories included eminent Hindu, Parsi, and Muslim men like T. Madhav Rao, Amir Ali, Dinsha Ardeshir Talyerkhanan; and British Liberals like Mary Carpenter, William Wedderburn, and William Gladstone. Malabari argued that child rape and widow celibacy were not sanctioned by Hindu, Muslim, or Parsi scriptures but were a "cold-blooded philosophy" devised by men. He also claimed that an apparently just Raj was needed to mediate between Indian society and its women. He pleaded:

> Emancipate the woman of India, ye English rulers! Restore to the widow her birth-right of which she is robbed by usurpers who owe no allegiance to God or to man. Give her back the exercise of free will. Is it meet that in the reign of the most womanly Queen the women of India should remain at the mercy of a foul superstition?[36]

Rakhmabai and Age of Consent Bill (1891)

In Maharashtra, female and male liberal reformers advocated legal intervention, although Hindu cultural nationalists like Bal Gangadhar Tilak (1856–1920) strongly disagreed. One case brought emotions to the surface. A woman named Rakhmabai was married at the age of 11 to Didaji Bhikaji, a man much older with little interest in education. On the other hand, Rakhmabai was taught by her stepfather who was a doctor, and resided with her parents. Upon her puberty, Bhikaji demanded that she live with him and give him conjugal rights, which she resisted strongly. The initial district court ruling in her favor as she was married without her consent was later overthrown by the Bombay High Court. Rakhmabai was now ordered to return to her husband or serve a prison sentence.[37] In 1885 under the pseudonym "A Hindu Woman," Rakhmabai wrote the article, "Indian Child Marriages," for an English newspaper. Her bitter denunciation of Indian men's laws confirmed British opinion on their civilizing mission:

> We Hindu women are treated as worse than beasts. We are regarded as playthings—objects of enjoyment to be unceremoniously thrown away

when the temporary use is over. Our law-givers (i.e., the writers of shastras) being men have painted themselves … noble and pure, and have laid every conceivable sin and impurity at our door.[38]

Controversy ensued, with British papers arguing that India was socially backward, and protests from Indian nationalists. The regressive B. G. Tilak opinions provoked Pandita Ramabai's spirited defense of Rakhmabai. In contrast, progressive men like Gokhale, Justice Telang, and T. Madhav Rao were incensed by the Bombay High Court's decision and immediately supported Sir Andrew Scoble's Age of Consent Bill (1891) in the Bombay legislature.[39] Even the more conservative Raghunatha Rao lamented that "the Modern Hindu Marriage has come to be but a sad travesty of the Grand Old Ideal."[40] Although the Age of Consent Bill cautiously raised the age for consensual sex for girls in marriage to 12 years, Tilak chastised it as a "foreign intrusion" and used the term "castration" to describe its effect upon Hinduism.[41]

The beneficial effect was that many Indians joined reform associations in the aftermath of the bill. Ordinary women in Madras boldly described their plight in Tamil journals, as seen in the introductory excerpt from *Mathar Manoranjani* (1898). Rakhmabai went to England to study medicine, and there probably met law student Cornelia Sorabji (1866–1954) who was the first Indian woman graduate of Bombay University. The daughter of Parsi converts to Christianity, Cornelia Sorabji shared Rakhmabai's dislike of some Hindu practices. In 1894, Sorabji returned to India ostensibly to serve its women but was interested only in aristocratic women in *pardah*. Her prolific literary output included her memoirs, *India Calling* (1934). An Anglophile loyalist, Cornelia Sorabji opposed the INC and Gandhi. She returned to England in 1944.[42]

It is moot here to state that in the late century, cultural nationalists often alienated feminists like Pandita Ramabai who broke free of even liberal supporters like Ranade. Indian society was ripe for change, but cultural nationalism was a knee-jerk response to British racist domination and aggressive evangelicals who wooed Hindu widows as trophies to justify Western rule. Women activists were in a dilemma. Were they to reject their culture completely, or just misogynist customs, while retaining its enlightened features? Unlike Rakhmabai and Cornelia Sorabji whose lives were guided by personal goals, Pandita Ramabai magnanimously chose to assist other women like herself. Her life is examined more closely in the next chapter.

REFORM ASSOCIATIONS AND WOMEN

Hindu and Muslim revivalists wished to resuscitate an ideal past marked by religious purity and social justice, while trying to carve out a modern power base through education. The late century, therefore, witnessed the crystallizing of the modern political identities of Hindus and Muslims. Like bourgeois Victorians who emphasized sexual sobriety and social progress, especially in women, revivalists romanticized women's chaste domesticity and patriarchal control over home and society. Hindu revivalists foisted their upper-caste values on non-Aryan matrilineal groups, while Muslim revivalists tried to expunge Hindu traditions borrowed by women over centuries.

Sectarian differences intensified due to the Raj policy of "divide and rule" and as colonial censuses and records revealed communal disparities in education and employment. As female literacy rates could trigger sectarian rivalries, Hindu, Sikh, and Muslim organizations sought to educate their girls, and female literacy rates rose after 1921. The most progressive on gender and caste rights were the PS, VS, and TS. The AS and some Muslim revivalists supported women's education but fomented sectarian xenophobia. Among Muslims, female seclusion through *pardah* was supported both by Sir Sayyid Ahmad's modernizing movement and by regressive conservatives. All reformers lauded women's chastity, spousal loyalty, and maternal power as the linchpins for the cultural survival of the group or nation. Their feminine paradigms thus shaped the contours of modern sectarian identity in the incipient nation-state.

Arya Samaj: Girls' Schools and Female Sexuality

Founded in Gujarat in 1875 by ascetic Dayananda Saraswati, the AS was intended as a means to restore Vedic fire rituals, education for women, and egalitarian social practices. However, Dayananda's anger over the perceived decay of Hindu society resulted in his Shuddhi (purification) movement through which Hindu converts to Islam and Christianity were restored to their ancestral faith. The ensuing communal vendettas instigated by later followers like Lekh Ram reached its apex in violent partition of India and Pakistan in 1947.[43] The bodies of Hindu, Sikh, and Muslim women then served as the sites to wage war against a sectarian enemy, and the scars are nearly irreparable in north India.[44]

Dayananda attempted to return to the Vedic era's occupational, non-hereditary caste system and women's human rights. He promoted education for women, adult marriages, and simplified marriage rituals, and he denounced child marriage as the accretion of a later age. The association started numerous schools for girls and boys in Punjab and north India, thus raising female literacy rates. Dayananda laid great emphasis upon women's chaste domesticity and the Vedic era custom of levirate remarriage (*niyoga*) through which a widow remarried her deceased husband's brother. However, under the guise of improving social morality, local AS leaders often attempted to control women's sexual and reproductive lives. After a visit to Calcutta, Dayananda became familiar with I. C. Vidyasagar's efforts for widows.

In 1875, he wrote the AS handbook, *Satyartha Prakash* (The Light of Truth).[45] This work urged proactive methods to restore Vedic/"Aryan" purity through better female health. Its implications for women as reproducers of an improved "Aryan" Hindu "race" were clearly apparent. Many later AS reformers also publicized adult marriages, as early marriages often resulted in higher child mortality rates. As Dayananda also felt that mothers were weakened by breast-feeding, he advised lower-caste wet nurses. He also devised meticulous rules on infant care, which would enhance the mother's reproductive energies. However, unlike some patriarchs who suspected women of inciting licentious behavior, Dayananda believed that both sexes were driven by sexual urges, which he believed should be restrained through gender segregation in schools. At first Dayananda distrusted widow remarriage among the high-caste *brahmans* and *kshatriyas* as likely to end in property disputes. However, he later changed this viewpoint and encouraged widow remarriage, as it prevented promiscuity, but only if there were no children from the previous marriage. The puritan reformer recommended levirate or *niyoga* remarriage as conducive to family stability.

The AS raised female literacy rates in Punjab where leader Lala Munshi Ram started national schools as a counterfoil to missionary schools. The Dayanand Anglo Vedic schools catered to upper-caste/middle-class Hindu girls whose parents refused to send them to mission and government schools where the teachers were often men or lower-caste women converts to Christianity. The teachers at AS girls' schools were Hindu women, and the students included young widows. The curriculum included traditional Indian texts and modern secular subjects, so that the girls would be suitable wives-companions for educated husbands. Widows were often encouraged to take up teaching as a profession. An important AS institution was the Great Girls' School or Kanya Mahavidyalaya (KMV) in Jalandhar, Punjab. It was founded in 1892 by the idealist Lala Devraj, after being inspired by his mother.[46]

A common theme that cuts across sectarian and regional lines for reformers was the inspiration of learned mothers. Thus, Tamil Christian writer Samuel Vedanayakam Pillai advocated girls' education in recognition of his learned mother Mariamma; and Sir Sayyid Ahmad Khan advocated home education for Muslim girls out of respect to his erudite mother. The AS schools also attempted to remedy the serious Punjab social problem of widespread widowhood. About 25 percent of Punjab's women were widows dependent on family charity, according to the 1881 Census. Whereas in earlier decades widows had sustained themselves through handicrafts like handloom spinning, their condition was precarious by the mid-nineteenth century when India's thriving textile industry declined under British rule. Christian missions often assisted indigent women but also converted the

women. AS schools trained widows to become teachers of women and to be
financially independent without losing their cultural traditions.

Other revivalist groups led by middle-class men and women attempted to
impose Victorian moralities upon subordinate communities with distinct
sexual norms. In the 1920s, they included Himalaya Vidya Parbandhani
Sabha (HVPS), Anjuman-I-Islamia, and Singh Sabha in Shimla, Himachal
Pradesh. The members of HVPS tried to shape laws to prohibit tribal
customs (*reet*) allowing women right to choose partners, cohabit, marry, or
seek divorce.[47] *Reet* was not subject to *brahmanical* Hindu laws (*shastras*),
and women could break free of an unhappy relationship by paying a sum
to the man. This offended the bourgeois sentiments of HVPS leaders who
influenced officials to abolish *reet* by associating it with prostitution rings
in 1924. While the HVPS thus used colonial bureaucratic authority to control tribal women's sexuality, enlightened reformers like Har Bilas Sarda
used the colonial state to raise the legal age of marriage for girls to 14 years
and thus prevented the sexual misuse of girls.

Ramakrishna Mission and Vedanta Society

The VS was inspired by the monism and universalism in the *Upanishads*
or Vedanta (last books of the *Vedas*). The *Upanishads* state that behind the
illusion of worldly diversities there exists a single cosmic entity (Brahman)
identical to the inner essence (Atman) in every living thing. This idea was
given a secular interpretation by Swami Vivekananda, who believed that a
spiritual unity lay behind India's social diversity, and his phrase "unity in
diversity" became the nationalist logo. In an inspirational lecture in 1900,
Vivekananda praised a "universal religion," which respected diverse sects
and cultures which enriched society, and that monotony was unnatural.[48]
Born in Bengal as Narendranath Dutta (1863–1902), Vivekananda received
a Western education, and he had friends in the BS.[49] At the age of 18, he
became a devoted monk-disciple of Sri Ramakrishna (1836–86), a Hindu
devotional (*bhakti*) saint with a broad social vision.[50] After his death,
Vivekananda and his monks formed the Ramakrishna Mission and VS to
serve humanity and to spread tolerance. The monks, nuns, and laymen and
laywomen disciples started schools and clinics, and fed the poor.

Ramakrishna and Sarada Devi

From early childhood, Ramakrishna felt great *bhakti* for the Mother
Goddess as Kali but was convinced of the unity of all religions. He believed
that the Buddha's teachings were integrated into Hinduism. In 1866, he took
instruction from a Muslim cleric, and in 1870, from a Christian teacher.
In each case, after observing their injunctions for weeks, he would go into a
complete trance (*samadhi*) when he had beatific visions from that religion.
Although he had not read many scriptures, Ramakrishna had a deep

knowledge of their teachings, and he was convinced that a fundamental truth lay behind disparate tenets. Ramakrishna once remarked to his disciples that "the same God" directed everyone, but through different paths, and that "the substance is One under different names."[51] This article of faith shaped the VS's programs for women.[52]

If the educated appreciated Ramakrishna's subtle wisdom, the poor were drawn by his compassion and childlike demeanor. He sought constantly for opportunities to serve others with humility, even when sweeping the hut of a Dalit scavenger.[53] The hermitage (ashram) housed monks like Vivekananda, and Ramakrishna's saintly wife Sarada Devi (1853–1920) who also had visions. The Kali temple and ashram were built in 1847 at Dakshineshwar near Calcutta on land with funds donated by Rani Rasmani, a wealthy but low-caste woman.[54] Ramakrishna was particularly respectful to women as the embodiments of the Divine Mother.[55] Although he had wanted an ascetic life, his family arranged his marriage to Sarada Devi. They took joint vows of celibacy and shared a tender, platonic friendship until his death. At one stage, Ramakrishna began a daily shoodasi puja in which he worshipped an image of Sarada Devi as Divine Mother. At first, followers were shocked by this reversal of gender roles, since custom required women to worship the husband as their lord.[56] However, later VS members revered Sarada Devi as a manifestation of the Divine Mother.[57]

Vivekananda and Women's Rights

Vivekananda's oratorical gifts stunned a Western audience at the World Parliament of Religions at Chicago in 1893. His speeches on Vedanta enlightened many who had previously regarded Hinduism as heathen polytheism. Vivekananda also honestly laid bare Hindu social flaws as deviations from the Upanishads, and that Hindus worshipped in different ways, but that the truth was found even among the unlettered. He asked educated Indians and Christians to respect them, as God lay in the poor (daridra narayan).[58] His modern vision of Vedanta involved renewed compassion and service, known to Indians before the advent of Christian missionaries.[59]

Vivekananda also delineated his views on women early in his career as spokesman for Hinduism. In a speech on "Ideals of Womanhood" to the Ethical Association of New York that was published in the Brooklyn Standard Union on January 21, 1895, he asked sternly that foreigners not judge Hinduism by its worst aspects, as rotten apples lie beneath the best apple trees. Although he credited the Enlightenment philosophers and John Stuart Mill for championing women's rights in the West, he praised Indian culture for honoring the mother above all (see introductory quotation). He traced the historical decline of educated women from Vedic age, and he blamed hereditary male brahman priests, Buddhist celibate monks, and Muslim invasions. He spoke romantically about Indian women's property rights, love of chastity, and the treatment of the mother as God. He blamed later eras for the custom of *sati*. He wrote:

> The ideal of womanhood centers in the Arian race of India, the most ancient in the world's history. In that race, men and women were co-religionists, as the Vedas called them. There every family had its hearth or altar, on which, at the time of the wedding, the marriage fire was kindled, which was kept alive, until either spouse died, when the funeral pile was lighted from its spark. There man and wife together offered their sacrifices ... But with the advent of a distinct and separate priest-class, the co-priesthood of the woman in all these nations steps back ... Another cause was instrumental in bringing this about—the change in the system of marriage. The earliest system was a matriarchal one; that is, one in which the mother was the center, and in which the girls acceded to her station ... when a man died without any children, his widow was permitted to live with another man, until she became a mother; but the children did not belong to their father, but to her dead husband. In later years the widow was allowed to marry again, which the modern idea forbids her to do.[60]

Sister Nivedita (1867–1911)

Vivekananda's idealizations fell like music upon nationalist ears and inspired Mahatma Gandhi. They were also an ideological wellspring for Margaret Noble, an Englishwoman who later became his disciple Sister Nivedita. She first met Vivekananda in 1895 at the home of Isabel Margesson in England where he spoke on Hinduism. As the daughter of an Irish Wesleyan minister, Margaret had begun to chafe under the constraints of Victorian, Christian life. Her search for fresh ideas led her first to George Bernard Shaw and William Butler Yeats, and she was also eager to experiment with new methods of teaching girls. She became enthralled by Vivekananda's talks from Sanskrit texts, and her desire for a broader humanism led her to attend his classes on Hinduism.[61] At one session, Vivekananda suggested that she teach Indian women but expressed concern for her health in the tropics. However, Margaret eagerly accepted this as her life mission.

In 1898, she stayed with Sarada Devi in Calcutta, and after intensive study, she became the lay nun Nivedita. She also became close friends with two American disciples named Sara Bull and Josephine McLeod. Her lay status allowed her to live, teach, and travel independently across India, which she loved deeply. In 1889, she started a girls' school in a crowded Calcutta community and taught 30 girls whom she encouraged to express themselves through art. She displayed their work in exhibitions and served in the local community by volunteering to clean the streets and to nurse the sick during plague and other epidemics. Returning from a fund-raising trip abroad in 1902, Nivedita began a new school with a class on reading, writing, and sewing for adult women whom she encouraged to discuss social issues openly with men.

Nivedita profoundly influenced later feminists like Sarojini Naidu and male nationalists like C. Subramania Bharati. Bharati was the author of Tamil poems, essays, and novels on women's rights, and he started the journal *Chakravartini* (Empress) in 1906 to promote women's emancipation. Another Tamil writer in the 1908 reform journal, *Viveka Bodhini* (Enlightened Intellect), described Nivedita's curriculum for Indian girls. Like Annie Besant, another British woman who had fled from domesticity in Christian Britain, Nivedita emphasized childcare, Hindu scriptures, arithmetic and accounts, and occupational skills for Indian girls, ideals that became central to the curriculum in nationalist girls' schools.[62]

Theosophical Society, Annie Besant, and Women

The Russian medium Mme. Blavatsky who was inspired by Asian religions chose to relocate the TS to India. She made a plea to Annie Besant to "come among us!" and appointed Besant as her successor.[63] Besant's life underwent several transformations before she became a Hindu Theosophist. From impoverished but educated Irish-English family, she resisted Victorian constraints on women's higher education by studying science instead of law.[64] She rejected Christian patriarchy by divorcing her domineering, pastor husband and fought for custody of her two children. Notoriety followed her tracts, "Marriage as It Was and as It Should Be" and "Law of Population" in which she advocated birth control. She became an atheist when living with trade unionist Charles Bradlaugh; as G. B. Shaw's friend, she adopted Fabian Socialism; as a feminist, she was elected to the London School Board. After becoming a Theosophist, she arrived in Bombay in 1893, remaining deeply committed to India till her death in 1933.

Although the TS first set up offices near the AS in Bombay, the TS soon left Bombay to establish its permanent base at Adyar, Madras. Besant now plunged into studies of Hinduism and Sanskrit, gave lectures on Indian cultural revival, and made contact with leaders of the INC. Besant's radical feminism was transformed in India. She promoted a system of national schools for girls and boys, gave assistance to the WIA in 1917, and championed women's suffrage in India. However, her speeches and pamphlets on girls' education reaffirmed their subordinate roles, which were enshrined in the curriculum in national girls' schools. She distinguished between Western and Eastern social mores on women and idealized the Indian woman as a chaste mother and selfless Sita or Savitri. She told women not to compete with men but to raise the future male leaders of India. Her feminism was subordinated by her interest in India's cultural rejuvenation and freedom.

This was first seen in her 1896 speech at Maharani Girls' School in the progressive princely state of Mysore. She advised the girls to "grow up to be Hindu wives and mothers," as there was "nothing nobler than loving, unselfish, spiritual Indian women."[65] By 1904, her pamphlet, "On the Education of Indian Girls," delineated her views on the curriculum at Indian girls' schools. She wrote:

> The national movement for girls' education must be on national lines: it must accept the general Hindu conceptions of woman's place in the national life, not the dwarfed modern view but the ancient ideal. It must see in the woman the mother and the wife, or, as in some cases, the learned and pious ascetic, the *Brahmavadini* of older days. It cannot see in her the rival and competitor of man in all forms of outside and public employment, as woman, under different economic conditions, is coming to be, more and more, in the West. The West must work out in its own way the artificial problem which has been created there as to the relation of the sexes. The East has not to face that problem and the lines of Western female education are not suitable for the education of Eastern girls.[66]

Besant began active in nationalist affairs, and she was elected INC president in 1917, the first woman of European ancestry to hold this post. She now urged Indian women to become activists for the nation and advised men to support them. In her 1932 book, *Higher Education in India,* she prophesied that "The future of Hinduism depends largely on women."[67] She also admonished men not to hinder their educational progress, since "exceptional girls" would require a "more profound and wider education" to lead India. She wrote:

> Such girls may be born into India in order to restore to her the learned women of the past, and to place again in her diadem the long lost pearl of lofty female intelligence. It is not for any to thwart them in their upward climbing—or to place unnecessary obstacles in their path.[68]

Madras philanthropic men like P. S. Sivaswamy Aiyar and Maranna Gounder joined the TS and financed its National Educational Trust, which established numerous schools attended by the middle-class intelligentsia. Here boys and girls studied the Indian languages, texts, and culture, as well as English and Western scientific disciplines. This type of curriculum attracted so many Indians that between 1902 and 1912, private schools doubled.[69] The TS also began schools for Dalits or the fifth caste (panchamas), often demeaned as "untouchable" pariahs. The initiative was taken by Colonel Olcott, an American Civil War veteran and Theosophist who outlined his goals in *The Poor Pariah* (1902).[70] Olcott began the Panchama Educational Trust, which had 757 boys and 193 girls in 1910. Students were taught academic subjects and given occupational training that made them economically independent of the high castes and also prevented their conversion by Christian evangelicals.[71]

The feminist and nationalist movements thus evolved together from the late nineteenth century when educated women began regional groups (*mahila samajs/parishads*) to assist their less fortunate Indian sisters. This was especially apparent after World War I when millions of women joined Mohandas K. Gandhi's (1869–1948) pacifist freedom campaigns (*satyagrahas*) based on nonviolence (*ahimsa*).[72] Among them were domiciled Irish women like Besant and Margaret Cousins who aligned Indian women's suffrage movement with feminism in the West. Initially, many Indian women rejected the term "feminist" as it seemed to imply a gender war. Supported by progressive men and guided by the culture of family solidarity under duress, they felt that they struggled jointly with men for rights and freedom.[73]

In return, male patriots idealized their women as unselfish and spiritual, in contrast to Western feminists who sought to wrest their individual rights from a patriarchal society marked by competitive materialism.[74] Gandhi or Mahatma (Great Soul) appealed to men to seek inspiration from women's daily abnegations for their families, and women now courted arrest and sacrificed for the nation's freedom.[75] In 1922, feminist Sarojini Naidu compared Gandhi's methods with Europe's wars:

> The difference between our warfare and the warfare of Europe, the warfare of the West, the accepted warfare of the world, is this, that while nations of another land win their victory slaying their enemies we win our victory by slaying only our sins.[76]

Assessment of Male Reformers

Recent critics argue that male reformers were too preoccupied with elite women's customs to consider the pressing problems of lower-class women.[77] As the elite, they filtered the benefits of modernity from themselves to women and the low castes, so that women became the *objects* of their reforming gaze and channels for India's regeneration. Moreover, critics point out that male reformers wished to educate elite girls by reaffirming their roles as "good wives and good mothers," an idea that was extended to their work as brave "mothers of the nation" (and its men).[78] In this highly political environment, missionary, government, and nationalist schools emphasized women's domestic and reproductive importance, since patriarchy demanded that men seek outside employment through a Western secular education. Nationalists did not try to educate their women for jobs but to maintain cultural stability in the midst of rapid social change.[79] The exception was the widow who became an ideal resource to teach other women. Without any substantive programs for women's economic independence, gender equality remained an elusive dream.[80] Moreover, nationalists used the colonial legal system to control female sexuality, fearing that women trained into other professions would shirk domestic duties or even become sexually independent like Western women. This appeared during Constituent Assembly debates after independence in 1949. Male legislators then opposed women's equal rights to property on the spurious logic that this would fragment the Indian family.[81]

These valid arguments may be understood better if placed in their historical context. Not only were patriarchal mores of over two millennia deeply ingrained in high-caste/class male nationalists, but also notions of caste hierarchy. They deeply resented the racist colonial hierarchy that allotted them a limited political niche. Neither colonial rulers nor Indian male nationalists wished to share authority equally with women or the lower orders, but rather to guide these paternalistically. Women thus became the means to attain freedom from Western rule. The idea of engendered spaces with men in the public sphere and women in the domestic arena had grown in the late Victorian consumerist economy.[82] When applied to India, the philosophy would postpone meaningful equality either for women or for the lower classes. As products of their era, male reformers shared the shibboleths of that time. Yet, the liberal first articulated the importance of human rights in India and fostered pride in its valuable traditions, but also criticized its weaknesses. As moderates, they were terrified by radical politics, whether by outspoken feminists or by cultural nationalists who wished to restore an outmoded past. Although born to privilege, elite nationalists forged a new philosophy that grafted spiritual equality from Indian scriptures onto recent Western innovations on social equality. This dual inspiration grounded their movement in the context of Indian historical dissent and tolerance, making it comprehensible to modern compatriots.[83] While the ideal of equality continues to entrance many, it requires constant vigilance. Ranade was convinced that his goals were innovative for his time, since more extreme changes would be socially convulsive and impermanent. He thus wished to proceed slowly, "along the lines of least resistance." In tune with current usage, Ranade used the term *mankind* for humanity, but his progressive views are evident throughout his speeches.[84] Reform was to be judicious, since despite "decay and corruption," "we cannot stop at a particular period without breaking the continuity of the whole." He sought to raise the low castes and women but criticized the revivalist who wished to restore Vedic levirate widow remarriage. Pointing to outmoded customs in *Manu Smriti,* Ranade asked sharply, "What shall we revive? Shall we revive the twelve forms of sons, or eight forms of marriage, which included capture, and recognized mixed and illegitimate intercourse?" He wrote:

All admit we have been deformed. We have lost our stature, we are bent in a hundred places ... and now we want this deformity to be removed; and the only way to remove it is to place ourselves under the discipline of better ideas and forms. Now this is the work of the Reformer.[85]

MUSLIM REFORMERS AND WOMEN

Modernist Movements

The most significant Islamic modernist movement was spearheaded by Sir Sayyid Ahmad Khan, an Urdu-speaking *ashraf* whose ancestors worked for the Mughal empire. Educated in Muslim schools (*madarssas*), Sir Sayyid became a scholar through personal diligence when serving as a minor judge in the British criminal court at Delhi. Convinced that the Raj would safeguard his Muslim community (*qwam*), Sir Sayyid was shaken by the 1857 Revolt, and in 1866, he founded the British Indian Association. In the late 1870s, he was dismayed by the rise of educated Hindus in the bureaucracy and derided the INC as a Hindu club. In order to promote a renaissance among Muslim men, he advocated a Western education along with studies in Arabic, Urdu, and Persian texts. He founded the Scientific Society to translate Western texts into Urdu, and the Mohammedan Anglo-Oriental University for men at Aligarh. However, Sir Sayyid believed that Muslim women should study only within the *zenana*. In 1886, Sir Sayyid also started the All-India Mohammedan Educational Conference (MEC), which met concurrently with the INC to siphon nationalist Muslims into his organization.

Women's Schooling and *Pardah*

Pan-Indian, Hindu, and Muslim identities were shaped by gender and class hierarchies. All reformers regardless of sect emphasized female education and women's domesticity as stabilizing influences on each community. Like the Hindu Ranade, Sir Sayyid and his successor Abd Ali Latif knew that the illiterate were likely to believe in miracles, and that as illiteracy was more common among women, they were susceptible to obscurantist ideas.[86] Conservative and modernist Muslim reformers sought to instruct women on the *Qur'an* and its verses outlining their rights. In 1905, Maulana Ashraf Ali Thanawi's Urdu guideline, *Bihishti Zewar* (Jewelry of Paradise), became a seminal influence upon Muslim women. A Sufi scholar of the revivalist Deoband school, Maulana Thanawi agreed with Sir Sayyid that an earlier tradition of wise Muslim women had deteriorated through contact with Hindus.[87] The Maulana argued that women must be taught, as Prophet Muhammad had emphasized that God had given both sexes natural intelligence. On a somber note, Thanawi wrote that he was "heartsick" at the "ruination of the religion of the women of Hindustan" and their "ignorance of the religious sciences." He urged women to shed ostentatious frivolity at weddings and rites.[88]

Modernist reformers drew attention to women's rights to property, adult marriages, and divorce as laid down by the *Qur'an*. They supported *pardah* as a way to promote respect for women but argued that many illiterate Muslim women had lost their *Qur'anic* rights to property, albeit half the amounts given to men. They felt that the important verse (4:32) advising men to manage female affairs and women to be "devoutly obedient" reflected female ignorance, and not censure by the Prophet who relied on the advice of his senior wives. Muslim women's property rights had eroded in India where such rights were customary, rather than textually mandated. Muslim reformers thus blamed Hindu society for such losses through cultural assimilation. This view was also accepted by British feminists like Eleanor Rathbone, a Parliamentary member who testified to the Census Board in 1934.[89]

Muslim reformers believed that women's lost rights to divorce and adult marriage in India could be rectified by education on the *Qur'an*. The progressive wished to also teach women some modern secular subjects but not commensurate to men's schooling. Most Muslim reformers also advocated some form of *pardah* as a distinguishing marker of high-class women. If the liberal advocated seclusion to safeguard women, the puritanical saw *pardah* as a way to punish women for inciting male lust. Muslim women faced the double indemnity of being both female and from a minority group, so that they could not easily explore the new freedoms that became available to Muslim men in the late colonial era. Lastly, incipient feminist aspirations were shadowed by sectarian contestations, so that decades passed before Muslim women could reassert their natural, human rights.[90]

Sir Sayyid's conservatism is evident in his advocacy of the *pardah* for women's chastity and *zenana* education. He distrusted Western gender norms as unsuitable for Muslim women and did not favor formal schools for Muslim girls.[91] His ideal was his aristocratic mother Azizunnissa Begam (d. 1857), who studied Arabic, Persian, and Urdu texts within the *zenana*. A similar vision was expounded nearly a century previously by Mirza Abu Talib in his *Vindication of the Liberties of Asiatic Women* (1801). Talib had witnessed the promiscuity of upper-class English women and men in Regency England. While Talib admired aristocratic Englishwomen, he disparaged their sexual escapades and praised Muslim women's secluded innocence. Thus, *pardah* became a significant cultural distinction between East and West.[92] Eighty years later, Sir Sayyid conflated several models of feminine perfection to create a modern Muslim woman with the grace admired by Talib, coupled with Victorian, educated domesticity. As his mother represented an ideal *zenana* woman, Sir Sayyid advised the Hunter Commission on Education in 1882 not to take the trouble to start formal schools for Muslim girls:

> The present state of education among Muhammadan females is, in my opinion, enough for domestic happiness, considering the present

social and economic condition of the life of the Muhammadans in India.[93]

The idea of a distinctive Muslim community was thus linked to gender ideals, their cultural spaces, and educational attainment. At the MEC in 1893, Sir Sayyid's son Sayyid Mahmoud (1850–1903), a judge at Allahabad High Court, gave a lecture on Muslim educational shortcomings.[94] Sayyid Mahmoud later published an erudite history on elite men's importance to his community, without any reference to women's public roles. Islamic nationalism was clearly in the hands of men.[95]

Islamic nationalism was also shaped by reformers who castigated the accretion of Hindu customs over a thousand years of historical interactions. The close proximity of Hindu and Muslim groups led to fuzzy cultural and ethnic markers, most noticeable among convert Muslims, but also true of elite *ashrafs* descended from West Asians. The Indian social mosaic is notable for the sharing of cultural ideas and practices across sects, often mediated by women. Shared regional vocabularies and languages, foods, music, litera-ture, art, social rites at births and marriages, and even religious rites at the tombs of Sufi saints. South Indian working Muslim women cover their heads but move freely out of *pardah,* speak Tamil or Malayalam and not Arabic or Urdu, and venerate the Sufi saints with plates of marigolds, ash, and fruits in rites that resemble Hindu temple offerings to icons.[96] Elite women in the *zen-ana* bridged disparate cultures through interactions with Hindu vendors and servants. In north India, mixed metaphors and language patterns with Hindu nuances was called the women's dialect (*begamati zabaan*).[97] Although soci-ety was enriched by such female mediations, male clerics (*maulvis*) frowned upon these as Hindu corruptions of the Islamic ideal.

However, some Muslims disagreed with purists and with Sir Sayyid on women's home education. The progressive thinker Mumtaz Ali (d. 1935) of Lahore, Punjab differed on the scope of women's domestic authority as delineated by the *Qur'anic* verse, which advised men to supervise household finances as women were unlettered. Mumtaz Ali proposed that female education would revive the example of powerful, literate women like the Prophet's chief wives.[98] Mumtaz Ali respectfully presented his manuscript on women's rights to Sir Sayyid Ahmad Khan but was shocked when the great man threw it into the waste basket. It was only after the great man's death in 1898 that Mumtaz Ali undertook to publish *Tahzib-E-Niswan* (The Women's Reformer), the first important Urdu women's journal.[99] Mumtaz Ali's wife Muhammadi Begam was his coeditor until her death, after which his daughter Waheeda Begam and later his son continued the journal till 1948.[100]

Fortunately, some of Sir Sayyid's students broke free of his dictates. Ibrahim Saber and his younger sister Rokeya, the first Muslim feminist, came from a distinguished Bengali family. Although their father had Ibrahim educated in Arabic, Persian, Urdu, and English, he restricted Rokeya and her sister to rote recitations from the *Qur'an* and forbade the girls from learning Bengali and English. Rokeya's eagerness to master Bengali led Ibrahim to teach his sister surreptitiously at night by candlelight. A grateful Rokeya dedicated her first novel *Padmarag* to him for having opened a window to Bengali literature.[101]

At the MEC at Allahabad in 1900, Muslims pledged to open more schools for both genders. They convinced British provincial governments to start girls' schools where teachers did not preach Christianity, and to arrange for closed *pardah* conveyances to transport the girls.[102] After the 1920s, liberal and patriotic Muslim families sent their daughters to college. Thus, the Gujarati Bohra Muslim merchant Badruddin Tyabji, a respected member of the INC, sent his elder daughters to a Bombay school and his younger daughter to college in England.[103] Similarly, Attia Hosain (b. 1913) of Lucknow was also educated abroad by her family, before she returned to write the English novel, *Sunlight on a Broken Column,* about a middle-class Muslim woman and the challenges faced by her family in the twentieth century.[104]

Muslim Laws for Women (Twentieth Century)

Muslims largely believed that the Sharia laws based on the *Qur'an* superseded the secular, civil laws of the colonial state. The Shariat governs both personal moralities and social responsibilities. However, many communities followed a combination of Shariat, local customs, and colonial government injunctions. Muslims gave charitable donations to religious endowments (*waqf*) administered by clerics (*mullahs, ulama*) to maintain indigents and widowed women. British colonial authorities often favored loyal but often reactionary landowners (*zamindars*) who sometimes misused their power over local *waqf* boards. Some *zamindars* allowed the endowments to become derelict and denuded widows of property, so that many became paupers. Liberal, Westernized Muslim nationalists joined hands with the clerics to reassert the primacy of the Shariat and *waqf* boards by forcing legislators to pass the Waqf Validating Act (1913).

Later, laws affecting women were instituted in the midst of several political movements. They included vibrant feminism, Pakistan separatist movement, and political divisions with secular Indian Muslim nationalists. The Muslim Personal Law (Shariat) Application Act of 1937 and the Muslim Dissolution of Marriage Act of 1939 (Divorce Act) were two laws that directly affected only Muslim women. Due to many regional inheritance practices among Muslims, the colonial government had enacted the Married Women's Property Act (1876), the Guardians and Wards Act (1890), and the Kazi Act (1880), the latter providing for a Muslim legal scholar (*kazi*) to advise civil courts on the Shariat. Many religious clerics of the Jamiat-ul-ulama-I-Hind organization supported the Shariat but rejected regional non-Islamic customs. Taking note of this movement, in 1927 at Peshwar, Punjab, Muslim leaders resolved to pass a civil law enforcing the Shariat and to reject local customs. Reactionary Muslim landlords of northern India loyal to the British deprived women of *Qur'anic* rights with impunity, and the colonial state overlooked their excesses. Patriotic Muslims like Mohammad Ali Jinnah (1871–1948), a Khoja from Bombay, believed that a secular law was necessary to help Muslim women. In 1934, a controversial bill was resisted by Gujarati Bohra and Khoja Muslims who followed a mix of Muslim and Hindu inheritance laws. Jinnah framed an amended bill allowing greater flexible transitions from local customs to Muslim Personal Law.[105] Although the Shariat Act appeared to promote religious over secular law, it partially restored Muslim women's rights, although some ensuing judgments were unfair to women.[106]

The Dissolution of Muslim Marriages Act (1939) had a more significant impact by replacing the Hanafi laws of Sharia that restricted women filing for divorce by the more lenient Maliki school of Sharia law that allowed women to dissolve marriages if the husband failed to support her or deserted her. The *Qur'an* accepts polygamy for men, but not all men are polygamous. The scripture allows women and men to divorce, especially if wives feared "cruelty or desertion" as there would be "no blame on them" (4:128). The *Qur'an* also states that a wife facing "prejudice" in marriage can break it (4:23–24), as long as she returns her dowry (*mehr*). While men can divorce even without the wife's presence by pronouncing the word "*talaq*" (divorce) three times, women need two (male) witnesses. The Maliki school of law prevailing in south India grants women divorce on several grounds. The strictest is the north Indian Hanafi school, which allows women to divorce only through the mediation of a clerical judge. It also does not accept divorce between Muslims if a non-Muslim judge is the mediator. Hanafi jurists also decreed that a woman be imprisoned if she married a non-Muslim or converted to another religion until she returned to the Islamic fold.[107] The clarity of the Dissolution of Muslim Marriage Act gave women ample reasons to divorce, and the law could be implemented justly and easily. Husain Iman, a Bihar legislator, explained the need for such a law, as the Hanafi Code had no provision if her husband "neglects to maintain her, makes her life miserable by deserting or persistently maltreating her, or absconds," which "entailed unspeakable misery to innumerable Muslim women in British India."[108]

Two secular laws applied to all Indian women irrespective of sect, caste, or class. They were the Age of Consent Bill (1927) introduced by Hari Singh Gour and the Child Marriage Restraint Act (1929) introduced by Har Bilas Sarda. Although intended to abolish child marriage most common among Hindus, both bills were supported by liberal Muslim women at local meetings and through national feminist organizations like the All India Women's Conference (AIWC), WIA, and the National Council of Women in India

(NCWI). Despite the growing rift between Muslim and Hindu male leaders, Hindu and Muslim feminists in the AIWC and WIA jointly denounced child marriage as an Indian custom. In her 1928 presidential address to the AIWC, the Begam of Bhopal described child marriage as an "evil" that debilitated women, took away their childhood, and denied them an education. Vocal Muslim supporters of the Sarda Bill were Begam Sharifa Hamid Ali, Lady Abdul Qadir, Begam Qudsia Aizaz Rasul, Mrs. Akhatar Husain, Mrs. Kazi Mir Ahmed, Begam Hamida Momin, and Mrs. I. F. Hasan. Similar support was forthcoming from Abru Begam, honorary secretary of AIWC chapter in Hyderabad princely state, and from Lady Ismail whose husband Mohammad Ismail was chief minister of Mysore, whose ruling dynasty was enlightened on women's rights.[109] Due to her husband's high rank, considerable weight was attached to her demand that the British legally raise the marriage age for girls to 16 years.[110] The Sarda Act of September 1929 made 14 the legal age of marriage for girls in British India.

Nation and Sect: Muslim Women and Politics

Many elite Muslim women began *pardah* clubs in the 1920s to articulate their ideas on reform for women. They included professionals like Dr. Rahamatunissa Begam of Madras and Sharifa Hamid Ali from the Tyabji family from Bombay, and aristocrats like the Begam of Bhopal. The AIWC represented a sisterhood embracing women of all communities. Muslim women's sectarian identity was reinforced in its debates over *pardah* and the Shariat Act. In the 1940s, feminists' united front was threatened by communal tensions, and they were forced to choose sides. Their family men espoused either the Muslim League's (ML) Pakistan cause or the Indian nationalist struggle led by Gandhi and the INC.[111] The less political returned to educational or quiet reform work that was not confrontational with their colleagues. The ML now organized women into political action groups, such as the All-India Muslim Women's Sub-Committee in 1938. Its leader Mohammad Ali Jinnah was interested in promoting women's involvement in the creation of Pakistan on August 14, 1947. Although in *pardah*, Muslim women participated in demonstrations by wearing a full-body cloak with veil (*burqah*). Others like the aristocratic Qudsia Aizaz Rasul discarded the *pardah*, if supported by their husbands.[112] She and her husband belonged to the ML but remained in India after India's partition.

Among the Muslim supporters of the INC was Sharifa Hamid Ali, from the affluent Bohra family of Badruddin Tyabji in Bombay. Sharifa's integrity and ability were respected by Jawaharlal Nehru (1889–1964), as she believed implicitly in a united India and represented the INC position against communal electorates at the Round Table Conference in 1933.[113] In 1939, Sharifa served on the National Planning Committee with two other Muslim women, under the direction of Prime Minister Nehru.

Two other important Muslim women were Kulsum Sayani and Sofia Khan. As Kulsum's father was Gandhi's physician, she regarded Gandhi as a favorite uncle and readily joined his *satyagraha* movement.[114] Sofia Khan (1916–61) was a devout Muslim and the daughter of the respected Justice Somjee of Bombay, and a relative of Khan Abdul Gaffar Khan of North West Province, also known as "Frontier Gandhi" due to his commitment to peace. Like other feminists, Sofia Khan joined the INC and took part in Salt Satyagraha of 1930. During this epoch-making event, Gandhi marched 240 miles from Sabarmati to Dandi, Gujarat. Gandhi made salt from seawater in defiance of the British monopoly over the manufacture and sale of salt, which was crucial to survival in the tropics. Although Gandhi had first objected to women in the arduous march, Sarojini Naidu, Kamaladevi Chattopadhyaya, and Khurshed Naoroji changed his mind. Elite and ordinary women became patriotic "salt thieves" who braved arrest by making and selling this commodity. Sofia Khan joined Nehru in protests against India's enforced involvement in World War II, and she was imprisoned in Yeravada Jail in Pune. Sofia Khan followed Gandhi's guidelines by spinning cotton cloth (*khaddar*) on the handloom (*charkha*).

A less prominent but enthusiastic follower of Gandhi was Sultana Hayat of Uttar Pradesh. Sultana later served as the president of an organization to promote the Urdu language in independent India. These were just a few examples of elite and middle-class Muslim women who fought to free India. Muslim women workers of Uttar Pradesh demonstrated for higher wages and lower prices, appearing in public in the full-body cloak (*burqah*). However, they did not often venture to public meetings unless the speakers were Muslim women or bore Muslim names like Aruna Asaf Ali (1906–95), a courageous feminist born Hindu and married to a Muslim who shared her commitment to leftist ideals.[115] Indira Gandhi was Jawaharlal Nehru's daughter, and the descendent of Kashmiri Hindu *brahmans*, married Feroze Gandhi whose parents were Zoroastrian and Muslim. The revolutionary freedom movement was marked by similar marriages transcending caste and sect in a search for national unity.

NOTES

1. Vivekananda, "Ideals of Womanhood," in *The Complete Works of Swami Vivekananda,* 9th ed. (Calcutta: Advaita Ashrama, 1995), 2:503–7.

2. Stanley Wolpert, *Tilak and Gokhale: Revolution and Reform in the Making of Modern India,* 2nd ed. (Berkeley and Los Angeles: University of California Press, 1961), 36.

3. *Bande Mataram* hymn appeared in Bankim Chandra Chatterji's Bengali novel, *Ananda Math.* Bankim Chandra Chatterji, *The Abbey of Bliss: A Translation of Bankim Chandra Chatterji's Ananda Math,* trans. Nares Chandra Sen Gupta (Calcutta: P. M. Neogi, 1906), 31–37.

4. I am indebted to Debashish Banerji for his comments during his exhibition of Bengal modern painters at Aurobindo Ashram at Pondicherry, Tamil Nadu, December 2001. Also cited in Raman and Surya, *A. Madhaviah,* 106, 114 nn. 3, 4.

5. Thanjavur state, now in Tamil Nadu, had many philanthropic kings and queens. Raman, *Getting Girls to School,* 1–6.

6. Gail Minault, "Introduction: The Extended Family as Metaphor and the Expansion of the Women's Realm," in *The Extended Family: Women and Political Participation in India and Pakistan,* ed. Gail Minault (New Delhi: Chanakya Publishers, 1981), 3–19, *vide,* 7–8.

7. Rabindranath Thakur's story was filmed by Satyajit Ray as *Home and the World* in 1961.

8. C. Subramania Bharati's Tamil writings on women include his journal editorial, "Statistics on Women's Education," *Chakravartini* (Empress), 1, no. 7 (February 1906), 1; his 1924 novella *Chandrikaiyin Kadai* (Chandrikai's Story; Madras: Sangam Publishers, 1982); *Katturaikal: Mathar* (Essays on Women; Triplicane: Bharati Publishing House, 1935); his four poems on the new Indian woman, in *Bharatiyar Kavitaikkal Muzhuvadum* (Bharatiyar's Complete Poems; Madras: Bharati Publishers, 1986), 207–12.

9. Madhu Kishwar, "Arya Samaj and Women's Education: Kanya Mahavidyalaya, Jalandhar," *Economic and Political Weekly* 21, no. 17 (April 1986): 9–10.

10. Raman, *Getting Girls to School,* 77–80.

11. Kumar, *History of Doing,* 14.

12. Forbes, *Women in Modern India,* 28–31.

13. Vedanayakam Pillai, *Pen Kalvi* (Female Education; repr., Tinnevelly: Saiva Siddhanta Publishing Society, 1950), frontispiece.

14. Raman, *Getting Girls to School,* 114–15; Raman, "Old Norms in New Bottles," 93–119, *vide,* 94–96.

15. Government of Madras, *Report of the Madras Provincial Committee with Evidence Taken Before the Committee and Memorials Addressed to the Education Commission, 1883,* 130; Government of India, *Report of the Indian Education Commission* (Hunter Commission), February 3, 1882, 542; and Raman, *Getting Girls to School,* 77–79, 99 nn. 48, 50.

16. Muthulakshmi Reddi, *My Experiences as a Legislator* (Triplicane: Current Thought Press, 1930); Muthulakshmi Reddi, *An Autobiography* (Adyar: Avvai Home, 1964); Muthulakshmi Reddi, *The Presidential Address of Dr. (Mrs) S. Muthulakshmi Reddi, Delivered at the Seventh Andhra Provincial Women's Conference* (pamphlet; Ellore: 1933); Muthulakshmi Reddi, *Why Should the Devadasi Institution in the Hindu Temples Be Abolished?* (Madras: Central Cooperative Printing Works, Ltd., 1927); S. Muthulakshmi Reddi Papers, Files 7–12, and All India Women's Conference Papers (New Delhi: Nehru Memorial Museum and Library [NMML]).

17. Pandita Ramabai, *The High Caste Hindu Woman* (New York: Fleming H. Revell Company, 1887); Tharu and Lalitha, *Women Writing in India,* 1:243–55, 340–52; Kosambi, *At the Intersection of Gender Reform and Religious Belief;* Forbes, *Women in Modern India,* 46–49; Chakravarti, "Whatever Happened to the Vedic *Dasi?*" 27–87; Kumar, *History of Doing,* 26–27, 32–34; Bharati Ray, *Early Feminists of Colonial India: Sarla Devi Chaudhurani and Rokeya Sakhawat Hossain* (New Delhi: Oxford University Press, 2002); Minault, *Secluded Scholars,* 256–62.

18. Sumit Sarkar, "The Women's Question in Nineteenth Century Bengal," in *Women and Culture,* ed. Kumkum Sangari and Sudesh Vaid (Bombay: SNDT Women's University, 1985), 157–72; Partha Chatterjee, "The Nationalist Resolution of the Women's Question," in *Recasting Women,* ed. Sangari and Vaid, 232–53, *vide,* 235.

19. John Greenfield Leonard, *Kandukuri Viresalingam: A Biography of an Indian Social Reformer* (Hyderabad: Telugu University, 1991), 58.

20. Raman, *Getting Girls to School,* 119–27.

21. Leonard, *Kandukuri Viresalingam,* 155–56.

22. Ibid., 56–59, 75–81, 85–90, 119–29; also Y. Vaikuntham, *Education and Social Change in South India: Andhra 1880–1920* (Madras: New Era, 1982), 221–22.

23. Kishwar, "Arya Samaj and Women's Education," 9.

24. R. Raghunatha Rao, "The Method of Social Reform," in *Hindu Social Progress,* ed. N. Subbarau Pantulu Garu (Madras: G. A. Natesan & Co., 1904), 66–67.

25. Rosalind O'Hanlon, *A Comparison between Women and Men: Tarabai Shinde and the Critique of Gender Relations in Colonial India* (New Delhi: Oxford University Press, 1994), 100–25; Tharu and Lalitha, *Women Writing in India,* 1:221–35.

26. Padma Anagol, *The Emergence of Feminism in India, 1850–1920* (Hampshire, England and Burlington, Vermont: Ashgate Publishers, 2005); Rosalind O'Hanlon, "Issues of Widowhood: Gender and Resistance in Colonial India," in *Contesting Power: Resistance and Everyday Social Relations in South Asia,* ed. Douglas Haynes and Gyan Prakash (Berkeley: University of California Press, 1991), 62–108; Rosalind O'Hanlon, *Caste, Conflict and Ideology: Mahatma Jotirao Phule and Low Caste Protest in Nineteenth Century Western India,* 2nd ed. (Cambridge: Cambridge University Press, 2002).

27. Gail Omvedt, *Cultural Revolt in a Colonial Society* (Bombay: Scientific Socialist Education Trust, 1976); and Gail Omvedt, "Hinduism as Patriarchy: Ramabai, Tarabai and Others," in *Dalit Visions,* ed. Gail Omvedt, 2nd ed. (Mumbai: Orient Longman, 2002), 25–42; Tharu and Lalitha, *Women Writing in India,* 1:211–14.

28. Kosambi, *At the Intersection of Gender Reform and Religious Belief,* 29.

29. Kumar, *History of Doing,* 37–38; Ray, *Early Feminists of Colonial India,* 152–53.

30. Forbes, *Women in Modern India,* 26–27.

31. Ibid., 66.

32. D. D. Karve, ed. and trans., *The New Brahmins: Five Maharashtrian Families* (Berkeley: University of California Press, 1963), 50–51.

33. Forbes, *Women in Modern India,* 51–53.

34. Annie Besant, "Address Delivered to the Children of the Maharani's Girls' School at Mysore on the Occasion of Her Recent Visit to That Institution, December 24, 1896," *Arya Bala Bodhini,* January 1897; Annie Besant, "An Interview," *Arya Bala Bodhini,* January 1899, 44–48; Besant, *On the Education of Indian Girls;* Besant, *Higher Education in India.* See also Raman, *Getting Girls to School,* 132–37.

35. Behramji M. Malabari, *Infant Marriage and Enforced Widowhood in India* (Bombay: Voice of India Press, 1887), v, 10–105; also Rajendra Singh Vatsa,

"The Movement against Infant Marriages in India, 1860–1914," *Journal of Indian History* 44, no. 145–47 (April 1971): 294–300; Rajendra Singh Vatsa, "The Remarriage and Rehabilitation of Hindu Widows in India, 1856–1914," *Journal of Indian History* 4, no. 3 (December 1976): 722–33; Raman, *Getting Girls to School,* 124–27; Kumar, *History of Doing,* 25–27.

36. Malabari, *Infant Marriage and Enforced Widowhood in India,* 5.

37. Kosambi, *At the Intersection of Gender Reform and Religious Belief,* 41–42.

38. See Ibid., 26–27.

39. Wolpert, *Tilak and Gokhale,* 37, 59–60.

40. R. Raghunatha Rao, *The Aryan Marriage with Special Reference to the Age Question: A Clinical and Historical Study* (1908; repr., New Delhi: Cosmo Publication, 1975), ix; also Rao, "The Method of Social Reform," 64–69.

41. Chakravarti, "Whatever Happened to the Vedic *Dasi?*" 73–75; Kumar, *History of Doing,* 25–27; Forbes, *Women in Modern India,* 22, 46–49.

42. Tharu and Lalitha, *Women Writing in India,* 1:296–98; Antoinette Burton, " 'Stray Thoughts of an Indian Girl' by Cornelia Sorabji, *The Nineteenth Century, October 1891,*" in *Feminism in India,* ed. Maitrayee Chaudhuri (New Delhi: Women Unlimited and Kali for Women, 2004), 94–102, *vide,* 94–95.

43. Kenneth W. Jones, "Communalism in the Punjab: The Arya Samaj Contribution," in *Modern India: An Interpretive Anthology,* ed. Thomas Metcalf (New Delhi: Sterling Publishers, 1990), 261–77.

44. Urvashi Butalia, *The Other Side of Silence: Voices from the Partition of India* (New Delhi: Penguin, 1998); Ritu Menon and Kamla Bhasin, *Borders and Boundaries: Women in India's Partition* (New Brunswick, New Jersey: Rutgers University, 1998).

45. Chakravarti, "Whatever Happened to the Vedic *Dasi?*" 55–60.

46. Kishwar, "Arya Samaj and Women's Education," 9–13.

47. Snehi, "Conjugality, Sexuality and *Shastras,*" 176, 178–81.

48. Vivekananda, "The Way to the Realization of a Universal Religion," Lecture at the Universalist Church, Pasadena, California, January 28, 1900, in *The Complete Works of Swami Vivekananda,* 2:359–96, *vide,* 381–83.

49. Swami Nikhilandanda, *Sri Ramakrishna: A Biography* (Madras: Sri Ramakrishna Math, 2002), 94–184; "Anna," *Saints of India* (Madras: Sri Ramakrishna Math, 1990), 77–97.

50. Nikhilandanda, *Sri Ramakrishna,* 106–9; "Anna," *Saints of India,* 70–76.

51. Advaita Ashrama, *A Short Life of Sri Ramakrishna* (Mayavati, Himalayas: Advaita Ashrama, 1940), 61.

52. Nikhilandanda, *Sri Ramakrishna,* 53–58.

53. Ashrama, *A Short Life of Sri Ramakrishna,* 69–70; "Anna," *Saints of India,* 73–74.

54. Nikhilandanda, *Sri Ramakrishna,* 10–11.

55. Ashrama, *A Short Life of Sri Ramakrishna,* 71, 90–92; "Anna," *Saints of India,* 40–45, 75.

56. Swami Tapasyananda, *Sri Sarada Devi, the Holy Mother: Life and Teachings* (Madras: Sri Ramakrishna Math, 2003), 24–25.

57. Ibid., 71–140.

58. Vivekananda, "Addresses at the World Parliament of Religions, Chicago, 11th September, 1893," in *The Complete Works of Swami Vivekananda,* 1:3–24, *vide,* 15.

59. Dietmar Rothermund, "Swami Vivekananda (1863–1902), Hindu Religious Leader," in *Encyclopedia of India*, ed. Stanley Wolpert (Detroit and New York: Thomson Gale, 2006), 4:222–23.

60. Vivekananda, "Ideals of Womanhood," 2:503–7.

61. Kumari Jayawardena, *The White Woman's Other Burden: Western Women and South Asia during British Colonial Rule* (New York and London: Routledge, 1995), 183–94; Pravrajika Atmaprana, *The Story of Sister Nivedita* (Calcutta: Ramakrishna Sarada Mission and Sister Niveditta Girls' School, 1991).

62. "Aa.chi.ka" (a pseudonym), "The Education of Women" (Tamil), *Viveka Bodhini* 1, no. 1 (August 1908): 39–41; also Raman, *Getting Girls to School*, 155, 192 n. 12.

63. Annie Besant, *An Autobiography* (1893; repr., Adyar: Theosophical Publishing Society, 1984), 311.

64. Jayawardena, *The White Woman's Other Burden*, 107–34; Raman, *Getting Girls to School*, 39, 132–36, 154, 168–73, 190, 219, 229; Barbara Ramusack, "Catalysts or Helpers? British Feminists, Indian Women's Rights, and Indian Independence," in *The Extended Family*, ed. Minault, 109–50; Arthur H. Nethercott, *The First Nine Lives of Annie Besant* (London: Rupert Hart-Davis, 1961); Anne Taylor, *Annie Besant, a Biography* (Oxford and New York: Oxford University Press, 1992); Jyoti Chandra, *Annie Besant: From Theosophy to Nationalism* (Delhi: K. R. Publications, 2001); Indra Gupta, *India's 50 Most Illustrious Women* (New Delhi: Icon Publications Pvt. Ltd., 2003), 57–66.

65. Besant, "Address to Maharani Girls' School"; also Raman, *Getting Girls to School*, 166–77.

66. Besant, *On the Education of Indian Girls*, 3.

67. Annie Besant, "An Appeal: Higher Education for Indian Girls" (Adyar: Theosophical Society, January 1915), 1–3.

68. Besant, *On the Education of Indian Girls*, 10.

69. Government of India, *Report on the Progress of Education in India, Fourth Quinquennial Review, 1897–1898 to 1901–1902*, Table 61, 106; *Report on the Progress of Education in India, Fifth Quinquennial Review, 1902–1907*, Table 174, 134; and *Report on the Progress of Education in India, Sixth Quinquennial Review*, Table 161, 285.

70. Henry S. Olcott, *The Poor Pariah* (Adyar: Theosophical Society, 1902), 16–17; Raman, *Getting Girls to School*, 160–66.

71. *Report of the Olcott Panchama Free Schools*, December 1, 1909–November 30, 1910 (Adyar: Theosophical Society Press, 1910), 3; C. Kofel, "Education of the Depressed Classes, Particularly in Southern India" (Adyar: 1913), handwritten report of the Superintendent of Olcott Panchama Free Schools.

72. R. K. Prabhu and U. R. Rao, *The Mind of Mahatma Gandhi* (1945; repr., Ahmedabad: Navajivan Trust Publishing House, 1967); B. R. Nanda, *Mahatma Gandhi: A Biography* (New Delhi: Oxford University Press, 1958); Joan Bondurant, *Conquest of Violence* (Princeton: Princeton University Press, 1988); Suzanne H. Rudolph and Lloyd I. Rudolph, *Gandhi: The Traditional Roots of Charisma*, 2nd ed. (Chicago: University of Chicago Press, 1983); Judith Brown, *Gandhi's Rise to Power* (London: Cambridge University Press, 1972); Judith Brown, *Gandhi and Civil Disobedience* (London: Cambridge University Press, 1977); Judith Brown, *Gandhi: Prisoner of Hope* (New Haven: Yale University Press, 1989); Dennis Dalton,

Mahatma Gandhi: Nonviolent Power in Action (New York: Columbia University Press, 1993); Stanley Wolpert, *Gandhi's Passion: The Life and Legacy of Mahatma Gandhi* (New York: Oxford University Press, 2001); Louis Fischer, *Gandhi: His Life and Message for the World* (New York: New American Library, 1954); Erik H. Erikson, *Gandhi's Truth: On the Origins of Militant Nonviolence* (New York: W. W. Norton & Co., 1969).

73. Suma Chitnis, "Feminism: Indian Ethos and Indian Convictions," in *Feminism in India,* ed. Chaudhuri, 8–25; Kamla Bhasin and Nighat Said Khan, "Some Questions on Feminism and Its Relevance in South Asia," in *Feminism in India,* ed. Chaudhuri, 3–7.

74. K. Sudarshana Rao, "Hindu Social Reform," in *Hindu Social Progress,* ed. Garu, 89–90; Maitrayee Chaudhuri, "The Indian Women's Movement," in *Feminism in India,* ed. Chaudhuri, 117–33.

75. Shahid Amin, "The Making of the Mahatma," in *Subaltern Studies 3,* ed. Ranajit Guha (New Delhi: Oxford University Press, 1984), 1–55; David Arnold, *Gandhi: Profiles in Power* (Harlow, U.K.: Longman and Pearson Education, 2001); Partha Chatterjee, *Nationalist Thought and the Colonial World* (Minneapolis: University of Minnesota Press, 1993); D. C. Ahir, *Gandhi and Ambedkar* (New Delhi: Blumoon Publishers, 1995).

76. Sarojini Naidu, "Presidential Address to the Ahmedabad Students' Conference, 1922," in *Women Writing in India,* ed. Tharu and Lalitha, 1:335–40, *vide,* 337–38.

77. Partha Chatterjee, "The Nation and Its Women," in *The Nation and Its Fragments: Colonial and Post-Colonial Histories* (New Delhi: Oxford University Press, 1995), 116–34; Chatterjee, "The Nationalist Resolution of the Women's Question," 233–53; Sumit Sarkar, *A Critique of Colonial India* (Calcutta: Papyrus, 1985), 1–17, 71–76; Chakravarti, "Whatever Happened to the Vedic *Dasi?*" 27–87; Joanna Liddle and Rama Joshi, *Daughters of Independence: Gender, Caste and Class* (New Brunswick, New Jersey: Rutgers University, 1986).

78. Chatterjee, *The Nation and Its Fragments,* 127–30.

79. Raman, *Getting Girls to School,* 19–21, 50–54, 166–69.

80. Bina Agarwal, "The Idea of Gender Equality: From Legislative Vision to Everyday Family Practice," in *India: Another Millennium?* ed. Romila Thapar (New Delhi: Penguin Books, 2000), 41–42.

81. Ibid., 39.

82. Chatterjee, *The Nation and Its Fragments,* 117.

83. Raman and Surya, *A. Madhaviah,* x, 18–19, 25–31.

84. Quotation in Sumit Sarkar, *Modern India, 1885–1947* (Madras: Macmillan India, 1983), 70.

85. Cited in Hay, *Sources of Indian Tradition: Modern India and Pakistan,* 2:104–9.

86. Hafeez Malik, "Sayyid Ahmed Khan and the Aligarh Movement," in *Encyclopedia of India,* ed. Stanley Wolpert (Detroit and New York: Thomson & Gale, 2006), 4:11–14.

87. Barbara Daly Metcalf, "Islamic Reform and Islamic Women: Maulana Thanawi's *Jewelry of Paradise,*" in *Moral Conduct and Authority,* ed. Metcalf, 184–95; Minault, *Secluded Scholars,* 62–72; and Minault, "Other Voices, Other Rooms," 108–24.

88. Cited by Minault, "Women, Legal Reform and Muslim Identity in South Asia," 2–3.

89. Lateef, *Muslim Women in India*, 62.

90. Gail Minault, "Sisterhood or Separatism? The All-India Muslim Ladies' Conference and the Nationalist Movement," in *The Extended Family*, ed. Minault, 83–108.

91. Minault, *Secluded Scholars*, 19–31.

92. Michael H. Fisher, "Representing 'His' Women: Mirza Abu Talib Khan's 1801 'Vindication of the Liberties of Asian Women,' " *The Indian Economic and Social History Review* 37, no. 2 (2000): 215–37, *vide*, 226–29.

93. Minault, *Secluded Scholars*, 18–19.

94. Ibid., 188.

95. Sayyid Mahmoud, *A History of English Education in India (1781–1893)* (Aligarh: Mohammedan Anglo-Oriental College, 1895), 37, 59.

96. My research in Muslim prayer offerings at the sixteenth-century Sufi *dargah* to *pir* Miran Sahib and his wife Sultana Bibi at Nagur (Nagapattinam), Tamil Nadu. Like priests at temples, Muslim clerics offer personalized Tamil and Arabic prayers to devotees regardless of sect. Devotees offer flowers, fruits, coconuts, a form of ash, and sometimes meat to the saints' tombs. The informational booklet describes this as *bhakti*, a Hindu term used also by Christian and Muslim converts. Raman, "Popular Pujas in Public Places," 165–98, *vide*, 168, 189 n. 3. Similar cultural borrowings form one theme in Bayly, *Saints, Goddesses and Kings*.

97. Minault, "Other Voices, Other Rooms," 108–24.

98. Ali, *The Meaning of the Illustrious Qur'an.*

99. Minault, *Secluded Scholars*, 62–95.

100. Azra Asghar Ali, *The Emergence of Feminism among Indian Muslim Women 1920–1947* (Karachi: Oxford University Press, 2000), 214–15.

101. Ray, *Early Feminists of Colonial India*, 20–21.

102. Raman, *Getting Girls to School*, 157–60.

103. Minault, *Secluded Scholars*, 183–87.

104. Attia Hosain, *Sunlight on a Broken Column* (New Delhi: Penguin, 1961).

105. Ali, *The Emergence of Feminism among Indian Muslim Women*, 147–51.

106. Lateef, *Muslim Women in India*, 66–73, 94.

107. Ali, *The Emergence of Feminism among Indian Muslim Women*, 152–61. Also Ramala Baxmulla, "Need for Change in the Muslim Personal Law Relating to Divorce in India," in *Problems of Muslim Women in India*, ed. Engineer, 18–29; Sherebanu Malik, "Divorce in Indian Islam," in *Problems of Muslim Women in India*, ed. Engineer, 30–33; and Appendix II, "Revised Memorandum by the Muslim Women's Research and Action Front to the Committee on Proposed Reforms to the Muslim Personal Law, 1987," in *Problems of Muslim Women in India*, ed. Engineer, 183–92.

108. Ali, *The Emergence of Feminism among Indian Muslim Women*, 144–45.

109. *Salana Report: All-India Muslim Ladies Conference at Hyderabad, February 1929*, cited by Ali, *The Emergence of Feminism among Indian Muslim Women*, 144–45, 163 n. 62; and Lateef, *Muslim Women in India*, 66–73.

110. *The Indian Ladies' Magazine* 3, no. 3 (October 1929): 145, cited by Ali, *The Emergence of Feminism among Indian Muslim Women*, 146, 163 n. 67.

111. Minault, "Sisterhood or Separatism?" 83–108.

112. Forbes, *Women in India,* 198–99.

113. Memorandum of Rajkumari Amrit Kaur, Dr. Muthulakshmi Reddi, Mrs. Hamid Ali to the AIWC, WIA, and NCWI from London, August 9, 1933, in "All-India Women's Conference Papers," File no. 10 (NMML).

114. Forbes, *Women in Modern India,* 198–201.

115. Suruchi Thapar-Björket, *Women in the Indian National Movement: Unseen Faces and Unheard Voices, 1930–42* (New Delhi and Thousand Oaks: Sage Publications, 2006), 96–97.

4

FEMINISTS AND NATIONALISTS

Patriotism is not a thing divorced from real life. It is the flame that
burns within the soul, a gem-like flame that cannot be extinguished.
The Congress-League scheme is a little thing. If you are not united
and earnest, even that little is too much of a burden for you to sustain,
but if you are united, if you forget your community and think of the
nation, if you forget your city and think of the province, if you forget
you are a Hindu and remember the Musalman, if you forget you are
a Brahmin and remember the Panchaman, then and then alone will
India progress.

Sarojini Naidu, 1917[1]

SISTERS, MATRIARCHS, WIVES, AND WIDOWS

Unlike women's earlier resistances to patriarchy, modern feminism
attempted to realign the gender hierarchy through programs to educate the
sisterhood, emancipate the nation, and fight for equal rights in the
democratic state.[2] Feminist and nationalist identities crystallized during the
nineteenth century from social angst over problems that affected women.
The fearful shadows of child marriage, debilitating pregnancies, and possible death fell upon girls while they played hopscotch, hide-and-seek, and
board games with conch shells and beads. Education was haphazard, as
the lucky imbibed Sanskrit verses (*slokas*), epic legends, and household rules
from mothers and aunts, but others languished in ignorance, prey to superstitions. Working women toiled in fields and huts with no time for study.
A mother's death was a catastrophe that brought other misfortunes, as
described by A. Madhaviah in *Muthumeenakshi* (1903), a Tamil novella
later published in a reform journal.[3] Celibate widows lived in perpetual
mourning as household drudges preyed upon by lechers, but discarded by
family and caste if they sought affection.[4] The bright spots for a married
woman were motherhood, friends' visits, *bhakti* songs, and festivals when
she decorated the home with tracings of rice powder (*rangoli, kolam*).

In 1899, an anonymous woman described the effects of child marriage and widowhood in the journal *Mathar Manoranjani* (Brightener of Women's Minds):

> Educated people outwardly revile the custom of child-marriages, but marry off their own daughters who are children. Wherever there are child marriages, there are child widows. The homes of astrologers and priests swarm with child wives and widows. Perhaps God is punishing them for performing the marriages of the innocent children of others! Fathers, mothers, elders! Stop this iniquity! Why do you push your offspring into a well with your hands! Why are your houses full of widows? Why don't you recognize the force of reason?[5]

Rank and education did not preclude such suffering. In her 1906 inaugural address to the Ladies' Social Conference, which Ramabai Ranade (1862–1924) had earlier established with her husband M. G. Ranade, the young widow reformer described herself as the unsullied floral offering to God (*nirmalya*) whose touch alone granted grace.[6] Christian missionaries and Muslims argued that conversion alleviated the widow's plight, but their women also endured some harsh restrictions. Thus, the talented Christian widow and first woman graduate from Madras University remained celibate and wore mourning till her death. Kamala had married educationist Samuel Sattianadhan, only to become a widow at the age of 27. She had ironically lauded Vedic women's rights and their abject condition in her time in an article, "Position of Women in Ancient and Modern India" (1901), for *Indian Social Reform* journal.[7] Her daughter wrote:

> It was a tragedy to Kamala that as a widow she could not wear flowers in her hair, as is the custom in South India. For some years after the death of her husband she dressed only in white, black, gray and dark red. But when we (children) grew up, we insisted on her wearing brighter colors, and as she disliked posing as a martyr under any circumstances, she willingly acquiesced. Flowers, however, she could never bring herself to don in her hair, thereby pandering to the strong convention prevailing that widows should not wear them. She always bemoaned this sad custom but nevertheless followed it herself.[8]

In one respect, a gendered world fostered a feminist network of sisterly companions (*sakhis*) and motherly mentors. Such solidarity was nurtured by Hindu, Muslim, and Christian women during celebrations, childbirth, and sickness. Feminists now projected this woman-centered view onto the national or international canvas of sisterhood, transforming patriarchal constraints into empowering ties binding all women.[9] Moreover, the educated feminist matriarch emerged as the natural leader in a culture where

motherhood elevated even the youngest daughter-in-law.[10] All Indian
women aspired eventually to be a mother-in-law whose opinions mattered
to the family.

The first women's society was the Arya Mahila Samaj (Aryan Women's
Society) formed by Pandita Ramabai Saraswati in Maharashtra ca. 1883.
Some early local groups were the Tamil Mathar Sangam (Tamil Women's
Organization) which met in Madras (1906) and Kanchipuram (1907,
1914);[11] the Gujarati Stree Mandal in Ahmedabad (1908);[12] and the Banga
Mahila Samaj (1909) and the Aghorekamini Roy's Nari Samiti (Women's
Society, ca. 1910) in Bengal to help women workers on tea plantations.[13]
In 1910, Sarala Devi Chaudhurani (1872–1945), daughter of composer
Swarnakumari Devi, started the nationalist Bharat Stri Mahamandal (Indian
Women's Great Circle) in north India.[14] Local sectarian groups included
Stri Zarthoshti Mandal (Parsi Women's Circle) in 1903 in Bombay;[15]
Anjuman-e-Khawatin-e-Islam (Muslim Women's Conference) established
in 1914 by the radical writer Rokeya Sakhawat Hossain (1880–1932);[16]
and the Ladies' Auxiliary of the YMCA, later known as the Young Women's
Christian Association (YWCA).[17] Using the core membership of the Madras
society and the institutional framework of the Theosophical Society (TS),
the first secular national women's group, the Women's Indian Association
(WIA), began in 1917.[18] Two later organizations were the broad-based
nationalist All India Women's Conference (AIWC; 1927) and the loyalist
National Council of Women in India (NCWI; 1925) supported by the
British.[19]

Yet, Indian women activists were initially reluctant to use the term
"feminist," which had negative connotations in late Victorian culture,
which caricatured feminists as "desexed" or "unnaturally" prone to lesbian
desires for resisting male dominance. These ideas spilled over to colonial
India where elite nationalists feared that feminists would destroy the joint
family and its gender mores. Some Indian feminists thus painstakingly demonstrated their domestic loyalties and refined "womanliness" as a survival
strategy for their organizations.[20] Space precludes the retelling of all their
narratives, but these biographies give a glimpse of some early educators,
writers, suffragists, and nationalists, categories that were not mutually
exclusive. The first feminist stirrings were expressed in literature, and by
teaching girls, forming clubs to assist less fortunate women, and supporting
female suffrage and Indian freedom.

When the Pakistan movement gathered momentum around 1930, Muslim
women faced the dilemma of choosing between a secular sisterhood and
their male relatives' agenda in the ML. Despite this, many educated Muslim
and Hindu women forged a bond that bridged sect, class, and caste in their
struggle for suffrage and to pass laws favorable to women. Many worked
as doctors, teachers, lawyers, and nurses to ameliorate the lives of women
in slums and villages. When the idea of an international sisterhood gathered

adherents, Indian feminists also cemented bonds with counterparts in colonialist regimes and in the West. A revolutionary band of non-pacifist, socialist communist women established contacts with Russians.[21] Indian feminism continues to evolve after independence in 1947 by addressing problems like dowry, rape, inflation, environmental decay, tribal displacement, and globalization.

FEMINIST REFORMERS

Savitribai Phule (1831–97)

The first modern woman humanitarian was Savitribai Phule, who was born into a middle-class farming family in Naigaum village near Satara, Maharashtra. At the age of nine, Savitribai was married to 13-year-old Jotiba Phule (d. 1890), a member of the lower ranking Mali caste of flower gardeners. Educated in village and missionary schools, Jotiba encouraged his young wife also to attend the village school so that she could later teach girls. However, his father was furious that the couple had broken the convention that forbade girls to attend a public school. When he threatened to evict them unless Savitribai desisted, Jotiba refused, and the couple left their family home, thus striking their first blow against unjust mores.[22] Jotiba was inspired by the revolutionary Maratha emperor Shivaji (d. 1680), George Washington (d. 1799), and Thomas Paine who advocated resistance to tyranny in *Rights of Man* (1791).[23] In 1848 when the lower ranking Jotiba was prevented from joining his high-caste friend's wedding procession, he began zealously to fight caste discrimination. Jotiba focused especially on helping the Mang and Mahar castes of Dalits, then called untouchables.

Savitribai attended teacher training classes with Fatima Sheik, a Muslim woman who became her friend and colleague. Savitribai founded the first girls' school in Pune in 1848, her nine students belonging to various castes. Although the village folk heaped insults and physical abuse when she walked to and from the school, she and Jotiba established five other schools in Pune. In 1851 the Phules began their first school for Dalits among whom they lived and shared a well, so that high-caste villagers regarded them also as Dalits. The Phules also assisted widows and promoted their remarriage. Their first major step for widow relief was taken when Jotiba rescued a pregnant, *brahman* widow who tried to commit suicide. As no one wished to help her, they brought her to their home for her confinement. As they had no children of their own, they adopted the boy Yasavantrao who later became a doctor.[24]

The Phules shared a common vision on social change. If Jotiba was the force, Savitribai was his active colleague and staunch defender. They organized the first strike against barbers who performed the ritual tonsure of widows, and they assisted other raped widows who were pregnant and destitute. In 1873, Jotiba and Savitribai founded Satyashodhak Mandal to help the needy, irrespective of caste. They were probably inspired by the medieval woman *bhakti* saint Muktabai whose Varkari sub-sect defied the caste system. In an era when men and women feared to move out of the rutted path of convention, Savitribai was unique as she was guided by her conscience. She and Jotiba's revolutionary ideology preceded that of Dr. Ambedkar (1891–1956), the twentieth-century Dalit legalist and reformer. When her affectionate, but conservative brother challenged their work with Dalits, she chastised him and defended Jotiba as her lord whom she helped to do "God's work." Savitribai was ready to break many conventions, but not that of a loyal, even subservient wife when she wrote:

Bhau [brother], your point of view is extremely narrow and, moreover, your reason has been weakened by the teachings of the Brahmins. You fondle even animals like the cow and the goat... But you consider the mangs and mahars, who are as human as you, untouchables... Learning has great value. One who masters it loses his lowly status and achieves the higher one. My master [swami] is a godlike man. No one can ever equal him in this world... Jotiba confronts the dastardly brahmins, fights with them and teaches the mangs and mahars because he believes they are human beings and must be able to live as such. So they must learn. That is why I also teach them. What is so improper about that? Yes, we teach the girls, the women, the mangs and the mahars... It's such a pleasant task and I feel immeasurably happy.[25]

Savitribai's 41 poems published in 1854 as *Kavyaphule* (Poetic Blossoms) had a didactic message on shunning caste and educating girls and boys. When Jotiba died, she published *Bhavankashi Subodha Ratnakar* (Ocean of Pure Gems), a prose biography about his legacy. The couple received awards from the British Raj for their humanitarian work in the devastating 1876–77 Deccan drought and famine.[26] When cholera struck in 1897, widowed Savitribai helped its victims until she finally contracted the fatal disease.

Pandita Ramabai Saraswati (1858–1922)

The foremother of Indian feminism is Pandita Ramabai Saraswati who challenged both Hindu and British colonial patriarchs in her efforts to educate widows and girls. Like her friend Ramabai Ranade, Pandita Ramabai belonged to the Chitpavan *brahman* caste of Maharashtra. However, she was an unusual, radical female scholar who not only married a lower-caste lawyer from Bihar but also adopted Christianity in 1883. Her conversion occurred in the wake of a spiritual crisis following the loss of her entire natal family, widowhood at the age of 22, and the suicide of a female companion on a ship bound for England. Pandita Ramabai's candid views and refusal to toe the line demarcated by male liberals led to her alienation from the reform community. Only recently have feminists resurrected her pioneering work, although its scope was limited by her ostracism by the orthodox whose very widows she wished to help. This message was understood by D. K. Karve and Sahodari (Sister) Subbalakshmi (1886–1969) who pragmatically worked with caste families so that they could educate their widowed daughters.

Life and Achievements

Ramabai's parents were the scholarly Ananta Sastri Dongre and his second wife Lakshmi. Dongre had tried to teach his first wife before she died, and he remarried at the age of 40. Lakshmi was then nine years old, and her father was impressed by his scholarship. Dongre instruction of Lakshmi in Sanskrit texts led to his ostracism by the *brahmans*. Dongre and Lakshmi were forced to resettle in the Gangamul forests of Karnataka where Ramabai, a brother Srinivas, and a sister were born. The family live peripatetically, as the father eked out a living from lectures on the *Puranas* in villages.[27] Ramabai describes her early studies with her mother, a scholarly emphasis that allowed her to elude child marriage. She wrote:

> When I was about eight years old my mother began to teach me and continued to do so until I was about fifteen years of age. During these years she succeeded in training my mind so that I might be able to carry on my education with very little aid from others.[28]

Ramabai's parents and sister all died in the 1877 Deccan famine. She and Srinivas continued on their lecture tours until word of her Sanskrit erudition reached scholars in Calcutta. She was invited to Bengal and awarded the title of Saraswati in honor of the Hindu goddess of wisdom. She became friendly with Keshab Chandra Sen, leader of the BS whose members advocated women's study of the *Vedas*. Pandita Ramabai was attracted to the BS as an enlightened Hindu sect, but a series of personal tragedies changed her life. The tragic death of her brother in 1880 led her to marry his close friend Bipin Behari Das Medhvi, a *shudra* lawyer from Bihar with whom she shared ideals on girls' education. After the birth of their daughter Manorama in 1881, Medhvi died in an epidemic. The bereft young widow returned to Maharashtra, resolving to teach widows.

In Pune she joined the PS, and at public lectures spoke out against child marriage and advised women to study Sanskrit and vernacular Hindu texts.[29] Supported by M. G. Ranade and his wife Ramabai Ranade, Pandita Ramabai started the women's club, Arya Mahila Sabha, which had centers in smaller towns. She and her friend Ramabai Ranade also studied English with a woman missionary at home. Around this time, Pandita Ramabai became unhappy over some PS reformers whose oratorical platitudes did not match the effectiveness of their work with women. She had admired the programs of the BS and was so impressed by Christian missionary work that she readily believed the Anglican Reverend Goreh who misinformed her that the BS "was not taught by the Vedas as I had thought, but it was the Christian faith."

Pandita Ramabai wished to study medicine in England, and to finance this journey, she wrote *Stri Dharma Niti* (Morals for Women) in 1881. In this first book, Ramabai urged women to become more independent of men. She left for England in 1883, declaring that she would not convert, but the suicide of her young woman friend on board ship produced a spiritual crisis. Eager for a religious community that would promote women's advancement, she sought baptism upon landing in England. However, when a woman missionary at Wantage expressed disgust over her daughter Manorama who scooped food with her fingers while seated on the ground, Ramabai retorted, "I want her to be one of us, and love our country people as one of them."[30] Moreover, her increasing deafness cut short medical studies, and Ramabai returned home to her Indian women friends like Ramabai Ranade.[31]

Missionaries often tried to convert high-caste widows or talented women like her cousin Anandibai Joshi, India's first woman doctor. Anandibai resisted them and the pressure of her recently baptized husband. Orthodox Indians attacked Pandita Ramabai's apostasy as abetting the colonial enemy, and even her former supporter M. G. Ranade believed she had become too Westernized.[32] If she lost her progressive friends, the West lauded her baptism, although Pandita Ramabai despised Anglophiles and the colonial hierarchy. She nearly ruptured her relationship with the Anglican Church by probing into its theology and organization.[33] She remained sharply critical of Hindu misogynist customs but drew attention to spiritual similarities between Vedic monism and Christian monotheism. In 1885, she described these thoughts in a letter to missionary Dorothea Beale at St. Mary's Home in Wantage, England:

> Is not the same God who dwells in Christ dwelling in you and me, yet can we ever say that our lower nature can touch Him? No, the Upanishads—the revelation of God to the Hindoos, if I may call them so—teach that the Great Brahma which is in a manifest atom, yet is in His nature unbounded, and most pure, dwelling in everything, yet untouched by the lower nature, just as the lotus leaf, though it grows in water, yet is not wetted by the water.[34]

In a letter to Ramabai's mentor Sister Geraldine, Beale feared that she would "easily pass into Unitarianism."[35] When chided by the Church, Ramabai proudly retorted that she was unlikely to accept Christian patriarchy after having rejected Hinduism for its inequalities.[36] She wrote:

I am, it is true, a member of the Church of Christ but I am not bound to accept every word that falls from the lips of priests or bishops ... Obedience ... to the Word of God is quite different from perfect obedience to priest only. I have just, with great effort, freed myself from the yoke of the Indian priestly tribe, so I am not at present willing to place myself under another similar yoke.[37]

Pandita Ramabai was angered also by the colonial state which did not educate women or safeguard their rights.[38] In 1882, she informed the Hunter Educational Commission that the extreme shortage of women doctors jeopardized the health of sick women who rejected male doctors. Her recommendations led to the Women's Medical Movement led by Lady Dufferin, wife of the Viceroy.[39] However, Ramabai blamed the British for racist cultural arrogance and impotence in educating and helping women. During the plague epidemic in Bombay in 1897, she protested to Governor Sandhurst that it was callous to expect "modest" women to submit to male doctors, and chided him for the special treatment given to European women in clinics and hospitals. Sandhurst dismissed her protests as "grossly inaccurate."[40] In 1892, when a prison sentence was accorded to a young woman Rakhmabai for refusing her husband's conjugal demands, Pandita Ramabai bitterly remarked:

We cannot blame the English Government for not defending a helpless woman; it is only fulfilling its agreement with the male population of India ... Should England serve God by protecting a helpless woman against the powers and principalities of ancient institutions, Mammon would surely be displeased, and British profit and rule in India might be endangered thereby.[41]

In 1887, Ramabai wrote *The High Caste Hindu Woman* to pay for a visit to the United States to attend her cousin Anandibai Joshi's medical school graduation. At Philadelphia, Anandibai's successful treatment of Ramabai's daughter Manorama cemented their bond, despite differences over religion. Ramabai's new book on the decline of Indian women's conditions after the Vedic era financed her lecture tours across America. Evangelicals and British colonials lauded the book as proof of the West's civilizing mission, and Ramabai took note of their praise in her lectures, which financed her plans for a girls' school in India. She informed her readers and audience that she wished to educate the "half-caste widow" as a teacher, nurse, or doctor. Her popularity is evident in the numbers of "Ramabai Associations" that sprang up in Boston in 1887 and across the east coast. They helped to implement her goals.

She founded Sharda Sadan, a widows' home and school at Chowpatty, Bombay in 1889. She named it after the Hindu goddess Saraswati (or Sharada), indicating her intention to educate, not proselytize, supported by trustees like Ranade and scholar R. G. Bhandarkar. Financial difficulties led her to move her school to more conservative Pune where cultural nationalist B. G. Tilak accused Ramabai of converting Hindu widows in his journal *Kesari.* The trustees began an investigation and cleared Ramabai; conservative parents withdrew their daughters. Even progressive, friendly reformers now severed their ties with Pandita Ramabai. However, she did not give up easily, and in 1896 started Mukti Sadan (Freedom Institute) for girls with her daughter Manorama. At Mukti Sadan in rural Khedgaon, Ramabai openly embraced Christian festivals, rites, and subjects, but she had lost opportunities to assist high-caste Hindu widows. The school catered to Christians and low-caste Hindus orphaned by famine and epidemics. Ramabai made one last effort to help Hindu widows by touring Brindavan and Benares where widows lived in temples, exploited by priests and pilgrims, but she did not achieve much success here. In 1919, the British awarded Pandita Ramabai the prestigious Kaiser-I-Hind for her service, although she scorned their racist hierarchies and cultural ignorance. A year after Manorama's death in 1921, Ramabai died leaving an enormous legacy for women.[42]

Tarabai Shinde (ca. 1850–1910)

In 1882, Tarabai Shinde wrote "Stri Purush Tulana" (A Comparison between Women and Men), a satirical protest against elite men who supported the court sentence meted to the *brahman* widow Vijayalakshmi for killing her illegitimate child in Surat, Gujarat.[43] This 40-page essay is one of the earliest modern Indian feminist works. Jotiba Phule admired her free spirit and defended Tarabai's booklet in an 1885 issue of *Satsar,* his journal for Satyashodhak Mandal. Tarabai's trenchant comments are at variance with her self-description as a "powerless dull woman, prisoner in a Maratha household." Probably born into a high-caste family, she was educated in Marathi, Sanskrit, and English. Her angry feminism may have resulted from a cold marital household. She seems to have had little regard for her ineffective husband, and they apparently had no children.[44] Tarabai boldly attacked marriages of convenience, as men bought rich wives to further their careers, and then neglected them, so that the women were inevitably disappointed. Tarabai accused men of lust and infidelity, and defended an outcaste prostitute as an innocent woman seduced by a married man. With biting wit and a compelling logic, she demanded conjugal fairness so that women could choose their spouses. She wrote:

> You would not like a bad, ugly, cruel, uneducated wife, full of vices; why then should a wife like such a husband? Just you desire a good wife, she also longs for a good husband.[45]

In another section, she accused men of hypocrisy when they accused women of lust, greed, and subterfuge although the prisons overflowed with men:

> You men are all very clever, it's true. But you just go and look in one of our prisons—you'll find it so stuffed full of your countrymen you can hardly put your foot down. Oh yes, they're all very clever there, aren't they? One's there for making counterfeit notes, another for taking bribes, another for running off with someone else's wife, another for taking part in a rebellion, another for poisoning, another for treason, another for giving false evidence, another for setting up a raja and destroying the people, yet another for doing murder. Of course, it's these great works of thought that make the government offer you a room so reverently in their palatial prisons! What women do things like these? How many prisons are filled with women?[46]

Tarabai attacked men's false adherence to *brahman* laws and rites, and their love of legends marked by male lust and trickery, so that even God seemed to have deserted women. She wrote:

> What he [God] gave you was just one great intelligence—he made you the greatest and best of all forms of life in the universe. So you should behave in a way that suits this high rank. But that would be hoping for too much, wouldn't it?[47]

Tarabai ended with a poignant prayer exhorting women to remain virtuous, "to conduct themselves properly," and "to live up to the name of Lakshmi." She ended with these words:

> So I pray to the great God who disposes over all, who is eternal, true and merciful, a river of compassion, a sea of forgiveness, brother of the poor. I pray women may shine like lightning by means of their conduct as pativratas (chaste loyal wives) in their husbands' families and their own.[48]

Rokeya Sakhawat Hossain (1880–1932)

The Muslim feminist writer Rokeya Sakhawat Hossain's achievements are quite astounding, as she was raised in an aristocratic *zenana*, yet started girls' schools. Her family of landed *ashraf* émigrés from Persia in the 1850s ensured that sons received an extensive education. However, her father insisted that Rokeya and her sister Karimunissa learn the *Qur'an* largely by rote and acquire enough Urdu to read Muslim guidelines on female decorum. However, Rokeya shaped her own destiny in defiance of his injunctions by requesting her elder brother Ibrahim Saber to teach her Bengali and English by candlelight. In gratitude, Rokeya later dedicated her Bengali novel *Padmarag* to Ibrahim.[49] Her first journal essays were "Pipasha" (Thirst, 1901) and "Alankar Na Badge of Slavery" (1903) on jewelry as chains of bondage.[50] Two volumes in *Motichur* (Pearl Dust, 1905) included the essays "Ardhangi" (Female Half) and "Borka" (*Burqah*), the women's cloak worn in public. Rokeya's hatred of *pardah* seclusion was explicit in her final set of essays, *Abarodhbhasini* (Secluded Women), in the journal *Muhamadhi* (1928–30).[51] She described her unpleasant experiences with *pardah* from the age of five. So indoctrinated was she that when even women visited their *zenana*, she would run "helter-skelter as if I were in mortal fear of my life" so that they did not see her unveiled.[52]

Eighteen-year-old Rokeya married Sayyid Sakhawat Hossain, a magistrate many years senior to her. She moved to Bihar where Sakhawat Hossain encouraged her to study and enjoyed hearing her read aloud in English.[53] After his death 11 years later, Rokeya used a part of her inheritance to start a girls' school in Bhagalpur, Bihar, and she now spent her time writing her first Bengali works. However, a property tussle with her stepdaughter forced her to leave for Calcutta in 1911, but here too she started a girls' school. She also cofounded Anjuman-e-Khawatin-e-Islam (Association for Muslim Women) in 1915 with Amir-Unissa, mother of Begam Shah Nawaz Khan of the NCWI. Rokeya continued to write until her death at the age of 53.[54]

Rokeya's works demonstrate her challenges to male dictates on female clothing, seclusion, education, and marriage. She used logic and personal experience to argue her case, rather than Western feminist and other literature. Her most famous work was the pungent short story, *Sultana's Dream* (1905), depicting a topsy-turvy universe in which men were secluded in segregated male rooms (*mardana*), and women ran public affairs. Rokeya's inspiration stemmed almost exclusively from Bengali literature, and the focus was solely upon Indian Muslim culture. Although she wrote *Sultana's Dream* first in English, and then translated it into Bengali, it is likely that she had not read Mary Wollstonecraft's *A Vindication of the Rights of Women* (1792), or Olympe de Gouge's *Declaration of the Rights of Women* (1791) in French.[55] However, three decades later in 1932, Rokeya left an unfinished work, "Narir Adhikar" (Women's Rights), whose title indicates that by now she was familiar of women's long struggle for rights in the West.[56] *Sultana's Dream* emerged from her experiences in running a girls' school in Bihar, when she had reassured parents by transporting their daughters in *burqah* to class in covered carriages. However, the public regarded her indictment of *pardah* as too extreme. Rokeya stated that it was contrary to the *Qur'an* and jeopardized women's mental and physical health. She called *pardah* an insidious "silent killer like carbon monoxide gas." She described how her aunt died on a train, unable to break *pardah*'s strict rules by soliciting help from men.[57] She used satire and the first person singular to describe her young heroine's dream walk in another world where the gender order was reversed, and her talks with the older woman Sister Sara. She wrote:

> I became very curious to know where the men were. I met more than a hundred women while walking there, but not a single man. "Where are the men?" I asked her. "In their proper places, where they ought to be." "Pray let me know what you mean by 'their proper places.'" "Oh, I see my mistake, you cannot know our customs, as you were never here before. We shut our men indoors." "Just as we are in the zenana?"
>
> "Exactly so." "How funny." I burst into a laugh. Sister Sara laughed too. "But, dear Sultana, how unfair it is to shut in the harmless women and let loose the men." "Why? It is not safe for us to come out of the zenana, as we are naturally weak." "Yes, it is not safe so long as there are men about the streets, nor is it so when a wild animal enters the marketplace."[58]

Sister Subbalakshmi (1886–1969)

Born into an enlightened *brahman* family, R. S. Subbalakshmi Ammal was a pioneer educationist of widows in colonial Madras.[59] Her students and coworkers affectionately called her *Sahodari* (Sister) Subbalakshmi.[60] In an era when high-caste female education was dependent on family whim, her father, who was a college professor, supervised her education, supported by her mother and a widowed aunt (or Chithi) Valambal Ammal. Subbalakshmi was married before puberty but widowed at the age of 11 when her bridegroom died in an epidemic. Subbalakshmi's family was determined not to let her languish in illiteracy, perennially tonsured, and in drab attire. They defied the censure of family and caste by moving to Madras city where she attended Presidency Convent Higher Secondary School. Although the nuns tried to convert this brilliant girl, her mother and Chithi instilled the *Bhagavad Gita,* so that she remained philosophical despite the burden of virgin widowhood. Subbalakshmi took comfort from the *Upanishads,* the *Gita,* and fervent Hindu *bhakti* saints. After winning gold medals at school, Subbalakshmi entered Madras Presidency College as a mathematics and botany major, graduating with a BA in 1912 as the first Hindu widow to receive this degree in Madras.[61]

Nearly 18 percent of the female population of Madras in 1910 consisted of widows.[62] Here Subbalakshmi began her first widows' home, aware of earlier efforts by Viresalingam Pantulu in Madras, D. K. Karve in Maharashtra, in the princely Mysore state (1907), and in Bangalore (1908). Her work began after the grieving parents of child widows requested her to start a school, after hearing of her graduation from college as the first *brahman* widow in Madras. Her first student Ammukutty was a child widow whose father approached Subbalakshmi to teach his daughter.[63] Subbalakshmi also began teaching at Presidency Convent, but despite minimal pay and proselytizing efforts of the nuns, she liked her former teachers. She knew that to help other caste widows, she would have to win the confidence of their conservative parents.

Her pragmatism enabled her venture to succeed and to attract the attention of Christina Lynch, a progressive Inspector of Government Girls' Schools. They jointly started a government teachers' training institute for widows, with a secular academic curriculum bolstered by Indian texts. On July 1, 1912, Sarada Widows' Ashram opened its doors, named for the goddess of wisdom. A later niece compared Subbalakshmi with Pandita Ramabai and their use of honorifics. While Christian Ramabai retained the Hindu title "Pandita," Hindu Subbalakshmi was endearingly known as "Sister" ("Sahodari"), a term used for Catholic nuns. Each drew strength from her religious beliefs but crossed cultural boundaries in order to serve other widows.[64]

Subbalakshmi became a beacon for women whose schooling had been curtailed by early marriage, like celebrated author Rajeshwari Padmanabhan whose pseudonym was "Anuthama."[65] Subbalakshmi also trained widows as teachers, the most famous being S. Chellammal, principal of Lady Sivaswamy Ayyar Girls' High School in Madras.[66] In January 1912, Subbalakshmi began Sarada Ladies Union (SLU) to promote intellectualism in women. A nationalist dedicated to women's rights, her post in a government school prevented her from being an active member of the WIA. However, as an unofficial colleague of WIA members, she assisted in their campaigns for women.[67] In 1919, Subbalakshmi started Sarada Vidyalaya school for destitute, unmarried girls. In 1921, she addressed the AIWC on more teacher training institutes and occupational programs that would induce parents to educate their daughters. She was respected by a broad spectrum of men and women conservatives and reformers, colonial officials, and nationalists. On July 28, 1928, SLU and WIA jointly hosted a public meeting to pledge support for Har Bilas Sarda's bill on child marriage and Hari Singh Gour's Age of Consent Bill, then being debated in the Central Legislative Council. Dr. Muthulakshmi Reddi took the first pledge, Subbalakshmi Ammal the second, and they were supported by Gandhian Ambujammal and by Rukmini Lakshmipathi.[68] In 1947, SLU was formally affiliated with the WIA. After India's independence, Subbalakshmi served on the Madras Legislative Council, a national and private icon to students and family.

WOMEN WRITERS

Despite constraints, women produced a corpus of remarkable literature using the prose genres of the novel, short story, essay, and biography to explore their turmoils and the contours of their lives. The late century saw a spate of journals in regional languages and in English. The authors included women from the literate middle class who resented educational discrimination and their plight as child brides and widows. The authors were Hindu, Christian, and Muslim women, but their writings are relatively free of sectarian prejudices. Instead, they evoke a broader sisterhood burdened by male laws and mores.

Rassundari Devi

The first notable Bengali woman writer was Rassundari Devi (born ca. 1810) whose *Amar Jiban* (My Life, 1876) is the first autobiography in that language. Its poignant elegance was recognized by gifted writer Rabindranath Thakur who first read it simply because its author was an elderly woman. However, Rassundari's unusual text preceded by 20 years the autobiography of his father Debendranath Thakur, writer and Brahma Samajist.[69] Rassundari Devi conquered her natural timidity by teaching herself to read and write. Her work is a paean to her religious faith, and her writing allowed to voice a subdued anger at injustice in her life. Rassundari Devi describes her mother as her one true friend and her silent grief at her death. She speaks of her "bondage" in marriage to an otherwise "likable man" who helped her to resist the cruelties meted out to daughters-in-law. In her hunger for study, she stealthily stole sheets of writing, which she taught herself to read without any help. She states simply that she worked long, arduous hours at servile chores, and that she had numerous children and duties, and describes her widowhood and tonsure as "more painful than death."[70] Self-deprecating and stoic, she corrected occasionally outbreaks of anger with such words:

> Wasn't it a matter to be regretted, that I had to go through all this humiliation just because I was a woman? Shut up like a thief, even trying to learn was considered an offense. It is such a pleasure to see the women today enjoying so much freedom. The parents of a single girl child take so much care to educate her. But we had to struggle so much for just that. The little that I have learned is only because God did me the favor.[71]

Swarnakumari Devi

Among the most astounding writers was Swarnakumari Devi of Bengal.[72] Daughter of Debendranath Thakur, Swarnakumari was married at the age of 13 but remained in close touch with her natal family. In 1878, she founded *Bharati* with her brothers Jyotindranath and Rabindranath Thakur, and she edited this journal for 30 years. A gifted artist, she composed over 25 works in a range of genres. She perfected the poetic of the *gatha* before

Rabindranath won the Nobel Prize for *Gitanjali* (Garland of Hymns), and to whom she addressed her first book of poems:

> "To My Younger Brother"
> Let me present these poems: carefully
> gleaned and strung
> To the most deserving person
> But you are so playful. I hope you will not
> Snap and scatter these flowers for fun.[73]

Swarnakumari published the first Bengali opera, *Basanta Utsav* (Spring Festival), which inspired Rabindranath's later work. Her first novel at the age of 18 was *Deep Nirban* (Snuffing Out of the Lamp), which received praises in contemporary journals. Two other novels, *Chinna Mukul* (Plucked Flower) and *Phuler Mala* (Flower Garland), were translated into English. She wrote historical novels about tribal revolts and the 1857 Mutiny, two popular farces, and several short stories. Although acclaimed by many, her younger brother's phenomenal fame eluded her.

Kripabai Sattianadhan

Other women writers paid respect to parents, brothers, and husbands for educating them. In return, they started girls' schools to refute the charge of women's intellectual inferiority. Christian Kripabai Sattianadhan (1862–94) and Kamala Sattianadhan both broke free of foreign missionary misconceptions to depict the real texture of south Indian women's lives. Before her premature death at 32, Kripabai wrote two English novels, namely the semiautobiographical *Saguna: The Story of Native Christian Life* (1886) and the fictional *Kamala: The Story of a Hindu Life* (1887). Both works testify to her ability to evoke picturesque images and Hindu characters without enveloping them with Christian rhetoric. Born into the first family of *brahman* converts in Bombay, Kripabai's faith was shaped by her mother Radhabai Khisty, while her elder brother Bhaskar directed her education. Intended for medical college in England, weak health compelled her to study at Madras Medical College as an early woman student. Despite her brilliance, she had to discontinue her studies because of ill health. Deeply chagrined, she married Samuel Sattianadhan, famed Tamil educationist and founder of the National Missionary Society. Kripabai taught girls and even started a school for Muslim girls in the hill station of Ootacamund.[74] In her first novel *Saguna*, Kripabai explored racism among European women missionaries and caste prejudices among Indian converts through the character who was her alter ego.[75] In *Kamala*, she sensitively portrayed a Hindu heroine's mystical philosophy, and social criticism of misogynist customs against widows.[76] Unfortunately, Kripabai's early death ended her promising career as writer of English novels, which revealed that this genre had easily adapted to its Indian environment.

Kamala Sattianadhan

Several years later, Samuel Sattianadhan married Kamala, daughter of Sivarama Krishnamma, a high-caste Telugu convert. Although a devout Christian, Kamala studied Sanskrit and Indian literature, and English, and graduated at 19 from Madras University. She was the first Indian woman to receive a BA in this province. Naturally ebullient, Kamala became famous as an educator of women and a writer of three novels, several sundry works, and the reform journal, *Indian Ladies' Magazine* (1901). Contributors to *Indian Ladies' Magazine* included nationalist Sarojini Naidu and British missionary Isabella Thoburn.[77] Widowed in 1906, Kamala educated her son and daughter in Indian Christian cultural values and formed a network with Christian women educators like Swarnam Appasamy and Mona Hensman.[78] These women also belonged to a larger circle of women activists who crossed sectarian boundaries to help indigent women in slums. They included the Hindu doctor Muthulakshmi Reddi and the Muslim doctor Rahamatunissa Begam who jointly founded Muslim Women's Association in 1928.[79] Kamala Sattianadhan reviewed Katherine Mayo's *Mother India* (1927), whose sensationalist indictment of India offended many nationalists.[80] This unpleasant controversy probably expedited the Sarda Act (1929) raising the age of marriage for girls to 14 years. Kamala Sattianadhan and Rokeya Sakhawat Hossain agreed that Mayo was insensitive to Indians, but they agreed with some of her allegations. Kamala also stated that biased patriotism would hinder Indians from redressing misogynist customs.[81] Kamala was an Honorary Magistrate in South India and served on the Central Advisory Board of Women's Education. She admired Gandhi's methods, and she started cooperative societies. She died after independence in 1950.[82]

Journal Writers

Other women's voices appeared in regional language journals started either by men or in conjunction with women. In Madras alone, 40 journals with reform themes were addressed solely to women or had a special section devoted only to women's issues. These vernacular journals fostered ideas of women's rights while fostering a regional language renaissance. In 1891, a Nagaratnam Pillai and his anonymous wife began the Tamil journal, *Penmathi Bodhini* (Women's Enlightenment). Two years later, *Chintamani* was dedicated to Tamil literary awakening, with stories on women's rights. In 1895, *Maharani* was started as the organ of the Madras Reform Association. In 1898, *Mathar Manoranjani* (Brightener of Women's Minds) provided quality reading for women, often by women. In the first issue of *Tamil Mathu* (Tamil Woman) in 1905, woman editor Ko. Svapneshwari stated that her goal was to provide excellent literature for women. She advised them that education prevented them from being duped of their property.[83]

Other women's journals emerged in this period across India. They included *Stree Subodh* (Women's Wisdom) in Gujarati (1901); the Hindi language *Bala Bodhini* (1874), Rameshwari Nehru's *Stree Darpan* (Women's Pride) in 1909 at Allahabad, and *Kumari Darpan* (Young Women's Pride). The most significant and successful was *Stree Darpan* whose women writers examined provocative issues like *pardah,* sexual exploitation, and marriages between older widowers and young girls. The journal also contained entertaining plays, stories, and poems.[84] In 1918, two British women Theosophists domiciled in South Asia founded *Stri Dharma,* the official organ of WIA, their chief contributions being to women's rights. Margaret Cousins (née Gillespie, 1878–1954) was a more ebullient suffragist and a strong believer in working-class rights. Her participation in Gandhi's freedom struggle led to her arrest, just as she was jailed earlier in Britain for joining the Irish Home Rule movement. Dorothy Jinarajadasa (née Graham), wife of a Sri Lankan Buddhist and Theosophist, was a founder of WIA, an editor of *Stri Dharma,* and a member of the first Indian women's suffrage deputation to the Viceroy.

Although aristocratic Muslim women wrote various pieces of literature, there was a spurt in Urdu women's journals after the Muslim middle class expanded in 1920. Moreover, initially, they had prescriptive articles by men for women, but later, the journals provided a forum for women to voice opinions on social issues and to disseminate information on political issues for the larger community. The first Urdu journal was *Akbar-E-Nisa* (Women's Newspaper) started in 1887 by *maulvi* Sayyid Ahmad for women's moral welfare. However, the first important paper was *Tahzib-E-Niswan* begun in 1898 by Mumtaz Ali and his wife Muhammadi Begam and later edited by his daughter Waheeda Begam.[85] There were few women writers until the Islamic separatism grew between 1930 and 1940, a popular editorial theme of "Woman, Not Slave," provoking debates on women in public roles.[86] Some women's papers like *Ismat* (Chastity) were published and written by men using a feminine pseudonym, and this encouraged women to express their views in print. In 1904, Sheik Abdullah began *Khatoon,* the most successful Urdu women's journal. His aim was to encourage women to speak bravely on a broad range of subjects. Sheik Abdullah urged them to study geography, history, and mathematics equally with men. Its women authors formed a Muslim feminist network.[87] Surprisingly, Christian missionaries often opposed these, as the women expressed their aversion for evangelicalism.[88]

SUFFRAGISTS AND NATIONALISTS

The nationalist and feminist movements intersected closely during the twentieth century, after the emergence of substantial numbers of educated women. Although female literacy in British India in 1921 was still just 1.8 percent (male, 13%), it rose after 1911 due to intensive work by reformers, especially in Bengal, Madras, and Bombay.[89] Private reform schools taught the scientific disciplines, math, and also Indian languages and culture, which drew Indian girls.[90] In Madras, for example, female enrollment doubled between 1902 and 1912.[91]

Until the WIA (1917), earlier twentieth-century women's societies often had a parallel focus on the nation, region, or sect. The latter included Stri Zarthoshti Mandal (1900), YWCA, and Anjuman-e-Khawatin-e-Islam (1915). Patriotic associations were started by women from prominent nationalist families. They included Ramabai Ranade's Ladies' Social Conference (1906) begun as an arm of the INC; and Bharat Stri Mahamandal (Greater Society of Indian Women, 1910) started in Allahabad by Sarala Devi Chaudhurani, gifted niece of Rabindranath Thakur whose poetry she set to music. Sarala Devi's Bharat Stri Mahamandal spread to just three centers in north India. At the 1901 INC session in Calcutta, Sarala Devi sang her patriotic hymn, *Arise, Bharata Lakshmi,* with 50 young women. A product of Bethune School, she was one of Calcutta's first women graduates of Bethune College with a degree in botany and science. During the British partition of Bengal in 1905, she lived with her husband in Punjab but registered her protest by wearing Indian (*swadeshi*) cloth. She later joined Gandhi's peaceful movement but remained a revolutionary at heart. Sarala Devi succeeded her mother Swarnakumari Devi (Ghosal) as editor of the journal *Bharati.*[92]

Women's associations in multiethnic Madras province reflected its diverse population of doctors, teachers, and magistrates. In 1910, Telugu-Indian reformer Viresalingam Pantulu founded Andhra Mahila Sabha (Andhra Women's Club) to educate and give vocational training to disadvantaged women. The Tamil Mathar Sangam (Tamil Women's Organization) met intermittently in Madras (1906) and in Kanchipuram (1907, 1914), while All-India Ladies' Congress (*parishad*) met in 1908. The Tamil Mathar Sangam became the seedbed for the WIA, the first secular organization to serve all Indian women of all regions and sects. According to Rajkumari Amrit Kaur (1889–1964), later president of the AIWC, WIA members expressed their desire for female liberation in Tamil, Malayalam, Telugu, Kannada, Marathi, and English.

The WIA and AIWC had sophisticated feminist agendas. The AIWC was established in 1927 as an educational forum for women of all regions, religions, and castes. Its founders included Margaret Cousins and Muthulakshmi Reddi who had started the WIA as an inclusive group, in marked contrast to the era's growing sectarian divisions. The first AIWC president was the Begam of Bhopal, a princely state now in Madhya Pradesh. The Muslim begam had hesitated to shed *pardah* and her personal name even when addressing the AIWC. The NCWI (1925) was loyal to the British Raj.

Women's Indian Association

On May 8, 1917, in Adyar, Madras, a multiethnic women's group started the WIA, which remains in operation today. WIA's success can be attributed to its secular agenda and effective use of the TS's organizational framework. TS President Annie Besant was chosen as president along with Margaret Cousins. Other founding matriarchs included Dr. Muthulakshmi Reddi (Vice President), Malathi Patwardhan (Hon. Secretary), Ammu Swaminathan (Treasurer), Dorothy Jinarajadasa, Dr. Joshi, Sarlabai Naik, Mangalammal Sadasivier, Herabai Tata, Dr. Poonen Lukhose, Sarojini Naidu, Begam Hazrat Mohani, and Dhanavanti Rama Rao.[93] Using the Tamil Mathar Sangam's idea of a multicultural association, Cousins sounded out her proposal to a TS gathering after she arrived in 1915. Besant was largely a silent member, and Cousins disagreed occasionally with her methods.[94] WIA first linked women's subjugation with poverty and disenfranchisement in colonial India. The members called themselves "daughters of India," dedicated to a sisterhood beyond sect, class, and caste:

The aims and ideals and work of the Association are on a religious, but non-sectarian basis.

To present to women their responsibilities as daughters of India

To help them to realize that the future of India lies largely in their hands for as wives and mothers they have the task of guiding and forming the character of the future rulers of India.

To band women into groups for the purpose of self-development and education, and for the definite service of others.

To secure for every girl and boy the Right to Education through schemes for Compulsory Primary Education including the teaching of religion.

To secure the abolition of child marriage and to raise the Age of Consent for married girls to sixteen.

To secure for women the vote for Municipal and Legislative Councils as it may be granted to men.

To secure for women the right to be elected as members on all Municipal and Legislative Councils.[95]

Social Service

By the end of 1918, the WIA had 33 self-governing local branches that served a sisterhood transcending creed, class, and caste. However, despite this ambition, its leaders stemmed from the elite for decades. In 1920, Cousins began *Stri Dharma*, a quarterly English newsletter with Tamil and Hindi sections, which later became a monthly journal. *Stri Dharma* publicized WIA activities and its agenda to abolish child marriage and *pardah*. Its membership grew quickly, so that by 1924 there were 51 branches and

2,500 members across India, and by 1926, it was the largest women's organization with 80 branches and 4,000 members.

Education was a key thrust of WIA activities, since less than 5 percent of Indian women were recorded as literate in the colonial census. The feminists blamed child marriage, polygamy, and *pardah* for adversely affecting girls' health and obstructing their school enrollment.[96] They discussed this in *Stri Dharma* and in articles to *Indian Social Reformer, The Commonweal,* and other regional journals. The national movement after World War I opened new forums for feminists to publicize their agenda. WIA held free literacy classes, and others on hygiene, child welfare, and vocational skills, and the ideal of social service spilled over to other feminist programs. Thus, doctors Muthulakshmi Reddi and Rahamatunissa Begam initiated a clinic for poor women; in 1930 Dr. Reddi started Avvai Home for destitute girls; and WIA members held vocational classes at Madras Seva Sadan. The WIA continues to serve women through numerous regional branches after independence in 1947.

Women's Suffrage: WIA and AIWC

One of the architects of the Indian women's suffrage movement was Margaret Cousins who had been jailed earlier in Britain as a suffragist and as an activist for Irish Home Rule. In 1915 she arrived with her musicology degree to teach at TS schools with her husband James.[97] Soon afterward, Margaret helped to organize the WIA with civic-minded, educated women like Sarojini Naidu (1879–1949). In August 1917, Sarojini appealed for support for female suffrage from the INC. They assured male nationalists that they would not usurp their authority, but that as matrons they would inspire the nation's children.[98] On December 18, 1917, a WIA delegation led by Sarojini met Viceroy Chelmsford and Secretary of State Edwin Montagu to request equal suffrage in the coming expanded provincial legislatures following the 1919 Indian Councils Act.[99] Margaret Cousins's outspoken opinions led her inexorably into Gandhi's movement, for which she was imprisoned in 1932 at Vellore.

In *We Two Together,* coauthored with her husband James, Margaret stated that her Indian women colleagues hesitated to speak boldly to the Viceroy, perhaps as they were quenched by the presence of imperious European rulers. However, Margaret probably exaggerated, as Sarojini Naidu was equally feisty, and moreover, had shed her fears of Europeans when educated in England. Sarojini's declamations at INC meetings were praised by men, yet Margaret Cousins remembered this scenario:

> Curiously enough, though I had the backing of some of the best women in India, I was the one voice publicly explaining and proclaiming the suffrage cause; not because I had any special fitness, but simply because the womanhood of India had not yet found its authoritative voice.[100]

The imperial Southborough Franchise Commission in London did not sanction their request, despite the support of Sir C. Sankaran Nair and Mr. Hogg in the commission. Sarojini Naidu, Besant, and Herabai Tata then appealed their case in London, and eventually, the provincial legislatures were authorized to decide on an individual basis. With the help of some male nationalists on the councils, a few women were granted the vote first in Madras in 1920, and then in Bombay in 1921. Thus, in the first elections of 1923, roughly a million women went to the polls, constituting between 5 percent and 8 percent of the electorate.[101]

There were other outspoken Indian women leaders like Dr. Muthulakshmi Reddi, a cofounder of WIA, and Kamaladevi Chattopadhyaya (1903–88) who helped her to organize the AIWC in 1927. Socialist Kamaladevi participated in Gandhi's peaceful resistance campaigns (*satyagraha*) and was jailed during the 1942 Quit India Movement led by Jawaharlal Nehru. Yet, Kamaladevi openly disagreed with Gandhi and Nehru on some issues. She and Margaret helped to organize the AIWC in 1927.

As the freedom movement intensified, feminists in WIA and AIWC passed resolutions on female suffrage. Earlier in 1926, five delegates had attended the Congress of International Women Suffrage Alliance in Paris and encouraged Indian women to stand for election as magistrates. In 1928, WIA supported Dr. Muthulakshmi's nomination to the Madras Legislative Council as India's first woman legislator, and she became its deputy president. Dr. Reddi introduced bills to expand women's education, raise the minimum marriage age for girls to 14, and support women's health programs. In 1929, she pushed legislation to discontinue temple endowments that maintained *devadasis* and thus helped to end this custom.[102]

The second phase in the fight for female suffrage began in 1929, when the Simon Commission arrived in India to work out the details of the Indian Councils Act of 1935. WIA supported the INC plank against separate electorates for minorities and boycotted the Simon Commission. WIA and AIWC feminists asked for an expanded electoral base, unlike the loyalist NCWI whose members stemmed from the landed gentry. When British Prime Minister Irwin called for Round Table Conferences in London, Sarojini Naidu, Muthulakshmi Reddi, and Rameshwari Nehru were the feminist delegates, but following Gandhi's lead, they boycotted the conference. Muthulakshmi thus described women in Gandhi's *satyagraha* campaigns:

> Women, both non-*pardah* and *pardah,* who came out in thousands not only picketed foreign and toddy [liquor] shops, but they also broke the salt law and courted imprisonment, faced lathi charge [police beatings] and police terrorism. It was a revolution of a non-violent nature in which students, men and women, all participated facing many a police atrocity during this period.[103]

Gandhi was released from jail in 1931, and a new Round Table Conference on Indian franchise was organized. The AIWC selected eight delegates, including Hansa Mehta, Sarojini Naidu, Sharifa Hamid Ali, and Hilla Fardoonji. The feminists asked for a united Indian front and "equality and no privileges" based on either class or sect.[104] The NCWI sent two British-nominated delegates, Begam Jahan Ara Shah Nawaz and Radhabai Subbarayan. Over the next decades, WIA and AIWC members spoke passionately in favor of adult franchise and against the criterion of wifehood for women to vote. However, the Lothian Committee rejected adult franchise in the 1935 India Act, supported separate electorates for Muslims, but conceded a marginally expanded female electorate.[105] In 1933, Rajkumari Amrit Kaur, Muthulakshmi Reddi, and Begam Sharifa Hamid Ali went to London to ask for adult women's suffrage, irrespective of literacy or wifehood. However, 1935 Act did not grant adult suffrage but emphasized literacy although the majority in India were illiterate and poor. Many feminists now eagerly joined Gandhi's struggle to overthrow the colonial regime.

Child Marriage and Age of Consent

In the mid-1920s, the Indian feminist and nationalist movements were well on its way. Women of all sects and ethnicities publicly voiced their opinions in journals, speeches, and dialogues with men. Feminists joined hands with male compatriots, whether Hindus, Muslims, Sikhs, or Christians, in the struggle to shape the political future of the subcontinent. In this period, feminists promoted a few laws with the potential to affect millions of ordinary women, some of them reflecting a closer global interaction after World War I.

The League of Nations attempted to control the traffic and sexual exploitation of women across the world. In India, although Hindus believed that sexual relations with a prepuberty girl was against the *shastras,* no civil injunction existed in the colonial state to punish such offenses. The 1891 Age of Consent Act simply made sex within marriage illegal before the age of 10. The growth of elected Indian officials to the central and provincial legislatures meant that reformers tried to pass laws against child marriage and sexual relations with minor girls.

In 1924–25, Dr. Hari Singh Gour's Age of Consent Bill in the Central Legislative Assembly attempted to raise the legal age of sexual consent to 16 for unmarried girls and to 14 for married girls. At first accepted, the bill was denied by 16 of the 30 British legislators.[106] Thereupon, progressive Indians, supported by the WIA, AIWC, and local women's groups, tried to pass a similar law in the provincial legislatures.[107] In the Madras Council in 1927, Muthulakshmi Reddi proposed a bill raising the age of consent to 18 for unmarried women, and within marriage to 16 for girls and 21 for boys. A similar bill was introduced by Jayaramdas Doulatram in the

Bombay Council. Neither bill passed, perhaps due to the escalating freedom movement, although many legislators believed that a child marriage law was desperately needed.

In 1928, central legislator Har Bilas Sarda framed a bill that would criminalize marriage and sex with a girl below the age of 12. Thousands of conservative Hindus and Muslims protested against Sarda's Bill and in favor of Gour's Bill, and voiced anger against British laws on Indian cultural customs.[108] Sarda's amended bill passed into law (1929), which stipulated that all girls, irrespective of sect and caste, had to be at least 14 years of age before marriage and sexual relations. The civil, secular implications of Gour's Bill and the Sarda Act evoked different sectarian responses based on perceived notions of identity. Although both Hindus and Muslims allowed child marriage, polygamy, and *pardah,* many Muslim legislators resisted bills on child marriage as not directly affecting their community. Conservative Hindu men did not support feminist arguments against polygamy and *pardah*, erroneously viewing these as only Muslim cultural norms. Progressive men like Sir C. Sankaran Nair supported feminists on all three issues.

Feminist Solidarity

Between 1925 and 1929, the WIA, AIWC, and local associations like the Madras Ladies Samaj held grassroots meetings promoting both Gour's Bill and Sarda's Act as conducive to female health and to a more protracted education. There was a general feminist consensus that girls less than 16 should not engage in sexual relations.[109] Three AIWC feminist delegations met the Viceroy and the Indian and European legislative members to support the Sarda Act. AIWC Muslim feminists praised the law that would protect all Indian women.[110] Initially a women's educational conference, AIWC took on social and political issues after a meeting at Patna, Bihar in 1929. Socialist nationalist Kamaladevi Chattopadhyaya and Hilla Fardoonji introduced a resolution that the organization of diverse Indian women should become a political voice to articulate wider social concerns.[111] Margaret Cousins helped to organize local cells to gather information on women's educational status, but the meetings were marked by discussions on other issues, beginning with their inauguration by Hindu or Muslim queens from progressive princely states. Thus, the first meeting of 2,000 delegates was led by the Rani of Sangli and the Maharani Chimnabai Gaekwad of Baroda. The Begam of Bhopal gave the presidential address the following year.[112]

The Sarda Act forced the conservative to conduct a daughter's marriage only when she was 14 years of age and encouraged the progressive to delay her nuptial consummation till the age of 16. Muslim women who supported the law included the Begam of Bhopal, Sharifa Hamid Ali as secretary of AIWC, and Mrs. Mir Muzeruddin of the Madras Muslim Women's

Association. The bills were also supported by Christian feminists like Swarnam Appasamy and Rajkumari Amrit Kaur.

In an era marked by deepening sectarian divisions among male leaders, it is remarkable that feminists presented a nonsectarian united front. If Muslim women supported raising the age of marriage, Hindu feminists raised awareness against polygamy and *pardah,* more common among Muslims. The WIA journal *Stri Dharma* supported the Muslim Women's Association of Madras, which demanded more government girls' high schools, but opposed the MWA's resolution on "pardah parks" for affluent members alone. *Stri Dharma* revealed that tuberculosis thrived among women in *pardah,* especially in "congested city gullies" without air circulation.[113] Muthulakshmi Reddi, a cofounder of MWA, informed the Hartog Committee on education in 1928 that Muslim women universally desired more girls' schools, even in conservative Sind where *pardah* was rigidly enforced.[114]

In her 1928 address to the AIWC, the Begam of Bhopal advocated Sarda's Bill then being examined by the legislature. Declaring that child marriage and *pardah* were common among Hindus and Muslims, she pleaded that "it is incumbent upon us to stop this evil" of child marriage.[115] Seconded by the Rani of Mandi, a resolution was taken to propose that government raise the legal age of marriage for girls to 16 years, since a law that simply raised the age of sexual consent was insufficient. They inaugurated a small standing committee to report on the progress of bill in the legislature and to raise public awareness.[116] The Begam of Bhopal stated:

> Another handicap to the education of our girls is the custom of child marriage. The evil custom exists practically in every part of the country, and in almost all sections of the people. Owing to it the best part of life which ought to be devoted to the physical, mental and moral growth of a girl, is wasted, and, besides, she often falls a victim to various kinds of disease and physical disability ... Another custom that needs re-adjustment is the *purdah.* Just as early marriage is largely common among the Hindus, the *purdah* is to be met with mostly among the Musalmans. There can be no denying the fact that the present strictness of the *purdah* system among Musalmans does not form a part of their religious obligations. It is based on purely local considerations and is not found in other Islamic countries.[117]

After 1920, Muslim feminists had been raising awareness against the deleterious effects of *pardah.* The Begam of Bhopal described it as contrary to the *Qur'an* and a "hindrance" to women's education and health. However, no Muslim or Hindu legislators attempted to abolish the veil by law, as had Kamal Ataturk of Turkey. Indian Muslim women like Begam Habibullah and Lady Abdul Qadir shed the veil but supported gender segregation in schools where girls were inhibited by competitive boys. The AIWC chose to spread awareness about its medical problems and to encourage women to move freely in mixed gatherings. In Patna, "anti-*pardah*" drives were planned in the 1930s and 1940s. In Calcutta in 1944, Radhadevi Goenka took part in a procession in which Marwari Hindu women rode horses.[118] The most significant change was the participation of Hindu and Muslim women in Gandhi's nonviolent campaigns.

WOMEN IN THE FREEDOM MOVEMENT

Gandhi, Women, and Kasturba

Revered as the father of independent India, Mohandas Karamchand Gandhi (1869–1948) is a unique personage in its protracted history. At once astute politician and visionary statesman, Gandhi's *satyagraha* campaigns based on nonviolence were instrumental in wresting India's freedom from a mighty British Empire.[119] Gandhi's decision to adopt celibacy (*brahmacharya*) after many years of marriage and fatherhood has been discussed by his biographers. Gandhi was married at the age of 13 to Kasturba (1869–1944), a wife chosen by his wealthy merchant caste family in Surat, Gujarat. Kasturba bore four sons and was his colleague for 62 years, supporting him in his ventures in South Africa and India.[120]

In *My Experiments with Truth,* Gandhi candidly described their mutual passion and a traumatic event in their early married life. Gandhi had spent hours in vigil beside his sick father's bed, but when released, he had rushed to his bedroom to make love to a pregnant Kasturba. However, Gandhi was soon awoken by the news of his father's sudden death. Soon thereafter, Kasturba miscarried, so that Gandhi agonized that he had been distracted from his filial duties. He now became convinced that sexual desire was destructive except for procreation within marriage. Gandhi also described his youthful squabbles with his spirited wife whom he tried to teach but felt impatient at her slow progress. A mature Gandhi understood that kindness brought him closer to God, whom he and other Hindus revered as Truth (*satya*). From his devout mother Putlibai, Gandhi learned self-discipline, fasting for spiritual purposes, and nonviolence (*ahimsa*), a Jaina-Buddhist precept absorbed by Hindus. Gandhi's quest for moral perfection became inextricably tied to *ahimsa,* which he stated was lived most perfectly by women like Putlibai and Kasturba. Gandhi's inspiration for *satyagraha* thus stemmed from his observations of women, and this in turn inspired other women and men.

In South Africa, Gandhi began to practice sexual restraint in his marriage, driven to a complete vow in 1906 after the birth of his fourth son Devadas. He had been searching for an ethical principle upon which to found his programs on constructive social activism, and he did not choose this path due to loss of affection for his wife. He and Kasturba had dreaded enforced separations, when he sailed alone in 1893 to South Africa to work as a barrister for an Indian firm. Rejoicing in their reunion, their marriage was strengthened by a shared commitment to promote justice, and belief in asceticism as a means to purify mind and body. Kasturba may thus have accepted his celibacy as conducive to the serenity required for his nonviolent work. Gandhi wrote that Kasturba was unafraid and candid, and "made no objection." He stated that carnal desire led to violence, but women exemplified nonviolence.[121] He wrote:

> Perhaps only a Hindu wife would tolerate these hardships, and that is why I have regarded woman as an incarnation of tolerance ... The canker of suspicion was rooted out only when I understood *Ahimsa* in all its bearings. I saw then the glory of *Brahmacharya* and realized that the wife is not the husband's bond slave, but his companion and his helpmate, and equal partner in all his joys and sorrows—as free as the husband to choose her own path.[122]

On women's role in spreading the idea of nonviolence, Gandhi wrote:

> I have hugged the hope that in this, woman will be the unquestioned leader and, having thus found her place in human evolution, will shed her inferiority complex. If she is able to do this successfully, she must resolutely refuse to believe in the modern teaching that everything is determined and regulated by the sex impulse.[123]

Gandhi and Kasturba shared certain Indian beliefs, beginning with the principle that God is Truth (*satya*) and can be spiritually known through a life of *ahimsa*, nonattachment to material goods (*asteya*), and *brahmacharya*. They also accepted the view that life had four phases, i.e., of the celibate student (*brahmacharya*), householder (*grihastha*), middle-aged forest contemplative (*vanaprastha*), and ascetic (*sanyasa*). Celibacy and poverty were required for all stages except that of the householder. Gandhi modified the *vanaprastha* ideals by taking a vow to serve others unselfishly without violence. In addition, Gandhi believed in the Hindu *Bhagavad Gita*'s delineation of three paths (*yogas*) to salvation, i.e., through asceticism, selfless action (*karma yoga*), and loving devotion (*bhakti*). He ardently upheld *karma yoga* or unselfish, nonviolent action as his path to God. In 1899, Gandhi combined public, nonviolent service by volunteering as an ambulance worker for the Natal government during the Boer War. He wrote:

> It became my conviction that procreation and the consequent care of children were inconsistent with public service ... the idea flashed upon me that if I wanted to devote myself to the service of the community in

this manner I must relinquish the desire for children and wealth and live the life of a *vanaprastha*—of one retired from household cares.[124]

However, after witnessing South African racist brutality against Zulu Africans and Indians in 1906, Gandhi felt morally compelled to strive to change attitudes without destroying his opponents. He defended the cause of Indian indentured workers, merchants, and clerks in public talks and writings. In Johannesburg, he organized his first nonviolent campaign (*satyagraha*) against the Asiatic Ordinance Bill compelling Indians to register and be fingerprinted like criminals. His vow of permanent celibacy has led psychobiologists to argue that Gandhi equated men's carnal use of women with white men's barbaric blood lust against dark-skinned people.[125] He certainly became a gentler husband and humanitarian. He wrote:

> Perhaps only a Hindu wife would tolerate these hardships, and that is why I have regarded woman as an incarnation of tolerance ... The canker of suspicion was rooted out only when I understood *Ahimsa* in all its bearings. I saw then the glory of *Brahmacharya* and realized that the wife is not the husband's bond slave, but his companion and his helpmate, and equal partner in all his joys and sorrows—as free as the husband to choose her own path.[126]

Despite personal hardships, Kasturba supported his mission by helping to establish his first communal hermitage (*ashram*), the Phoenix Settlement in Africa, and his later Sabarmati Ashram in India. She was also unafraid to challenge his "cruel-kind" shibboleths, for example, by initially resisting his order to clean latrines as the work of "untouchables" but later acquiescing, while he regretted his authoritarian commands. Yet, Kasturba herself became transformed through service to Dalit women and children, and worked for their uplift. So implicit was her faith in Gandhi's idea of justice that she staunchly defended him to their son Harilal.[127] Gandhi's views on women's patience and *ahimsa* were thus shaped by his observations of Putlibai and Kasturba. While many men saw women's loving service as a sign of weakness, he argued that it was a strength that men could cultivate. If humanism means love of humankind, women were its embodiments. He wrote:

> Woman is the incarnation of *ahimsa*. *Ahimsa* means infinite love, which again means infinite capacity for suffering. And who but woman, the mother of man, shows this capacity in the largest measure? ... Let her transfer that love to the whole of humanity ... And she will occupy her proud position by the side of man as his mother, maker and silent leader. It is given to her to teach the art of peace to the warring world thirsting for that nectar. She can become the leader

in *satyagraha* which does not require the learning that books give but does require the stout heart that comes from suffering and faith.[128]

Satyagraha and Women Patriots

In 1915, Gandhi returned to India and joined the INC. His success was his ability to utilize earthy, domestic symbols to challenge political and economic threats to India. Two important emblems associated with women and the peasant world were handloom spinning and the manufacture of salt, a staple in the poor person's diet. Women enthusiastically joined his campaigns to promote handloom spinning and to resist the British monopoly on salt. They embraced his directive to wear cotton cloth (*khaddar*) spun on the handloom wheel (*charkha*), and they became *satyagraha* protestors. Handloom textiles were India's chief cottage industry often produced by village women. Gandhi launched his *charkha* protest against British policy to inundate the Indian market with mill cloth from Lancashire. Gandhi personally learned to spin on the *charkha* from women whose dexterous hands he envied. His masterly campaign combined economic resistance, pride in craft labor, and the ancient view of the wheel of law (*dharma chakra*). Elite and working Indians now wore *khaddar* as an emblem of democratic pride. For example, Sridevi Tiwari was an ardent handloom spinner of little education and wealth. Yet, her motive was not personal gain but the altruistic conviction that *khaddar* sales supported women whose handicrafts were being replaced by machines.[129]

Gandhi defended workers' rights through *satyagraha* campaigns against British indigo planters in Champaran, Bihar (1917) and at Ahmedabad, Gujarat (1918) where the industrialist was Ambalal Sarabhai, an INC supporter of Gandhi. Gandhi answered an appeal by Sarabhai's sister Ansuyaben, an advocate for the workers over the withdrawal of a "plague bonus" granted by the company a year earlier. Gandhi negotiated with Sarabhai who restored the bonus, while Ansuyaben founded the Ahmedabad Textile Labor Union. In 1930, her niece Mridula Sarabhai and mother Sarla Devi both joined the INC and the AIWC. The Sarabhai women took part in several *satyagraha* campaigns in which ordinary women beat drums and cymbals, and paraded in small streets calling attention to the nationalist cause.[130]

Women Activists after Jallianwala Bagh

In April 1919 at Jallianwala Bagh, Punjab, British troops opened fire upon an intersect festival, killing over 400 and injuring 1,200 women, children, and men. This watershed event spurred Gandhi to declare his mission to end Britain's "evil" rule, and many elite Indians discarded foreign cloth for *khaddar*. In December, nationalists converged as pilgrims upon Jallianwala Bagh. They included women political activists like Lajjavanti of Punjab and Lado Rani Zutshi of the aristocratic Nehru family. Motilal's charismatic son Jawaharlal (1889–1964) became Gandhi's closest colleague, and both father and son were arrested in *satyagraha* campaigns in 1921. Nehru's vision of democratic equality is enshrined in free India's laws on female property, marriage, and divorce when he was elected as the first prime minister (1947–64). Several Nehru women were involved in Gandhian politics. Feminist Rameshwari Nehru began Prayag Mahila Samiti (Allahabad Women's Society) in 1909 with two hundred members. Jawaharlal's mother Swarup Rani and his shy wife Kamala were unwillingly drawn into the struggle, but both took part eagerly in the 1930 Salt Satyagraha. Yet, women's political activity took a toll of their family duties, as occasionally stated by his patriotic sisters Vijayalakshmi Pandit and Krishna Hutheesing. As a mother of three children, Vijayalakshmi spent months in jail for taking the freedom pledge in 1928. Her niece Indira Gandhi (1917–84) largely raised her two sons alone, yet found time for family when prime minister (1966–77, 1980–84).[131]

Women answered Gandhi's call, convinced that he respected their work and rights. Gandhi's paternalism was complex. On the one hand, he described them as mothers, sisters, and wives, and thus reinforced patriarchal notions of gender. On the other, he spoke of them idealistically as the social conduit through which ethical ideals were transmitted to boys and men. He reiterated that woman was "the companion of man, gifted in equal mental capacities," a social being whose purpose was to purify male intemperance.[132] He spoke to elite women in many cities, appealing to wealthier women to donate jewelry, wear *khaddar,* and picket shops selling liquor and foreign goods. He asked Hindu women to sacrifice like the heroine Sita. To Muslim women, he compared Britain to a Satanic colonial power.

Ordinary women joined INC demonstrations in full force after 1921. Gandhi asked the educated to rehabilitate *devadasis* as they were victims of male lechery. When Telugu social worker Durgabai Deshmukh organized an audience of *devadasis* to hear him speak, Gandhi's compassion elicited such a generous flood of contributions to the freedom struggle that he was visibly overwhelmed.[133] He especially requested women to shun caste and to serve the "untouchables" whom he renamed Harijans (God's folk). In Punjab, AS leaders like Lala Lajpat Rai feared the arrest of middle-class women and curtailed their demonstrations. However, women in Bombay and Calcutta were freer in their protests, and south Indian women eagerly took part in his reform programs. Many women attended INC meetings and continued their activism after returning home. In Bombay, women formed the Rashtriya Stri Sabha to distribute *khaddar* and picket liquor shops. Among those who were jailed was Basanti Devi of Bengal, wife of INC leader C. R. Das.[134]

Madras nationalist-feminists were preoccupied by problems like prepuberty marriages, *devadasi* prostitution, caste harmony, and poverty. They spoke out on improving women's lives in villages and slums, and advocated cautious cooperation with nationalist men like V. S. Srinivasa Sastri, and even liberal British officials. Subbalakshmi Ammal addressed the importance of a female board to shape girls' school curriculum in the context of an impending law on education. They shared Gandhi's views on improving education and health facilities for the poor, and raising the age of marriage. The austere felt that the nation must channel its energies from sexual and alcoholic indulgence into social regeneration.[135]

After Dr. Reddi's return in 1926 from an international women's conference in Paris, the WIA nominated her for the Madras Legislative Council. As its deputy president, she received a unique legal opportunity to chip away at gender inequalities.[136] When Gandhi visited Madras in September 1927, WIA feminists led by Muthulakshmi Reddi asked him to speak about India's social problems that directly affected women.[137] Gandhi was somewhat critical of middle-class women's domestic preoccupations. He advised them to donate generously to help disadvantaged women, educate their daughters, and delay their marriage. He also asked them to remove the "blemish" of the *devadasi* system through which women fell into prostitution. Suffragists had recently won some electoral gains in Madras and Bombay, and Muthulakshmi Reddi had just been appointed to the Legislative Assembly. In 1933, Gandhi made a longer visit, and he jokingly remarked that he must be mistaken for a woman, as he was attending a women's meeting. The audience included both housewives and feminist leaders of the WIA, Madras Seva Sadan, SLU, and the Ladies Samaj. Dr. Reddi translated Gandhi's speech into Tamil in which he urged them to become activists, to donate money and jewelry for Harijan uplift, and to love them as family members.

Leaders like Durgabai Deshmukh and Soundram Ramachandran described the great poverty in villages and slums, which often lacked amenities and health facilities. Both women were members of the INC and started constructive programs for poor women. Dr. Reddi and Dr. Rahamatunissa Begam treated poor women in the slums, while nationalist Christians like Swarnam Appasamy and Mona Hensman ran classes and raised funds for women workers. Dr. Soundram Ramachandran asked women social workers to cultivate compassion and serve the poor in villages. Other women leaders spoke of the relative cultural and sectarian unity in south India. Kerala Muslim social worker Ayesha Bibi described Hindus and Muslims as working together in south Indian villages but not in towns. The queen of Vizianagaram princely state gave a generous donation to the national cause.[138]

Women *Satyagrahis:* Salt March (1930) and Quit India Movement (1942)

In the context of Depression and wartime penury during the 1930s–40s, millions of Indian women and men demonstrated against British rule. Two major noncooperation campaigns were the 1930 Salt Satyagraha led by Gandhi with a women's group led by Sarojini Naidu, and the Quit India Movement (1940–42) organized by Jawaharlal Nehru in which countless ordinary women took part. The 240-mile Salt March from Sabarmati to Dandi was Gandhi's masterly stroke against the British monopoly over the production and sale of salt, crucial for life in the tropics. After Gandhi scooped up some salt water and simply manufactured salt, others like Kamaladevi Chattopadhyaya boiled seawater in pots on the beaches. The Quit India Movement was a massive protest against India's enforced involvement in World War II, although Gandhi, Nehru, and INC members opposed Hitler and Mussolini as fascists. War meant heavier taxes, military spending, and deaths of Indian soldiers. This exacerbated the devastating effects of the 1942–43 Bengal famine in which millions died.

The idea of self-rule (swaraj) for India (Bharat) became an enticing slogan for everyone. Yet, Gandhi cautiously advised women leaders to not push female demonstrators onto the streets, in case they were mistaken for prostitutes. He also shielded them from arduous satyagraha campaigns like the Dandi Salt March but was dissuaded by feminists Sarojini Naidu, Kamaladevi Chattopadhyaya, and Khurshed Naoroji (1894–1996). In the end, thousands of women were jailed for "stealing" salt from India's beaches in contravention of the British colonial monopoly and tax on a commodity that was essential in the tropics. Many poor Indians contented themselves with the barest meal of salt with a chapatti or rice.

Many feminists joined in this momentous satyagraha, including Aruna Asaf Ali (1906–96), a Bengali Hindu (née Ganguly) whose Muslim husband shared her views on freedom and socialism. Aruna and Asaf Ali also participated in the 1942 Quit India demonstrations and were arrested numerous times. Aruna's prison hunger strike against the ill-treatment of political prisoners resulted in her solitary confinement. Her courage and leadership earned her the sobriquet, "Heroine of the 1942 Movement." After independence, Aruna started the National Federation of Indian Women as a wing of the Communist Party.[139]

Two other women in the Salt Satyagraha were Durgabai Deshmukh (1909–81) of Andhra Pradesh and Rajkumari Amrit Kaur (1889–1964) of Punjab. At the age of 12, Durgabai heard him speak to an audience urging resistance to colonialism. She then made a bonfire of her foreign clothes and learned to spin on the charkha. Unhappy over her arranged marriage, since it cut her education short, she requested her husband for a separation. She bore him no ill will and later helped him to remarry. She now devoted her life to the cause of national freedom, and service to women and children. In 1922, she founded Balika Hindi Pathasala (Hindi Girls' School) where she taught girls Hindi and Telugu. In 1923, she organized a Girls' Volunteer Corps.

As a young woman, Durgabai began to travel across the country with Gandhi and other leaders to raise awareness about their struggle. At a meeting in south India, she asked him for a separate address to Muslim women in *pardah* as they could not appear in public. During the 1930 Salt Satyagraha, she raised the national flag in Madras beaches, organized processions, and bore police beatings with the *lathi* stick. She refused special treatment as a political prisoner and was incarcerated in jail with ordinary women for whose rights she pleaded. After release in 1933, she studied and received her BA, MA, and law degrees. At a meeting when Gandhi addressed Madras middle-class women, Durgabai spoke of sexual exploitation, of village women's poverty and basic lack of amenities, and of dedicated women social workers. She proposed that the Kasturba Fund be used for village women in south India. In 1937, Durgabai founded the Andhra Mahila Samaj (Andhra Women's Society, AMS) with funds donated by south Indian queens of Pithapuram, Mirzapur, Bobbili, and Hyderabad.[140] After Indian independence, she was appointed to the Indian Planning Commission and the Central Society Welfare Board. In 1953, Durgabai married Finance Minister C. D. Deshmukh of Maharashtra. The AMS continues to treat women's health and to support welfare activities in Madras.[141]

Rajkumari Amrit Kaur was a Christian from the royal family in Kapurthala, Punjab. She imbibed her patriotism from her father, a friend of reformer G. K. Gokhale. After her father's death, she joined Gandhi's cause and served as his secretary for 16 years.[142] In 1937, she was arrested on sedition in the North West Frontier Province, and in the 1942 Quit India Movement, suffered brutal police beatings with the *lathi* when she led processions demonstrating against British rule. She was passionately convinced that *pardah* and child marriage were "cankers" that vitiated the nation and prevented women from rising to their full potential. She strongly advocated free, compulsory schooling for girls, more teacher training schools for women, and health care for girls and infants at school. After independence, she was the first woman central minister for health and later the president of the United Nations World Health Assembly. She helped to establish the All India Institute of Medical Sciences and used her contacts in New Zealand, the United States, and West Germany to promote research on tuberculosis.[143]

Personal conviction and family affiliation brought many women to Gandhi's cause. The young medical student Sushila Nayar of Punjab arrived with her brother Pyarelal Nayar at Gandhi's Sevagram Ashram in Wardha, Maharashtra. Pyarelal later became Gandhi's secretary, but Sushila was inspired also by the doctrine of selfless service and began to view Gandhi in a paternal light.[144] Throwing herself into the treatment of cholera victims, an observant Gandhi chose her as his personal physician. She participated in numerous *satyagraha* campaigns and was imprisoned with Gandhi during the Quit India Movement. She remained with him till his assassination by a Hindu fanatic in 1948. She then went to the United States for further medical studies, and after her return, she began a sanatorium for TB patients in a cooperative township started by Kamaladevi Chattopadhyaya outside Delhi.

Dr. Nayar's first clinic at Wardha developed into the Kasturba Memorial Hospital (1944), the Mahatma Gandhi Institute of Medical Sciences (1969), and the Gandhi Memorial Leprosy Foundation. In 1952, Nehru appointed her as Health Minister, and she was elected several times to Parliament. However, her differences with Indira Gandhi made her join the opposition Janata Party in 1971. Sushila Nayar's contributions to the treatment of cholera, leprosy, and tuberculosis have earned her a respected place in modern India.

The prominent feminist Hansabehn Mehta (1897–1995) was one of the first Gujarati women college graduates. Although her intercaste marriage to Dr. Jivraj Mehta led to family ostracism, the progressive maharaja of Baroda attended their wedding. Hansabehn joined Gandhi's movement, picketed shops that sold liquor and foreign goods, and was jailed during one of his *satyagraha* campaigns. She and fourteen women were included in the Constituent Assembly to frame India's constitution in December 1946. On the transfer of power on August 14, 1947, as a representative of Indian women, Hansabehn Mehta presented the tricolor flag to the Constituent Assembly. In her 1946 presidential address to AIWC, Hansabehn proposed a Women's Charter of Rights, and as India's representative to the UN Human Rights Commission, she helped to frame its Universal Declaration of Human Rights.

Usha Mehta (b. 1920) was born in Surat to a Gujarati couple. She became a follower of Gandhi after meeting him at the age of five. Her father was a judge, and while her mother was not highly educated, she inspired Usha to attend college and acquire a BA and a law degree. In an era when marriage was considered essential for a woman, Usha Mehta boldly remained unmarried. She emulated Gandhi by remaining celibate and wearing only homespun *khaddar*. She participated in anti-British demonstrations from 1928 with the tacit support of her extended family, and her father joined her after resigning as a judge in 1930. During the salt *satyagraha*, Usha and her family broke the law by making salt on the beaches of Bombay. The high point of her career was in 1942 when Gandhi, Nehru, and key INC officials were jailed in the Quit India Movement. She operated an underground radio station, later called "Congress Radio," to disseminate news and also surreptitiously unfurled the Indian tricolor flag in public places. She was then incarcerated in isolation and interrogated for four years. Although her health suffered permanently, she bravely remained silent. Usha Mehta received India's Padma Vibhushan award in 1998.[145]

Sarojini Naidu (1879–1949)

Sarojini Naidu's nationalism was underscored by her feminism. Her BS parents had nurtured her creative talents, and their home in Hyderabad princely Muslim state, now in Andhra Pradesh, was open to diverse intellectuals of all communities. Her mother Varada Sundari Devi wrote Bengali lyrics, and her father Dr. Aghorenath Chattopadhyaya was a scientist who founded Nizam's College. Sarojini's poetic collections in English, *Songs* (1895), *The Golden Threshold* (1905), *The Bird of Time* (1912), and *The Broken Wing* (1917), were acclaimed in her lifetime for evocative descriptions of India.[146] Sarojini would later make passionate speeches on women's education. As a 12-year-old in 1891, she received the highest marks in the Madras Presidency matriculation exams, a feat that impressed the Nizam into granting her a scholarship to attend Girton College, Cambridge. She now made friends with famous writers and traveled in Europe, but ill health brought her home to India. In 1898, Sarojini defied caste rules by marrying Dr. Govindarajulu Naidu, a non-*brahman* Telugu widower with whom she had four children.[147]

Sarojini's oratory drew large crowds after 1904. At Framji Cowasji Institute, she recited her poem *Ode to India* asking Mother India to awaken from slumber. This was in sharp contrast to Ramabai Ranade's practical plea to affluent women to help their poorer sisters. In 1906 she spoke on women's education to INC members at Calcutta and to male reformers at the ISC. She was a close associate of G. K. Gokhale, Gandhi, Rabindranath Thakur, and Sarala Devi Chaudhurani. In Madras in 1909, she met Muthulakshmi Reddi, her future colleague and cofounder of WIA in 1917. Although she received the colonial government Kaiser-I-Hind award for flood relief work in 1911, she remained an ardent nationalist.

In 1917, Sarojini appealed to INC men to support women's equal voting rights and emphasized that as the mothers of the nation, women did not wish to overturn male authority. On December 18, 1917, Sarojini led the WIA delegation to Edwin Montagu to request women suffrage in the 1919 elections. At Madras, Bombay, and Secunderabad, Sarojini told women that their low status was due to child marriage, *pardah* seclusion, and bigamy. However, Sarojini also romantically referred to female sacrifice as *sati,* although she ironically supported the 1829 colonial law against widow immolation on the husband's pyre. This has led some scholars to describe her as a "traditional feminist," as she reified certain feminine stereotypes.

Sarojini's speeches were a poetic cascade of idealism, humanism, and humor. She lauded patriotism as "the flame that burns within the soul" and condemned communal separatism.[148] At Lucknow and Patna, she urged Muslims and Hindus to remember their shared national identity and common humanity. On December 21, 1917, she pleaded with Madras Special Provincial Council to support the INC-Muslim League Pact.

Sarojini was key player in Gandhi's *satyagrahas* after 1917 when she began to speak about nonviolent resistance. In 1925, she was appointed the first INC woman president. When Gandhi hesitated to have women in the 1930 Salt March as it would be arduous, he was dissuaded from this view by Sarojini, Kamaladevi Chattopadhyaya, and Khurshed Naoroji, a granddaughter of Zoroastrian leader Dadabhai Naoroji. Sarojini led the women marchers and was jailed. She was also imprisoned in the 1942 Quit India struggle, as was her brother's wife Kamaladevi Chattopadhyaya, a cofounder of AIWC. The two women are respected as India's nationalist-feminist luminaries. After independence, Sarojini Naidu was appointed governor of Uttar Pradesh, and all Indians mourned her death in 1949.

Muthulakshmi Reddi (1886–1968)

Feminist Muthulakshmi Reddi was a founding member of WIA, the first Hindu woman doctor in Madras Presidency (province), and the first woman legislator in India. Born in Pudukottai princely state in Tamil Nadu, her upper-caste father S. Narayanaswami was principal of Maharaja's College. Her mother Chandrammal belonged to a family of musician dancers (*devadasis*). Although her father had initial reservations about educating girls, except to teach them to keep "milk and dhoby (laundry) accounts," Muthulakshmi's scholastic talents attracted the attention of her teachers. Narayanaswami then encouraged his daughter to study further and even relocated to Madras so that she could attend medical college. Muthulakshmi thus respected her father more greatly than her fairly illiterate mother who feared that higher education would prevent her daughter from marriage and domestic fulfillment. Muthulakshmi blamed her mother's *devadasi* ancestry for her superstitious fears, and lack of enthusiasm for her education.

In 1912, Muthulakshmi graduated with higher grades than her all-male class at Madras Medical College. She immediately threw herself into the service of women and children in this province, by treating women and children at a government hospital and the poor in Madras slums.[149] She chose medicine as her profession, attracted by its scientific answers to the world's problems. Convinced that illiteracy bred irrational fears and beliefs, she used her knowledge and position in society to educate women, as she was convinced that it would improve their physical and mental condition. She also had a strong distaste for sectarian and caste divisions, which she felt were irrational and misogynist traditions that obstructed women's modernization.

In 1913, she became resident doctor for R. S. Subbalakshmi Ammal's Brahmin Hostel for Widows. In 1914, her parents persuaded her to marry Dr. Sundara Reddi despite their different castes. The couple shared an interest in medicine and welfare work, and they jointly established a girls' orphanage and rehabilitation center for destitute women. When she first attended to sick, vagrant children at Dr. Varadappa Naidu Home in 1919, she perceived the direct connections between women's low status, family neglect, illiteracy, early marriage, childbirth death, prostitution, and disease. Muthulakshmi then became politically active in the struggle for women's rights.

In 1917, she joined Margaret Cousins and other feminists to found the WIA, and in 1928, she, Dr. Rahamatunissa Begam, and Sharifa Mazeruddin cofounded the Muslim Women's Association. The first MWA president was Rani Begam Yukub Hasan of Arcot. She also worked with women of several communities in Madras Seva Sadan (1923) which assisted indigent women; the Madras Vigilance Society which retrieved girls from brothels; and the Indian Ladies' Samaj. Her colleagues included Hindus like Parvati Ammal Chandrasekharan and Mangalammal Sadasivier; Muslims like Rahamatunissa Begam and Shafia Mazeruddin; Christians like Swarnam Appasamy and Poonen Lukhose; Parsis like Herabai Tata; and the British Annie Besant and Margaret Cousins. She joined the 1917 WIA delegation to Edwin Montagu to request provincial female suffrage under the 1919 Constitutional Reform Act. In 1926, she represented India at the International Suffrage Conference of Women in Paris, and in 1933, at the Congress of Women in Chicago.

As the first woman legislator in 1927–28 and deputy president of the Madras Legislative Council, Muthulakshmi first formulated a bill to raise the age of sexual consent to 16 for girls. However, she and her WIA colleagues soon campaigned for the Sarda Act, which raised the age of marriage for girls to 14 years. She also campaigned for increased state funding for girls' schools and occupational centers, Dalit (Adi Dravida) girls' teacher training programs, and Muslim girls' education. As a member of the 1928 Hartog Committee, she investigated the state of female education in India. Although she believed that the *pardah* promoted female ill health, as a pragmatist, she passed an Assembly resolution for separate wards and doctors for Muslim women in *pardah*.

Her personal dislike of her maternal ancestry probably led her to frame a 1927 bill. This bill eventually led to the abolishing of *devadasi* dedication to Hindu temples as musician dancers. The subject had attracted the attention of legislators after World War I. In 1922, Hari Singh Gour tried to change the penal code on minor girls' prostitution under a religious pretext; and in 1924, Government of India Act XVIII guaranteed protection to temple girls below 18 years of age. However, *devadasi* dedication continued in Madras until Muthulakshmi formulated her new bill. She resigned in 1929 when Gandhi called for civil disobedience, so that the bill lay dormant. It was finally passed as Madras Hindu Religious Endowments Act V (1947). Muthulakshmi's bill undercut the economic basis of this cultural system by denying temples certain land revenues to maintain *devadasis*. This endorsed Gandhi's views on moral purification to renew the nation and to emancipate women.

Muthulakshmi and Gandhi respected each other's constructive programs for the discriminated poor and low caste. In one letter, she praised his "moving appeal" to help *devadasis* as "victims of tradition, custom or mistaken religious fervor" due to male lechery, and spoke of "a few good and pure" women rehabilitated into "virtuous" vocations.[150] Gandhi admired Muthulakshmi for going beyond speeches and slogans, and for organizing pragmatic programs.

Not only did she tend to their health, but she and other feminists of Madras Vigilance Society, Ladies Samaj, and WIA rehabilitated *devadasis*. She also started Avvai Home and Orphanage for Girls to teach them other trades so that financial independence would prevent a lapse into prostitution. Addressing Gandhi respectfully as "Beloved Mahatmaji," in 1937, she wrote:

> I was simply touched by your moving appeal in the *Harijan* in support of the Bill for the abolition of the dedication of girls to the Hindu temples in this Presidency. As you might remember, I introduced an amendment to the Hindu Religious Endowments Act, which has now become law to dispense with the Devadasi service in the Hindu temples ... But I have found soon after that a large number of women and girls are allowed to be dedicated in the large as well as in the small temples for the purpose of prostitution ... The saddest part is that these girls while they are young, innocent and helpless are coached up and trained purposely for a life of prostitution ... Therefore, I have introduced another measure, *viz.,* a bill for the prevention of dedication of girls ... As I resigned soon after, the work was left incomplete ... I may also add that some of us women have done propaganda against this custom through lectures and pamphlets both in English and in the vernacular but without much effect. Therefore, I feel strongly that legislation for the prevention of this evil is absolutely necessary.[151]

Kamaladevi Chattopadhyaya (1903–88)

Kamaladevi Chattopadhyaya was a dynamic nationalist-feminist, a prolific writer on diverse topics, and a cultural enthusiast who helped to revive Indian theater and handicrafts. Kamaladevi's interest in acting began when she met her husband Harindranath Chattopadhyaya, but it persisted even after her divorce, as in 1944 she spearheaded the Bharatiya Natya Sangha (Indian Drama Council). Her work for Indian cottage industries led to her appointment as Chairman of the Indian Handicrafts Board in 1952. At the age of 18, she joined INC and accompanied Gandhi across the country, appealing to youths to join their struggle. She was then appointed as president of the national Youth Conference. In 1930, she was one of the first women appointed to break the salt laws at Dandi. She was commander of the Women's Volunteer Corps in the Quit India Movement, and her key role in numerous *satyagraha* campaigns resulted in her jail sentence for five years, one in solitary confinement. At the 1927 meeting of the Women's Educational Conference, she and Hilla Fardoonji introduced a resolution to expand its focus, which led to AIWC's political involvement in *satyagraha* campaigns. As AIWC general secretary, she helped to establish branches across India, and in 1934 she became AIWC president.[152] In 1926, Kamaladevi represented AIWC at the International Congress of the Women's League for Peace and Freedom at Prague. As a socialist, she openly disagreed with Gandhi and questioned even Nehru's plan to retain colonial institutions. However, her indefatigable service inspired their respect.

Early Life

She was from a prominent high-caste family of Konkan Saraswat *brahmans* from Mangalore. When her father, a distinguished District Collector, died intestate, his son by an earlier marriage claimed his entire property. Kamaladevi's mother Girijabai was a second wife now entirely dependent on her own dowry.[153] In 1914, Girijabai arranged for her daughter's marriage according to social custom, but the groom died the next year, leaving Kamaladevi as a child widow. However, her educated mother and grandmother did not allow Kamaladevi to languish, and they sent her to a convent girls' school. Girijabai's resolve stemmed from her personal admiration for Pandita Ramabai and Ramabai Ranade, and her anger at the caste ostracism of Pandita Ramabai's father for educating his widowed daughter. Kamaladevi always remembered how her mother and grandmother read and discussed Sanskrit texts and the Marathi newspaper *Kesari* edited by Tilak, the cultural nationalist.[154]

In 1917 the family moved to Madras city where Kamaladevi was now exposed to speeches by Annie Besant who admired Indian handicrafts and culture, and by WIA feminists like Margaret Cousins. Kamaladevi attended St. Mary's College and met the talented Chattopadhyaya siblings, namely Sarojini (later Naidu) and Harindranath, a mercurial poet and actor. In 1919, Kamaladevi and Harindranath were married in a civil ceremony, and in 1921 they left for England, he to Cambridge, she to study sociology at Bedford College. Kamaladevi's eagerness to join Gandhi's movement led to their return the following year. After the birth of her son Ramakrishna in 1923, she accompanied Gandhi in his journeys to exhort young Indians to resist British rule. Harindranath's philandering led to their separation in 1927 and divorce many years later. Kamaladevi was now befriended by Margaret Cousins with whom she founded AIWC. In the first general elections with women candidates to Madras Legislative Council, she unsuccessfully contested a seat from Mangalore. The WIA had the right to select another female candidate, and Muthulakshmi Reddi was chosen as India's first woman legislator.

Activist and Writer

In 1930, she, Sarojini Naidu, and Khurshed Naoroji convinced Gandhi to include women in the Salt March to Dandi. After his arrival at Dandi, he symbolically broke the salt law on April 6, the anniversary of the Jallianwala Bagh massacre. The next day the feminists Kamaladevi and Avantibai Gokhale marched onto the beaches with five male *satyagrahis,* lit the fires, and made salt by boiling seawater.[155] In her later work, *Inner Recesses, Outer Spaces: Memoirs* (1986), Kamaladevi described her excitement "at the enormity of the occasion and my own good fortune" at being one of the first women to take part in the event.[156]

By 1934, she joined the newly formed Congress Socialist Party in the belief that justice was possible only through left-wing politics. The conviction remained in a muted form till her final years. It appears in her early work, *At the Crossroads* (1947), which described the perfect welfare state, cooperative unions, public education, and programs to free women from domestic bondage.[157] During the 1940s' civil disobedience campaigns, especially after the 1942 Quit India demonstrations, her socialist involvement increased, and she disagreed even with socialist Nehru who wanted to retain some colonial institutions after independence. Ideological tensions and personal sorrows led her to focus again on the AIWC in 1944 and to help revive Indian theater and handicrafts. Gandhi lauded her constructive plans to help women through the handloom before his assassination. In 1951, Prime Minister Nehru endorsed her candidacy in the Bombay elections, although on a Socialist Party ticket. Upon her defeat she resigned from the Socialist Party and accepted Nehru's offer to organize the All India Handloom Board in 1952. In this post, she served her country with creative vision and talent.[158]

Despite their extraordinary contributions to women's social and political equality, recent feminists have criticized Kamaladevi, Sarojini Naidu, and others for disclaiming the title of "feminist." Feminism is rooted in the historical struggle for women's rights, and the first women to challenge patriarchy are surely entitled to this term, even if they did not describe themselves as feminists. Indian nationalist-feminists believed that their fledgling movement would be jeopardized if they antagonized male nationalists in power. An earlier generation of elite reformers had focused solely on female illiteracy, early marriage, and widowhood. The nationalist-feminists were faced with the compelling social problems of grueling poverty and misrule. They joined men of all castes, sects, and classes who were energized by the idea of self-rule (*swaraj*). As their generation's goal was freedom, nationalist women like Kamaladevi agreed with men like Gandhi that political unity was essential across gender and class lines. Moreover, like Nehru, Kamaladevi believed that freedom with democracy and socialism would guarantee class and gender equality, and that an all-out "gender war" would delay freedom. Kamaladevi's socialism is evident in *The Awakening of Indian Women* (1939), in which she blamed feudalism for women's thralldom. However, in 1983, the 80-year-old feminist glanced back with satisfaction over her generation's feminist achievements in the *Indian Women's Battle for Freedom*.

Kamaladevi's writings include a broad range of books, pamphlets, and essays. They are carefully researched, elegant works imbued with her characteristic passion for each subject, enlivened by translations from Indian literature. Apart from the two works listed above, others include the books *At the Crossroads* (1947); *Carpets and Floor Coverings of India* (1966); *The Glory of Indian Handicrafts* (1976); *Indian Embroidery* (1977); *Tribalism in India* (1978); and *Inner Recesses, Outer Spaces* (1986); and essays such as "In War-Torn China" (1944), "America: The Land of Superlatives" (1946), "Socialism and Society" (1950), and "Towards a National Theatre" (post-1947) for the AIWC.[159]

Women Revolutionaries with Alternative Ideologies

Other twentieth-century women wielded arms for the nation, in the martial tradition of Raziyya who died struggling for her throne (d. 1240), Abakka Devi who died fighting the Portuguese (d. 1598), and Lakshmibai of Jhansi who died on the battlefield of the 1857 Revolt. In 1905, the British Bengal partition on communal lines provoked militancy among Indian youths who threw bombs and assassinated officials, after listening to the oratory of Bipin Chandra Pal and Lala Lajpat Rai. Several notable women wrote inflammatory journal articles. For example, Sarala Devi Chaudhurani (née Ghosal) redirected her rebellion into writing editorials for *Bharati*.[160] Kumudini Mitra, whose father was a respectable nationalist, published the inflammatory journal *Suprabhat* in 1907. Other women's incendiary activities were noted by the British police. Moreover, unlike mainstream worshippers of Kali, newer violent cults believed that the goddess blessed the martyrs who died for Mother India.

To control Indian discontent in World War I, the British passed the Defense of India Act (1915) and expanded its constraints through 1918 Rowlatt Acts. In angry response, young Indian men excited by recent Marxist successes in Europe took pride as revolutionaries (*krantis*) by forming societies to overthrow the British Empire. They saw themselves as socialists, rather than as anarchists (*biplabi*). However, the colonial government categorized them all simply as terrorists. Amarendranath Chattopadhyaya who founded the revolutionary Jugantar Party lived with his aunt Nanibala Devi (d. 1967). This widow since childhood was not simply his housekeeper but his assistant in revolutionary activities.[161] Revolutionary news journals referred often to the courage of Mazzini and Garibaldi of Italy.

Bhikaiji Cama

These inspired Bhikaiji Cama (née Patel, 1866–1936), a wealthy Zoroastrian patriot of India. Unhappily married to a wealthy man, she became involved with women's groups that spread ideas of sectarian and class unity for the nation, and worked with Bombay plague victims. When her health deteriorated, her father sent her to recuperate in Europe where she associated with exiled Indian nationalists. In 1907, she attended a socialist conference at Stuttgart, Germany and unfurled the Indian tricolor flag for the first time. This was construed as treason by the British, but Hindus praised Bhikaiji as a patriot and as an incarnation of goddess Kali, although she was a Zoroastrian.[162] In 1909, Bhikaiji moved to Paris where she launched *Vande Mataram* journal and smuggled revolvers to distribute in British India.[163] While patriots often accepted nonviolent methods as effective in the long run, they sometimes felt that violence was necessary when family, religion, or homeland was in danger. While Gandhi's followers spun peacefully on the *charkha,* some would occasionally resort to sabotage. The Mahatma would then anxiously educate them on the nuances of *satyagraha.* Aruna Asaf Ali and Kamaladevi Chattopadhyaya were two women who occasionally went underground as revolutionary socialists.

After 1930 when harsher colonial laws tried to curb nationalist activity, the young sometimes resorted to violence. In the Chittagong Armory Raids, the British arrested young Bengali men for making arms. However, their wives and sisters continued manufacturing bombs until they too were jailed as terrorists. They included Mrinalini, her daughter Jogmaya, and Radha Rani Debi of the Bengal Youth League.[164] In 1931, Shanti Ghosh and Suniti Choudhury shot at the magistrate who promulgated harsh ordinances, and Bina Das's attempt to kill Governor Stanley Jackson led to a life sentence in a penal colony.[165] Bina Bhowmich's 1932 attempt to kill the governor led to her confession that she was "entirely responsible." She wrote:

> My object was to die, and if to die, to die nobly fighting against this despotic system of Government, which has kept my country in perpetual subjection to its infinite shame and endless suffering. I have been thinking—is it worth living in an India, so subject to wrong and continually groaning under the tyranny of a foreign Government or is it not better to make one supreme protest by offering one's life away?[166]

Lakshmi Sahgal and the Indian National Army

During World War II, Indians endured economic hardships and also Japanese coastal attacks from Singapore, Malaya, and Burma. Indians led by Subhas Chandra Bose (d. 1944) now courted the Axis Powers as a counterfoil against British imperialism. Bose established the India Independence League (IIL) from exile in Singapore, while followers like General Mohan Singh used Japanese aid to organize the Indian Liberation Army (ILA). An ILA battalion of women was the Rani of Jhansi Regiment, founded by Dr. Lakshmi Sahgal (b. 1914), a Tamil woman, and daughter of WIA feminist Ammu Swaminathan, a Gandhian member of INC. At first, Lakshmi also joined INC, but she was disillusioned by the hanging of revolutionary patriot Bhagat Singh. Lakshmi entered medical college, became a gynecologist, and started a medical clinic for women in

Singapore in 1939. Here she met Bose, joined the IIL, and was chosen as
its president. In 1942, Bose set up his Provisional Government of Free
India in exile, and he appointed Dr. Lakshmi Swaminathan as Minister
of Women's Organization. Upon Bose's request, she formed the Rani of
Jhansi Regiment, holding the rank of captain and later as colonel. When
her regiment was in combat in Burma, Lakshmi conducted a hospital for
the wounded. In 1945, she was captured by the Allies during the Japanese
retreat into Thailand and taken to Rangoon where she treated patients in a
clinic. Due to her continued involvement with ILA, she was later imprisoned at Red Fort in Delhi. However, Indians accorded her heroine's
welcome upon her return. Here she met the political prisoner Prem Kumar
Sahgal whom she married in 1947 after independence. In October 1984,
she once again showed her personal courage while living with her family
in Kanpur, Uttar Pradesh, by confronting mob attacks on innocent Sikhs
after Prime Minister Indira Gandhi was assassinated by Sikh guards.
In 1998, Lakshmi Sahgal was awarded the Padma Vibhushan by the
Government of India for exemplary services.[167]

Independence and Partition

When early reformers tried to guarantee modern women's rights, they did
not imagine that women would one day fight beside men to free the nation.
By 1930 it was apparent to the liberal Nehru, socialist Jayaprakash Narayan
(1902–79), and legalist B. R. Ambedkar (1891–1956) that gender equality
had to be a cornerstone of the Indian democracy. In Nehru's *The Discovery
of India* written while in prison, he described how women resisted British rule:

> Most of us men folk were in prison. And then a remarkable thing hap-
> pened. Our women came to the front and took charge of the struggle.
> Women had always been there, of course, but now there was an ava-
> lanche of them, which took not only the British government but their
> own men folk by surprise. Here were these women, women of the
> upper or middle classes, leading sheltered lives in their homes, peasant
> women, working-class women, rich women, poor women, pouring out
> in their tens of thousands in defiance of government order and police
> lathi. It was not only that display of courage and daring, but what
> was even more surprising was the organizational power they showed.
> Never can I forget the thrill that came to us in Naini Prison when news
> of this reached us, the enormous pride in the women of India that filled
> us. We could hardly talk about all this among ourselves for our hearts
> were full and our eyes were dim with tears.[168]

Indian women's activism invited the admiration both at home and abroad.
In recognition, 14 AIWC and WIA feminists were appointed as members

of the Constituent Assembly to draft the constitution. They included Ammu Swaminathan, Kamala Chaudhuri, Begam Qudsia Aizaz Rasul, Sarojini Naidu, Hansa Mehta, Sucheta Kripalani, Dakshayani Velayudhan, Durgabai Deshmukh, Purnima Banerjee, Begam Ikramullah, Lila Roy, and Vijayalakshmi Pandit.[169]

Vijayalakshmi Pandit (1900–1990), Nehru's talented sister, began her political career at the age of 16 by joining Besant's Home Rule League. In 1928, the young married mother of three was elected to Allahabad Municipal Board. In 1937, Vijayalakshmi Pandit became minister for health in pre-independence Uttar Pradesh. She was first jailed in 1928 for taking the public oath of freedom and was imprisoned twice during Gandhi's *satyagrahas*. Born to affluence and prestige, Vijayalakshmi contributed generously to the nation's cause, but when widowed at the age of 44, she was swindled by her husband's relatives of his estate, like many widows. Vijayalakshmi volunteered her services for women and child victims of cholera and famine in Bengal in 1944. She was elected AIWC president for two terms and appointed to the Constituent Assembly in 1946. She was India's first emissary to the USSR and to the United Nations where in 1953, she was elected as the first woman president of the General Assembly.

In 1946, Vijayalakshmi attended a conference for the UN Commission on the Status of Women, which passed a Charter of Women's Rights under the aegis of Eleanor Roosevelt, India's well-wisher and Nehru's personal friend. The AIWC endorsed the UN charter and also prepared its own Charter of Women's Rights and Duties.[170] In Nehru's records during his first trip abroad as prime minister in 1948, he described Mrs. Roosevelt's respectful praise for Indian feminists, with a special reference to Professor Lakshmi N. Menon (1899–1994), an AIWC founder, and later president.[171] Lakshmi Menon also served as delegate to the United Nations, and in 1949 she headed the UN Human Rights Division on the Status of Women. She was appointed to the Rajya Sabha, India's Parliamentary upper house, and received the Padma Bhushan in 1959.

Partition

On the independence day of August 15, 1947, Prime Minister Jawaharlal Nehru spoke eloquently of "India's tryst with destiny," while women leaders hoisted the tricolor flag. Yet, behind this momentous event lurked the tragedy of Partition, "an undeclared civil war" that began months earlier and escalated like a wildfire after August 16.[172] About 10 million Hindus, Sikhs, and Muslims fled to and from India and Pakistan across boundaries demarcated rapidly by British jurist Cyril Radcliffe and accepted prima facie by the INC and the ML.[173] Although often described as the world's largest peacetime migration, it was hardly peaceful, especially for women. Roughly a million people died, the roads were strewn with corpses, and Punjab rivers ran blood. Convoys and trains meant to safeguard migrants often arrived eerily at destinations with dead bodies. Some 75,000 Hindu, Muslim, and Sikh women were raped and brutalized, their bodies serving as the sites to wage war for the nation and male honor.[174] In a culture that places great value upon female honor (*izzat* [Urdu]; *abhiman* [Hindi]), patriarchal families often rejected raped women, forcing them into prostitution or to commit suicide. Those who became pregnant occasionally married the rapist and converted to forget painful memories, but the offspring were living reminders of a traumatic event.

Fearing that the stories of abducted, raped, and converted women would raise "popular passions" leading to a communal frenzy, Nehru urged that "recovery" proceed quickly, as the "trouble will simmer and might blaze out."[175] Condemning such "heinous" treatment of women, INC leaders urged that women be restored to their homes in India and Pakistan in a humane manner. On December 6, 1947, discussions began at Lahore, Pakistan. Mridula Sarabhai was appointed Chief All India Organizer of the women's recovery program, and Rameshwari Nehru was Honorary Advisor for rehabilitation.[176] The two women humanely and creatively used welfare program funds, named Kasturba Gandhi and Kamala Nehru.

The Indian and Pakistani governments set up transit refugee camps with police inspectors to send abducted women back to their homelands. Unfortunately, the official discourse often treated women as national property to be claimed or rejected, so that occasionally they were even raped by supervisory officials appointed for their help. There were continuous press and government complaints until 1949 that Pakistan returned fewer women (6,272) than India (12,500). One Indian legislator suggested that communal retaliation was required, since Hindu men were "descendants of Ram" whose duty it was to "bring back every Sita that is alive."[177] It was left to veteran feminists like Ammu Swaminathan to point out that women were not mythic ideals but flesh and blood victims:

> I think that is a most inhuman thing to do because after all, if two Governments are not agreeing with each other, that is not the fault of these innocent girls who have been victims of cruel circumstances. We should not think in terms of retaliation at all.[178]

A major problem was that the large population of discarded widows, wives, and orphaned children were paupers after Partition. Rehabilitation centers were set up, including the Karnal Mahila Ashram with a sewing center; the Kasturba Niketan; the Trust for Sindhi Women and Children; and the Nari Seva Sangh. While women did find employment as leather workers, producers of apparel, dairy and vegetable farmhands, accountants, and stenographers, they were often underpaid and received little for their products.[179] The cruelties perpetuated on innocent women and children so dismayed Gandhi that this apostle of peace retreated to Sabarmati Ashram, making rare appearances till a Hindu fanatic assassinated him on January 30, 1948.

NOTES

1. Sarojini Naidu, *Speeches and Writings* (Madras: G. A. Natesan, 1919), 219.

2. Sita Anantha Raman, "Crossing Cultural Boundaries: Indian Matriarchs and Sisters in Service," *Journal of Third World Studies* 18, no. 2 (Fall 2001): 131–48.

3. A. Madhaviah, *Muthumeenakshi* (1903; repr., Chennai: Vanavil Press, 1984); Raman and Surya, *A. Madhaviah*, 87–98, 127–86.

4. My father's maternal cousin, a *brahman* widow, eloped with a Mudaliyar and was never heard of again. See also the fictional tale of a *brahman* widow's seduction, her death in childhood, and the adoption of her son by missionaries in Madhaviah, *Satyananda.*

5. "A Woman" (anon.), *Mathar Manoranjani* (Brightener of Women's Minds), a Tamil journal for women, 1, no. 8 (October 1899): 125.

6. Kosambi, *At the Intersection of Gender Reform and Religious Belief,* 25.

7. Padmini Sengupta, *The Portrait of an Indian Woman* (Calcutta: Y.M.C.A., 1956), 45–47.

8. Ibid., 61–62.

9. Minault, "Introduction: The Extended Family," 3–19, *vide,* 5.

10. Raman, "Crossing Cultural Boundaries," 131–36.

11. Ibid., 131–33.

12. Aparna Basu and Bharati Ray, *Women's Struggle: A History of the All India Women's Conference, 1927–2002,* 2nd ed. (New Delhi: Manohar Publishers, 2003), 18–19.

13. Kumar, *History of Doing,* 45, 54.

14. Ray, *Early Feminists of Colonial India,* 15; Kumar, *History of Doing,* 38–39.

15. Forbes, *Women in Modern India,* 67–68.

16. Minault, "Sisterhood or Separatism?" 83–108, *vide,* 86–87.

17. Sengupta, *Portrait of an Indian Woman,* 52; Raman, *Getting Girls to School,* 210–11.

18. Women's Indian Association, "History of the Women's Indian Association," in *Golden Jubilee Celebration Souvenir, 1917–1967* (Madras: Women's Indian Association, 1967), 1–10.

19. Basu and Ray, *Women's Struggle,* 17–29.

20. Anagol, *The Emergence of Feminism in India, 1850–1920,* 62.

21. Women's Indian Association, *Annual Reports for 1928 & 1929; All Asian Conference on Women* (Adyar: Women's Indian Association, 1930); Reddi, *An Autobiography,* 88–96; Raman, "Crossing Cultural Boundaries," 140–42, 148 nn. 48–51.

22. O'Hanlon, *Caste, Conflict and Ideology,* 118.

23. Ibid., 110.

24. Ibid., 135.

25. Savitribai Phule, "Letter to Jotiba Phule," October 10, 1856, full text in Tharu and Lalitha, *Women Writing in India,* 1:213–14.

26. Tharu and Lalitha, *Women Writing in India*, 1:211–12.

27. Kosambi, *At the Intersection of Gender Reform and Religious Belief*, 28–32.

28. Tharu and Lalitha, *Women Writing in India*, 1:243–55.

29. Jayawardena, *The White Woman's Other Burden*, 54.

30. Cited by Kosambi, *At the Intersection of Gender Reform and Religious Belief*, 87–88.

31. Ibid., 72–73.

32. Maratha feminist wrote Anandibai's biography in 1912, *vide*, Kosambi, *At the Intersection of Gender Reform and Religious Belief*, 18. See also S. J. Joshi, *Anandi Gopal*, trans. Asha Damle (Calcutta: Stree, 1992), 229, 236–39.

33. Gauri Vishwanathan, "Silencing Heresy: Feminist Struggle and Religious Dissent," in *Outside the Fold: Conversion, Modernity and Belief* (Princeton: Princeton University Press, 1998), 118–52.

34. Tharu and Lalitha, *Women Writing in India*, 1:243–55, *vide*, 253.

35. Vishwanathan, *Outside the Fold*, 149.

36. Gauri Vishwanathan argues that her conversion was due to changed spiritual faith, and rebellion against Hindu social misogyny, unlike most feminists who believe it was in rejection of Hindu patriarchal norms. They include Kosambi, *At the Intersection of Gender Reform and Religious Belief*; Inderpal Grewal, *Home and Harem: Nation, Gender, Empire, Cultures of Travel* (Durham, North Carolina: Duke University Press, 1996); Antoinette Burton, *Burdens of History: British Feminists, Indian Women, and Imperial Culture, 1865–1915* (Chapel Hill: University of North Carolina, 1994); and Jayawardena, *The White Woman's Other Burden*, 53–62.

37. Mary Rama (Pandita Ramabai), "Letter to Miss Dorothea Beale, Cheltenham," in *Women Writing in India*, ed. Tharu and Lalitha, 1:245.

38. Tharu and Lalitha, *Women Writing in India*, 1:245.

39. Kumar, *History of Doing*, 26; Forbes, *Women in Modern India*, 46.

40. Quoted by Tharu and Lalitha, eds., *Women Writing in India*, 1:246.

41. Quoted by Kosambi, *At the Intersection of Gender Reform and Religious Belief*, 89.

42. Ibid., 31; Gail Omvedt, *Dalit Visions: The Anti-Caste Movement and the Construction of an Indian Identity*, 2nd ed. (Mumbai: Orient Longman, 2006), 17–24.

43. Rosalind O'Hanlon, *A Comparison between Women and Men: Tarabai Shinde and the Critique of Gender Relations in Colonial India* (New Delhi: Oxford University Press, 1994), 100–125; and O'Hanlon, "Extract from *Stri Purush Tulana (A Comparison between Women and Men)*: Tarabai Shinde and the Critique of Gender," in *Feminism in India*, ed. Maitrayee Chaudhuri, 2nd ed. (New Delhi: Women Unlimited and Kali for Women, 2005), 82–93.

44. O'Hanlon, "Extract from *Stri Purush Tulana*," 88; Tharu and Lalitha, *Women Writing in India*, 1:221–35.

45. Tharu and Lalitha, *Women Writing in India*, 1:228.

46. O'Hanlon, "Extract from *Stri Purush Tulana*," 83–84.

47. Ibid., 91.

48. Ibid.

49. Ray, *Early Feminists of Colonial India*, 20.

50. Ibid., 22–23.

51. Tharu and Lalitha, *Women Writing in India,* 1:340–42.

52. Ray, *Early Feminists of Colonial India,* 19.

53. Forbes, *Women in Modern India,* 55–57.

54. Tharu and Lalitha, *Women Writing in India,* 1:340–42.

55. Thomas Noble, Barry Strauss, Duane Osheim, Kristen Neuschel, and William Cohen, *Western Civilization: The Continuing Experiment* (Boston and Toronto: Houghton Mifflin Company, 1994), 746–47, 794, 826.

56. Tharu and Lalitha, *Women Writing in India,* 1:341.

57. Forbes, *Women in Modern India,* 56.

58. Rokeya Sakhawat Hossain, "Sultana's Dream," trans. Roushan Jahan, in *Feminism in India,* ed. Chaudhuri, 103–14, *vide,* 104–5; also in Tharu and Lalitha, *Women Writing in India,* 1:344–45.

59. *Primary sources:* R. S. Subbalakshmi Ammal, "My Diary," handwritten account from 1899 to 1935 (Tamil and English); Government of Madras (Educ), G.O. 504, June 4, 1913, Tamil Nadu Archives, Chennai (TNA); S. Chellammal, "Sister Subbalakshmi Ammal," in *Sister Subbalakshmi Ammal First Anniversary Commemoration Souvenir* (Tamil; T. Nagar: Sarada Ladies Union, 1970), 50–53; Interview with S. Chellammal, 1987 at Madras; "Origin and Growth of Sri Sarada Ladies Union," in *Sister Subbalakshmi Ammal First Anniversary Commemoration Souvenir* (T. Nagar: Sarada Ladies Union, 1970).

60. *Secondary references:* Monica Felton, *A Child Widow's Story* (London: Gollancz, 1966); K. Krishnaveni, *Sahodari Subbalakshmi* (Tamil; Madras: Sarada Ladies Union, 1962); Kokila Sastri, "Sister R. S. Subbalakshmi," in *Women Pioneers in Education (Tamil Nadu),* ed. T. M. Narayanaswamy Pillai (Madras: National Seminar on the Role of Women in Education in India, 1975); Raman, *Getting Girls to School,* 186–92; Raman, "Crossing Cultural Boundaries," 131–48; Muthulakshmi Reddi, "Messages," in *Sister Subbalakshmi Ammal Souvenir* (T. Nagar: Sarada Ladies Union, 1953), 29–32; Malathi Ramanathan, "Preface," in *Sister Subbalakshmi Ammal Birth Centenary Souvenir* (T. Nagar: Sarada Ladies Union, 1986), 57–58; S. Chellammal, "Avar Oru Daivam" (She Was a Divine Person), in *Sister Subbalakshmi Birth Centenary Souvenir* (T. Nagar: Sarada Ladies Union, 1986), 1–4; Radha Sadasivan, "A Centenary Tribute: Sister Subbalakshmi Ammal," *Bhavan's Journal* 32, no. 24 (July 16–31, 1982): 21–23.

61. Raman, *Getting Girls to School,* 186–92.

62. Government of India, *Census, 1911,* Volume 12, Madras, part 1, 28.

63. Subbalakshmi Ammal, "My Diary," entry dated September 27, 1910 on Ammukutty.

64. Ramanathan, "Preface."

65. Interview with Rajeshwari Padmanabhan (Anuthama) in Madras on July 28, 1987; also Raman, *Getting Girls to School,* 191–92, 202 n. 181.

66. Interview with S. Chellammal, January 8, 1990; interview with Radha Sadasivan, November 30, 1989; interview with V. S. Shankar, December 16, 1989.

67. Nallamuthu Ramamurthi, "Messages," in *Souvenir Presented to Sister Subbalakshmi Ammal,* November 29, 1953 (Madras: Sarada Ladies' Union, 1953), 35–37; "Sister Subbalakshmi's Talk on Compulsory Primary Education for Girls at the Indian Women's Conference," *Stri Dharma* 4, no. 1 (January 1921): 4; S. Chellammal, "Sister Subbalakshmi Ammal," in *Sister Subbalakshmi Ammal First Anniversary Commemoration Souvenir,* 50–53.

68. "Legislation on Child Marriage," S. Muthulakshmi Reddi Correspondence, File no. 8, Nehru Memorial Museum and Library, New Delhi.

69. Tharu and Lalitha, *Women Writing in India,* 1:190.

70. Ibid., 190–202.

71. Ibid., 201–2.

72. Ibid., 256–43; Kumar, *History of Doing,* 38.

73. Tharu and Lalitha, *Women Writing in India,* 1:237.

74. Krupabai Sattianadhan, *Kamala: The Story of a Hindu Life,* ed., Chandani Lokuge (New Delhi: Oxford University Press, 1998), xiii–xv.

75. Krupabai Sattianadhan, "Saguna: A Story of Native Christian Life," in *Women Writing in India,* ed. Tharu and Lalitha, 1:277–81.

76. Sattianadhan, *Kamala,* 57–87.

77. Sengupta, *The Portrait of an Indian Woman,* 41–43, 191–92; also *Indian Ladies' Magazine* 2, no. 6–9 (January–April 1929).

78. Raman, *Getting Girls to School,* 210–13.

79. Raman, "Prescriptions for Gender Equality in South India," 331–66; and Raman, "Crossing Cultural Boundaries," 131–37.

80. Katherine Mayo, *Mother India* (New York: Harcourt Brace, 1927), 319–23; also Forbes, *Women in Modern India,* 85, 88, 108.

81. Sengupta, *The Portrait of an Indian Woman,* 179–81.

82. Ibid., 182–84.

83. Raman, *Getting Girls to School,* 130–31, 142; also *Mathar Manoranjani* 1, no. 7 (September 1899), and 3, no. 6 (August 1901); *Tamil Mathu* 1, no. 1 (April 13, 1905).

84. Vir Bharat Talwar, "Feminist Consciousness in Women's Journals in Hindi, 1910–1920," in *Recasting Women,* ed. Sangari and Vaid, 207–15.

85. Ali, *The Emergence of Feminism among Indian Muslim Women,* 24–25.

86. Ibid., 215.

87. Ibid., 25–26.

88. Ibid., 228–29.

89. Government of India, Hartog Committee Report, *Review of Growth of Education in British India by the Auxiliary Committee Appointed by the Indian Statutory Commission,* September 1929, 45, 145; Appendix, Fig. I.

90. *Theosophical Society:* "An Indian Lady," "Girls' Education," read to the Mahila Parishad, Kanchipuram, in *The Commonweal,* vol. 1 (April 3, 1914), 267, Adyar: TS; Besant, "Address to Maharani Girls' School"; Besant, "An Appeal: Higher Education for Indian Girls"; Besant, *An Autobiography;* Besant, *Higher Education in India.*

91. Government of India, Hartog Committee Report, Table 71, 147; Appendix. Fig. J.

92. Ray, *Early Feminists of Colonial India,* 1, 7–15.

93. *Primary sources: Stri Dharma* 3, no. 4 (December 1920); 5, no. 1–4 (January–December 1921); 7, no. 3 (January 1924); 8, no. 3–8 (January–June 1925); 11, no. 6–8 (April–June 1928); Women's Indian Association, *Annual Reports, 1927–1928, 1928–1929;* WIA, "Demand for the Grant of the Vote Placed before Lord Chelmsford and Mr. Montagu by the Representatives of All India Women's Deputation on December 18, 1917" with a photograph; WIA, "Franchise for Women: Views of Prominent Men" (pamphlet), 1918; WIA, *Golden Jubilee Celebration: 1917–1967* (Adyar: WIA, 1967).

94. Jayawardena, *The White Woman's Other Burden*, 147–55, *vide*, 151.

95. "Goals of the Women's Indian Association," May 8, 1917, in WIA, *Report of the Women's Indian Association* (Adyar, Madras: Theosophical Society Publishers, 1928).

96. *Some secondary sources:* Geraldine Forbes, "The Indian Women's Movement: A Struggle for Women's Rights or National Liberation?" in *The Extended Family*, ed. Minault; Gail Minault, "Introduction: The Extended Family"; Manmohan Kaur, *Role of Women in the Freedom Movement (1857–1947)* (Delhi: Sterling, 1968); Shahida Lateef, "Indian Women's Movement and National Development: An Overview," in *The Extended Family*, ed. Minault; Lateef, *Muslim Women in India;* Vishwanath S. Naravane, *Sarojini Naidu: Her Life, Work, and Poetry* (1980; repr., Delhi: Orient Longman, 2001); Ramusack, "Catalysts or Helpers?"

97. Cousins, *The Awakening of Indian Womanhood;* James H. Cousins and Margaret Cousins, *We Two Together* (Madras: Ganesh, 1950); Margaret Cousins, "Women's Indian Association: Summary of Women's Suffrage Work in India," letter to Annie Besant, June 4, 1919, Madras; Dorothy Jinarajadasa and Margaret Cousins, letter to Annie Besant, March 21, 1922.

98. Forbes, *Women in Modern India,* 78–83.

99. Rajkumari Amrit Kaur, Sharifa Hamid Ali, and Muthulakshmi Reddi, "Statement of the Elected Representatives of the All-India Women's Conference, the Women's Indian Association, and the National Council of Women in India, to the Joint Select Committee," London, August 1, 1933, File no. 10 (Nehru Memorial Museum and Library, New Delhi); joint letter to All-India Women's Conference Papers, London, August 9, 1933, File no. 10 (NMML); Letter of Support for the Indian Women Suffrage Delegation from the British Commonwealth League, Women's Freedom League, Six Point Group, St. Joan's Social and Political Alliance, and Women's International League, April 10, 1934, File no. 12 (NMML).

100. Cousins and Cousins, *We Two Together,* 370; also Ramusack, "Catalysts or Helpers?" 109–43, *vide,* 127.

101. Basu and Ray, *Women's Struggle,* 70.

102. Reddi, *My Experiences as a Legislator;* Reddi, *An Autobiography;* Reddi, *Presidential Address;* Reddi: *Why Should the Devadasi Institution in the Hindu Temples Be Abolished?* Pamphlet, S. Muthulakshmi Reddi Papers, Files 7–12 (NMML).

103. Reddi, *An Autobiography,* 87.

104. *The Hindu,* November 17, 1931, as cited by Forbes, *Women in Modern India,* 107.

105. Basu and Ray, *Women's Struggle,* 69–73.

106. Dorothy Jinarajadasa, *Stri Dharma* 8, no. 6 (1925): 82–83.

107. Muthulakshmi Reddi, letter to Kamaladevi Chattopadhyaya, February 6, 1927, "S. Muthulakshmi Reddi Correspondence, 1925–53," 1–8; also Indian National Social Conference, Madras Session, 1927, agenda pamphlet, signed by Muthulakshmi Reddi, Kamaladevi Chattopadhyaya, K. Natarajan, File no. 8.

108. Kumar, *History of Doing,* 71–72.

109. Muthulakshmi Reddi papers, "Resolution at the Public Meeting of the Hindu Women of Madras, April 7th, 1928," File no. 7 (NMML); "Public Meeting Under the Auspices of the Sri Sarada Ladies' Union, Women's Indian Association, Indian Ladies' Samaj, Women Graduates' Union, and Mothers' Union on July 28th,

1928" in Madras, signed by Malathi Patwardhan, Mrs. Muzeruddin, Sister Subbalakshmi, Swarnam (Mrs. Paul) Appasamy, File no. 7 (NMML).

110. Basu and Ray, *Women's Struggle,* 58–60.

111. Reena Nanda, *Kamaladevi Chattopadhyaya: A Biography* (New Delhi: Oxford University Press, 2002), 33.

112. Forbes, *Women in Modern India,* 79.

113. *Stri Dharma,* "Madras Women's Muslim Association," April 1928, 49.

114. Government of India, Hartog Committee Report, 181–83.

115. Basu and Ray, *Women's Struggle,* 59.

116. Ibid., 55–60.

117. Begam of Bhopal, "Presidential Address at the Second All-India Women's Educational Conference," February 7–10, 1928 at Delhi, in *The Indian Social Reformer* 38, no. 25 (February 18, 1928): 391.

118. Basu and Ray, *Women's Struggle,* 85–87.

119. *Gandhi's writings:* M. K. Gandhi, *An Autobiography or My Experiments with Truth,* translated from Gujarati by Mahadev Desai (1927; repr., Ahmedabad: Navajivan Publishing House, 1996); M. K. Gandhi, *The Collected Works of Mahatma Gandhi,* 2 vols. (New Delhi: Government of India Publications Division, 1958); M. K. Gandhi, *Hind Swaraj and Other Writings,* ed. A. J. Parel (Cambridge: Cambridge University Press, 1997).

120. Arun Gandhi, Sunanda Gandhi, and Carol Lynn Yellin, *The Forgotten Woman: The Untold Story of Kastur Gandhi, Wife of Mahatma Gandhi* (Arkansas: Zark Mountain Publishers, 1998).

121. Gandhi, *An Autobiography,* 174.

122. Ibid., 21.

123. M. K. Gandhi, "What Is Women's Role?" February 12, 1940, in *The Penguin Gandhi Reader,* ed. Rudrangshu Mukherjee (New Delhi: Penguin India, 1993), 194.

124. Gandhi, *An Autobiography,* 172–73.

125. On his celibacy, see M. K. Gandhi, *An Autobiography,* 171–76; Erikson, *Gandhi's Truth,* 192–95, 224; Gandhi, Gandhi, and Yellin, *The Forgotten Woman,* 138–40.

126. M. K. Gandhi, *An Autobiography or My Experiments with Truth,* 21.

127. Gandhi, Gandhi, and Yellin, *The Forgotten Woman,* 212–15, 221–27, 235–39, 241–43.

128. Gandhi, "What Is Women's Role?" 194.

129. Thapar-Björket, *Women in the Indian National Movement,* 109.

130. Ibid., 59–60.

131. Ibid., 65, 81, 100–101, 106–7.

132. M. K. Gandhi, *Young India,* March 26, 1918, cited by Thapar-Björket, *Women in the Indian National Movement,* 79.

133. Forbes, *Women in Modern India,* 125, 127–28, 145–46, 229, 236.

134. Kumar, *History of Doing,* 63–64.

135. Raman, "Prescriptions for Gender Equality in South India," 331–66; Raman, *Getting Girls to School,* 212–13, 227–40.

136. Reddi, *My Experience as a Legislator;* Reddi, *An Autobiography.*

137. Muthulakshmi Reddi, letters to M. K. Gandhi, July 31, 1927, and January 24, 1946, Muthulakshmi Reddi Papers (NMML).

138. Reddi, *An Autobiography,* 110–12.

139. Kaur, *Role of Women in the Freedom Movement,* 236–38.

140. Durgabai Deshmukh, *Stone That Speaketh: The Story of the Andhra Mahila Sabha* (Hyderabad: Andhra Mahila Sabha, 1980).

141. Reddi, *An Autobiography,* 110–12.

142. Gupta, *India's 50 Most Illustrious Women,* 11–18, 87–93; Forbes, *Women in Modern India,* 129, 205–7.

143. Gupta, *India's 50 Most Illustrious Women,* 90–92.

144. Forbes, *Women in Modern India,* 129.

145. Gupta, *India's 50 Most Illustrious Women,* 100–106.

146. Sarojini Naidu, *Speeches and Writings;* S. Naidu, *The Bird of Time: Songs of Life, Death and the Spring,* 5th ed. (1912; repr., London: William Heinemann, 1926); S. Naidu, *Broken Wing: Songs of Love, Death, and Destiny* (London: William Heinemann, 1917); Muthulakshmi Reddi, "Letter to Sarojini Naidu on Her Diamond Jubilee Celebration," February 9, 1946, Muthulakshmi Reddi Correspondence, 1917–53 (NMML); Sarojini Naidu, "Bangle Sellers," "The Temple, a Pilgrimage of Love," and "Presidential Address at the Ahmedabad Students' Conference," in Tharu and Lalitha, *Women Writing in India,* 1:331–40.

147. Tara Ali Baig, *Sarojini Naidu: Portrait of a Patriot* (New Delhi: Congress Centenary Celebration Committee, 1985); Hasi Banerjee, *Sarojini Naidu: The Traditional Feminist,* University of Calcutta monograph #16 (Calcutta: K. P. Bagchi, 1998); Bipin Chandra, *India's Struggle for Independence,* 2nd ed. (Delhi: Penguin, 1989); Partha Chatterjee, "The Nationalist Resolution of the Woman Question," in *Recasting Women,* ed. Sangari and Vaid, 233–53; Neera Desai, *Woman in Modern India* (Bombay: Vora, 1977); Mukul C. Dey, *Twenty Portraits* (Calcutta: Thacker, Spink and Company, 1953); Forbes, "The Indian Women's Movement," 49–82; Sarla Jag Mohan, *Remembering Sarojini Naidu* (Delhi: Children's Book Trust, 1978); Devaki Jain, *Indian Women* (Delhi: Government of India Publication Division, 1976); Kaur, *Role of Women in the Freedom Movement;* V. S. Navaratne, *Sarojini Naidu: Her Life, Work and Poetry* (Delhi: Orient Longman, 1980); G. Venkatachalam, *My Contemporaries* (Bangalore: Hosati Press, 1966).

148. Naidu, *Speeches and Writings,* 219.

149. Avvai Ashram, Adyar: *14th–15th Annual Report, 1943–44 & 1944–45; Avvai Home Completes Fifty Years: A Golden Centenary Souvenir* (Adyar: Avvai Ashram, 1980); *Avvai Home Silver Jubilee Souvenir, 1955;* "Yengal Amma" (Our Mother), *Avvai Home School Calendar, 1986–87;* Government of India, (Home), Judicial, Part A, May 1905, nos. 130–44, "Legislating for the Protection of Minor Girls Found in the Custody of Women of Ill-Fame"; Govt. of India, (Home), Jails, Part B, May 1918, nos. 7–8, "The Madras Children's Bill"; (Home), Jails Branch Proceedings, December 1920, nos. 35–36, "Madras Children's Law," no. 15, 63–66; (Home), Jails, December 1920, nos. 35–36, "The Madras Children's Law"; (Home), Judicial File 791, August 24, 1927, 1–4; (Home), Judicial File 791, 1927, 1–4, "Legislation to Prohibit Dedication of Girls at Temples as Devadasis"; Government of Madras, (Educational), G.O. 504, June 4, 1913, "Brahmin Widows' Hostel"; *Legislative Council Proceedings,* v. 51 (July 1915–June 1916); v. 53 (July 1919–June 1920); v. I-A, No. 1 (July 1920–June 1921); Dorothy Jinarajadasa, "The Age of Consent Bill," *Stri Dharma* (Adyar: Women's Indian Association), 8, no. 6 (April 1925): 82–83; Margaret Cousins, "Children's Protection Bill,"

Stri Dharma 8, no. 11 (September 1925): 129; Anon., "Social Evil in Madras," *Stri Dharma* 8, no. 12 (October 1925): 130; Anon., "The Madras Muslim Ladies Association," *Stri Dharma* 11, no. 6 (1928): 47; S. Bhagirathi Ammal, "Raising of the Marriage Age," *Stri Dharma* 11, no. 6 (April 1928): 12–13; C. V. Vishwanatha Sastri, "The Child Marriage Bill," *Indian Social Reformer* (Bombay), 38, no. 26 (February 1928): 407; K. Natarajan, "Haribilas Sarda's Bill," *Indian Social Reformer* 38, no. 31 (March 1928): 487–89; Kamala Sattianadhan, "The Society for the Protection of Children in Madras," *Indian Ladies' Magazine* 2, no. 7 (February 1929): 355–57; Kamala Sattianadhan, "Dr. Muthulakshmi's Achievement," *Indian Ladies' Magazine* 2, no. 8 (March 1929): 447; Reddi, *An Autobiography;* Reddi, *My Experience as a Legislator;* Reddi, *A Brief Autobiographical Sketch of Dr. (Mrs.) Muthulakshmi Reddi* (Adyar: Avvai Home, 1957); Reddi, *The Life of Dr. T. Sundara Reddi: The Story of a Dedicated Life* (Madras: Shakti Karyalayam, 1949); and Madras Seva Sadan, *Silver Jubilee Souvenir, 1953* (Madras: 1953).

150. Reddi, *An Autobiography,* 140–41, 145.

151. Muthulakshmi Reddi, letter to M. K. Gandhi, September 29, 1937, Adyar, Madras, Muthulakshmi Reddi Papers, File no. 11, Part I (NMML).

152. Basu and Ray, *Women's Struggle,* 221.

153. Nanda, *Kamaladevi Chattopadhyaya,* 10–16.

154. Ibid., 33–39; Basu and Ray, *Women's Struggle,* 19, 106–7, 221; Kumar, *History of Doing,* 55, 57–58.

155. Nanda, *Kamaladevi Chattopadhyaya,* 48–49.

156. Kamaladevi Chattopadhyaya, *Inner Recesses, Outer Spaces* (New Delhi: Navrang Publications, 1986), 152–53; Forbes, *Women in Modern India,* 132.

157. Nanda, *Kamaladevi Chattopadhyaya,* 96–97.

158. Ibid., 114–20.

159. Kamaladevi Chattopadhyaya, *The Awakening of Indian Women* (Madras: Everyman's Press, 1939); K. Chattopadhyaya, *Indian Women's Battle for Freedom* (New Delhi: Abinav Publications, 1983); Chattopadhyaya, *Inner Recesses, Outer Spaces;* K. Chattopadhyaya, *At the Crossroads,* collection of essays on socialism and other topics (Bombay: Yusuf Meherally and Nalanda Publications, 1947); K. Chattopadhyaya, *Tribalism in India* (New Delhi: Vikas, 1978); K. Chattopadhyaya, *Carpets and Floor Coverings of India* (New Delhi: Handicrafts Board, 1966); K. Chattopadhyaya, *The Glory of Indian Handicrafts* (New Delhi: Indian Book Co., 1976); K. Chattopadhyaya, *Indian Embroidery* (New Delhi: Wiley Eastern, 1977).

160. Ray, *Early Feminists of India,* 3–16; Kumar, *History of Doing,* 38–41.

161. Forbes, *Women in Modern India,* 123.

162. Gupta, *India's 50 Most Illustrious Women,* 67–75.

163. Kumar, *History of Doing,* 46–47.

164. Thapar-Björket, *Women in the National Movement,* 124–32.

165. Kumar, *History of Doing,* 86–87.

166. Ibid., 91.

167. Gupta, *India's 50 Most Illustrious Women,* 80–87.

168. Jawaharlal Nehru, *The Discovery of India* (New York: The John Day Company, 1946), 29, 239–40, 265.

169. Kiran Devendra, *Changing Status of Women in India* (New Delhi: Vikas Publishing House, 1996), 43.

170. Basu and Ray, *Women's Struggle,* 65.

171. Sarvepalli Gopal, ed., *Selected Works of Jawaharlal Nehru*, 2nd series (New Delhi: Jawaharlal Nehru Memorial Fund, 1989), 8:296–300, *vide*, 299.

172. Menon and Bhasin, *Borders and Boundaries*, 21, 33–35.

173. Butalia, *The Other Side of Silence*, 83–86.

174. Ibid., 3–4.

175. Cited by Menon and Bhasin, *Borders and Boundaries*, 68.

176. Ibid., 69–71.

177. Butalia, *The Other Side of Silence*, 175–78.

178. Ibid., 179.

179. Menon and Bhasin, *Borders and Boundaries*, 148–58.

5

CONCLUSION: WOMEN IN INDIA TODAY

Achieving gender equality is therefore not just women's concern—it deeply concerns men.

Bina Agarwal, economist[1]

IDEALS AND REALITIES

India's secular, democratic constitution is formulated on the principle of social justice for all. Its laws give women equal rights to property (1956) and prohibit dowry (1984), child labor (1987), and female feticide (1984), and its press is vigilant and relatively free. Indian women made notable strides in literacy by 2001 (53.7%) from the abysmal 7.30 percent at the end of colonial rule. This is especially significant as the population tripled, thus raising the number of literate women from 11.7 million (1951) to 255 million (2001).[2] Other achievements include the appreciable drop in the fertility rate (1990: 4 children per woman; 2007: 2.7), as women wait longer to marry and to have children.[3] Women of the expanding middle class have garnered high professional honors at home and abroad, although these benefits have not yet accrued fully to the lowest-caste and tribal women. A growing number contest and win elections to village councils (*panchayats*), provincial councils, and Parliament, while dissident women challenge corrupt officials and multinational corporations to change the power structure. Despite poverty and patriarchal traditions, women juggle family duties and work to be their own agents. They care for children and seniors at home, while bringing in an income as farmers, herders, weavers, craftswomen, teachers, doctors, scientists, pharmacists, lawyers, judges, administrators, bankers, businesswomen, nurses, soldiers, policewomen, computer technicians, tailors, artists, performers, shop assistants, and construction laborers.

They maneuver village and urban streets on foot, bikes, scooters, buses, trams, and cars to reach these places of work. Many take up contractual jobs in the Persian Gulf and elsewhere abroad, thus ensuring the family's prosperity, boosting India's economy, and reshaping gender norms and ethnic identities. Erstwhile elite feminist associations have been penetrated by working-class leaders, and their societies have multiplied since 1970. Clearly, Indian women are productive agents today.[4]

Government welfare departments, nongovernmental organizations (NGOs), and some UN agencies have started cooperatives for marginalized women. One such is SEWA or help (Self-Employed Women's Association) started by Ela Bhatt in Ahmedabad as a union for workers in bidi (local cigarette) and other small industries, and for self-employed vendors of vegetables and small products. Today, numerous SEWA branches across Gujarat offer women loans for small businesses, conduct classes to expand employment skills, and publish their activities in *Shramshakti* (Working Power) journal founded in 1989.[5] Following the model of Grameen Bank in Bangladesh, micro-credit banks in India give poor women loans to buy livestock, start small handicraft shops, repair homes, and acquire skills to earn a better living.[6] The repayment rates are sometimes as high as 98 percent despite extensive female poverty.[7] Indian micro-credit unions are run by NGOs and by government, examples of the latter being the Tamil Nadu Women's Development Project and the Maharashtra Rural Credit Project. A small NGO micro-credit bank is BISWA (Bharat Integrated Social Welfare Agency) in operation in Sambalpur, Orissa since 1984. By assisting women to educate their daughters or halt the sale of children into servitude, micro-credit banks stall the cycle of poverty and empower women.[8]

Despite such gains, gender equality remains elusive for many Indian women for complex reasons. These obstacles include entrenched patriarchal cultural norms; a residual colonial legal framework; persistent high-caste male domination in the bastions of power; electoral politics in a multiethnic nation; and commercial globalization that thrives on female and child labor, and reduces them to pawns for large corporations. Modernization is not always commensurate with progress, since moribund traditions do not all simply fade away but are often reinvented in the relentless drive for wealth and power. While there is broad consensus that women are more assertive, and that a democracy can be guided into promoting the disadvantaged, even such a state can be coercive under corrupt leaders, unless humane attitudes are assiduously cultivated and just laws duly enforced.

In the crucial markers of sex ratio (933 females per 1000 males), literacy, nutrition, wages, and wealth, India's gender anomalies are startling, and women walk a sedate two paces behind men, like the dutiful housewives of a bygone era.[9] Although women are visible on rural paths and the Bollywood silver screen, in some conservative circles, the *pardah* threatens to make a comeback. The goddess of wisdom, Saraswati, beckons girls to schools that are passports to opportunity. However, female dropout rates are high, as girls perform many domestic chores or labor to augment the family income.[10] Women have equal property rights, yet many daughters are denied their inheritance by male relatives, and many widows own property jointly with sons.[11] Although the legal marriage age is 18 for women and 21 for men (1978), child marriage is common, thriving where female literacy is negligible, and infant mortality is high.[12] Destitution sometimes drives parents to sell daughters into prostitution and children into bonded labor for the family to survive, making these a lurking threat for young working women.[13] These poignant themes are encountered in daily life and portrayed in journals like *Manushi* and *Economic and Political Weekly*, and in regional films and literature.[14]

India's 35 states and territories are diverse in culture, language, history, and governance by political party. Comparisons between Kerala and Uttar Pradesh reveal statistical links between female education, sex ratio, and infant mortality.[15] This has led scholars like Nobel Laureate Amartya Sen to emphasize a holistic approach to female "well-being" and agency, which are shaped by many factors such as education, income, and property. In their absence, women suffer domestic violence, and the whole family is affected. Sen argues persuasively that gender inequality cannot therefore be simply dismissed as a "female problem," when it jeopardizes the larger community and shakes India's foundations of freedom and democracy.[16] In view of these complex developments after 1947, this chapter is divided into four broad but interrelated sections, viz., survival (sex ratio, education, and employment); women in power (politics and laws); women as dissidents; and some notable women in the arts.

SURVIVAL

Sex Ratio and Violence to Women

Statistics and studies now show that India's population is growing at a slower pace, as women wait longer to marry and have children. The fertility rate (children per woman) has thus taken a significant dip (2007: 2.7; 1990: 4), and other favorable signs are the decline in maternal and infant mortality after 1970.[17] However, the intelligentsia is alert to the problem of "missing women" in the population ever since the United Nations published its report *Towards Equality* (1974), which inaugurated the International Women's Decade (1975–85). While praising elite women in India for their high educational honors, the report revealed that most ordinary women lagged far behind. It also revealed that India's low sex ratio (females per 1000 males) had been plummeting since 1901. The Census of India 2001 gives these figures: 1901 (972); 1911 (962); 1921 (955); 1931 (950); 1941 (945); 1951 (946); 1961 (941); 1971 (930). Since the report, the census records indicate a slight rise in 1981 (934), but then a sharp slump in 1991 (927). Although it appears to improve in 2001 (933), it is actually 927 for infants less than six years. It is clear that girls are being aborted, despite a higher chance of survival at birth than boys.[18]

The declining sex ratio indicates a disturbing trend toward sex-selective abortion. Abortion was first legalized in 1971 (Medical Termination of Pregnancy Act) for humane reasons, namely to safeguard women after rape, if they are physically or mentally unfit to bear a child, or in other extreme circumstances, and in 1978, ultrasound and amniocentesis were introduced to detect fetal abnormalities. However, due to a growing number of female feticides, these modern technologies were soon legally prohibited except in extreme cases (Penal Code, sections 312 and 316). Ironically, in order to maintain their traditions of patriarchal descent and inheritance, some affluent urban families bribe local doctors or visit the United States to have these procedures. The sex ratio is now alarmingly askew in Daman and Diu (710 females/1000 males), Haryana (819), Chandigarh (777), and Delhi (821).[19] Female feticide is also more common among those aspiring for social mobility, by emulating the misguided lifestyles of the wealthy. The sex ratio is higher in areas with some matrilineal traditions (e.g., Kerala, Tamil Nadu, and Assam) and in small states like Goa (2003) where a recent law protects girls based on the UN Convention on the Rights of the Child.[20] The sex ratio is lower in the north and west (Haryana, Punjab, Uttar Pradesh, Madhya Pradesh, Bihar, Gujarat, and Rajasthan).

A comparison of Kerala and Uttar Pradesh reveals the links between female literacy, sex ratio, and the infant mortality. Kerala is home to more than one matrilineal community, and its former kings and queens invested in primary education, a thrust maintained by the Communist Party of India (CPI) whose political clout dates from 1952. Kerala has the highest female literacy (87.7%), the highest sex ratio (1028), and the lowest infant mortality rate in the nation. Uttar Pradesh on the Gangetic plain is home to a conservative Hindu and Muslim population, and it remains a major stronghold of the Congress Party, which has done little to help its women. Its record of female literacy (42.2%) and sex ratio (916) is among the lowest, while its infant mortality rate is four times higher than that of Kerala.[21] The link between "missing women" and general "female well-being" was first brought out in 1992 by Amartya Sen in a medical journal. Since then, other scholars like Bina Agarwal have shown that women's agency and equality cannot be dismissed as simply "female" issues, as they profoundly affect the community's survival.

Sen argues that a 75 percent female literacy will lead to a plummeting of child mortality rates. However, wealth alone does not guarantee a lower fertility rate or a higher sex ratio, as seen in wealthy Punjab and Haryana where birth rates are higher than in poorer southern states. Despite Punjab's fair record in female literates, there is a substantial gap between literate men and women, and its sex ratio, especially in two districts, is among the lowest in the nation.[22] Traditional gender inequity is being abetted by modern technology and commercialization. The tradition of bequeathing property to sons drives even educated parents to bribe doctors to abort girls.[23] This defies the Constitutional guideline "to renounce practices derogatory to women" and to break the law against sex-selective amniocentesis. "Gender cleansing"

Census of India 2001[25]

	Sex Ratio (Lowest to Highest)	Sex Ratio (0–6 Years)
India	933	927
Daman & Diu	710	926
Dadra & Nagar Haveli	812	979
Haryana	819	861
Delhi	821	868
Chandigarh	845	777
Andaman & Nicobar	846	957
Punjab	876	798
Sikkim	875	964
Jammu & Kashmir	892	941
Arunachal Pradesh	893	964
Nagaland	900	964
Uttaranchal	908	962
Uttar Pradesh	916	898
Madhya Pradesh	919	932
Bihar	919	942
Gujarat	920	883
Goa	920	938
Rajasthan	921	909
Maharashtra	922	913
West Bengal	934	960
Assam	935	965
Mizoram	935	964
Jharkhand	941	965
Tripura	948	966
Lakshadweep	948	959
Karnataka	965	946
Himachal Pradesh	968	896
Orissa	972	953
Meghalaya	972	973
Manipur	974	957
Andhra Pradesh	978	961
Tamil Nadu	987	942
Chhattisgarh	989	975
Pondicherry	1001	967
Kerala	1058	960

has insidiously crept even into Tamil Nadu whose Dravidian culture once exalted women. Tamil Nadu once had the second highest sex ratio in India (1991: 975), but this has now fallen (2001: 942).[24] The Indian sex ratio in the 0–6-year range is noticeably lower in some urban states like Chandigarh and Delhi (see chart of sex ratio in each state).

Domestic Violence

Female feticide has also spread from the urban wealthy to the rural poor, thriving in the tradition of extravagant weddings for daughters and of lavish dowry gifts to the groom's family. Dowry demands have grown with the commercial economy. In the earlier tradition, dowry consisted of jewelry, clothes, cash, and linen for the girl as *stridhan,* or personal property. In the modern era, the groom's family now often demands real estate, an apartment, or a car as the price for their son. Such demands are illegal under India's Dowry Prohibition Act (1961), which has been amended twice (1984, 1986). However, dowry continues to extract its toll of verbal and physical abuse of the bride, sometimes even death at the hands of the groom's mother or father. Young brides were sent back to their natal family until they returned with a second dowry. As few could remarry with ease, they often became permanent dependents of their natal families; if they remained with the husband, violence was their lot. Newspaper reports of "bride burning" increased in the 1970s–80s, although the groom's family whitewashed these as kitchen "accidents" or "self-immolations" using kerosene.[26]

Feminists publicized the cruel incidents through assistance groups like Nari Raksha Samiti (Women's Protection Group), Mahila Dakshata Samiti (Society for Women as Gifts), and Stri Sangharsh (Women's Welfare Organization) in Punjab, Maharashtra, Gujarat, West Bengal, Madhya Pradesh, and Karnataka. So common were these incidents that even left-wing politicians conceded that their party members were guilty. The deaths of young Shakuntala Arora and Tarvinder Kaur in north India thus led to outraged demonstrations by feminists and benign patriarchs until the perpetrators were arrested.[27] Debates in the Lok Sabha (Parliamentary Lower House) in 1987 revealed that the dowry issue was the cause of at least half the reported cases of domestic violence.

Domestic violence also occurs when women defied fathers and brothers who believed they defended her honor. In 1982, Kiran Singh, a Ph.D. zoology student at Patna University in Bihar, filed a petition in the Supreme Court charging her father with violence. This was reported in the journal *Manushi.* Although Kiran's father was the university's vice-chancellor, she claimed that he had taken away her fundamental rights for dating a Muslim student named Anwar Ahmad, and that he had coerced her friends.[28] Violence also takes more subtle, chronic forms due to poverty, as girl children are more likely to be undernourished, and marriage in adolescence takes its toll through early pregnancy and death. Early malnutrition also leads to physical and cognitive stunting with long-term effects during pregnancy, maternity, and old age. Its cross-generational effect is profound, as the children of malnourished women are often born underweight and remain so for years.[29] However, a recent study (Rajasthan) shows that some poor parents strive to nourish their daughters before marriage, as young brides in a new home often face nutritional deprivation.[30] Young brides can also be physically or verbally abused by in-laws for not conforming to gender roles (Maharashtra).[31] As some ignorantly believe that a child's sex depends on the mother, she can be abused at the birth of a girl child.[32] A young bride's lot improves with age and the birth of sons. It is best for a mother-in-law but worst for a propertyless widow, whose numbers are greater in the northern states.[33]

A serious health issue today is AIDS which affects over two million Indian women. Although only 1 percent of Indian men and women are affected by the HIV, India has the second largest population of those infected with HIV. Although once feared as a homosexual disease, it is clear now that heterosexual women and men are equally vulnerable to this virus. While it was probably introduced to wives after the husband frequented a brothel, only 1 percent of the sex workers actually carry the HIV. It is expected that in the near future, Indian women will comprise the majority of victims, and as this ignorance and fear accompany this epidemic, victims are sometimes shunned and refused treatment. In recent years, government and UN agencies have worked to educate the population and to curb the spread of this fatal disease.[34]

Education

Girls' schools were inadequate under the colonial government whose Hunter Educational Commission (1882) noted that female literacy was a low .02 percent. Conscious efforts by feminists and nationalist reformers raised it to 1.8 percent in 1921, but it was still just 7.3 percent in 1947. Independent India has improved primary school enrollment, but budget allocations remain low, and secondary school is not compulsory. In the first stage of national planning (1950–60), officials viewed women as welfare recipients. Between 1970 and 1980, planners addressed working women's problems, and rates rose in 1981. The 1986 National Educational Policy specifically addressed enrollment and literacy (see chart).

Literacy rates in India (%), 1947–2001[35]

Year	Female	Male
1947	7.3	22.6
1961	15.3	40.4
1981	28.5	53.5
2001	53.7	76

Since 2001, girls' primary school enrollment has risen, even in states with low female literacy rates like Rajasthan and Bihar. The National Literacy Mission has also percolated into rural areas where older women have been eager to learn. In 1997, female literacy rose significantly in Maharashtra after an aggressive drive to commemorate Savitribai Phule, the state's first woman teacher. Most girls in Maharashtra now complete secondary school, and many urban dwellers send daughters to college.[36] The chart reveals that female literacy is often higher in smaller states that are easier to administer

Census 2001: Literacy rates (%) by state (from highest to lowest)[37]

State	Female	Male
Kerala	87.7	94.2
Lakshadweep	80.5	92.5
Mizoram	86.7	90.7
Chandigarh	76.5	86.1
Goa	75.4	88.4
Andaman & Nicobar	75.2	86.3
Delhi	74.7	87.3
Pondicherry	73.9	88.6
Maharashtra	67	86
Himachal Pradesh	67.4	85.3
Daman & Diu	65.6	86.8
Tamil Nadu	64.4	82.4
Tripura	64.9	81
Punjab	63.4	75.2
Nagaland	61.5	71.2
Sikkim	60.4	76
Uttaranchal	59.6	83.3
West Bengal	59.6	77
Meghalaya	59.6	65.4
Karnataka	56.9	76.1
Gujarat	57.8	79.7
Manipur	56.8	75
Haryana	55.7	78.5
Assam	54.6	71.3
Chhattisgarh	51.9	77.4
Orissa	50.5	75.3
Andhra Pradesh	50.4	70.3
Madhya Pradesh	50.3	76.1
Rajasthan	43.9	75.7
Arunachal Pradesh	43.5	63.8
Jammu & Kashmir	43	66.6
Uttar Pradesh	42.2	68.8
Dadra & Nagar Haveli	40.2	71.2
Jharkhand	38.9	67.3
Bihar	33.1	59.7

like Lakshadweep islands and a city like Delhi. It is also true of Kerala with its history of educational commitment, former Portuguese or French colonies (Goa and Pondicherry), or tribal states (Mizoram). In states like Rajasthan with low female literacy, there is often a considerable disparity between the literacy rates of men and women (see chart).

Literacy empowers women by increasing skills for better paying jobs and more voice in decisions on the family budget. Evidence shows that most women spend the household income on food, health, and education for boys and girls. If these allocations are met, the family's chances of survival are greater in the leaner years. Educated women often have fewer children, and their energies are spent in other productive activities that generate income for the whole family. Educated women bring down infant mortality rates, and they are more receptive to ideas on conserving the environment. Girls fare better when state governments promote gender equality (e.g., in Kerala, Pondicherry, and Tamil Nadu).[38]

Some activists argue that "literacy by itself is meaningless" unless society is mobilized to appreciate women's rights and to reject gender biases in nutrition, education, and employment. They point out that in Chandigarh, many women are literate, but the sex ratio is the worst in the nation, and many girls drop out of school. Government textbooks are also discriminatory, as they marginalize women's contributions and diminish their self-esteem. This perpetuates some men's stereotypes of women as useful largely for reproduction, and not productive enterprise.[39]

Yet it is patently clear that literacy leads to more educated women who are empowered to demand more rights. This reduces domestic violence, raises child survival rates, and ensures better nutrition for girl children. Educated women also make wiser choices on family expenditure and other decisions concerning sanitation, and this benefits the whole family.[40] They also are better equipped to learn ecologically sound practices that improve the environment for the family and community. Today, primary and secondary education are within the reach of many women, and more girls are visible in schools. However, there still remains much to be achieved in terms of the content, standards, and affordability of textbooks, and whether schools can satisfy the expectations of ordinary women to an improved quality of life. Rural peasants often keep their daughters to care for the family, so that fewer girls finish school than boys. Literacy rates are far higher in cities and towns than in the rural areas, and since over 70 percent of India's population is rural, the impact upon females is most significant.

Employment

As stated earlier, independence has witnessed a significant growth in literate women and in highly educated women who are professional teachers, lawyers, judges, doctors, news editors, and businesswomen. Yet, even in

college, middle- and high-caste boys have the advantage, since a degree in science and technology is largely a male preserve, and over 72 percent of the
girls are found in the arts. This means that girls potentially earn less, are more
likely to be financially dependent on men, and are more likely to remain poor
even with an education.[41] Many highly qualified women scientists face a
"glass ceiling," as they are kept from attaining a faculty post in universities.
The first women at Raman Research Institute, Bangalore faced restrictions
from the founder Dr. C. V. Raman, a Nobel Laureate. Dr. Sunanda Bai completed her dissertation but was not given a Ph.D., and later committed
suicide. However, Dr. Anna Mani went on to become Deputy Director-
General, Indian Meteorological Department.[42] Despite obstacles, many
brilliant women today strategize in forums like Third World Organization
of Women Scientists. A small sample of those in major institutions includes
National Brain Research Center director Dr. Vijayalakshmi Ravindranath,
and Dr. Shyamala Mani who researches stem cells; Dr. Kiran Majumdar
Shaw, biotechnologist, founder of BIOCON; Dr. Maria Lisette D'Souza of
the National Institute of Oceanography in Goa; theoretical physicist
Dr. Sumati Surya at Raman Research Institute; Dr. Vineeta Bal of the
National Institute of Immunology; Dr. Manju Sharma, Executive Director,
Indian Institute of Advanced Research; and Dr. Shobhana Narasimhan at
Jawaharlal Nehru Center for Advanced Scientific Research.[43]

Most women do not fall into this elite category, however, as they are
either low skilled or unskilled workers who face discrimination in hiring
and wage, and are harassed by male supervisors. These issues shape public
perceptions of their work as insignificant, and they are rendered "invisible"
in some records. This lowers women's self-esteem, they demand less rights,
and the cycle of discrimination is perpetuated.[44] Often denied access to better paying jobs, girls and older women go into domestic service, and females
constitute the bulk of such workers. One out of every three girls between the
ages of six and eleven is outside school and at work, compared to the high
rate of male school enrollment. Illiteracy also further marginalizes Dalits,
low-caste Hindus, Christians, and Muslims.

Women workers cannot be categorized easily as they perform a wide
range of jobs, each with its own type of discrimination or abuse. Economic
globalization has pushed unskilled girls and women into the informal sector
as casual labor with lower wages, no job security, and long hours in hazardous conditions. More women have been pauperized by globalization than
men, an affliction that is greater as they largely care for the family. Although
laws dictate that certain industries establish crèches (Factories Act 1948,
Mines Act 1952, Plantation Act 1957, and Labour Act 1970), other industries have escaped through legal loopholes. Thus, workers' children play in
the rubble near dangerous construction sites, although mothers nurse and
other workers care for the babies while she is busy. Some women do piece
work for cottage industries that are lauded as beneficial to the nation.

However, most women, girls, and boys are paid trifles for their piece work, while profits accrue to rich intermediaries and corporations.

In 2007, international corporations like GAP reported the semi-slavery conditions of child laborers.[45] Gender inequalities have also heightened in the global market economy. Formal industries rely heavily on cheap female labor from the informal sector. Unskilled women often do not unionize, as they cannot easily find jobs in the formal sector. In the formal sector, gender labor divisions have widened, and discrimination is subtle.[46] The benefits of industrial technology do not always filter down to women. Global demands have increased for Indian cloth made often in power loom mills. Women constitute around 40 percent of the workers in power loom mills, unlike their numbers in traditional mills and the cottage handloom industry. A study of the textile power loom industry in Coimbatore, Tamil Nadu reveals that the women workers are more educated, younger, and fairly well trained before being inducted as mill weavers, winders, and reelers of thread. Immediately after independence, there were less gender divisions in labor in the mills and annual wage increases, and the state paid women three months leave at half wages after childbirth due to the Maternity Act.[47] Yet, women's voices are being heard through their unions, and there is a growing social acceptance of women as factory workers. Most scholars agree that mill workers are more empowered than those in the informal sector.

Even in the domestic service industry marked by low wages and few rights, women are beginning to organize and receive publicity for their difficulties. Domestic service draws upon the pool of unskilled female labor, and although it appears to be set in a relatively benign environment, abuse and rape are commonly reported to social workers. Domestic workers are often expected to perform dangerous and difficult tasks, and to use hazardous cleaning agents without protection. Despite the law against child labor, young girls are often employed in such work, and they are easily exploited. Their protests gathered momentum in the 1980s when their first union was formed in Bombay and spread to Chennai, Patna, Varanasi, and Bangalore. In 2004, Karnataka became the first state to pass a minimum wage law. Two years later, 10,000 women domestic workers organized by Stree Jagruti Samiti (Society of Awakened Women) took out a prolonged national strike for better conditions.[48]

Most Indian women workers perform various agricultural functions. Yet, a mere 3–10 percent of the women own the land which they till and harvest, and this creates the public perception that they are not farmers, and certainly not as productive as men. This affects their bargaining power within the household and in public village *panchayats*. Women farm vegetables for the kitchen pot, which provide the nutrients necessary for subsistence families. Such kitchen gardens sustain the family during leaner years. Commercial cultivation is by men who are respected as farmers, since land titles are largely in their hands and as commercial crops fetch more income than women's kitchen plots.[49] Property ownership is necessary to emancipate women, but it also empowers the community. Thus, women's economic power benefits everyone.

Since the 1990s, some favorable changes have occurred, especially after government and NGOs have tried to "mainstream" women into development programs. Women's voices are heard more loudly now in local councils, and they do not easily submit to pressure from the men. Indian women are now expanding their traditional role in vegetable farming to commercial agriculture which fetches a larger income, and this increases their bargaining power. In a comparable example, Bangladeshi women now often hold on to their rights to fish they raise in hatcheries, but they are willing to share ownership of ponds with men.[50]

WOMEN IN POWER

Democratic Idealism and National Realities

Democratic idealism was most evident in the two decades before independence. It appeared in the 1931 INC Resolution of the Fundamental Rights of Citizenship in India introduced by Jawaharlal Nehru at Karachi. This important document laid the groundwork for the free India's Constitution (1950) by declaring a strong commitment to human rights and legal equality "irrespective of religion, caste, creed or sex." Its goals were to prevent all forms of discrimination in public employment, to adopt universal adult suffrage, and to ensure women's right to vote and to hold office. In addition, in 1939, when a National Planning Committee was created to prepare for independence to be headed by Nehru, he followed the AIWC recommendations by appointing a special Sub-Committee on Women to study their legal, social, political, and economic status. This Sub-Committee was authorized to examine familial and traditional constraints upon women, as well as legal deterrents to their education, employment, and full participation in national life.[51] The Sub-Committee re-endorsed the Fundamental Rights of individual women, irrespective of marital status. It reminded the incipient state that women bore an unequal burden, and that it was the state's responsibility to ensure female "equal status and equal opportunity" through laws against unjust practices and through local and other governing bodies. Emphasis was laid upon the special health needs of all females and the vulnerability of orphan girls to various kinds of exploitation. The document highlighted the contributions of women workers to the economy. It also emphasized that they needed equal wages, better crèches to remove anxiety over their children, and trade unions to protect them during economic slumps or from employers' whims. Idealism is apparent in the discussions on women's education and right to personal earnings, equal property, and status in the family.[52]

Hindu Code Bill and Implications for Women

In this era, many male nationalists lauded the contributions of ordinary women and of feminist organizations to freedom. However, there were growing expressions of different views on legal measures to guarantee women's rights. After 1935, Indian members of the provincial and central legislatures began to introduce a number of separate bills to amend local customary laws on female property and divorce, and also the existing colonial Women's Rights to Property Act (1937). By 1940, senior legislators were clear that a cohesive law was necessary to guarantee women's rights to property and divorce. Based on recommendations by the AIWC, the Rau (Hindu Law) Committee was appointed in 1941 to consider an amendment to the existing law of 1937. However, the complexities in framing a new law and also the disruptions to legislative continuity caused by mass resignations during the Quit India Movement meant that these changes were shelved temporarily, and the 1937 law remained intact until independence.

Although many AIWC feminists supported Gandhi and Nehru, the feminists disagreed among themselves and with some nationalists on how best to change colonial family laws on monogamy, property, and divorce. Gandhi's noncooperation movement led many Indian legislators and officials to resign en masse, and this delayed the process of making legal changes to help women. Gandhi urged elite feminists to help their disadvantaged sisters and to take part in the nation's struggle, but he also advised them not to engage in prolonged legal battles that were divisive and debilitating to the nation. Although respectful to Gandhi, Rajkumari Amrit Kaur, Hansa Mehta, and Durgabai Deshmukh openly dissented on this issue.[53] Nehru advised patience, since his party was committed to women's rights, and he would support them.[54] One Indian who remained at his post as Law Minister was B. R. Ambedkar, a senior Dalit leader with ideological differences with Gandhi. However, as both Nehru and Ambedkar believed implicitly in a secular democracy, they agreed that a civil code was needed to guarantee women's rights to property and divorce. Moreover, Nehru and Gandhi recognized that Ambedkar's legal insights would be invaluable when framing the Constitution.

After independence, the Constituent Assembly began to draft the Constitution and review changes in Hindu law. The feminists in this august assembly included Ammu Swaminathan, Hansa Mehta, Sucheta Kripalani, Vijayalakshmi Pandit, Sarojini Naidu, Purnima Banerjee, Begam Qudsia Aizaz Rasul, Malti Chowdhury, Kamala Chaudhuri, Durgabai Deshmukh, Begam Ikramullah, Dakshayani Velayudhan, and Lila Roy.[55] In 1949, debate accelerated on a Hindu Code Bill (HCB) whose important provisions included women's right to paternal and family property, and to divorce. Although framed as a Hindu bill, its scope also included Sikhs, Buddhists, and Jainas. Both Nehru and Ambedkar had accepted the UN Charter of

Women's Rights (1946) and the AIWC's own Charter of Women's Rights and Duties (1946). Nehru stated, "I am personally anxious to do everything in my power to advance the cause of women in the country."[56] In the opposite camp were powerful traditionalists like C. Rajagopalachari, first Indian governor-general (1947), and Rajendra Prasad, India's first president (1950). In a letter to Nehru, Prasad voiced his view that social precept, not state law, should change attitudes to monogamy and women's right to marital separation, since Hindu law already gave women right to property (*stridhan*).[57] Other patriarchs in the Assembly and press threatened that the HCB would cause the dissolution of the Indian family because financial independence would make women spurn marriage and adopt permissive Western mores.

Nehru's declaration indicates that he agreed with Ambedkar on the principle of secular laws to guarantee women's rights, but when facing the opposition of powerful men like Rajagopalachari and Prasad, Nehru procrastinated over the HCB, and Ambedkar resigned in protest.[58] However, the Indian Constitution bears the unmistakable stamp of Ambedkar's legal insights and Nehru's statesmanship. The Constitution ushered in a democratic, secular republic on January 30, 1950, declaring justice, liberty, equality, and fraternity for all citizens; legal equality and suffrage irrespective of gender, sect, caste, or class; and the individual rights of women and men regardless of marital status. These aspirations are clearly stipulated in Part III (Fundamental Rights), Articles 14–16 and 23 (equality in law, of opportunity, employment, and prohibition of traffic in humans and forced labor); and Part IV, Article 29 (equal pay and freedom from exploitation), Article 42 (humane work conditions and maternity relief), and Article 44 (uniform civil code for all).[59] A few years later, controversies over women rights were resolved when Parliament enacted the Hindu Marriage Act (1955) sanctioning female divorce and the Hindu Succession Act (1956) giving females equal shares in family property. These laws still operate today.

Modern Indian family laws on women's property, marriage, divorce, and maternal rights are based primarily upon elite interpretations of Hindu and Muslim legal texts, of which there were many schools. These were also shaped by British law, which were patriarchal, and by Victorian imperial attitudes. Indian paternalism was thus reinforced by English common law in which the father is the head of the family, and by Biblical strictures on adultery that penalized women for extramarital sex. In contrast, in India, unregistered marriages were once common, and sometimes even legally valid; a mother's primary rights over her young child were recognized by many men; and matrilineal societies exalted the family matriarch. Yet, the Colonial Guardians and Wards Act of 1890, which still operates in independent India, requires the father's permission if a mother considers it necessary for her child to have a medical procedure, to enter school, or to have a passport. On the one hand, ideas of gender equality are now written into the legal system, yet residual colonial laws on divorce are too stringent for a woman to escape, except in marital rape. However, as India is a signatory of the bilateral Convention on the Elimination of All Forms of Discrimination against Women (CEDAW), a case can be taken to the UN court after having first explored legal avenues within India. This treaty has also led to some reforms in India on inheriting citizenship through the mother, but in the cases of women's conflicts with religious authority, the power lies with religious clerks, and not the state.[60]

Despite the important law on women's right to an equal share of family property, recent studies show that the reality is somewhat different. As few as 13 percent of the daughters and 51 percent of the widows actually get a share of the family estate, and nearly half the widows own this jointly with sons on whom they are effectively dependant. Sons can also disinherit the woman using their power in the village *panchayat,* which often rule for men. Matriliny in Kerala suffered due to colonial prejudice against the poly-androus Nayars, and it eroded further when the Communist Party's Kerala Agrarian Bill (1957) redistributed land among the poor but effectively penalized Nayar women with property.[61] Similarly, the HCB's application to tribal (Adivasi) women has been challenged by the Jharkhand Nari Mukti Samiti (Women's Freedom Forum of Jharkhand) and the Shramik Stri Mukti Sanghatana (Working Women's Freedom Organization) in Shahada, Maharashtra.[62]

Women Politicians

Soon after independence, elite women nationalists attained high-ranking appointments as central government ministers, governors of provinces, and emissaries to other nations. They were immediately granted the right to hold top executive and legislative posts, and this has continued as a feature of the Indian democracy. The first women in high political offices included AIWC feminist patriots like Sarojini Naidu (first governor of Uttar Pradesh), Rajkumari Amrit Kaur (first central minister for health), Hansa Mehta (UN Human Rights Commission), and Sharifa Hamid Ali (UN Commission on the Status of Women).[63] Women patriots from influential families were recognized for their contributions, the foremost being Vijayalakshmi Pandit, India's first emissary to the United Nations where she was elected as the first woman president of the General Assembly. In 1975, the aging matriarch came out of retirement to denounce the semi-dictatorial powers assumed by her niece Prime Minister Indira Gandhi (1917–84) under Emergency Rule (1975–77).

As prime minister, Indira Gandhi was in office for two long terms (1966–77, 1980–84). Sometimes described as one of India's most popular leaders, the high point of her regime was the assistance she provided to the Bangladesh freedom movement against West Pakistan's military dictatorship in 1971.

However, she also authorized an army raid of the Sikhs' holiest shrine, the Golden Temple at Amritsar, Punjab, in which the militants inside were killed. Their martyrdom fueled a protracted struggle with Sikhs and led to her assassination in 1984. During the Emergency, she imprisoned political opponents without legal cause, yet democratically called for an election in which she was defeated. She also allowed her son Sanjiv to authorize the compulsory sterilizations of disadvantaged men, a move that retarded the family planning program through persuasion. Lauded abroad as a powerful Third World woman leader, Indira Gandhi's gender neutral policies did not specifically help women's causes. This is in contrast to the first woman legislator, Dr. Muthulakshmi Reddi, who used her short tenure (1927–28) to introduce numerous bills for women. Ironically, it was during Indira Gandhi's regime that the United Nations published *Towards Equality*. The UN report lauded elite Indian women's achievements but noted that other Indian women trailed in nutrition, education, employment, and the sharp plummet in a declining sex ratio. While Mrs. Gandhi was not responsible for these figures, neither did she pursue programs to rectify these problems.

For generations, dominant men in the village assemblies or *panchayats* have silenced women who wish to speak on public issues.[64] However, in central and provincial councils, this has not always been true. Women have contested elections, and they hold power as the wives, widows, mistresses, daughters, sisters, and heirs of male politicians. Indians believe implicitly in democracy, despite corruption and nepotism, and view elections as the *vox populi*. A vibrant vernacular language and English press quickly report scandals about corruption in the teeth of dangerous reprisals. The vast majority of women whose rights are tenuously held are not the women in power. Some women like Sheila Dixit, chief minister of Delhi, champion women's causes, while others follow Indira Gandhi's policies of downplaying gender and focusing on the economy or communal tensions that also interest male voters.

Tamil Nadu's former chief minister Jayalalitaa (All India Anna Dravida Munnetra Kazhagam, AIADMK) has bestowed upon herself the honorific of "Amma" (Mother) but rather resembles a quixotic stepmother. The former mistress of former chief minister M. G. Ramachandran, a flamboyant film idol, Jayalalitaa's brand of fascist politics has kept her intermittently in power for over a decade. She has garnered millions, bullied recalcitrant bureaucrats, and used the media to denounce enemies but done virtually nothing for women.

South Asians laud the dutiful wife and daughter-in-law, but widows are often disregarded. It is thus interesting that elite widows hold some of the highest offices in India. Sonia Gandhi was unwillingly inducted into politics after her husband Prime Minister Rajiv Gandhi, a son of Indira Gandhi, was assassinated. Sonia was chosen leader of the Congress Party, whose electoral successes in 2004 led to the United Progressive Alliance (UPA) coalition government. Although legally entitled to be India's prime minister, she quickly ceded this posit to her next in command in Congress and remained behind the scenes in the party.

Sushma Swaraj is the moral arbiter of the Hindu right-wing Bharatiya Janata Party (BJP) and also the wife of former Mizoram governor Swaraj Kaushal. Rabri Devi of Rashtriya Janata Dal (RJD) was three times chief minister of Bihar (1997–2005) and is the wife of Union Railway Minister Lalu Prasad Yadav. Vasundhara Raje (BJP) was the chief minister of Rajasthan (2003–2008) and also the dutiful daughter-in-law of former rani Gayatri Devi of Jaipur. Pratibha Patil became the first woman president of India (2007), after serving as governor of Rajasthan, positions accruing from her loyalty to the Congress Party and Indira Gandhi's family.

One of the most colorful is Rabri Devi who uses a housewife's efficiency to run Bihar. Rabri Devi is the wife of Lalu Prasad Yadav who was the chief minister into whose office she would rush at will, claiming her right as his "*aurat*" (wife). In 1997, Rabri Devi charmed voters with her homespun imagery, devotion to her husband, and maternal references to her nine children. Despite her rustic background, she is not easily manipulated, but when conscious of her deficiencies in finance or other areas, she appoints trained bureaucrats to guide her. She preaches the importance of less talk and more help to the poor, and appeals to women journalists by accusing male reporters of misguiding the world about India.[65] Yet, Rabri Devi has done almost nothing to help Dalit women in her decade of power. Like the entrenched feudal attitudes in Madhya Pradesh, Bihar is marked by human rights violations against Dalits and tribals by caste landlords. Its sex ratio is one of India's lowest (919), and its female literacy is the lowest (33.1%), with Dalit women lagging even further behind men.

A controversial woman leader is Mayawati of the Bahujan Samaj Party of Uttar Pradesh. Mayawati provides a role model to other Dalit women and men as she has a college degree. Her political mentor was Kansi Ram who founded this party in 1984 to mobilize Dalits and poor Muslims against the high-caste politicians in the BJP and in most other parties.[66] Despite the strength of her ideology, Mayawati's two earlier stints as chief minister were marked by charges of corruption. In the "Taj Corridor" scandal, she stands accused of diverting huge sums meant for tourist purposes into her private coffers.[67] After Kansi Ram's death in 2006, Mayawati lit the funeral pyre claiming that she was his political heir, and that women had this final right just like men. After her landslide victory in 2007, she proclaimed her intention to adopt Buddhism like Ambedkar, the great Dalit leader. However, Mayawati's political moves also include wooing voters from higher castes or accusing Gandhi of having divided Hindus and Muslims.[68]

To win votes, some women politicians assume traditional gender roles and pay lip service to morality (*dharma*). The moral arbiter of Hindu right-wing politics (Hindutva) is self-styled ascetic (*sadhvi*) Uma Bharati

(BJP) of Madhya Pradesh. The Hindutva uses rhetoric laced with images of goddess Durga as Shakti (female power). Uma Bharati depicts herself as a champion of Hindu traditions, so that elite and middle-class voters regard her as a mortal shakti. Winning her first Parliamentary victory in 1989 from Bundelkhand, Uma Bharati kept this seat in three elections. However, she did not improve the state's record of violence against women or its low sex ratio (919/1000), nor raise these issues in Parliament. Many BJP-run states like Madhya Pradesh, Rajasthan, Gujarat, Maharashtra, and Uttar Pradesh have poor records on female literacy, violence, and female feticide, according to the National Family Health Survey (2007).[69] The press reports that in these states, most court cases revolve around women's shooting, torture, and rape, and subsequent suicide, and that police and officials are often complicit. The NGO network Samaan (Equal) raises awareness on this issue.[70]

Rajasthan is India's largest state. The 2001 census records that it has the lowest female literacy (43.9%) that is far below the male (75%), and also a low sex ratio (921).[71] However, a decade ago, conditions were far worse as female literacy was just 20.44 percent, with the district of Barmar registering 7.68 percent.[72] Rajasthan's desert region has meant less population density and less productivity than many states. Half the population is less than 20 years of age, child marriage is common, and the lurking threat of *sati* became a public nightmare when an 18-year-old widow named Roop Kanwar was cremated on her husband's pyre. Roop Kanwar's *sati* had little to do with spousal loyalty, as the couple did not live together for more than a few months. Rather, the spectacle was intended to revive Hindu Rajput identity and the state's autonomy over the 1829 colonial-federal law banning *sati*.[73] Roop Kanwar created a furor in the national press but sidetracked attention from feudal traditions oppressing peasants.

Yet, after Vasundhara Raje's landslide victory as chief minister in 2003, she attempted to showcase Rajasthan's modernizing programs and some changes in its feudal attitudes to women. As the educated, royal daughter-in-law of powerful Gayatri Devi (b. 1919), former Jaipur rani, Vasundhara's programs benefit women. At the same time, she speaks patriotically of female "full honor" through literacy and its "empowerment" of women. She also lauds tribal resistance to colonialism and refers to the education of women weavers whose handicrafts are popular among foreign tourists.[74] The press release extols newly established scores of maternity centers; 500 crèches (*anganbadis*) for rural working women; 35,000 women helpers at the crèches; 1,200 policewomen to protect women's honor; and thousands of women's self-help groups. Vasundhara is clearly fueled by the desire to remain in power by winning the votes of an expanded, educated female electorate and the subsequent boost from tourists. They have already garnered the state two UNESCO awards for combating illiteracy. Meanwhile, Gayatri Devi has taken up a crusade against violence against women, using her popular image of benign victim and defender, as she was incarcerated for opposing Indira Gandhi's Emergency. Although misogyny has a stranglehold on Rajasthan, these two women leaders have tried to remedy some crucial problems of women.

The Hindutva Right challenges the Constitutional premise of secularism and uses Hindu emblems to mobilize women into militant cadres like Durga Vahini in honor of the goddess and Rashtriya Swayamsevika Samiti (National Women's Service League).[75] A secular intelligentsia was shocked in 1989 at media portrayals of women who helped to demolish the sixteenth-century mosque known as Babri Masjid in Ayodhya, Uttar Pradesh. In the ensuing communal clashes, Uma Bharati urged Hindu women to fight Muslims who opposed the construction of a new Rama temple at this site. The BJP ideologue is Sushma Swaraj whose middle-class, educated female followers are apparently liberated but are cultural reactionaries. Hindu and Muslim women are thus prominent both in religious and in secular politics, and are found as leaders of several parties. In contrast, Communist parties claiming to rise above religion have yet to produce notable women leaders.[76] Hindutva appeals to a segment of conservative women, but many educated female voters vote for parties with broad-based programs for all women. Moreover, lower-caste rural Hindus are also known to forge alliances with poor Dalits, Muslims, and Christians.

Women's Reservation Bill

Group representation is essential in a democracy, and women fall into the category of the underrepresented, especially those in rural India and also from the minorities or low castes. While women vote in large numbers in both provincial and central government elections, there have been relatively fewer women members of local councils, provincial assemblies, or Parliament. The custom of veiling, particularly in northern India, has restricted many Hindu and Muslim women from participating in village councils (*panchayats*). In the early 1980s, the main women's organizations refused any move toward quotas in Parliament on the grounds that separate electorates would fragment Indian democracy. Instead, they suggested a 30 percent quota for women in the village *panchayats* where they had almost no voice, and possibly a special quota for Dalit and tribal women. They also requested regular elections for local councils as a path to later elected offices in the provincial and central legislatures. A local women's movement in Maharashtra (1985) began to demand a female quota in *panchayats,* leading to political party debates on gender representation in local government. The next years saw a growth in all-women *panchayats,* e.g., in Bengal, and in 1993, a Parliamentary amendment guaranteed women a one-third representation in *panchayats,* once the preserve of high-caste men. The momentous act enabled women to make significant changes in local governance by working with various NGOs on programs to improve literacy, health, and sanitation for the whole community. The women learned to become more adept as public leaders, serving as role models for younger women.[77]

In 1988 the Draft National Perspective Plan introduced the idea of giving women a 30 percent quota in Parliament. Many women's groups now supported Parliamentary quotas, and a new Women's Reservation Bill was introduced in 1998 with some significant changes. Opposition came from some women who asked for higher quotas, since they formed half the population (ideally!), and from socialist and people's parties, e.g., Samajwadi and RJD, whose leaders argue that quotas were needed for the poor, rather than for elite women. If the bill is ideally revised, women would contest open seats, there would be separate quotas for Dalits and underrepresented minorities, and men would be less threatened that they would lose their seats to women's "reserved" seats. At present, just 8.3 percent of the seats in Parliament are held by women, far less than in Muslim Pakistan (21%), so that women's quotas would bring India closer to the democratic ideal of proportional representation.[78] In 2003, a revised Women's Reservation Bill (WRB) was supported by the ruling BJP, although leaders Murli Manohar Joshi and L. K. Advani have shown scant respect for women.[79] Congress leaders support the WRB and have made it clear after their victory in 2005 when they formed UPA coalition government. Sushma Swaraj took the opportunity to blame Congress leadership and Sonia Gandhi for the bill's impasse at a BJP women's convention titled Matrushakti (Mother Strength). However, the impasse is due to opposition from leftist parties in the UPA, while some male legislators are apprehensive over women holding 33 percent of Parliamentary seats.[80] Mohini Giri, chairperson for the National Commission for Women, spoke at an interview of the need to expand women legislators in all councils and described *panchayat* women leaders' plans to improve water, sanitation, and electricity facilities in the villages.

WOMEN DISSIDENTS

Class and Gender

In the late 1960s, class and gender struggles for justice began to converge, and there brewed a simmering discontent due to high food prices, a doldrums economy, droughts, and famines. A marginalized peasant population created the platform for the CPI's new wing, the CPI-ML (Marxist-Leninist), with a Maoist ideology of rural insurrection. The CPI often mobilized urban working women in street demonstrations against price hikes, poor wages, and liquor consumption among working men.[81] The CPI-ML organized peasant associations (*kisan sabhas*), inspired by a violent revolt in Naxalbari district of Bengal, where the leaders were peasants, and there was a militant women's wing. In Telegana, Andhra Pradesh, a festering movement against upper-caste landlords erupted in the 1970s, and women were again trained to use rifles. In the context of drought and forest encroachments in Shahada, Maharashtra, tribal Bhil women took up arms against oppressive landlords.[82] In response to agrarian crises, Vinobha Bhave, a respected Gandhian, appealed to the rich to donate viable land to the poor (Bhoodan movement), but such land was often arid and rocky.[83] Bhave undertook fasts with Mira Behn (Madeleine Slade), another Gandhian, but the crisis escalated.

Oppressed peasant movements often had a militant female cadre demanding a minimum wage, Food for Work programs, forest rights, water, and fuel. Although they were rarely supported by middle-caste/class women, feminist groups were also shaken by the searing discontent among low castes, laborers, and various minorities.[84] Their newspapers reported urban, middle-class women's problems such as the "dowry murders" often whitewashed as "accidental" deaths of young women in kitchen fires when the groom's family was dissatisfied with the girl's dowry. Although these reflected a raging undercurrent of misogyny, working women's problems eclipsed the scale and magnitude of dowry deaths. Meanwhile, in the late 1970s, newspapers also described escalating communal tensions due to minority anxieties over identity and status, and issues like sexual taunts ("eve teasing") in city streets across northern India. However, most rapes occur nearer the home and by men known to the woman or girl.

More serious were rapes by police and other state officials when the woman was held in custody over an alleged offence. Police were known to single out women for rape as a warning to others who protested against uniformed authority. One of the brutal incidents of police rape occurred in December 1978 at the village of Beldhia, Bihar as a reprisal against tribals who decided to farm land that belonged to a wealthy merchant. That night, some two hundred Central Reserve and Bihar Police forces surrounded and attacked the sleeping villagers and gang-raped girls and women.[85] The Hindi poem *Ballad of Budhini* (1988) tells another tale of police terror in a village in Madhya Pradesh, where fears of molestation led women to suffer thirst in the grueling summer, rather than to walk to the well.[86] In Jharkhand in 1979, Santhal women were raped after protesting against high-caste takeover of tribal land and forced labor.

Feminists were divided on how to resolve these serious problems affecting women in various cadres of society. Left-wing feminists believed these incidents preceded a revolutionary class upheaval that would bring benefits to all women. Other feminists charged all politicians, including the leftists, of paying scant attention to violence against women and of subsuming gender issues under the umbrella of minority rights. It is now clear that gender and class are not mutually exclusive categories, and that women's issues need to be addressed specifically on their own merit, but also within the separate contexts of sect, caste, class, and ethnicity in India.

The issue of rape as assault brought many women activists together, as it is one of the most underreported types of violence, and it often accompanies a political struggle. In the 1970s–80s, ordinary women took to the streets of Bombay, Mathura, Patna, Delhi, and Bangalore to demonstrate against police rape. Their protests compelled the new feminists to demand that policemen be retried if earlier charges had been dismissed too easily. Communal tensions are not simply a result of religio-cultural differences, but they are due to perceived grievances over the distribution of economic benefits or the political power. This fact has been proven repeatedly after Partition in 1947; in the 1990's rapes of Tamil Dalit women by higher-caste *tevar* men who resented government benefits to Dalits;[87] in Gujarat where the BJP condoned the gang-rape of hundreds of Muslim women (2002); in the Narmada dam controversy over displacements of low-caste and tribal groups;[88] and at Nandigram, Bengal (2007) where police assaulted protestors against the privatization of tribal lands.

Environmental Struggles

Chipko Movement

In contrast to Naxalite rebellions in Bengal and Andhra, and tribal women's violent protests in Shahada, tribal women led peaceful protests during the Chipko Movement in Tehri Gahrwal (1970s). When loggers encroached on tribal forest preserves in these Himalayan foothills, women obstructed them by clinging (*chipko*) to huge ash and pine trees. The protestors had almost no political power, while the loggers represented the might of wealthy companies and the state. The Chipko Movement began with the demonstration by 10,000 working women against liquor vendors who supplied men with drink in the town. Male alcoholism depleted small family incomes and led often to rape, assault, and burning when women resisted men's advances. Chipko women organized patrol squads to ferret out distillers, tied them to buffalo poles, and gave evidence against them in the local court.[89]

Discontent had also been brewing ever since the colonial government established a Forestry Department to provide timber for railway carriages and sleepers. After 1960, the Indian government began to intrude further in tribal lands, although its rhetoric included a claim to protect forests and their inhabitants. The government also sanctioned logging by outside contractors for whom roads were built into the forests, and this eroded the fragile soil around trees. Diminishing patterns of rainfall caused huge fires, which the local people refused to help extinguish as they felt that their way of life was being threatened.[90] In the ensuing drought, women continued in the customary manner to collect water and fuel for the household, but the walks became longer and more arduous. They often worked for 14 hours a day in these and other chores, returning in the evening to light the kitchen fires with insufficient fuel. Their caloric expenditure far exceeded their intake, especially as women ate after feeding the family. Women's health was thus severely compromised, and in these decades, half the women of India fell below the poverty line.[91] Although government laid faucets in central areas, water was siphoned off by the road contractors, and few women had access to these taps.[92]

Tribal women began the struggle to protect the forests from loggers, although the movement was later shaped by Sunderlal Bahuguna and Chandi Prasad Bhatt, two followers of Gandhi. They described how they drew inspiration from the women's commitment to preserving the forests. In Gopeswar town in 1973 and 1975, women and men resisted contractors who felled ash trees to make sporting goods. Women then dressed the axe "wounds" with mud and sacking, and bemoaned the hurt to the ancient pine trees. In Almora, women peacefully obstructed soapstone mining contractors who cut across their fields to reach the mines. When contractors tried to stifle women's protests by stoning their homes, burning children, and bribing men, the women took their case to court and revealed their damage to the magistrate. When the contractors realized its extent, they pleaded guilty, and the women won their case.[93]

Narmada Bachao Andolan and Medha Patkar

While these struggles in the 1970s were marked by at least a modicum of government interest in social welfare, these benign interests have been sacrificed by its commitment to a market economy since the 1990s. Not all tribal protests have been nearly as successful as the Chipko, as seen in the Narmada Bachao Andolan (NBA) or Movement to Protect the Narmada. This is led by humanitarians who wish to protect tribal villages from government dams (35 large, 135 medium, and 3,000 small) to be built across the Narmada river in western India. The project is the largest in the world, and government argues that it would "develop" India by bringing electricity and other modern benefits. The opponents argue that this huge project would flood low-caste and tribal villages, disturb the water tables, and have profound environmental results.

The chief spokeswoman for the NBA is Medha Patkar (b. 1954), a believer in Gandhian nonviolent resistance, who also heads the National Alliance of People's Movements. When she first learned in the 1980s that the dams would evacuate 100,000 tribal Adivasis, she began to live among them and alerted them about the effects of large dams. When NBA members voiced protests to government officials, they were threatened. More than 35,000 poor Dalits and tribals have already been displaced, and many have not received compensation for having vacated their ancient villages. The NBA work of publicizing these issues led the World Bank to conduct an independent review before sanctioning further loans. The World Bank report first criticized the dam proposal as being poorly conceived. Medha Patkar and the NBA also appealed to the Supreme Court to stop construction of the huge Sardar Sarovar Dam, while displaced tribals conducted their protests. The Supreme Court later ordered construction to proceed, and the World Bank has also now resumed its loan agreement. However, Medha continues to fast and conduct "monsoon *satyagrahas*" on the banks of a rising Narmada in order to demonstrate how its flood waters could engulf thousands.[94] Her life is now legendary, since she is a courageous individual defending the poor against corporate and state power.[95] Medha Patkar herself appears unfazed by failures, and she relies on two tactics that have sustained her movement. The first is struggle (*sangarsh*), which has resulted in considerable international publicity for this cause. The second is constructive work (*nirman*) through which she helps villagers to discover the best ecological methods to conserve soil and water in their region. Patkar's numerous awards include the Mahatma Phule Award (India), the prestigious Goldman Environmental Prize, and the Human Rights Defender Award (Amnesty International).

Women in Other Struggles

In December 2007, three women received awards for fighting battles against corporations for polluting the environment and exploiting Indian workers. The first was Mukta Jodia, an Adivasi from Rayagad, Orissa who received the Chingari Award for Women Against Corporate Crime. She and her fellow tribeswomen consistently waged a battle for traditional usufruct rights to forest products and to fair wages as workers in companies that mined bauxite in the forests. Rasheeda Bee and Champa Devi were two women who received the Goldman Environmental Prize for their fight for adequate compensation from Union Carbide Corporation at whose factory in Bhopal over 3,000 people died and others maimed in 1984. Union Carbide was a subsidiary of Dow Chemical (U.S.), and this industrial disaster is one of the worst in the world.[96] Corporate negligence led to poisonous methyl isocyanate leaks, but the company refused to bear its full responsibility. When India charged CEO Warren Anderson with manslaughter, he conveniently escaped to the United States where the case was tried. Although Union Carbide paid some damages, the charges were diluted considerably.

NOTABLE WOMEN IN THE ARTS

It is impossible to do justice to all the numerous and extraordinary women writers, artists, musicians, and dancers in independent India, so this brief section confines itself to a few in each category. Among the writers, Arundhati Roy (b. 1961) is one of the most articulate champions of the weak. Arundhati Roy is an impassioned supporter of Medha Patkar's struggle against dams on the Narmada, and she has given this international publicity through her writings, speeches, and media presentations. Born to a Kerala mother and a Bengali father, Arundhati Roy is an architect who had written two film scripts before her English novel, *The God of Small Things* (1997), which won the Commonwealth Booker Prize.[97] Her phenomenal success from the prize and the sale of her book, which has been translated into numerous languages, has enabled Arundhati Roy to pick up her pen for social justice. Her searing, forthright prose exposes misanthropic governments that wage war for profit, and multinational corporations that sacrifice the weak.[98] Her first article, "Lies, Dam Lies and Statistics" (1999), called attention to the human toll of big dams (50 million Adivasis and Dalits). Her other works include *The Algebra of Infinite Justice* (2001) and *An Ordinary Person's Guide to Empire* (2006). In 2002, she was imprisoned for a day for challenging the Supreme Court's order to resume construction of the Narmada dams.[99] In 2004, Arundhati Roy received the Sydney Peace Prize at Australia. Another writer in English is the prolific Anita Desai (b. 1937), whose canvas is largely one of fiction. Anita Desai has published at least 12 volumes of novels, short stories, and poetry, and has taught at universities in Delhi and the United States. She has received awards like the Padma Shri from India, the Guardian Prize for Children's Fiction, and the Taraknath Award.[100]

Many women authors have also produced some splendid works in regional languages, some of which have been retrieved and translated by scholars. Mahasweta Devi (b. 1926) has written over a hundred Bengali novels and short stories on the oppression of women, Adivasis, and Dalits who are trapped by feudal landlords who conspire with high-caste bureaucrats in the climate of droughts and famines in the 1970s.[101] Mahasweta Devi's initial fascination for literary composition soon graduated to literature as activism. In "Witch Hunt," she describes the panic caused by a tribal Oraon woman who predicts famine in a village. "Paddy Seeds" concerns the devious revenge taken by a powerless Dalit upon a merciless landlord. "Dhowli" is a poignant story about a Dalit woman's love affair with a *brahman* man whose family will not allow their marriage.[102] Mahasweta Devi received the national Padma Shri (1986) and the prestigious Jnanpith (1996) awards for her literary contributions.

Mahadevi Verma (1907–87) is widely regarded as one of the greatest writers of Hindi poetry in the twentieth century. Mahadevi Verma received her education at home due to liberal parents who encouraged her literary and artistic talents. A devout woman of compassion, Mahadevi Verma was inspired by Gandhi to become an advocate of women's liberation. She served this cause through the Prayag Mahila Vidhyapith (Allahabad Women's Educational Institution). She used to host Hindi poetry festivals, even as she published five volumes of poetry and others of prose. Her essays on women's liberation were compiled in *Shrnkhla Ki Kadiyaan* (Chains of Subjugation), and her paintings appeared in her poetry collection, *Sandhyageet* (Evening Songs). She used the proceeds of her Padma Bhushan and Jnanpith awards to support aspiring writers.[103]

Women write most often in the regional languages, and these few examples of those that have been translated represent a small tip of a vast iceberg available in English translations. The Urdu short stories of Ismat Chugtai (d. 1991) depict middle-class Muslim family life, its suppressions and emotional opportunities. This is visible in "The Quilt," a subtle short story describing a young girl's humorous discovery of a lesbian relationship between a mistress and a servant.[104] "Anil" (Squirrel) by the Tamil author Ambai (C. S. Lakshmi) is a reflective journey into how women write their life stories. Vaasanthi's recent work "Birthright" on female feticide is an ironic story of a woman doctor who aborts girls out of her fury at misogyny.[105] Its compelling translation into English is by Vasantha Surya, a seasoned poet with volumes of her own poetry collections and a translator from Tamil, Hindi, and even German.[106] The Kannada author Veena Shanteswar wrote "Avala Svatantrya" (Her Independence) to explore how and if women were yet free in India.

A discussion of painters must include Amrita Sher-Gil (1913–41), an innovative but short-lived artist. Born to a Hungarian mother and a Sikh father, her European upbringing and marriage left her with little curiosity about Indian culture or its independence movement. Poverty merely provided her with an opportunity to paint people whom she described as "strangely beautiful in their ugliness." These shortcomings can be partly understood by the fact that she died at 29 and thus never arrived to a philosophical middle age. She hardly had time to explore her own vibrant, original talent. Yet, Amrita Sher-Gil painted and sketched landscapes, monuments, and portraits with lyrical melancholy, as seen in "Hill Men," "Hill Women," "Mother India," and "The Beggars." The profusion and scope of her paintings attest to her great talent, so that India's government has declared them to be National Treasures.

In music, dance, film, and theater, there continue to be a stream of extraordinary women performers. If earlier reformers had viewed women performers derogatively as *devadasis* or "*nautch*" girls, the national movement also led to a growing pride in Indian cultural traditions that helped to legitimize their art. A growing film world absorbed and glamorized musicians, actresses, and dancers, so that erstwhile *devadasis* merged into the general population. In south India, the community assumed the caste name of *isai vellalas* (musicians), and their dance traditions were elevated under the title of classical Bharata Natyam. Bharata Natyam luminaries include Theosophist Rukmini Arundale who reshaped its format and styles; Balasaraswati, a genius in dance emotive expression (*abhinaya*); Kamala Lakshman who made it dramatic; and Padma Subrahmanyam who researched temple sculptural depictions of dancers. In north India, Muslim and Hindu Kathak dancers reinvigorated a court dance, a famous danseuse being Sitara Devi.

Other famous dancers like Yamini Krishnamurthy and Mallika Sarabhai strengthened the Kuchipudi dance of Orissa, while Sanjukta Panigrahi and Sonal Mansingh brought innovations to Odissi. The wide popularity of regional films incorporated folk traditions, e.g., *koratthi* dances in Tamil cinema and Bhojpuri group dances on the Hindi screen (Bollywood).

A unique south Indian (Karnatak) classical musician was M. S. Subbulakshmi (1916–2004), whom Nehru described as the "Nightingale of India." Subbulakshmi's golden voice haunted audiences from her first performance at the age of six and her first record at the age of ten. Born in Madurai, Tamil Nadu near the great temple to goddess Meenakshi Amman, she and her siblings were raised in a household dedicated to music. Her mother was gifted *veena* instrumentalist Shammukhavadivu of the community of musicians (*isai vellalas*), and her father was a *brahman* lawyer. Subbulakshmi's extraordinary gifts soon led to extensive training in Karnatak music. She later studied with a seasoned *guru* in north Indian (Hindustani) classical music, enabling her to sing its *ragas* (melodic arrangements) with subtle understanding. Subbulakshmi's rendering of *bhakti* hymns by woman saint Mira and the Gujarati Narsinh Mehta profoundly touched Gandhi. Upon his assassination, the nation mourned as she sang his favorite hymn on religious unity. Subbulakshmi also sang in other Indian languages at the UN General Assembly, as an ardent believer in peace among all nations. M. S. Subbulakshmi was married to Thyagarajan Sadasivam, a prominent journalist and INC nationalist. Subbulakshmi lived serenely immersed in music in Chennai until her death. Other legendary women Karnatak music singers include D. K. Pattammal and Vasantha Kumari.

In north India, one of the most powerful women singers was Begam Akhtar (1910–73). Begam Akhtar set the benchmark for the performance of Urdu *ghazals* set to the musical form of *thumri*. Born in Faizabad, Uttar Pradesh to a professional woman singer of moderate means, Begam Akhtar learned to play the folk *dholak* drum as a girl of six. After training under venerable *ustads* (scholarly virtuosos), she gave her first performance at the age of 15. Begam Akhtar's powerful voice and her aesthetic musical renditions of the *ghazal* soon earned her fame. She also began to sing for films after 1930, as *ghazals* are ideally suited for romantic themes. She also performed in the affluent courts of the erstwhile royalty of India, and she came to be known as the Queen of the Ghazal (Mallika-e-Ghazal). She was posthumously awarded the national Padma Bhushan award, and in 1996, a stamp was issued portraying her face.[107] Other northern Indian women classicists are Gangubai Hangal, Girija Devi, and Prabha Atre.

In the field of film music, mention must be made of Lata Mangeshkar (b. 1929) whose legendary voice has been the most significant influence upon women singers of the Hindi cinema. Her singing career spans six decades and includes some 30,000 songs in many languages.[108] Raised in a family of theatrical singers, Lata and her siblings like Asha Bhonsle quickly took to the lessons in light music imparted by their father, which were strengthened by lessons in classical music, especially after her singing debut in a Marathi film in 1942. She acted in some films for a decade, but her magic lies in her voice which has retained its innocent quality. Her greatest hits occurred after 1950, when her repertoire included Urdu *ghazals* and trendy songs. Famous singer Noor Jehan predicted that the phenomenal Lata would overtake her own popularity. Often called the Melody Queen, Lata Mangeshkar received both the Padma Bhushan and the Padma Vibhushan awards, and numerous minor awards.

The Indian film screen has provided thoughtful artistes with the opportunity to explore their personal talents and to expose injustice of various sorts. The best films depict women as victims, as well as agents unfazed by overwhelming odds. For example, in *Mother India* (1950), Nargis acts as a long-suffering, rural housewife, and this served as a metaphor for the nation and its women. In the Hindi art film *Ankur* (1974), Shabana Azmi gave a stellar performance as a low-caste woman who triumphs over a predatory landlord. In Satyajit Ray's *Ghare Bhaire* (1984), a cinematic masterpiece based on Tagore's story, Swatilekha Chatterjee is a woman whose new explorations into freedom turn into tragedy. In the popular Hindi film *Aradhana* (1961), actress Sharmila Tagore became an irate mother defending her son. A merged metaphor connects her to both goddess Durga who conquers male lust and sacrificial Sita whose virtue is her own reward. Two women directors have produced significant award-winning films. Mira Nair's *Salaam Bombay* portrays prostitutes who are essentially purer within than the men who frequent them. Deepa Mehta uncovers thick veils of misogyny and homophobia in *Fire* (1996), *Earth* (1999), and *Water* (2000).

CONCLUSION

This chapter concludes a two-volume history of women in India from its beginnings to the present era. Its focus has been on society, culture, and religion as framed by economic and political systems, and it attempts to highlight the strengths and weaknesses of this civilization. It is impossible to narrate the stories of Indian women without placing them in their historical contexts. Early Indian women's rights appear to have lessened over the millennia with each successive wave of immigration and settlement on the subcontinent. A simple reliance on male texts to tell the multiple feminine stories may lead us into the false impression of women's powerlessness in each phase of India's history. Although regional governments and institutions were dominated by elite men, women enjoyed both domestic and local authority in communities outside the mainstream. India's geographical and social complexities gave opportunities to wield certain types of power, in certain spaces and in certain times. However, during crises, women were compelled to bear the brunt of misogynist laws. Thus, during wars and invasions, patriarchal rules were enforced more stringently upon women whose sexual vulnerability was exploited through rape, child marriage, widowhood, and *sati*. Despite these constraints, Indian women managed to rule kingdoms, either by occupying the throne or from behind the scenes as advisors. They used wealth often for philanthropy, as well as for art. They have produced an enormous corpus of regional language literature. They have farmed, crafted, and sustained their families, done math, supported men in their endeavors, and are rewarded through respect as virtuous mothers and wives. They have often been *agents* of destinies circumscribed by men, but their writings show that they did not regard themselves completely as victims. In the past century, women's social roles have expanded greatly, and they are now vocal and dissident when necessary. However, as modernity is accompanied by new forms of exploitation, they need to strengthen the legal institutions that protect them. The pitfalls include the Internet that can prey on girls and women, international corporations enriched through cheap labor, and governments that wage wars using a profitable arms industry. These prevent all Indian women from farming and industry, writing and artistry, feeding and nurturing families, healing and researching illnesses, and governing society in a peaceful, humane manner.

NOTES

1. Agarwal, "The Idea of Gender Equality," 36–65, *vide,* 36.

2. Government of India, Office of the Registrar General and Census Commissioner, *Census 2001*, Series 1, India, vol. 4 (Primary Census Abstract, and Total Population Table A-5), vol. 9 (Report and Tables on Age C-14), New Delhi: Controller of Publications, 2003. See also Government of India National Portal at http://www.india.gov.in/knowindia/literacy.php; National Literacy Movement in India, "Female Literacy in India," with Census 2001 statistical tables at http://www.nlm.nic.in/women.htm; Azad India Foundation, "Literacy in India," at http://azadindia.org/social-issues/literacy-in-india.html; and Victoria A. Velkoff, "Women's Education in India," U.S. Department of Commerce, Economics and Statistics Administration, Bureau of the Census, International Programs Center, October 1998, 1–5, at http://www.census.gov/ipc/prod/wid-9801.pdf.

3. Government of India updated information on the sex ratio has been cited by researchers from United Nations International Children's Educational Fund at http://www.unicef.org/india/resources_4458.htm. See also O. P. Sharma and Carl Haub, "Sex Ratio at Birth Begins to Improve in India," for Population Reference Bureau, August 2008, at http://www.prb.org/Articles/2008/indiasexratio.aspx; and editorial article, "Adverse Child Sex Ratio in India," *The Financial Express,* Mumbai, October 27, 2003, at http://www.financialexpress.com/news/advers-child-sex-ratio-in-india/48979/.

4. Kurien, *Kaleidoscopic Ethnicity,* 30–36, 58, 94–100, 127–30, 139–56, 164–70.

5. SEWA at http://www.sewa.org. Also the documentary *Kamala and Raji,* produced by Michael Camerini and Shari Robertson, 1991. The film examines two women workers, and their empowerment through SEWA.

6. Gawzi Hamad Al Sultan, in *Frontline* 17, no. 25 (December 9, 2000), at http://www.flonnet.com/fl2024/stories.

7. Amartya Sen, *Development as Freedom* (New York: Anchor Books, 1991), 197–98.

8. BISWA at http://www.biswa.org.

9. Raman, "Walking Two Paces Behind," 375–95.

10. Myron Weiner, *The Child and the State in India: Child Labor and Education Policy in Comparative Perspective* (Princeton: Princeton University Press, 1991), 59–64, 114, 161, 175, 184; Meena Verma and Neeta Verma, "Incidence of Female Child Labour in Bihar," in *Children at Work: Problems and Policy Options,* ed. Bhagwan Pd. Singh and Shukla Mahanty (New Delhi and Patna: B. R. Publishing Corporation and Indian Society of Labour Economics, 1993), 105–15; Kumudini Sinha, "Female Child Labour in Bihar: Incidence and Their Conditions," in *Children at Work: Problems and Policy Options,* ed. Singh and Mahanty, 117–32.

11. Agarwal, "The Idea of Gender Equality," 37.

12. Indu Grewal and J. Kishore, "Female Foeticide in India," *International Humanist and Ethical Union,* May 1, 2004, http://www.iheu.org/female-foeticide-in-india.

13. Madhu Kishwar and Ruth Vanita, "Drought—Women Are the Worst Victims" (1980), in *In Search of Answers: Indian Women's Voices from Manushi,* ed. Madhu Kishwar and Ruth Vanita (New Delhi: Manohar, 1996), 80–93.

14. Personal experience with two working women whose fathers sold them into prostitution in Bengal, but who escaped due to good Samaritans. See also Manik Bandhopadhyaya, "A Female Problem at a Low Level" (1963), in *Women, Outcastes, Peasants, and Rebels: A Selection of Bengali Stories,* trans. Kalpana Bardhan (Berkeley: University of California, 1990), 152–57; Mahasweta Devi, "Dhowli" (1979), in ibid., 184–205; Hasan Aizul Huq, "The Daughter and the Oleander" (1966), in ibid., 290–98. Hindi films on girls forced into prostitution include Shakti Samanta's *Amar Prem* (Eternal Love, 1971) and Mira Nair's *Salaam Bombay* (1988).

15. Anirudh K. Jain and Moni Nag, "Importance of Female Primary Education for Fertility Reduction in India," *Economic and Political Weekly* 21, no. 36 (1986): 1602–7; Leela Visaria, "Infant Mortality in India: Levels, Trends, and Determinants," *Economic and Political Weekly* 20, no. 34 (1985): 1447–50; Santosh Mehrotra, "Child Malnutrition and Gender Discrimination in South Asia," *Economic and Political Weekly* 41, no. 10 (2006): 912–18.

16. Sen, *Development as Freedom,* 187–203; Amartya Sen, "Gender Inequality and Theories of Justice," in *Women, Culture, and Development: A Study of Human Capabilities,* ed. Martha Nussbaum and Jonathan Glover (Oxford: Clarendon Press, 1995); and Amartya Sen, "Agency and Well-Being: The Development Agenda," in *A Commitment to the Women,* ed. Noeleen Heyzer (New York: UNIFEM, 1996).

17. Leelamma Devasia, "Maternal and Girl Child Care in India," in *Girl Child in India,* ed. Leelamma Devasia and V. V. Devasia (Springfield, VA: Nataraj Books, 1992), 133–52, *vide,* 140–43; United Nations Children's Fund (UNICEF) Statistics on India at http://www.unicef.org/india/resources_4458.htm.

18. Asok Mitra, *Implications of Declining Sex Ratio in India's Population,* Indian Council of Social Science Research (ICSSR), Women's Studies, and Jawaharlal Nehru University (Bombay: Allied Publishers, 1979), 1–11.

19. The 2001 Census records the sex ratio as 933 females/1000 males, but since 1991, it is closer to 800/1000. Punjab and Haryana have 10 districts with lower ratios, e.g., Fatehgarh Sahib with 766/1000. See Kalpana Sharma's "No Girls Please, We're Indian," *The Hindu,* August 29, 2004, 1–3; and Vaasanthi, *Kadaisee Varai* (Birthright), trans. from Tamil by Vasantha Surya (New Delhi: Zubaan Books, 2004).

20. J. Venkatesan, "Unique Legislation to Protect Girl Child," *The Hindu,* May 12, 2003, at http://www.hinduonnet.com/2003/05/12/stories/200305120 4460100.htm.

21. Visaria, "Infant Mortality in India," 1447–50.

22. Sen, *Development as Freedom,* 197–98, 217–18.

23. K. P. Srikumar, "Amniocentesis and the Future of the Girl Child," in *Girl Child in India,* ed. Devasia and Devasia, 51–65; Sharma, "No Girls Please, We're Indian," at http://www.hindu.com/mag/2004/08/29/stories/2004082900130100 .htm.

24. Barbara Hariss-White, "Gender Cleansing: The Paradox of Development and Deteriorating Female Life Chances in Tamil Nadu," in *Signposts: Gender Issues in Post-Independence India,* ed. Rajeswari Sunder Rajan (New Brunswick: Rutgers University, 2001), 125–54, 132–33.

25. Government of India, *Census 2001,* Series 1, vol. 4 (Primary Census Abstract, and Total Population Table A-5), vol. 9 (Report and Tables on Age C-14), New Delhi: Controller of Publications, 2003.

26. Ranjana Kumari, "Dowry Victims: Harassment and Torture," in *Widows, Abandoned and Destitute Women in India,* for Mahila Dakshata Samiti (Society for Women as Wealth), ed. Pramila Dandvate, Ranjana Kumari, and Jamila Veghese (New Delhi: Radiant Publishers, 1989), 10–26; Pramila Dandvate, "Social Legislation and Women," in ibid., 84–89.

27. Kumar, *History of Doing,* 115–26.

28. Kiran Singh, "It's Only a Family Affair!" in *In Search of Answers,* ed. Kishwar and Vanita, 186–90; Madhu Kishwar, "Denial of Fundamental Rights to Women," in ibid., 191–203.

29. Mehrotra, "Child Malnutrition and Gender Discrimination in South Asia," 912–18. Mehrotra cites United Nations, *Second Report on the World Nutrition Situation,* vol. 1 (Geneva: United Nations, 1992). See also V. Ramalingaswami, U. Jonsson, and J. Rohde, "The Asian Enigma," in *Progress of Nations* (New York: United Nations Children's Fund, 1996).

30. Alka Barua, Hemant Apte, and Pradeep Kumar, "Care and Support of Unmarried Adolescent Girls in Rajasthan," *Economic and Political Weekly* 42, no. 45–46 (November 3–23, 2007), 54–62.

31. Kavita Sethuraman and Nata Duvvury, "The Nexus of Gender Discrimination with Malnutrition: An Introduction," *Economic and Political Weekly* 42, no. 45–46 (November 3–23, 2007): 49–52.

32. Personal experience with a Punjabi friend after the birth of her daughter in 1965.

33. Agarwal, *A Field of Ones Own,* 30, 257 n. 24. Also Deepa Mehta's film *Water* (2000) on destitute widows in north India. On Bangalore slums, see Sarayu Pani, "Poverty, Ageing and Gender," *India Together,* November 14, 2007, at http:// www.indiatogether.org.

34. Smita Jain, "Bringing the Virus Home," *The Hindu,* November 27, 2005, at http://www.thehindu.com/thehindu/mag/2005/11/27/stories/2005112700190400 .htm; "Cutting Across Barriers," *The Hindu,* November 24, 2004, at http:// www.hinduonnet.com/thehindu/mag/2002/11/24/stories/2002112400400400.htm; Dilip D'Souza, "The AIDS Challenge" (Review of Siddharth Dube), *Sex, Lies and AIDS* (New Delhi: Harper Collins, 2000), *Frontline* 18, no. 19 (September 15, 2001); Madeleine Morris, "Indian Women Face Peril of HIV," BBC World News, September 21, 2005, at http://news.bbc.co.uk/2/hi/south_asia/4260314.stm.

35. Pratima Chaudhary, *Women's Education in India* (New Delhi: Har Anand Publications, 1995), 40; Usha Agrawal, *Indian Woman Education and Development* (Ambala: Indian Publications, 1995), 15; Raman, "Walking Two Paces Behind," 375–95; and Sita Anantha Raman, "Women's Education," in *Encyclopedia of India,* ed. Stanley Wolpert, 4:237–38.

36. Vibhuti Patel, "Schools to Empower Women," *Frontline* 20, no. 15 (2003), at http://www.flonnet.com/fl2015/stories/20030801006209600.htm.

37. *Census of India 2001,* Series 1, vol. 4 (Primary Census Abstract, and Total Population Table A-5), vol. 9 (Report and Tables on Age C-14). See also Government of India National Portal at http://www.india.gov.in/knowindia/literacy.php. Also see National Literacy Movement in India, "Female Literacy in India," with tables from Census 2001 at http://www.nlm.nic.in/women.htm; and Azad India Foundation, "Literacy in India," at http://azadindia.org/social-issues/literacy-in-india.html.

38. Sen, *Development as Freedom,* 187, 191–203, 336 n. 15.

39. Anil Sadgopal, "Gender and Education," *Frontline* 20, no. 24 (2003), at http://www.flonnet.com/fl2024/stories/20031205006910000.htm.

40. Mehrotra, "Child Malnutrition and Gender Discrimination in South Asia," 912–18.

41. Agarwal, "The Idea of Gender Equality," 43.

42. Lalitha Subrahmanyam, *Women Scientists in the Third World: The Indian Experience* (New Delhi and Thousand Oaks: Sage Publications, 1998).

43. Personal knowledge of some of these scientists. Also see Vineeta Bal, "Women Scientists in India: Nowhere Near the Glass Ceiling," *Current Science* 88, no. 6 (March 25, 2005): 872–82; Parvati Menon, "For More Women in Science," *Frontline* 22, no. 26 (December 2005).

44. Bina Agarwal, "Gender Inequalities: Neglected Dimensions and Hidden Facts," a Malcolm Adiseshiah Memorial Lecture, Madras Institute of Developmental Studies (MIDS), November 2004 (printed copy), Adyar: MIDS.

45. Ela Bhatt, *National Commission on Self-Employed Women and Women in the Informal Sector* (Ahmedabad: SEWA, 1988), 3–6.

46. Mythili Sivaraman, "A Struggle Without Borders: The World March for the Eradication of Poverty and Violence against Women," *Frontline* 17, no. 25 (December 9–22, 2000), at http://www.frontlineonnet.com/fl1725/17250460.htm.

47. Isa Baud, "In All Its Manifestations: The Impact of Changing Technology on the Gender Division of Labour," in *Indian Women in a Changing Industrial Scenario,* ed. Nirmala Bannerjee (New Delhi and Thousand Oaks, CA: Sage, 1991), 35, 78, 98–100.

48. Areeba Hamid, "Domestic Workers: Harsh Everyday Realities," *Economic and Political Weekly* 41, no. 13 (April 1–7, 2006): 1235–37.

49. Agarwal, *A Field of Ones Own,* 19–33; also Govind Kelkar, "Development Effectiveness Through Gender Mainstreaming: Gender Equality and Poverty Reduction in South Asia," *Economic and Political Weekly,* Review of Women's Studies, 40, no. 44–45 (October 29–November 4, 2005): 4690–95.

50. Kelkar, Ibid.

51. Agarwal, *A Field of Ones Own,* 206–10.

52. Leela Kasturi, "Report of the Sub-Committee, Women's Role in Planned Economy, National Planning Committee Series (1947)," in *Feminism in India,* ed. Chaudhuri, 136–55.

53. Basu and Ray, *Women's Struggle,* 62–65.

54. Renuka Ray, *My Reminiscences: Social Development during Gandhian Era and After* (New Delhi: Allied Publishers, 1982), 148–49.

55. Kiran Devendra, "Redefining Hindu Family: The Hindu Code Bill," in *Changing Status of Women in India,* 3rd ed. (New Delhi: Vikas Publishing House, 1996), 43, 84.

56. Basu and Ray, *Women's Struggle,* 65.

57. Letter from Rajendra Prasad to Jawaharlal Nehru on the Hindu Code Bill, September 14, 1951, Appendix III, in Devendra, *Changing Status of Women in India,* 183–90.

58. Agarwal, *A Field of Ones Own,* 209–10; and Agarwal, "The Idea of Gender Equality," 37–39.

59. Appendix V, "Rights of Women under the Constitution," in Devendra, *Changing Status of Women in India,* 199–210.

60. Savitri Goonesekere, "Sex Equality in South Asia," in *Men's Laws, Women's Lives,* ed. Jaising, 217, 223–24; Parmar, "Gender Equality in the Name of Religion," 245–51.

61. Agarwal, *A Field of Ones Own,* 175, 249–50, 279, 292; Agarwal, "The Idea of Gender Equality," 37.

62. Gail Omvedt, "New Movements and New Theories in India," in *Feminism in India,* ed. Chaudhuri, 291.

63. Basu and Ray, *Women's Struggle,* 112.

64. Agarwal, "Gender and the Environment" lecture at Santa Clara University, May 2000, and personal communication.

65. Farzand Ahmed and Sanjay Kumar Jha, "Mother's Methods," *India Today,* October 13, 1997.

66. A. K. Verma, "Backward Caste Politics in Uttar Pradesh," *Economic and Political Weekly* 40, no. 36 (September 3, 2005): 3889–92.

67. Purima S. Tripathi, "Delay and Doubts," *Frontline* 20, no. 21 (October 11, 2003).

68. Editor, "Political Tour De Force," *The Hindu,* May 12, 2007.

69. T. K. Rajalakshmi, "Miles to Go," *Frontline* 24, no. 22 (November 3–16, 2007), http://www.flonnet.com/fl2422/stories/20071116506309000.htm.

70. Aditi Kapoor, "Break the Silence," *The Hindu,* November 21, 2004.

71. National Literacy Movement in India, "Female Literacy in India," with Census 2001 statistical tables at http://www.nlm.nic.in/women.htm; and Azad India Foundation, "Literacy in India," at http://azadindia.org/social-issues/literacy-in -india.html.

72. Government of India, Census of 1991, Series 1, Paper 2 of 1992, Statement 21, p. 70.

73. On Roop Kanwar's *sati,* see Neerja Mishra, "The Murder of Roop Kanwar," in *Widows, Abandoned and Destitute Women in India,* ed. Dandvate, Kumari, and Verghese, 49–53; Indu Prakash Singh and Renuka Singh, "Sati: Its Patri-Politics," in ibid., 54–61; Kumar, *History of Doing,* 172–81.

74. Special Correspondent, "Special Feature: Rajasthan," *Frontline* 22, no. 27 (January 13, 2006): 85–204, *vide,* 99–103, showcasing Vasundhara Raje's work.

75. Tanika Sarkar and Urvashi Butalia, eds., *Women and the Hindu Right: A Collection of Essays* (New Delhi: Kali for Women, 1995).

76. Gail Omvedt, "Women in Governance in South Asia," *Economic and Political Weekly* 40, no. 44–45 (October 29–November 4, 2005): 4746–52.

77. Ibid., 4746–49.

78. Ibid., 4750.

79. Staff Correspondent, "We Will Go Ahead with the Women's Bill: P.M.," *The Hindu,* March 8, 2003, at http://www.thehindu.com/2003/03/08/stories/2003030804350100.htm.

80. Special Correspondent, "UPA Blamed for Delay on Women's Reservation Bill," *The Hindu,* December 4, 2005, at http://www.hindu.com/2005/12/04/stories/2005120406110700.htm.

81. Kumar, *History of Doing,* 96, 100–101.

82. Ibid.

83. Mahasweta Devi, "Paddy Seeds," in *Women, Outcastes, Peasants, and Rebels,* trans. Bardhan, 158–84.

84. Madhu Kishwar, "Introduction: Indian Women—The Continuing Struggle," in *In Search of Answers,* ed. Kishwar and Vanita, 31–40.

85. Darryl D'Monte, "Mass Rape in Bihar by Police" (1979), in *In Search of Answers,* ed. Kishwar and Vanita, 206–7.

86. This ballad is based on real events at Pipariya, Madhya Pradesh. Vasantha Surya, trans., *The Ballad of Budhini,* from the Bundeli Hindi poem by Veerendra Kumar, Narendra Kumar, and Raghuvanshi Krishnamurthi (Calcutta: Writers' Workshop, 1992).

87. Handwritten records shown to me by an official of All India Democratic Women's Association (AIDWA), Chennai in 1997.

88. Arundhati Roy, *An Ordinary Person's Guide to Empire* (London: Penguin Books, 2006), 96–106.

89. Sunderlal Bahuguna, "The Chipko Movement, Part I—Women's Non-Violent Power" (1980), in *In Search of Answers,* ed. Kishwar and Vanita, 149–53; Gopa Joshi, "The Chipko Movement, Part II—Community Opposes Activists" (1981), in ibid., 153–57.

90. Guha, *Unquiet Woods,* 152–64.

91. Bina Agarwal, "Neither Sustenance Nor Sustainability: Agricultural Strategies, Ecological Degradation and Indian Women in Poverty," in *Structures of Patriarchy,* ed. Agarwal, 83–120, *vide,* 104–13.

92. Bahuguna, "The Chipko Movement, Part I," 152.

93. Kumar, *History of Doing,* 183.

94. "Medha Patkar Ends Fast," *The Hindu,* September 28, 2001; "Medha Patkar Mobbed, Scribes Injured in Police Lathi Charge," *The Hindu,* April 8, 2002; "Medha

Patkar Continues Fast," *The Hindu,* January 28, 2004; "Medha Patkar Held," *The Hindu,* February 17, 2004, at http://www.hinduonnet.com.

95. Gupta, *India's 50 Most Illustrious Women,* 159–64.

96. Kalpana Sharma, "Unrecognized Heroines," *India Together,* December 21, 2007, at http://www.indiatogether.org/2007/dec/ksh-heroines.htm.

97. Arundhati Roy, *The God of Small Things* (New York: Harper Collins, 1997).

98. Roy, *An Ordinary Person's Guide to Empire,* 96–106. See also Sanjay Sanghvi, *The River and the Life: People's Struggle in the Narmada Valley* (Mumbai: Earth Care Books, 2000).

99. Gupta, *India's 50 Most Illustrious Women,* 205–12.

100. Ibid., 199–204.

101. Tharu and Lalitha, eds., *Women Writing in India: 600 B.C. to the Present: The Twentieth Century* (New Delhi: Oxford University Press, 1995), 2:234.

102. Devi, "Paddy Seeds," 158–84; Devi, "Dhowli," 185–205; Mahasweta Devi, "The Witch-Hunt," in *Women, Outcastes, Peasants, and Rebels,* trans. Bardhan, 242–71.

103. Gupta, *India's 50 Most Illustrious Women,* 213–18.

104. Ismat Chugtai, "Lihaf" (The Quilt), trans. Syed Sirajuddin, in Tharu and Lalitha, eds., *Women Writing in India: 600 B.C. to the Present: The Twentieth Century,* 2:129–38.

105. Vaasanthi, *Kadaisee Varai* (Birthright).

106. Vasantha Surya, *The Stalk of Time* (Chennai: K. Suryanarayanan, 1985); Vasantha Surya, *A Word Between Us* (Chennai: Sandhya, 2003); Chudamani Raghavan, *Yamini,* trans. from Tamil by Vasantha Surya (Chennai: Macmillan, 1996).

107. Gupta, *India's 50 Most Illustrious Women,* 241–47.

108. Ibid., 27–37.

BIBLIOGRAPHY

PRIMARY AND SECONDARY

"A.D." *Until the Shadows Flee Away: The Story of the C.E.Z.M.S.* London: Church of England Zenana Mission Society, 1920.

"Aa.chi.ka" (pseudonym). "The Education of Women" (Tamil). *Viveka Bodhini* 1, no. 1 (August 1908): 39–41.

Advaita Ashrama. *A Short Life of Sri Ramakrishna.* Mayavati, Himalayas: Advaita Ashrama, 1940.

Agarwal, Bina. *A Field of Ones Own: Gender and Land Rights in South Asia.* Cambridge: Cambridge University Press, 1994.

———. "Gender Inequalities: Neglected Dimensions and Hidden Facts." A Malcolm Adiseshiah Memorial Lecture, Madras Institute of Developmental Studies. Adyar: MIDS, November 2004.

———. "The Idea of Gender Equality: From Legislative Vision to Everyday Family Practice." In *India: Another Millennium?* Edited by Romila Thapar, 36–65. New Delhi: Penguin, 2000.

———, ed. *Structures of Patriarchy: State, Community and Household in Modernizing Asia.* New Delhi: Kali for Women, 1988.

Agnes, Flavia. "Women, Marriage, and the Subordination of Rights." In *Subaltern Studies XI: Community, Gender and Violence.* Edited by Partha Chatterjee and Pradeep Jeganathan, 106–37. New York: Columbia University Press, 1995.

Agrawal, Usha. *Indian Woman Education and Development.* Ambala: Indian Publications, 1995.

Ahir, D. C. *Gandhi and Ambedkar.* New Delhi: Blumoon Publishers, 1995.

Ahmed, Leila. *Women and Gender in Islam.* New Haven: Yale University Press, 1992.

Ali, Allama Abdullah Yusuf, trans. *The Meaning of the Illustrious Qur'an.* 1934. Reprint, Lahore: Shaikh Muhammad Ashraf, 1946.

Ali, Azra Asghar. *The Emergence of Feminism among Indian Muslim Women 1920–1947.* Karachi: Oxford University Press, 2000.

All India Women's Conference Papers, Nehru Memorial Museum & Library, New Delhi

- British Commonwealth League, Women's Freedom League, Six Point Group, St. Joan's Social and Political Alliance, Women's International League, letter in support of Indian woman suffrage, April 10, 1934, File 12.
- Rajkumari Amrit Kaur, Shareefa Hamid Ali, Muthulakshmi Reddi, letter to All-India Women's Conference, London, August 9, 1933, File no. 10.
- Rajkumari Amrit Kaur, Shareefa Hamid Ali, Muthulakshmi Reddi, "Statement of the elected representatives of the All-India Women's Conference, the Women's Indian Association, and the National Council of Women in India, to the Joint Select Committee," London, August 1, 1933, File no. 10.

Amin, Shahid. "The Making of the Mahatma." In *Subaltern Studies 3*. Edited by Ranajit Guha, 1–55. New Delhi: Oxford University Press, 1984.
Anagol, Padma. *The Emergence of Feminism in India, 1850–1920*. Hampshire, England: Ashgate Publishers, 2005.
Anand, Mulk Raj. *Sati: A Writeup of Raja Ram Mohan Roy about Burning of Widows Alive*. Delhi: B. R. Publishing Corporation, 1989.
Andrews, Charles Freer. *The Indian Question in East Africa*. Nairobi, Kenya: The Swift Press, 1921.
"Anna." *Saints of India*. Madras: Sri Ramakrishna Math, 1990.
Arasaratnam, Sinnappa. *Indians in Malaysia and Singapore*. Kuala Lumpur: Oxford University Press, 1979.
Arnold, David. *Gandhi: Profiles in Power*. Harlow, U.K.: Longman and Pearson Education, 2001.
Arora, G. S. *Indian Emigration*. New Delhi: Puja Publishers, 1991.
Arunima, G. *There Comes Papa: Colonialism and the Transformation of Matriliny in Kerala, Malabar c. 1850–1940*. Delhi: Orient Longman, 2004.
Arya, Anita. *Indian Women: Society and Law* (vol. 1); *Education and Empowerment* (vol. 2); *Work and Development* (vol. 3). New Delhi: Gyan Publishing House, 2000.
Asani, Ali S. "Creating Tradition Through Devotional Songs and Communal Script: The Kojah Isma'ilis of South Asia." In *India's Islamic Traditions, 711–1750*. Edited by Richard M. Eaton, 285–310. Delhi: Oxford University Press, 2003.
Atmaprana, Pravrajika. *The Story of Sister Nivedita*. Calcutta: Ramakrishna Sarada Mission and Sister Niveditta Girls' School, 1991.
Avvai Ashram Records, Adyar, Tamil Nadu

- *14th–15th Annual Report, 1943–44 & 1944–45.*
- *Avvai Home Completes Fifty Years: A Golden Centenary Souvenir, 1980; Avvai Home Silver Jubilee Souvenir, 1955.*
- "Yengal Amma" (Our Mother, Dr. Muthulakshmi Reddi), *Avvai Home School Calendar, 1986–87.*

Bacon, Leonard, trans. *The Lusiads of Luiz de Camoes*. New York: Hispanic Society of America, 1950.
Bahuguna, Sunderlal. "The Chipko Movement, Part I—Women's Non-Violent Power" (1980). In *In Search of Answers: Indian Women's Voices from Manushi*. Edited by Madhu Kishwar and Ruth Vanita, 149–57. New Delhi: Manohar, 1996.

Baig, Tara Ali. *Sarojini Naidu: Portrait of a Patriot.* New Delhi: Congress Centenary Celebration Committee, 1985.

Bal, Vineeta. "Women Scientists in India: Nowhere Near the Glass Ceiling." *Current Science* 88, no. 6 (March 25, 2005): 872–82.

Balasaraswati, T. "Presidential Address (1975): Bala on Bharatanatyam." *Sruti 5* (March 1, 1984), Chennai, 11–16.

Balchin, Cassandra. "Law Reform Processes in Plural Legal Systems." In *Men's Laws, Women's Lives: A Constitutional Perspective on Religion, Common Law and Culture in South Asia.* Edited by Indira Jaising, 87–108. New Delhi: Women Unlimited, 2005.

Banerjee, Hasi. *Sarojini Naidu: The Traditional Feminist.* University of Calcutta monograph #16. Calcutta: K. P. Bagchi, 1998.

Banerjee, Nirmala. "Working Women in Colonial Bengal: Modernization and Marginalization." In *Recasting Women: Essays in Colonial History.* Edited by Kumkum Sangari and Sudesh Vaid. New Delhi: Kali for Women, 1989.

Banerjee, Sumanta. "Marginalization for Women's Popular Culture in Nineteenth Century Bengal." In *Recasting Women: Essays in Colonial History.* Edited by Kumkum Sangari and Sudesh Vaid, 127–79. New Delhi: Kali for Women, 1989.

Banu, Zenab. "Muslim Women's Right to Inheritance: Sharia Law and Its Practice among the Dawoodi Bohras of Udaipur, Rajasthan." In *Problems of Muslim Women in India.* Edited by Asghar Ali Engineer, 34–39. Bombay: Orient Longman, 1995.

Barani, Ziuddin. *Tariq-I-Firuz Shahi.* Translated by Saiyid Ahmad Khan. Calcutta: Royal Asiatic Society, 1862.

Bardhan, Kalpana, trans. *Women, Outcastes, Peasants, and Rebels: A Selection of Bengali Stories.* Berkeley and Los Angeles: University of California, 1990.

Barnes, Irene H. *Behind the Pardah.* 1898. Reprint, London: Marshall Brothers, 1903.

Barua, Alka, Hemant Apte, and Pradeep Kumar. "Care and Support of Unmarried Adolescent Girls in Rajasthan." *Economic and Political Weekly* 42, nos. 45–46 (November 3, 2007): 54–62.

Basu, Aparna, and Bharati Ray. *Women's Struggle: A History of the All India Women's Conference 1927–2002.* 2nd ed. New Delhi: Manohar Publishers, 2003.

Baud, Isa. "In All Its Manifestations: The Impact of Changing Technology on the Gender Division of Labour." In *Indian Women in a Changing Industrial Scenario.* Edited by Nirmala Banerjee. New Delhi: Sage, 1991.

Baxamula, Ramala. "Need for Change in Muslim Personal Law Relating to Divorce in India." In *Problems of Muslim Women in India.* Edited by Ashgar Ali Engineer, 18–29. Bombay: Orient Longman, 1995.

Bayly, Susan. *Saints, Goddesses and Kings: Muslims and Christians in South Indian History, 1700–1900.* Cambridge: Cambridge University Press, 1989.

Behl, Aditya. "The Magic Doe: Desire and Narrative in a Hindavi Sufi Romance, Circa 1503." In *India's Islamic Traditions, 711–1750.* Edited by Richard M. Eaton. New Delhi: Oxford University Press, 2004.

Berinstain, Valérie. *India and the Mughal Dynasty.* New York: Harry N. Abrams, 1998.

Bernier, Francois. *Travels in the Mogul Empire.* Translated by Archibald Constable. Westminster, U.K.: 1891.

Besant, Annie (Theosophical Society Archives, Adyar, Tamil Nadu)

- "Address Delivered to the Children of the Maharani's Girls' School at Mysore on December 24, 1896." *Arya Bala Bodhini,* January 1897.
- "An Appeal: Higher Education for Indian Girls." Adyar: TS, January 1915.
- *An Autobiography.* 1893. Reprint, Adyar: TS, 1984.
- "An Interview with Annie Besant." *Arya Bala Bodhini,* January 1899, 44–48.
- *Higher Education in India: Past and Present,* Convocation Address at the University of Mysore, October 29, 1924. Adyar: TS, 1932.
- *On the Education of Indian Girls.* Series no. 25. Benares and London: TS, 1904.

Beveridge, Annette Susannah, trans. *The Baburnama in English (Memoirs of Babur).* Translated from the original Turki. 2 vols. London: Luzac, 1922. Reprint, New York: AMS Press, 1971.
Bharati, C. Subramania. *Bharatiyar Kavitaikkal Muzhuvadum* (Bharaityar's Complete Poems), 207–12. Madras: Bharati Publishers, 1986.
———. *Chandrikaiyin Kadai* (Chandrikai's Story). Madras: Sangam Publishers, 1982.
———. *Katturaikal: Mathar* (Essays on Women). Triplicane: Bharati Publishing House, 1935.
———. "Statistics on Women's Education." *Chakravartini* (in Tamil), 1, no. 7 (February 1906): 1.
Bhasin, Kamla, and Nighat Said Khan. "Some Questions on Feminism and Its Relevance in South Asia." In *Feminism in India.* Edited by Maitrayee Chaudhuri, 3–7. New Delhi: Women Unlimited and Kali for Women, 2004.
Bhatt, Ela R. *National Commission on Self-Employed Women and Women in the Informal Sector.* Ahmedabad: SEWA, 1996.
Borthwick, Meredith. "Bhadramahila and Changing Conjugal Relations in Bengal, 1850–1900." In *Women in India and Nepal.* Edited by Michael Allen and S. N. Mukherjee, 108–10. Delhi: Oxford University Press, 1982.
———. *Changing Role of Women in Bengal, 1849–1905.* Princeton: Princeton University Press, 1984.
Boxer, C. R. *Women in the Iberian Expansion Overseas, 1415–1815: Some Facts, Fancies and Personalities, 1415–1815.* London: Oxford University Press, 1975.
British Parliamentary Papers

- Colonies, East India, 1831–1832 (I, Public), Part B, Appendix (I), "On the Education of the Natives," Governor Thomas Munro's Minute, July 2, 1822, 413.
- Comins, D. W. D. *Note on Emigration from the East Indies to Trinidad,* 1893.
- Goeghegan, J. *Report on Coolie Emigration from India,* 1873.
- Grierson, G. A. *Report on the System of Recruiting Coolies for British and Foreign Colonies as Carried Out in the Lower Provinces of Bengal,* 1883.
- Hansard, Thomas Curson, ed. *Hansard's Parliamentary Debates.* Third Series. Vol. 41. 1837–1838.

Proceedings, Minutes, Letters, Reports

- 1837–38, LII, (100–101), (180), H. J. Princep to G. F. Dick, June 29, 1836; 1840, XXXVII, (58), (455), Despatch 57, Governor W. Nicolay to Lord

Glenglg, May 4, 1839; 1840, IX, (659), Despatch 62 from Glenglg to Nicolay; 1841, III, (137); 1841, III, Session 66; 1844, XXXV, (356–544); 1854 (393), XLVII, 155, Charles Wood, "Despatch on the Subject of General Education in India," July 19, 1854, no. 49; 1857–58, (72), XLII, 339, "Further Correspondence on Education," 390; 1875, XXXIV, (100–180).

- 1910, Lord Sanderson Report, XXVII (1), (Cmd. 5193 & 5194), *Report of the Committee of Enquiry on Emigration from India to the Crown Colonies and Protectorates*.
- 1914–16, McNeill Chiman Lal Report, XLVII (488 & 583), *Report to the Government of India on the Conditions of Indians in 4 British Colonies & Surinam*, led by Mr. James McNeill and Mr. Chiman Lal.

Brockway, Nora. *A Larger Way for Women: Aspects of Christian Education for Girls in South India, 1712–1948.* London: Oxford University Press, 1949.

Brown, Judith. *Gandhi: Prisoner of Hope.* New Haven: Yale University Press, 1989.

———. *Gandhi and Civil Disobedience.* London: Cambridge University Press, 1977.

———. *Gandhi's Rise to Power.* London: Cambridge University Press, 1972.

Burton, Antoinette. *Burdens of History: British Feminists, Indian Women, and Imperial Culture, 1865–1915.* Chapel Hill: University of North Carolina, 1994.

———. " 'Stray Thoughts of an Indian Girl' by Cornelia Sorabji, *The Nineteenth Century, October 1891.*" In *Feminism in India.* Edited by Maitrayee Chaudhuri, 94–102. New Delhi: Women Unlimited and Kali for Women, 2004.

Butalia, Urvashi. *The Other Side of Silence: Voices from the Partition of India.* New Delhi: Penguin, 1998.

Chakrabarty, Dipesh. *Rethinking Working-Class History: Bengal 1890–1940.* Princeton: Princeton University Press, 1989.

Chakravarti, Uma. "Whatever Happened to the Vedic *Dasi?* Orientalism, Nationalism and a Script for the Past." In *Recasting Women: Essays in Colonial History.* Edited by Kumkum Sangari and Sudesh Vaid, 27–87. New Delhi: Kali for Women, 1989.

Champakalakshmi, R., and S. Gopal, eds. *Tradition, Dissent and Ideology: Essays in Honor of Romila Thapar.* Delhi: Oxford University Press, 1996.

Chandeigne, Michel, ed. *Goa 1510–1685: Inde Portugaise, Apostolique et Commerciale,* Collection Memoires no. 41. Paris: Editions Autrement, 1996.

Chandler, John S. *Seventy-Five Years in the Madura Mission.* Madras: American Madura Mission, 1912.

Chandra, Bipin. *India's Struggle for Independence.* 2nd ed. Delhi: Penguin, 1989.

Chandra, Jyoti. *Annie Besant: From Theosophy to Nationalism.* Delhi: K. R. Publications, 2001.

Chatterjee, Partha. *The Nation and Its Fragments: Colonial and Post-Colonial Histories.* New Delhi: Oxford University Press, 1995.

———. "The Nationalist Resolution of the Women's Question." In *Recasting Women: Essays in Colonial History.* Edited by Kumkum Sangari and Sudesh Vaid, 232–53. New Delhi: Kali for Women, 1989.

———. *Nationalist Thought and the Colonial World.* Minneapolis: University of Minnesota Press, 1993.

Chatterjee, Partha, and Pradeep Jeganathan, eds. *Subaltern Studies XI: Community, Gender and Violence.* New York: Columbia University Press, 1995.

Chatterji, Bankim Chandra. *The Abbey of Bliss: A Translation of Bankim Chandra Chatterji's Ananda Math.* Translated by Nares Chandra Sen Gupta. Calcutta: P. M. Neogi, 1906.

Chattopadhyaya, Kamaladevi. *At the Crossroads,* collection of essays on socialism and other topics. Bombay: Yusuf Meherally and Nalanda Publications, 1947.

———. *The Awakening of Indian Women.* Madras: Everyman's Press, 1939.

———. *Carpets and Floor Coverings of India.* New Delhi: Handicrafts Board, 1966.

———. *The Glory of Indian Handicrafts.* New Delhi: Indian Book Co., 1976.

———. *Indian Embroidery.* New Delhi: Wiley Eastern, 1977.

———. *Indian Women's Battle for Freedom.* New Delhi: Abinav Publications. 1983.

———. *Inner Recesses, Outer Spaces.* New Delhi: Navrang, 1986.

Chaudhary, Pratima. *Women's Education in India.* New Delhi: Har Anand Publications, 1995.

Chaudhuri, Buddhadeb, ed. *Tribal Transformation in India.* Tribals of India Series. Vol. 1. Delhi: Inter-India Publications, 1992.

Chaudhuri, Maitrayee, ed. *Feminism in India.* 2nd ed. New Delhi: Women Unlimited and Kali for Women, 2005.

Chellammal, S. "Sister Subbalakshmi Ammal." In *Sister Subbalakshmi Ammal First Anniversary Commemoration Souvenir* (Tamil). T. Nagar: Sarada Ladies Union, 1970.

Chitnis, Suma. "Feminism: Indian Ethos and Indian Convictions." In *Feminism in India.* Edited by Maitrayee Chaudhuri, 8–25. New Delhi: Women Unlimited and Kali for Women, 2004.

Chowdhry, Prem. "Customs in a Peasant Economy: Women in Colonial Haryana." In *Recasting Women: Essays in Colonial History.* Edited by Kumkum Sangari and Sudesh Vaid, 79–89. New Delhi: Kali for Women, 1989.

Chugtai, Ismat. "Lihaf" (The Quilt). In *Women Writing in India: 600 B.C. to the Present: The Twentieth Century.* Edited by Susie Tharu and K. Lalitha, 2:129–38. New Delhi: Oxford University Press, 1995.

Church Missionary Intelligencer. London: Church Missionary Society, vols. 1851–1930.

Coates, Timothy. "State-Sponsored Female Colonization in the Estado da India, ca. 1550–1750." In *Sinners and Saints: The Successors of Vasco da Gama.* Edited by Sanjay Subrahmanyam. Delhi: Oxford University Press, 2000.

Cole, J. R. I. "Popular Shi'ism." In *India's Islamic Traditions, 711–1750.* Edited by Richard M. Eaton, 311–29. Delhi: Oxford University Press, 2003.

The Commonweal 1, no. 1 (April 3, 1914). Edited by Annie Besant. Adyar: Theosophical Society.

Coomaraswamy, Ananda K. "Sati: A Vindication of the Hindu Woman." Paper to the Sociological Society, November 12, 1912. In *The Sociological Review.* Edited by J. Mark Baldwin, 119–35. London: 1912.

———. "Status of Indian Women." In *The Dance of Shiva: On Indian Art and Culture.* Rev. ed., 100–126. New Delhi: Sagar Publications, 1991.

Cousins, James H., and Margaret Cousins. *We Two Together.* Madras: Ganesh, 1950.

Cousins, Margaret. *The Awakening of Indian Womanhood.* Madras: Ganesh, 1922.

———. Letter from Margaret Cousins and Dorothy Jinarajadasa to Annie Besant on men's support for the Women's Indian Association, March 21, 1922.

———. "Summary of Woman Suffrage Work Done in India." Letter to Annie Besant, Madras, June 4, 1919.

Cumpston, I. M. *Indians Overseas in British Territories (1834–1854)*. London: Oxford University Press, 1953.

da Silva Gracias, Fatima. *Kaleidoscope of Women in Goa, 1510–1961*. New Delhi: Concept Publishing Company, 1996.

Dalton, Dennis. *Mahatma Gandhi: Nonviolent Power in Action*. New York: Columbia University Press, 1993.

Dandvate, Pramila, Ranjana Kumari, and Jamila Verghese, eds. *Widows, Abandoned and Destitute Women in India*, for Mahila Dakshata Samiti (Society for Women as Wealth). New Delhi: Radiant Publishers, 1989.

Danvers, Frederick Charles. *The Portuguese in India: Being a History of the Rise and Decline of Their Eastern Empire*. 2 vols. 1894. Reprint, London: Frank Cass & Co., Ltd., 1988.

Darwin, Charles. *The Descent of Man and Selection in Relation to Sex*. 2nd ed. 1871. Reprint, New York: D. Appleton and Company, 1898.

———. *The Origins of Species by Means of Natural Selection, or the Preservation of the Favored Races in the Struggle for Life*. 6th ed. 1859. Reprint, New York: Appleton, 1892.

Das, M. N. *Studies in the Economic and Social Development of India, 1848–1856*. Calcutta: Firma KLM, 1959.

de Souza, Teotonio R., ed. *Indo-Portuguese History: Old Issues, New Questions*. New Delhi: Concept Publishing Company, 1985.

Desai, Neera. *Woman in Modern India*. Bombay: Vora, 1977.

Deshmukh, Durgabai. *Stone That Speaketh: The Story of the Andhra Mahila Sabha*. Hyderabad: Andhra Mahila Sabha, 1980.

Devasia, Leelamma, and V. V. Devasia. *Girl Child in India*. Springfield, VA: Nataraj Books, 1992.

Devendra, Kiran. "Redefining Hindu Family: The Hindu Code Bill." In *Changing Status of Women in India*, 84. New Delhi: Vikas Publishing House, 1996.

Devi, Mahasweta. "Paddy Seeds," "Dhowli," "The Funeral Wailer," "Strange Children," "The Witch-Hunt," "Giribala." In *Women, Outcastes, Peasants, and Rebels*. Translated by Kalpana Bardhan, 158–271. Berkeley and Los Angeles: University of California Press, 1990.

Dey, Mukul C. *Twenty Portraits*. Calcutta: Thacker, Spink and Company, 1953.

Dharampal. *The Beautiful Tree: Indigenous Education in the Eighteenth Century*. New Delhi: Biblica Implex, 1983.

Digby, Simon. "The Sufi Shaikh as a Source of Authority in Medieval India." In *India's Islamic Traditions*. Edited by Richard M. Eaton, 234–62. New Delhi: Oxford University Press, 2004.

D'Monte, Darryl. "Mass Rape in Bihar by Police" (1979). In *In Search of Answers: Indian Women's Voices from Manushi*. Edited by Madhu Kishwar and Ruth Vanita, 206–7. New Delhi: Manohar, 1996.

Doniger, Wendy, and Brian K. Smith, trans. *The Laws of Manu*. New York: Penguin, 1991.

D'Souza, Dilip. "The AIDS Challenge" (Review of Siddharth Dube). *Sex, Lies and AIDS* (New Delhi: Harper Collins, 2000). *Frontline* 18, no. 19 (September 15, 2001).

Earle, T. S., and John Villiers, eds. *Albuquerque, Caesar of the East: Selected Texts by Afonso de Albuquerque and His Son.* Warminster: Aris & Phillips, 1990.

Eaton, Richard M., ed. *India's Islamic Traditions, 711–1750.* Delhi: Oxford University Press, 2003.

———. "The Political and Religious Authority of the Shrine of Baba Farid." In *India's Islamic Traditions, 711–1750.* Edited by Richard M. Eaton, 263–84. New Delhi: Oxford University Press, 2003.

———. *The Rise of Islam and the Bengal Frontier, 1204–1760.* Berkeley and Los Angeles: University of California Press, 1993.

———. *The Sufis of Bijapur.* Princeton: Princeton University Press, 1978.

Elliot, Henry M., and John Dowson, eds. *The History of India as Told by Its Own Historians: The Muhammadan Period.* Vol. 2. London: Trübner & Co., 1869. Reprint, New York: AMS Press Inc., 1966.

Embree, Ainslie. "Comment: Widows as Cultural Symbols." In *Sati, the Blessing and the Curse: The Burning of Wives in India.* Edited by Jonathan Stratton Hawley, 149–59. Berkeley and Los Angeles: University of California Press, 1994.

———, ed. *Sources of Indian Tradition: From the Beginning to 1800.* Vols. 1 and 2. 2nd ed. New York: Columbia University Press, 1988.

Engels, Dagmar. "The Myth of the Family Unit: Adivasi Women in Coal-Mines and Tea Plantations in Early Twentieth-Century Bengal." In *Dalit Movements and the Meanings of Labour in India.* Edited by Peter Robb, 225–44. Delhi: Oxford University Press, 1993.

Engineer, Asghar Ali, ed. *Problems of Muslim Women in India.* Bombay: Orient Longman, 1995.

Erikson, Erik H. *Gandhi's Truth: On the Origins of Militant Nonviolence.* New York: W. W. Norton & Co., 1969.

Felton, Monica. *A Child Widow's Story.* London: Gollancz, 1966.

Figueira, Dorothy M. "Die Flambierte Frau: Sati in European Culture." In *Sati, the Blessing and the Curse: The Burning of Wives in India.* Edited by John Stratton Hawley, 55–72. New York: Oxford University Press, 1994.

Findly, Ellison Banks. *Nur Jahan: Empress of Mughal India.* New York: Oxford University Press, 1993.

Fischer, Louis. *Gandhi: His Life and Message for the World.* New York: New American Library, 1954.

Fisher, Michael H. "Representing 'His' Women: Mirza Abu Talib Khan's 1801 'Vindication of the Liberties of Asian Women.' " *The Indian Economic and Social History Review* 37, no. 2 (2000): 215–37.

Forbes, Geraldine. "The Indian Women's Movement: A Struggle for Women's Rights or National Liberation?" In *The Extended Family: Women and Political Participation in India and Pakistan.* Edited by Gail Minault, 49–82. Delhi: Chanakya, 1981.

———. *Women in Modern India.* Cambridge: Cambridge University Press, 1996.

Gandhi, Arun, and Sunanda Gandhi, with Carol Lynn Yellin. *The Forgotten Woman: The Untold Story of Kastur Gandhi, Wife of Mahatma Gandhi.* Arkansas: Zark Mountain Publishers, 1998.

Gandhi, M. K. *An Autobiography or My Experiments with Truth.* Translated from Gujarati by Mahadev Desai. 1927. Reprint, Ahmedabad: Navajivan Publishing House, 1996.

————. *The Collected Works of Mahatma Gandhi*. New Delhi: Government of India Publications Division, 1958.

————. *Hind Swaraj and Other Writings*. Edited by A. J. Parel. Cambridge: Cambridge University Press, 1997.

Gangulee, N. *Indians in the Empire Overseas: A Survey*. London: New India Publishing House, 1947.

Garu, N. Subbarau Pantulu, ed. *Hindu Social Progress*. Madras: G. A. Natesan & Co., 1904.

Gascoigne, Bamber. *The Great Moguls: India's Most Flamboyant Rulers*. 2nd ed. New York: Carroll & Graf Publishers, 2002.

Gibb, H. A. R., trans. *Travels of Ibn Battuta*. 2nd series. Vol. 3. Cambridge and London: Hakluyt Society at the University Press, 1958–94.

Gillion, K. L. *Fiji's Indian Emigrants: A History to the End of Indenture in 1920*. Melbourne: Oxford University Press, 1962.

Godden, Rumer. *Gulbadan: Portrait of a Rose Princess at the Mughal Court*. New York: Viking Press, 1981.

Goonatilleka, M. H. "A Portuguese Creole in Sri Lanka, a Brief Socio-Linguistic Survey." In *Indo-Portuguese History: Old Issues, New Questions*. Edited by Teotonio R. de Souza. New Delhi: Concept Publishing Company, 1985.

Goonesekere, Savitri. "Sex Equality in South Asia." In *Men's Laws, Women's Lives: A Constitutional Perspective on Religion, Common Law and Culture in South Asia*. Edited by Indira Jaising, 212–25. New Delhi: Women Unlimited and Kali for Women, 2005.

Government of India (National Archives, New Delhi)

Census 1911, Volume 12, Madras, Part 1.

Census 1921, ed. G. T. Boag, Volume 13, Part 1, Madras: Government Press, 1922.

Census 1991, Series 1, Paper 2 of 1992, p. 70.

Census 2001, Office of the Registrar General and Census Commissioner, *Census of India 2001*, Series 1, India, vol. 4 (Primary Census Abstract, and Total Population Table A-5), Educational Statistics, Part II-A, General Population Tables, Sex Ratio (Table 2.5), Sub-Table VI, vol. 9 (Report and Tables on Age C-14), New Delhi: Office of the Registrar General and Census Commissioner, Controller of Publications, 2003.

National Literacy Mission at http://www.nlm.nic.in/women.htm.

• Proceedings (unpublished), (Home), Judicial, Part A, May 1905, nos. 130–144, "Legislating for the Protection of Minor Girls Found in the Custody of Women of Ill-Fame"; (Home), Jails, Part B, May 1918, nos. 7–8, "The Madras Children's Bill"; (Home), Jails Branch Proceedings, December 1920, nos. 35–36, "Madras Children's Law," no. 15, 63–66; (Home), Jails, December 1920, nos. 35–36, "The Madras Children's Law"; (Home), Judicial File 791, August 24, 1927, 1–4; (Home), Judicial File 791, 1927, 1–4, "Legislation to Prohibit Dedication of Girls at Temples as Devadasis."

• Reports (published), *Report of the Indian Education Commission* (Hunter Commission), February 3, 1882, 542; *Report on the Progress of Education in India, Fourth Quinquennial Review, 1897–1898 to 1901–1902,* Table 61,

106; *Fifth Quinquennial Review, 1902–1907,* Table 174, 134; *Sixth Quinquen-nial Review,* Table 161, 285.

- Hartog Committee Report, *Review of Growth of Education in British India by the Auxiliary Committee Appointed by the Indian Statutory Commission,* September 1929.

Government of Madras (TNA)

Proceedings (unpublished)

(Education), G.O. 254, May 16, 1884; G.O. 504, June 4, 1913, "Brahmin Wid-ows' Hostel."

(Revenue), District Collectors' Reports: J. B. Huddleston, vol. 928, Tinnevelly, October 28, 1822, nos. 46–47, 9937; H. Vibart, vol. 929, Seringapatam, November 4, 1822, nos. 33–34, 10260–10262; L. G. K. Murray, vol. 931, Madras, November 14, 1822, nos. 57–58, 10512, 10512a, 10512b; J. Sulli-van, vol. 932, Coimbatore, December 2, 1822, no. 43, 10939–10943; R. Peter, vol. 942, Madura, February 13, 1823, no. 21, 2402–2406; William Cook, vol. 944, North Arcot, March 10, 1823, nos. 20–21, 2806–2816; E. Smalley, vol. 946, Chingleput, April 3, 1823, no. 25, 3494; J. Cotton, vol. 953, Tanjore, July 3, 1823, no. 61, 5347–5354; C. Hyde, vol. 954, South Arcot, July 7, 1823, nos. 59–60, 5622–5624; G. W. Sanders, vol. 959, Trichinopoly, August 28, 1823, nos. 35–36, 7456–7457A.

Government Proceedings and Reports (published)

- *Madras Legislative Council, (Proceedings),* v. 51 (July 1915–June 1916); v. 53 (July 1919–June 1920); v. I-A, no. 1 (July 1920–June 1921). Madras: Govern-ment Press, 1920.
- *Manual of the Administration of the Madras Presidency,* Records of the Government and the Yearly Administration Reports, Volume I, Part I. Madras: Government Press, 1885, 597.
- *Note on the Past and Present Administration of the Raja's Chattrams in the Tanjore and Madura Districts.* Tanjore: Government of Madras Press, 1908.
- Row, T. Venkasami, ed. *A Manual of the District of Tanjore.* Madras: Law-rence Government Press, 1883.

Grewal, Inderpal. *Home and Harem: Nation, Gender, Empire, Cultures of Travel.* Durham, North Carolina: Duke University Press, 1996.

Grewal, Indu, and J. Kishore. "Female Foeticide in India." *International Humanist and Ethical Union,* May 2004, at this URL: http://www.iheu.org.

Grewal, J. S. "Gender and Guru Nanak." In *Women in Indian History: Social, Eco-nomic, Political, and Cultural Perspectives.* Edited by Kiran Pawar, 141–58. Patiala and New Delhi: Vision and Venture Publishing Company, 1996.

Guha, Ramachandra. "Forestry and Social Protest in British Kumaun, c. 1893–1921." In *Subaltern Studies IV: Writings on South Asian History and Society.* Edited by Ranajit Guha. Delhi: Oxford University Press, 1994.

———. *Unquiet Woods: Ecological Change and Peasant Resistance in the Himalaya.* Berkeley and Los Angeles: University of California Press, 1989.

Guha, Ranajit, ed. *Subaltern Studies IV: Writings on South Asian History and Soci-ety.* Delhi: Oxford University Press, 1994.

Gupta, Indra. *India's 50 Most Illustrious Women.* New Delhi: Icon Publications Pvt. Ltd., 2003.

Hamid, Areeba. "Domestic Workers: Harsh Everyday Realities." *Economic and Political Weekly* 41, no. 13 (April 1–7, 2006): 1235–37.

Hardinge, Lord. *My Indian Years: 1910–1916.* London: Murray, 1948.

Hariss-White, Barbara. "Gender Cleansing: The Paradox of Development and Deteriorating Female Life Chances in Tamil Nadu." In *Signposts: Gender Issues in Post-Independence India.* Edited by Rajeswari Sunder Rajan, 125–54. New Brunswick: Rutgers University, 2001.

Harlan, Lindsey. "Perfection and Devotion: Sati Tradition in Rajasthan." In *Sati, the Blessing and the Curse: The Burning of Wives in India.* Edited by John Stratton Hawley. New York: Oxford University Press, 1994.

———. *Religion and Rajput Women.* Berkeley and Los Angeles: University of California Press, 1997.

Hasan, S. Nurul. *Religion, State and Society in Medieval India: Collected Papers of S. N. Hasan.* Edited by Satish Chandra. Delhi: Oxford University Press, 2005.

Hasan, Zoya, and Ritu Menon. *Unequal Citizens: A Study of Muslim Women in India.* New Delhi: Oxford University Press, 2004.

Hawley, John Stratton, ed. *Sati, the Blessing and the Curse: The Burning of Wives in India,* 79–99. New York: Oxford University Press, 1994.

Hay, Stephen, ed. *Sources of Indian Tradition: Modern India and Pakistan.* Vol. 2. 2nd ed. New York: Columbia University Press, 1988.

Hazareesingh, K. *History of Indians in Mauritius.* London: MacMillan Education Ltd., 1975.

Hickey, William. *Tanjore Maratha Principality in South India, Madras,* 36–37. Madras: 1872.

Horne, Sylvester. *The Story of the London Missionary Society, 1795–1895.* London: John Snow, 1894.

Hoyland, J. S., and S. N. Banerjee, trans. *The Commentary of Father Monserrate, S. J., on His Journey to the Court of Akbar.* London: Humphrey Milford, Oxford University Press, 1922.

Hyder, Qurratulain, trans. *Hasan Shah's The Nautch Girl.* New Delhi: Sterling, 2003.

Indian Council of Social Science Research and Central Statistical Organization. *Social Information of India: Trends and Structure,* 167. New Delhi: Hindustan Publishing Corporation, 1983.

Indian Ladies' Magazine. Edited by Kamala Sattianadhan, Madras
   "The Society for the Protection of Children in Madras," 2, no. 7 (February 1929): 355–57; "Dr. Muthulakshmi's Achievement," 2, no. 8 (March 1929): 447.

Indian Social Reformer. Edited by K. Natarajan, Bombay
   Begam of Bhopal, "Presidential Address at the Second All-India Women's Educational Conference," 38, no. 25 (February 18, 1928); "Haribilas Sarda's Bill," 38, no. 31 (March 1928): 487–89; Sastri, C. V. Vishwanatha, "The Child Marriage Bill," 38, no. 26 (February 1928): 407.

Ingham, Kenneth. *Reformers in India, 1793–1833.* London: Cambridge University Press, 1956.

Irvine, William, trans. *Storio Do Mogor or Mogul India, 1653–1708 by Nicolao Manucci Venetian.* Vol. 1. London: 1907.

Jackson, Peter. *The Delhi Sultanate: A Political and Military History.* Cambridge: Cambridge University Press, 1999.

Jag Mohan, Sarla. *Remembering Sarojini Naidu.* Delhi: Children's Book Trust, 1978.

Jain, Anirudh K., and Moni Nag. "Importance of Female Primary Education for Fertility Reduction in India." *Economic and Political Weekly* 21, no. 36 (1986): 1602–7.

Jain, Devaki. *Indian Women.* Delhi: Government of India Publication Division, 1976.

Jaising, Indira, ed. *Men's Laws, Women's Lives: A Constitutional Perspective on Religion, Common Law and Culture in South Asia*, 226–58. New Delhi: Women Unlimited and Kali for Women, 2005.

Jayawardena, Kumari. *The White Woman's Other Burden: Western Women and South Asia during British Colonial Rule.* New York and London: Routledge, 1995.

Jones, Kenneth W. "Communalism in the Punjab: The Arya Samaj Contribution." In *Modern India: An Interpretive Anthology.* Edited by Thomas Metcalf, 261–77. New Delhi: Sterling Publishers, 1990.

Joshi, Gopa. "The Chipko Movement, Part II—Community Opposes Activists," from *Manushi* journal (no. 7, 1981). In *In Search of Answers: Indian Women's Voices from Manushi.* Edited by Madhu Kishwar and Ruth Vanita, 153–57. New Delhi: Manohar, 1996.

Joshi, S. J. *Anandi Gopal.* Translated by Asha Damle. Calcutta: Stree, 1992.

Joshi, V. C., ed. *Rammohan Roy and the Process of Modernization in India*, 168–93. New Delhi: Vikas, 1975.

Karve, D. D., ed. and trans. *The New Brahmins: Five Maharashtrian Families.* Berkeley: University of California Press, 1963.

Kasturi, Leela. "Report of the Sub-Committee, Women's Role in Planned Economy, National Planning Committee Series (1947)." In *Feminism in India.* Edited by Maitrayee Chaudhuri, 136–55. New Delhi: Women Unlimited and Kali for Women, 2004.

Kaur, Manmohan. *Role of Women in the Freedom Movement (1857–1947).* Delhi: Sterling, 1968.

Kausar, Zinat. *Muslim Women in Medieval India.* Patna and New Delhi: Janaki Prakashan, 1992.

Keay, John. *India: A History.* New York: Grove Press, Harper Collins, 2000.

Kelkar, Govind. "Development Effectiveness through Gender Mainstreaming: Gender Equality and Poverty Reduction in South Asia." *Economic and Political Weekly,* special issue, Review of Women's Studies, 40, nos. 44–45 (October 29–November 4, 2005): 4690–95.

Kersenboom-Story, Saskia. *Nityasumangali: Devadasi Tradition in South India.* New Delhi: Motilal Banarsidass, 1987.

Khan, Mohammad Ishaq. "The Impact of Islam on Kashmir." In *The Rise of Islam and the Bengal Frontier, 1204–1750.* Edited by Richard M. Eaton, 342–62. Berkeley and Los Angeles: University of California, 1996.

Kishwar, Madhu. "Arya Samaj and Women's Education: Kanya Mahavidyalaya, Jalandhar." *Economic and Political Weekly,* Review of Women's Studies, 21, no. 17 (April 1986): 9–24.

Kishwar, Madhu, and Ruth Vanita, eds. *In Search of Answers: Indian Women's Voices from Manushi, 80–93.* New Delhi: Manohar, 1996.

Klass, Morton. *East Indians in Trinidad.* New York: Columbia University Press, 1961.

Kondapi, C. *Indians Overseas.* Bombay and Delhi: Oxford University Press, 1951.

Kosambi, Meera. *At the Intersection of Gender Reform and Religious Belief: Pandita Ramabai's Contribution and the Age of Consent Controversy.* Bombay: Research Centre for Women's Studies, 1993.

Krishnaraj, Maithreyi, ed. *Women in Indian Data Systems.* Contribution to Women Studies Series 6. Mumbai: Research Centre for Women's Studies, SNDT Women's University, 1990.

Krishnaveni, K. *Sahodari Subbalakshmi* (Tamil). Madras: Sarada Ladies Union, 1962.

Krynicki, Annie Krieger. *Captive Princess Zebunissa: Daughter of Emperor Aurangzeb.* Translated from French by Enjum Hamid. Oxford: Oxford University Press, 2005.

Kumar, Nita, ed. *Women as Subjects: South Asian Histories.* Calcutta: Stree, 1994.

Kumar, Radha. *The History of Doing: An Illustrated Account of the Movements for Women's Rights and Feminism, 1890–1990.* 2nd ed. New Delhi: Kali for Women, 1997.

Kurien, Prema. *Kaleidoscopic Ethnicity: International Migration and the Reconstruction of Community Identities in India.* Delhi: Oxford University Press, 2002.

Laine, James W. *Hindu King in Islamic India.* Delhi: Oxford University Press, 2003.

———. "Shivaji's Mother." In *Images of Women in Maharashtrian Literature and Religion.* Edited by Anne Feldhaus, 97–114. Albany: State University of New York, 1996.

Lal, Ruby. *Domesticity and Power in the Early Mughal World.* Cambridge Studies in Islamic Civilization. Cambridge: Cambridge University Press, 2005.

Lateef, Shahida. "Indian Women's Movement and National Development: An Overview." In *The Extended Family: Women and Political Participation in India and Pakistan.* Edited by Gail Minault. New Delhi: Chanakya, 1981.

———. *Muslim Women in India: Political and Private Realities, 1890's–1980's.* Delhi: Kali for Women, 1990.

Law, Narendranath N. *Promotion of Learning in India by Early European Settlers up to 1800 AD.* London: Longmans Green, 1915.

Lebra, Joyce, Joy Paulson, and Jana Everett, eds. *Women and Work in India.* New Delhi: Promilla Publishers, 1980.

Leonard, John Greenfield. *Kandukuri Viresalingam: A Biography of an Indian Social Reformer.* Hyderabad: Telugu University, 1991.

Leslie, I. Julia. *The Perfect Wife: The Orthodox Hindu Woman According to the Stridharmapadhati of Tryambakayajvan.* Delhi: Oxford University Press, 1989.

Lewis, Robin Jared. "Comment: Sati and the Nineteenth-Century British Self." In *Sati, the Blessing and the Curse: The Burning of Wives in India.* Edited by John Stratton Hawley, 72–78. New York: Oxford University Press, 1994.

Liddle, Joanna, and Rama Joshi. *Daughters of Independence: Gender, Caste and Class in India.* New Brunswick, New Jersey: Rutgers University Press, 1986.

London Missionary Society, Letters, Records, Reports, 1817–52 (microfilm, UCLA).

Madhaviah, A. *Muthumeenakshi.* 1903. Reprint, Chennai: Vanavil Prasuram, 1984.
———. *Padmavati Charitram.* 7th ed. 1898. Reprint, Chennai: Little Flower Book House, 1958.
———. *Satyananda.* Bangalore: Mysore Review, 1909.
Madras Seva Sadan. *Silver Jubilee Souvenir, 1953.* Madras: 1953.
Mahmoud, Syed. *A History of English Education in India (1781–1893).* Aligarh: Mohammedan Anglo-Oriental College, 1895.
Majumdar, J. K., ed. *Raja Rammohun Roy and the Progressive Movements in India: A Selection from Records, 1775–1845.* Calcutta: Art Press, 1941.
Malabari, Behramji M. *Infant Marriage and Enforced Widowhood in India.* Bombay: Voice of India Press, 1887.
Malik, Sherebanu. "Divorce in Indian Islam." In *Problems of Muslim Women in India.* Edited by Ashgar Ali Engineer, 30–33. Bombay: Orient Longman, 1995.
Malik, Z. U. "Profile of a Slave Girl Munny Begam, Widow of Meer Jafar." In *Women in Indian History: Social, Economic, Political, and Cultural Perspectives.* Edited by Kiran Pawar, 11–140. Patiala and New Delhi: Vision and Venture Publishing Company, 1996.
Mani, Lata. *Contentious Traditions: The Debate on Sati in Colonial India.* Berkeley and Los Angeles: University of California Press, 1998.
Mathar Manoranjani (Brightener of Women's Minds; Tamil journal), 1, no. 8 (October 1899).
Mayo, Katherine. *Mother India.* New York: Harcourt Brace, 1927.
McDonough, Shiela. "Muslim Women in India." In *Women in Indian Religions.* Edited by Arvind Sharma. 2nd ed., 166–88. New Delhi: Oxford University Press, 2004.
Meenakshi, Thiagarajan, trans. *Padmavati Charitram.* New Delhi: Katha, 2004.
Mehrotra, Santosh. "Child Malnutrition and Gender Discrimination in South Asia." *Economic and Political Weekly* 41, no. 10 (March 11, 2006): 912–18.
Mehta, Pratap Bhanu. "Reason, Tradition, Authority: Religion and the Indian State." In *Men's Laws, Women's Lives: A Constitutional Perspective on Religion, Common Law and Culture in South Asia.* Edited by Indira Jaising, 56–86. New Delhi: Women Unlimited, 2005.
Menon, Ritu, and Kamla Bhasin. *Borders and Boundaries: Women in India's Partition.* New Brunswick, New Jersey: Rutgers University, 1998.
Mernissi, Fatima. *Women and Islam: An Historical and Theological Enquiry.* Translated by Mary Jo Lakeland. Delhi: Kali for Women, 1991.
Metcalf, Barbara Daly. "Islamic Reform and Islamic Women: Maulana Thanawi's *Jewelry of Paradise.*" In *Moral Conduct and Authority: The Place of Adab in South Asian Islam.* Edited by Barbara Daly Metcalf, 184–95. Berkeley and Los Angeles: University of California, 1984.
Metcalf, Thomas. *Ideologies of the Raj.* Cambridge: Cambridge University Press, 1995.
Mill, James. *The History of British India.* Vols. 1–2. London: James Madden, 1826. Reprint, New York: Chelsea House, 1968.
Minault, Gail, ed. *The Extended Family: Women and Political Participation in India and Pakistan,* 3–19. New Delhi: Chanakya Publishers, 1981.
———. "Other Voices, Other Rooms: The View from the Zenana." In *Women as Subjects.* Edited by Nita Kumar, 108–24. Calcutta: Stree, 1994.

———. *Secluded Scholars: Women's Education and Muslim Social Reform in Colonial India.* New Delhi: Oxford University Press, 1998.

———. "Sisterhood or Separatism? The All-India Muslim Ladies' Conference and the Nationalist Movement." In *The Extended Family: Women and Political Participation in India and Pakistan.* Edited by Gail Minault, 83–108. New Delhi: Chanakya Publications, 1981.

Mishra, Neerja. "The Murder of Roop Kanwar." In *Widows, Abandoned and Destitute Women in India.* Edited by Pramila Dandvate, Ranjana Kumari, and Jamila Verghese. New Delhi: Radiant Publishers, 1989.

Misra, Rekha. *Women in Mughal India (1526–1748).* New Delhi: Munshiram Manoharlal, 1967.

Mitra, Asok. *Implications of Declining Sex Ratio in India's Population.* Indian Council of Social Science Research (ICSSR), Programme of Women's Studies, and Jawaharlal Nehru University. Bombay: Allied Publishers, Pvt. Ltd., 1979.

Mukherjee, Rudrangshu, ed. *The Penguin Gandhi Reader.* New Delhi: Penguin India, 1993.

Naidu, Sarojini. *The Bird of Time: Songs of Life, Death and the Spring.* 5th ed. 1912. Reprint, London: William Heinemann, 1926.

———. *Broken Wing: Songs of Love, Death, and Destiny.* London: William Heinemann, 1917.

———. "Presidential Address at the Ahmedabad Students' Conference." In *Women Writing in India: 600 B.C. to the Early Twentieth Century.* Edited by Susie Tharu and K. Lalitha, 1:331–40. New York: Feminist Press, 1991.

———. *Speeches and Writings.* Madras: G. A. Natesan, 1919.

Nambisan, Sobha. *Effective Enforcement of Social Legislation Pertaining to Women.* Bangalore: Indian Institute of Management, 2005.

Nanda, B. R. *Mahatma Gandhi: A Biography.* New Delhi: Oxford University Press, 1958.

Nanda, Reena. *Kamaladevi Chattopadhyaya: A Biography.* New Delhi: Oxford University Press, 2002.

Nandy, Ashis. *At the Edge of Psychology: Essays in Politics and Culture.* New Delhi: Oxford University Press, 1980.

———. "Sati: A Nineteenth Century Tale of Women, Violence and Protest." In *Rammohan Roy and the Process of Modernization in India.* Edited by V. C. Joshi, 168–75. New Delhi: Vikas, 1975.

———. "Sati as Profit Versus Sati as Spectacle: The Public Debate on Roop Kanwar's Death." In *Sati, the Blessing and the Curse: The Burning of Wives in India.* Edited by John Stratton Hawley, 131–49. Berkeley and Los Angeles: University of California Press, 1994.

Naravane, Vishwanath S. *Sarojini Naidu: Her Life, Work, and Poetry.* 2nd ed. Delhi: Orient Longman, 1996.

Natarajan, S *A Century of Social Reform in India.* Bombay: Asia Publishing House, 1959.

Nath, R. *Private Life of the Mughals of India (1526–1803 A.D.).* Delhi: Rupa & Co., 2005.

National Family Health Survey of India (2005–6), 24, no. 22 (November 3–16, 2007).

Navaratne, V. S. *Sarojini Naidu: Her Life, Work and Poetry.* Delhi: Orient Longman, 1980.

Nehru, Jawaharlal. *The Discovery of India.* New York: The John Day Company, 1946.

———. *Selected Works of Jawaharlal Nehru.* Edited by Sarvepalli Gopal. 2nd series. New Delhi: Jawaharlal Nehru Memorial Fund, 1989.

Nethercott, Arthur H. *The First Nine Lives of Annie Besant.* London: Rupert Hart-Davis, 1961.

Nikhilandanda, Swami. *Sri Ramakrishna: A Biography.* Madras: Sri Ramakrishna Math, 2002.

Nussbaum, Martha. "Religion, Culture and Sex Equality." In *Men's Laws, Women's Lives: A Constitutional Perspective on Religion, Common Law and Culture in South Asia.* Edited by Indira Jaising, 109–37. New Delhi: Women Unlimited, 2005.

O'Hanlon, Rosalind. *Caste, Conflict and Ideology: Mahatma Jotirao Phule and Low Caste Protest in Nineteenth Century Western India.* 2nd ed. Cambridge: Cambridge University Press, 2002.

———. *A Comparison between Women and Men: Tarabai Shinde and the Critique of Gender Relations in Colonial India.* New Delhi: Oxford University Press, 1994.

———. "Issues of Widowhood: Gender and Resistance in Colonial India." In *Contesting Power: Resistance and Everyday Social Relations in South Asia.* Edited by Douglas Haynes and Gyan Prakash, 62–108. Berkeley: University of California Press, 1991.

Olcott, Henry S. *The Poor Pariah.* Adyar: Theosophical Society, 1902.

Oldenburg, Veena Talwar. "Comment: The Continuing Invention of the Sati Tradition." In *Sati, the Blessing and the Curse: The Burning of Wives in India.* Edited by John Stratton Hawley, 159–73. Berkeley and Los Angeles: University of California Press, 1994.

Oldham, William F. *Isabella Thoburn.* Chicago: Jennings and Pye, The Student Volunteer Movement for Foreign Missions, 1902.

Omvedt, Gail. *Cultural Revolt in a Colonial Society.* Bombay: Scientific Socialist Education Trust, 1976.

———, ed. *Dalit Visions: Facts for the Times.* 2nd ed. Mumbai: Orient Longman, 2006.

———. "Hinduism as Patriarchy: Ramabai, Tarabai and Others." In *Dalit Visions: Facts for the Times.* Edited by Gail Omvedt. 2nd ed., 25–42. Mumbai: Orient Longman, 2002.

———. "New Movements and New Theories in India." In *Feminism in India.* Edited by Maitrayee Chaudhuri. 2nd ed., 177–86. New Delhi: Women Unlimited and Kali for Women, 2005.

———. *We Will Smash This Prison! Indian Women in Struggle.* London: Zed Books, 1980.

———. "Women in Governance in South Asia." *Economic and Political Weekly,* Review of Women's Studies, 40, nos. 44–45 (October 29–November 4, 2005): 4746–52.

———. "Women's Movement: Some Ideological Debates." In *Feminism in India.* Edited by Maitrayee Chaudhuri, 286–95. New Delhi: Women Unlimited and Kali for Women, 2005.

Orme, Robert. *Of the Government and People of Indostan.* Part 1. London: 1753. Reprint, Lucknow: 1971.

Pande, Rekha. *Succession in the Delhi Sultanate.* New Delhi: Commonwealth Publishers, 1990.

Parmar, Sharan. "Gender Equality in the Name of Religion." In *Men's Laws, Women's Lives: A Constitutional Perspective on Religion, Common Law and Culture in South Asia.* Edited by Indira Jaising, 226–58. New Delhi: Women Unlimited, 2005.

Pascoe, C. F. *Two Hundred Years of the S.P.G., 1701–1900.* Westminster: Society for the Propagation of the Gospel, 1900.

Patel, Vibhuti. "Problems Pertaining to Women's Work: Paid/Unpaid, Employment/Unemployment." In *Women in Indian Data Systems.* Women's Studies Series 6. Edited by Maithreyi Krishnaraj, 80–93. Mumbai: Research Centre for Women's Studies, SNDT Women's University, 1990.

———. "The Shah Bano Controversy and the Challenges Faced by Women's Movement in India." In *Problems of Muslim Women in India.* Edited by Asghar Ali Engineer, 140–48. Bombay: Orient Longman, 1995.

Pawar, Kiran, ed. *Women in Indian History: Social, Economic, Political and Cultural Perspectives,* 87–101. Patiala and New Delhi: Vision & Venture Publishers, 1996.

Pearson, M. N. *The Portuguese in India.* Cambridge: Cambridge University Press, 1987.

Phillips, Godfrey E. *The Outcastes' Hope.* London: United Council for Missionary Education, 1913.

Pillai, T. M. Narayanaswamy, ed. *Women Pioneers in Education (Tamil Nadu).* Madras: National Seminar on the Role of Women in Education in India, 1975.

Pillai, Vedanayakam. *Pen Kalvi* (Female Education). Reprint, Tinnevelly: Saiva Siddhanta Publishing Society, 1950.

———. *Pratapa Mudaliyar Charitram* (The Story of Pratapa Mudaliyar). 1879. Reprint, Madras: Vanavil Press, 1984.

Pinault, David. "Zaynab Bint' Ali and the Place of the Women of the Households of the Imāms in Shī'ite Devotional Literature." In *Women in the Medieval Islamic World,* 69–98. Edited by Gavin R. G. Hambly. New York: St. Martin's Press, 1998.

Prabhu, R. K., and U. R. Rao. *The Mind of Mahatma Gandhi.* 1945. Reprint, Ahmedabad: Navajivan Trust Publishing House, 1967.

Rajalakshmi, T. K. "A Dangerous Trend." *Frontline* 20, no. 23 (November 21, 2003): 95–96.

Ramabai, Pandita. *The High Caste Hindu Woman.* New York: Fleming H. Revell Company, 1887.

Ramalingaswami, V., U. Jonsson, and J. Rohde. "The Asian Enigma." In *Progress of Nations.* New York: United Nations Children's Fund, 1996.

Raman, Sita Anantha. "Crossing Cultural Boundaries: Indian Matriarchs and Sisters in Service." *Journal of Third World Studies* 18, no. 2 (Fall 2001): 131–48.

———. "From Chattrams to National Schools: Educational Philanthropy in South India, 18th–20th Centuries." Selected Papers in Asian Studies, #52, Western Conference of the Association for Asian Studies, 1994.

———. *Getting Girls to School: Social Reform in the Tamil Districts, 1870–1930.* Calcutta: Stree, 1996.

———. "Old Norms in New Bottles: Constructions of Gender and Ethnicity in the Early Tamil Novel." *Journal of Women's History* 12, no. 3 (Autumn 2000): 93–119.

———. "Prescriptions for Gender Equality: The Work of Dr. Muthulakshmi Reddi." In *Charisma and Commitment: Essays in South Asian History in Honor of Stanley Wolpert.* Edited by Roger Long, 331–66. Mumbai: Orient Longman, 2004.

———. "Walking Two Paces Behind: Women's Education in India." In *Ananya: A Portrait of India.* Edited by S. N. Sridhar and Nirmal Mattoo, 382. New York: SUNY Press, 1996.

Raman, Sita Anantha, and Vasantha Surya, trans. *A. Madhaviah: A Biography and a Novel.* New Delhi: Oxford University Press, 2005.

Ramanathan, Malathi. *Sister R. S. Subbalakshmi: Social Reformer and Educationist.* Bombay: Sukumar Damle, 1989.

Ramusack, Barbara. "Catalysts or Helpers? British Feminists, Indian Women's Rights, and Indian Independence." In *The Extended Family: Women and Political Participation in India and Pakistan.* Edited by Gail Minault, 109–50. New Delhi: Chanakya Publications, 1981.

Rao, R. Raghunatha. *The Aryan Marriage with Special Reference to the Age Question: A Clinical and Historical Study.* 1908. Reprint, New Delhi: Cosmo Publication, 1975.

———. "The Method of Social Reform." In *Hindu Social Progress.* Edited by N. Subbarau Pantulu Garu, 64–69. Madras: G. A. Natesan & Co., 1904.

Rao, Velcheru Narayana, David Shulman, and Sanjay Subrahmanyam. *Symbols of Substance: Court and State in Nayaka Period Tamilnadu.* Delhi: Oxford University Press, 1998.

Raverty, H. G., trans. *A General History of the Muhammadan Dynasties of Asia, Including Hindustan (810–1260),* 1:637–38. Calcutta: Asiatic Society of Bengal, 1881. Reprint, Delhi: Oriental Books Reprint Corp., 1970.

Ray, Bharati. *Early Feminists of Colonial India: Sarla Devi Chaudhurani and Rokeya Sakhawat Hossain.* New Delhi: Oxford University Press, 2002.

Ray, Renuka. *My Reminiscences: Social Development during Gandhian Era and After.* New Delhi: Allied Publishers, 1982.

Raychaudhuri, Tapan, and Irfan Habib, eds. *The Cambridge Economic History of India, c.1200–c.1750.* Vol. 1. Cambridge: Cambridge University Press, 1982.

Reddi, Muthulakshmi. *An Autobiography.* Adyar: Avvai Home, 1964.

———. *A Brief Autobiographical Sketch of Dr. (Mrs.) Muthulakshmi Reddi.* Adyar: Avvai Home, 1957.

———. "Legislation on Child Marriage," File 8; "Letter to Sarojini Naidu on Her Diamond Jubilee Celebration," February 9, 1946; "Speeches and Writings," 1917–53 (NMML).

———. *The Life of Dr. T. Sundara Reddi: The Story of a Dedicated Life.* Madras: Shakti Karyalayam, 1949.

———. *My Experience as a Legislator.* Triplicane: Current Thought Press, 1930.

———. *The Presidential Address of Dr. (Mrs.) S. Muthulakshmi Reddi.* Seventh Andhra Provincial Women's Conference. Ellore: 1933.

———. *Why Should the Devadasi Institution in the Hindu Temples Be Abolished?* A pamphlet. Madras: Central Cooperative Printing Works, Ltd., 1927.

Richards, John F. *The Mughal Empire.* 6th ed. New Delhi: Foundation Books, for Cambridge University Press, 2002.

Rizvi, Syed Abas A. "The Ruling Muslim Dynasties." In *A Cultural History of India.* Edited by A. L. Basham. 6th ed., 245–65. Delhi: Oxford University Press, 2002.

———. *The Wonder that Was India.* Vol. 2, *A Survey of the History and Culture of the Indian Sub-Continent from the Coming of the Muslims to the British Conquest 1200–1700.* 5th ed. 1987. Reprint, Delhi: Rupa & Co., 1996.

Robb, Peter, ed. *Dalit Movements and the Meanings of Labour in India.* Delhi: Oxford University Press, 1993.

Roy, Arundhati. *An Ordinary Person's Guide to Empire.* New Delhi: Penguin Books, 2006.

Roy, Shibani. *Status of Muslim Women in North India.* Delhi: B. R. Publishers, 1979.

Rudolph, Suzanne H., and Lloyd I. Rudolph. *Gandhi: The Traditional Roots of Charisma.* 2nd ed. Chicago: University of Chicago Press, 1983.

Ruswa, Mirza Mohammad Hadi. *Umrao Jan Ada, Courtesan of Lucknow* (1905). Translated by Khushwant Singh and M. A. Husaini. Bombay: Orient Longman and Disha Books, 1982.

Sadasivan, Radha. "A Centenary Tribute: Sister Subbalakshmi Ammal." *Bhavan's Journal* 32, no. 24 (July 16–31, 1982): 21–23.

Saha, Panchanan. *Emigration of Indian Labour (1834–1900).* New Delhi: People's Publishing House, 1970.

Sangari, Kumkum, ed. *Politics of the Possible: Essays on Gender, History, Narrative, Colonial English.* New Delhi: Tullika, 1999.

Sangari, Kumkum, and Sudesh Vaid, eds. *Recasting Women: Essays in Colonial History.* New Delhi: Kali for Women, 1989.

———, eds. *Women and Culture.* Bombay: SNDT Women's University, 1985.

Sanghvi, Sanjay. *The River and Life: People's Struggle in the Narmada Valley.* Mumbai: Earth Care Books, 2000.

Sarkar, Sumit. *A Critique of Colonial India.* Calcutta: Papyrus, 1985.

———. *Modern India, 1885–1947.* Madras: Macmillan India, 1983.

———. "The Women's Question in Nineteenth Century Bengal." In *Women and Culture.* Edited by Kumkum Sangari and Sudesh Vaid, 157–72. Bombay: SNDT Women's University, 1985.

Sarkar, Tanika, and Urvashi Butalia, eds. *Women and the Hindu Right: A Collection of Essays.* New Delhi: Kali for Women, 1995.

Sastri, K. A. Nilakanta. *Foreign Notices of South India from Megasthenes to Mahuan.* 1939. Reprint, Chennai: University of Madras, 2001.

Sattianadhan, Krupabai. *Kamala: The Story of a Hindu Life.* Edited by Chandani Lokuge. New Delhi: Oxford University Press, 1998.

Sattianadhan, Samuel. *History of Education in the Madras Presidency.* Madras: Srinivasa Varadachari, 1896.

Schimmel, Annemarie. *The Empire of the Great Mughals: History, Art and Culture.* London: Reaktion Books, 2004.

Scholberg, Henry. "The Writings of Francisco Luis Gomes." In *Indo-Portuguese History: Old Issues, New Questions*. Edited by Teotonio de Souza. New Delhi: Concept Publishing Company, 1985.

Sen, Amartya. "Agency and Well-Being: The Development Agenda." In *A Commitment to the Women*. Edited by Noeleen Heyzer. New York: UNIFEM, 1996.

———. *Development as Freedom*. New York: Anchor Books, 1999.

———. "Gender Inequality and Theories of Justice." In *Women, Culture, and Development: A Study of Human Capabilities*. Edited by Martha Nussbaum and Jonathan Glover. Oxford: Clarendon Press, 1995.

Sen, Samita. *Women and Labour in Late Colonial India: The Bengal Jute Industry*. Cambridge: Cambridge University Press, 1999.

Sengupta, Padmini. *The Portrait of an Indian Woman*. Calcutta: Y.M.C.A., 1956.

Sethuraman, Kavita, and Nata Duvvury. "The Nexus of Gender Discrimination with Malnutrition: An Introduction." *Economic and Political Weekly* 42, nos. 45–46 (November 3–23, 2007): 49–52.

Shanker, Rajkumari. "Women in Sikhism." In *Women in Indian Religions*. Edited by Arvind Sharma. 2nd ed. New Delhi: Oxford University Press, 2004.

Sharma, Radha Krishna. *Nationalism, Social Reform, and Indian Women*. Patna: Janaki Prakashan, 1981.

Sharrock, J. A. *South Indian Missions*. Westminster: Society for the Propagation of the Gospel, 1910.

Shepherd, Verene. "Gender, Migration and Settlement: The Indentureship and Post-Indentureship Experience of Indian Females in Jamaica, 1845–1943." In *Engendering History: Caribbean Women in Historical Perspective*. Edited by Verene Shepherd, Bridget Brereton, and Barbara Bailey. Kingston: Ian Randle Publishers, 1995.

Sherring, M. A. *The History of Protestant Missions in India*. London: Religious Tract Society, 1884.

Shiva, Vandana. *Staying Alive: Women, Ecology and Survival in India*. Delhi: Kali for Women, 1988.

Siddiqui, Iqtidar Hussain. "Socio-Political Role of Women in the Sultanate of Delhi." In *Women in Indian History: Social, Economic, Political and Cultural Perspectives*. Edited by Kiran Pawar. Patiala and New Delhi: Vision & Venture Publishers, 1996.

Siddiqui, Mohammad Abdul-Aleem. *Elementary Teachings of Islam*. Karachi: Taj Company Ltd., 1954.

Singh, Indu Prakash, and Renuka Singh. "Sati: Its Patri-Politics." In *Widows, Abandoned and Destitute Women in India*. Edited by Pramila Dandvate, Ranjana Kumari, and Jamila Verghese, 54–61. New Delhi: Radiant, 1989.

Singh, Kelvin. *Race and Class: Struggles in a Colonial State, Trinidad 1917–1945*. Jamaica: University of the West Indies, 1994.

Singh, Kiran. "It's Only a Family Affair!" In *In Search of Answers: Indian Women's Voices from Manushi*. Edited by Madhu Kishwar and Ruth Vanita, 186–90. New Delhi: Manohar, 1996.

Sinha, Kumudini. "Female Child Labour in Bihar: Incidence and Their Conditions." In *Children at Work: Problems and Policy Options*. Edited by Bhagwan Pd. Singh and Shukla Mahanty, 117–32. New Delhi: B. R. Publishing Corporation and Indian Society of Labour Economics, 1993.

Siraj, Minhaj-ud-din. *Tabaqat-I-Nasiri: A General History of the Muhammadan Dynasties of Asia, Including Hindustan (810–1260).* Translated by H. G. Raverty. Vols. 1–2. Calcutta: Asiatic Society of Bengal, 1881. Reprint, New Delhi: Oriental Books Reprint Corp., 1970.

Sivaraman, Mythili. *Fragments of a Life: A Family Archive.* Delhi: Zubaan Books, 2006.

Snehi, Yogesh. "Conjugality, Sexuality and *Shastras:* Debate on the Abolition of *Reet* in Colonial Himachal Pradesh." *Indian Economic and Social History Review* 43, no. 2 (2006): 163–97.

Spivak, Gayatri Chakravorty. "Can the Subaltern Speak?" In *Marxism and the Interpretation of Culture.* Edited by Cary Nelson and Lawrence Grossberg, 263–305. Urbana and Chicago: University of Chicago Press, 1988.

Srikumar, K. P. "Amniocentesis and the Future of the Girl Child." In *Girl Child in India.* Edited by Leelamma Devasia and V. V. Devasia, 51–65. Springfield, VA: Nataraj Books, 1992.

Srinivasan, Amrit. "The Hindu Temple-Dancer: Prostitute or Nun?" *Cambridge Anthropology* 8, no. 1 (1983): 73–99.

———. "Reform and Revival: The Devadasi and Her Dance." *Economic and Political Weekly* 20, no. 44 (November 2, 1985): 1869–76.

———. "Reform or Conformity? Temple 'Prostitution' and the Community in the Madras Presidency." In *Structures of Patriarchy: State, Community and Household in Modernizing Asia.* Edited by Bina Agarwal, 175–98. New Delhi: Kali for Women, 1988.

Stri Dharma (Adyar: Women's Indian Association), these issues:

- 2, no. 4 (December 1920); 4, no. 1 (January 1921); 5, nos. 1–4 (January–December 1921); Margaret Cousins, "Remarkable Reforms under a Woman Ruler (Begam of Bhopal)," 6, no. 5 (March 1923): 65; 7, no. 3 (January 1924); Anon., "Social Evil in Madras," 8, nos. 3–8 (January–June 1925); Margaret Cousins, "Children's Protection Bill," 8, no. 11 (September 1925): 129.
- 8, no. 12 (October 1925): 130; Anon., "The Madras Muslim Ladies Association," 11, no. 6 (1928): 47; Bhagirathi Ammal, S., "Raising of the Marriage Age," 11, no. 6 (April 1928): 12–13; Dorothy Jinarajadasa, "The Age of Consent Bill," 8, no. 6 (April 1925): 82–83; Nallamuthu Ramamurthi, "Sister Subbalakshmi's Talk on Compulsory Primary Education for Girls at the Indian Women's Conference," 4, no. 1 (January 1921).

Subbalakshmi Ammal, R. S. (private papers)

- "My Diary," handwritten (Tamil and English)
- *Sister Subbalakshmi Ammal Birth Centenary Souvenir,* T. Nagar: Sarada Ladies Union, 1986; *Sister Subbalakshmi Ammal First Anniversary Commemoration Souvenir,* SLU, 1970; *Sister Subbalakshmi Ammal Souvenir,* SLU, 1953.

Subrahmanyam, Lalitha. *Women Scientists in the Third World: The Indian Experience.* New Delhi and Thousand Oaks: Sage Publications, 1998.

Subrahmanyam, Sanjay, ed. *Sinners and Saints: The Successors of Vasco da Gama.* Delhi: Oxford University Press, 2000.

Surya, Vasantha. *The Stalk of Time.* Chennai: K. Suryanarayanan, 1985.

———. *A Word Between Us*. Chennai: Sandhya Publications, 2004.

———, trans. *The Ballad of Budhini,* from the Bundeli Hindi poem by Veerendra Kumar, Narendra Kumar, and Raghuvanshi Krishnamurthi. Calcutta: Writers' Workshop, 1992.

———, trans. *A Place to Live: Contemporary Tamil Short Fiction*. Edited by Dilip Kumar. New Delhi: Penguin, 1984.

———, trans. *Yamini,* from the Tamil novel by Chudamani Raghavan. Chennai: Macmillan, 1996.

Talwar, Vir Bharat. "Feminist Consciousness in Women's Journals in Hindi, 1910–1920." In *Recasting Women: Essays in Colonial History*. Edited by Kumkum Sangari and Sudesh Vaid, 204–32. New Delhi: Kali for Women, 1989.

Tapasyananda, Swami. *Sri Sarada Devi, the Holy Mother: Life and Teachings*. Madras: Sri Ramakrishna Math, 2003.

Taylor, Anne. *Annie Besant, a Biography*. Oxford and New York: Oxford University Press, 1992.

Thapar, Romila. *Early India: From the Origins to AD 1300*. Berkeley and Los Angeles: University of California Press, 2002.

———, ed. *India: Another Millennium?* New Delhi: Penguin Books, 2000.

———. "Perspective in History: Seminar 342 (February 1988)." In *Sati: A Writeup of Ram Mohan Roy about Burning Widows Alive*. Edited by Mulk Raj Anand, 83–95. New Delhi: B. R. Publishing Corporation, 1989.

Thapar-Björkert, Suruchi. *Women in the Indian National Movement: Unseen Faces and Unheard Voices, 1930–42*. New Delhi and Thousand Oaks: Sage Publications, 2006.

Tharu, Susie, and K. Lalitha, eds. *Women Writing in India: 600 BC to the Present*. Vols. 1 and 2. New York: Feminist Press, 1991.

Theosophical Society

- Kofel, C. "Education of the Depressed Classes, Particularly in Southern India." Adyar, 1913, Handwritten Report of the Superintendent of the Olcott Panchama Free Schools, Adyar.
- *Report of the Olcott Panchama Free Schools,* December 1, 1909 to November 30, 1910. Adyar: TS, 1910.

Tinker, Hugh. *A New System of Slavery: The Export of Indian Labour Overseas, 1830–1920*. London: Oxford University Press, 1974.

Tomlinson, B. R. *The Economy of Modern India, 1860–1970*. Cambridge: Cambridge University Press, 1993.

United Nations. *Second Report on the World Nutrition Situation*. Vol. 1. Geneva: United Nations, 1992.

Vaasanthi, K. *Kadaisee Varai* (Birthright; Tamil). Translated by Vasantha Surya. New Delhi: Zubaan Books, 2004.

Vaikuntham, Y. *Education and Social Change in South India: Andhra 1880–1920*. Madras: New Era, 1982.

Vatsa, Rajendra Singh. "The Movement against Infant Marriages in India, 1860–1914." *Journal of Indian History* 44, no. 145–47 (April 1971): 294–300.

———. "The Remarriage and Rehabilitation of Hindu Widows in India, 1856–1914." *Journal of Indian History* 4, no. 3 (December 1976): 722–23.

Venkatachalam, G. *My Contemporaries*. Bangalore: Hosati Press, 1966.

Verma, A. K. "Backward Caste Politics in Uttar Pradesh." *Economic and Political Weekly* 40, no. 36 (September 3, 2005): 3889–92.

Verma, Meena, and Neeta Verma. "Incidence of Female Child Labour in Bihar." In *Children at Work: Problems and Policy Options*. Edited by Bhagwan Pd. Singh and Shukla Mahanty, 105–15. New Delhi and Patna: B. R. Publishing Corporation and Indian Society of Labour Economics, 1993.

Visaria, Leela. "Infant Mortality in India: Levels, Trends, and Determinants." *Economic and Political Weekly* 20, no. 34 (1985): 1447–50.

Vishwanathan, Gauri. *Outside the Fold: Conversion, Modernity and Belief*. Princeton: Princeton University Press, 1998.

Vivekananda, Swami. *The Complete Works of Swami Vivekananda*. 2 vols. 9th ed. Calcutta: Advaita Ashrama, 1995.

Walther, Wiebke. *Women in Islam from Medieval to Modern Times*. Princeton and New York: Marcus Wiener Publishing, 1993.

Weiner, Myron. *The Child and the State in India: Child Labor and Education Policy in Comparative Perspective*. Princeton: Princeton University Press, 1991.

Wolpert, Stanley. *Gandhi's Passion: The Life and Legacy of Mahatma Gandhi*. New York: Oxford University Press, 2001.

———. *A New History of India*. 7th ed. New York: Oxford University Press, 2004.

———. *Tilak and Gokhale: Revolution and Reform in the Making of India*. 2nd ed. Berkeley and Los Angeles: University of California Press, 1961.

Women's Indian Association Papers and Reports (TSA)

- *All Asian Conference on Women*. Adyar: WIA, 1930.
- *Annual Reports, 1927–1928, 1928–1929*.
- "Demand for the Grant of the Vote Placed before Lord Chelmsford and Mr. Montagu by the Representatives of All India Women's Deputation on December 18, 1917," with photograph.
- "Franchise for Women: Views of Prominent Men," 1918.
- "Goals of the Women's Indian Association," May 8, 1917. In *Report of the Women's Indian Association*. Adyar: TS, 1928.
- *Golden Jubilee Celebration: 1917–1967*. Adyar: WIA, 1967.

Yesudas, R. N. *The History of the London Missionary Society in Travancore, 1806–1908*. Trivandrum: Kerala Historical Society, 1980.

Zakaria, Rafiq. *Razia: Queen of India*. 2nd ed. New Delhi: Oxford University Press, 1999.

INDEX

Verma, Mahadevi, 213
Vivekananda, Swami, xv, 101, 103,
 114–16. *See also* Ramakrishna
 Mission and Vedanta Society

Widow remarriage, 46, 48, 64, 76, 80,
 101–4, 106, 109, 113; levirate, 120;
 Remarriage Act, 78–80, 102, 107

Women workers, 82–84, 127, 137,
 164, 198–99, 200
Women's Indian Association (WIA),
 103, 117, 125–26, 137, 147, 151–
 58, 164, 168–72, 175–76
Women's Reservation Bill, 207–8
Wood, Charles (Educational Despatch
 of 1854), 69

About the Author

SITA ANANTHA RAMAN is Associate Professor Emerita, History, Santa Clara University, California; member of the Board of Directors, Pacific Coast Immigration Museum, California; and Adjunct at the University of Georgia, Athens. She is the author of *Getting Girls to School: Social Reform in the Tamil Districts, 1870–1930* (1996) and *A. Madhaviah: A Biography and a Novella* (2004).